Bahamas For Dummies

3rd Edition

Dining Out in Freeport/Lucaya

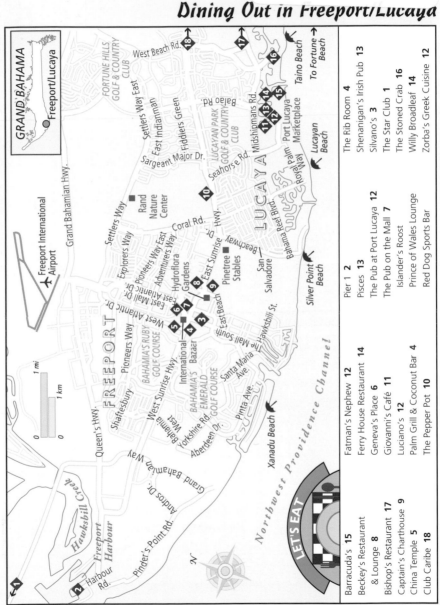

GRAND BAHAMA — Freeport/Lucaya

LET'S EAT

Barracuda's **15**
Beckey's Restaurant & Lounge **8**
Bishop's Restaurant **17**
Captain's Charthouse **9**
China Temple **5**
Club Caribe **18**

Fatman's Nephew **12**
Ferry House Restaurant **14**
Geneva's Place **6**
Giovanni's Café **11**
Luciano's **12**
Palm Grill & Coconut Bar **4**
The Pepper Pot **10**

Pier 1 **2**
Pisces **13**
The Pub at Port Lucaya **12**
The Pub on the Mall **7**
Islander's Roost
Prince of Wales Lounge
Red Dog Sports Bar

The Rib Room **4**
Shenanigan's Irish Pub **13**
Silvano's **3**
The Star Club **1**
The Stoned Crab **16**
Willy Broadleaf **14**
Zorba's Greek Cuisine **12**

Dining Out in Nassau

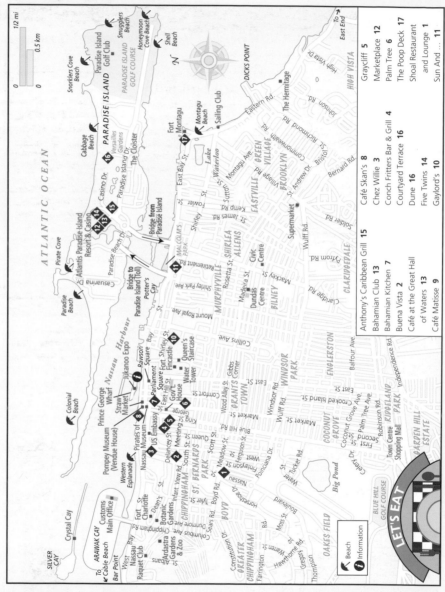

Anthony's Caribbean Grill **15**
Bahamian Club **13**
Bahamian Kitchen **7**
Buena Vista **2**
Cafe at the Great Hall
 of Waters **13**
Café Matisse **9**

Café Skan's **8**
Chez Willie **3**
Conch Fritters Bar & Grill **4**
Courtyard Terrace **16**
Dune **16**
Five Twins **14**
Gaylord's **10**

Graycliff **5**
Marketplace **12**
Palm Tree **6**
The Poop Deck **17**
Shoal Restaurant
 and Lounge **1**
Sun And **11**

FOR DUMMIES

The fun and easy way™ to travel!

U.S.A.

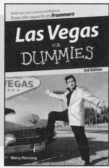

Also available:

Alaska For Dummies

Arizona For Dummies

Boston For Dummies

California For Dummies

Chicago For Dummies

Colorado & the Rockies For Dummies

Florida For Dummies

Los Angeles & Disneyland For Dummies

Maui For Dummies

National Parks of the American West For Dummies

New Orleans For Dummies

New York City For Dummies

San Francisco For Dummies

Seattle & the Olympic Peninsula For Dummies

Washington, D.C. For Dummies

RV Vacations For Dummies

Walt Disney World & Orlando For Dummies

EUROPE

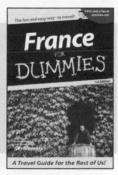

A Travel Guide for the Rest of Us!

Also available:

England For Dummies

Europe For Dummies

Germany For Dummies

Ireland For Dummies

London For Dummies

Paris For Dummies

Scotland For Dummies

Spain For Dummies

OTHER DESTINATIONS

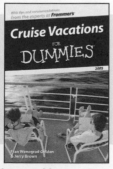

Also available:

Bahamas For Dummies

Cancun & the Yucatan For Dummies

Costa Rica For Dummies

Mexico's Beach Resorts For Dummies

Montreal & Quebec City For Dummies

Vancouver & Victoria For Dummies

Available wherever books are sold.
Go to www.dummies.com or call 1-877-762-2974 to order direct.

Bahamas
FOR
DUMMIES®
3RD EDITION

by Darwin Porter and
Danforth Prince

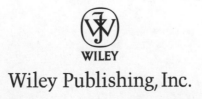

WILEY

Wiley Publishing, Inc.

Bahamas For Dummies,® 3rd Edition
Published by
Wiley Publishing, Inc.
111 River St.
Hoboken, NJ 07030-5774
www.wiley.com

Copyright © 2005 by Wiley Publishing, Inc., Indianapolis, Indiana

Published simultaneously in Canada

For general information on our other products and services or to obtain technical support, please contact our Customer Care Department within the U.S. at 800-762-2974, outside the U.S. at 317-572-3993, or fax 317-572-4002.

Wiley also publishes its books in a variety of electronic formats. Some content that appears in print may not be available in electronic books.

Library of Congress Control Number: Available From Publisher

ISBN: 0-7645-6939-2

Manufactured in the United States of America

10 9 8 7 6 5 4 3 2

3B/RY//RQ/QU/IN

WILEY

About the Authors

Darwin Porter, while still a teenager, began writing about The Bahamas for the *Miami Herald* and has been a frequent visitor ever since. His writing partner is Ohio-born **Danforth Prince,** formerly of the Paris bureau of the *New York Times,* who has co-authored numerous Frommer's best-sellers with Darwin, including the *Caribbean, Bermuda, Puerto Rico, Jamaica,* and the *Virgin Islands.* Together, they share their secrets, discoveries, and opinions about The Bahamas with you.

Publisher's Acknowledgments

We're proud of this book; please send us your comments through our Dummies online registration form located at www.dummies.com/register/.

Some of the people who helped bring this book to market include the following:

Editorial

Editors: Mike Baker, Project Editor; Myka Carroll Del Barrio, Editor

Copy Editor: Michelle Dzurny

Cartographer: Roberta Stockwell

Editorial Manager: Jennifer Ehrlich

Editorial Assistant: Nadine Bell

Senior Photo Editor: Richard Fox

Front Cover Photo: A woman savoring the view © Greg Johnston/ Lonely Planet Images

Back Cover Photo: Colorful huts in Junkanoo colors at Compass Point, Nassau © Christopher P. Baker/Lonely Planet Images

Cartoons: Rich Tennant, www.the5thwave.com

Composition

Project Coordinator: Kristie Rees

Layout and Graphics: Lauren Goddard, Michael Kruzil, Melanee Prendergast, Jacque Roth, Julie Trippetti

Proofreaders: David Faust, John Greenough, TECHBOOKS Production Services

Indexer: TECHBOOKS Production Services

Publishing and Editorial for Consumer Dummies

Diane Graves Steele, Vice President and Publisher, Consumer Dummies

Joyce Pepple, Acquisitions Director, Consumer Dummies

Kristin A. Cocks, Product Development Director, Consumer Dummies

Michael Spring, Vice President and Publisher, Travel

Brice Gosnell, Associate Publisher, Travel

Kelly Regan, Editorial Director, Travel

Publishing for Technology Dummies

Andy Cummings, Vice President and Publisher, Dummies Technology/General User

Composition Services

Gerry Fahey, Vice President of Production Services

Debbie Stailey, Director of Composition Services

Contents at a Glance

Maps at a Glance

● ●

Table of Contents

Introduction

• •

*L*ying just off the tip of Florida and stretching southeast across 258,998 sq. km (100,000 sq. miles) of the Atlantic Ocean, The Bahamas are often called the South Sea Islands of the Atlantic. Many of The Bahamas' thousands of miles of perfect coral sand beaches remain free of footprints.

Charting its own course from Britain since 1973, the archipelago is made up of a landmass of 700 islands. The prospect of deciding which island is right for you isn't as daunting as that figure suggests. Most of the islands — or islets, in some cases — aren't inhabited. Of those islands that are inhabited, only a few are graced with places to stay.

Don't come here looking for mountainous interiors like the ones found in Jamaica or Puerto Rico. Instead of hills, The Bahamas offer seascapes that seem to stretch forever. For the most part, beaches of white, golden, or, in some rare cases, pink sands ring the islands. If you're flying over them like a bird, you can see translucent waters shimmering in the sunlight — pale aquamarine, blue sapphire, or what an aerial photographer once called "dancing green."

Entire books containing only photographs of these swirling water patterns have been published. As more and more of the world's seas become polluted, the Bahamian waters alone make this island nation worth a trip.

In *Bahamas For Dummies,* 3rd Edition, we help you discover the islands, focusing on the high points but also warning you about some of the low points. Of course, we hit all the hot spots, like the well-touristed **Nassau, Paradise Island,** and **Freeport/Lucaya** on **Grand Bahama Island.** But we also take you to the less-visited and harder-to-reach islands, such as the **Exumas** in the southern Bahamas, perfect for those visitors seeking an escape for some serious R&R.

About This Book

You can use this book in three ways:

 ✔ **As a trip planner:** Whether you think you know where you want to go in The Bahamas or you don't have a clue, this book helps you zero in on the right island (or islands) for you. Expect plenty of insider advice — the kind you'd get from a trusted friend — about where to go and what to avoid. We guide you through all the necessary steps of making your travel arrangements, from finding the cheapest airfare, to figuring out a budget, to packing like a pro. All the chapters are self-contained, so you don't have to read them in order. Just flip to them as you need them.

 ✔ **As an island guide:** Pack this book alongside your sunscreen and it'll come in just as handy while you're away. Turn to the appropriate island chapters whenever you need to find the best beaches, a tasty place to eat, a great snorkel or sail, a challenging golf course, a hot nightspot, or tips on any other diversions.

 ✔ **For an overview:** If you want a feel for The Bahamas, peruse this guide from start to finish to figure out which of the archipelago's pleasurable pursuits are right for you.

Be advised that travel information is subject to change at any time — and this is especially true of prices. We suggest that you write or call ahead for confirmation when making your travel plans. The authors, editors, and publisher cannot be held responsible for the experiences of readers while traveling. Your safety is important to us, however, so we encourage you to stay alert and be aware of your surroundings. Keep a close eye on cameras, purses, and wallets — all favorite targets of thieves and pickpockets.

Dummies Post-it® Flags

As you're reading this book, you'll find information that you'll want to reference as you plan or enjoy your trip — whether it be a new hotel, a must-see attraction, or a must-try walking tour. Mark these pages with the handy Post-it® Flags included in this book to help make your trip planning easier!

Conventions Used in This Book

Bahamas For Dummies is a reference guide that allows you to read chapters in any order you want. Instead of providing guidebook "hieroglyphics," the book is user-friendly, keeping abbreviations and symbols to a minimum.

The following credit-card abbreviations noted are used for the establishments that accept them:

- ✔ AE: American Express
- ✔ DC: Diners Club
- ✔ DISC: Discover
- ✔ MC: MasterCard
- ✔ V: Visa

We use $ signs to indicate the costs of hotels and restaurants so that you can quickly determine whether you want to unpack your luggage at a hotel or dine on the local cuisine (see the price table later in this section). The $ system lists a range of costs so you can make fast comparisons.

The rates we use in our hotel recommendations are for two guests spending one night in a standard double room during the high season, which lasts from mid-December to mid-April. In the off-season, tariffs are sometimes lowered anywhere from 20 to 60 percent.

Most rates listed include only the room. In some cases, however, the stated price includes breakfast. And in the rare cases of all-inclusive hotels, the rates we present may initially seem very high, but we note that one price includes everything: your room, meals, drinks, and all those extra expenses, such as tips, taxes, most activities, airport pick-ups, and returns for your departing flight. For restaurants, we give the price range for a main course per person.

The following table shows the system of $ signs that we use to indicate a range of costs for one night in a hotel or the price of a dinner main course at a restaurant.

Cost	Hotel	Restaurant (Main Courses)
$	$100 or less per night	Less than $15
$$	$100–$150	$15–$20
$$$	$150–$225	$20–$25
$$$$	$225–$300	$25–$30
$$$$$	More than $300 per night	$30 and up

Foolish Assumptions

We made the following assumptions in preparing this guide:

- ✔ You may be a first-time visitor to The Bahamas in need of the "building blocks" to help you create a trip at a price that you can afford.

- ✔ You may have been to The Bahamas before, but you haven't explored them in a long time and you want sound advice about what's new and good and what's changed since your last trip.

- ✔ You're a busy person and don't want to read a lot of background and less-than-urgent information. After all, a vacation shouldn't be homework. You want a book that focuses quickly on the places that'll give you the best experience in the islands.

- ✔ Finally, we assume that you're seeking value — that you want to get the biggest bang for your buck in The Bahamas. So we help you steer clear of pricey tourist traps.

If you fall into any of these categories, *Bahamas For Dummies* is for you.

How This Book Is Organized

This book is divided into seven parts. The chapters within each part cover specific subjects in detail. You don't have to read this book in any particular order. In fact, think of these pages as an island buffet: You can consume whatever you want, and no one cares whether you eat the guava duff for dessert before you consume the conch chowder.

Part 1: Introducing The Bahamas

In this part, we offer our opinions on the best attractions and experiences The Bahamas have to offer, and we give you an overview of Bahamian customs, music, festivals, cuisine, and "thirst-busters." We also compare and contrast the most popular islands of The Bahamas so that you can decide which place (or places) best suits your tastes. Sure, they all have gorgeous beaches, but that's where the similarities end.

We also tell you the best and worst times of the year to travel to The Bahamas. We explain *high season* (when prices go up) and *low season* (when prices go down again), and we highlight the advantages and disadvantages of traveling during these times of year. We also provide a calendar of events in case you want to plan your trip to coincide with a festival, tournament, or local holiday.

Part II: Planning Your Trip to The Bahamas

Part II lays out everything you need to know about how to plan a worry-free trip. Because money is a primary consideration, we tell you how to access your funds, and we provide tips on how you can stay within your budget. We also help you decide how to travel to The Bahamas. If you're flying, you discover how to obtain the best fares, or, if you're traveling by cruise ship, we show you how to link up with some of the best deals for your "floating hotel" to The Bahamas.

To help you plan a stay that's tailored to your preferences, we explain in detail the various accommodation options awaiting you, from simple Bahamian inns and guesthouses to mega-resorts. We offer trip-planning tips for newlyweds, soon-to-be-newlyweds, families, singles, gays and lesbians, seniors, and travelers with disabilities. You also find out everything you need to know about the boring but vital stuff, such as getting a passport and purchasing travel insurance.

Parts III through VI: The Islands

These parts are where we dish out the main course. The chapters in Parts III through VI are the juiciest morsels of the book because they're packed with all the fun stuff that makes a vacation a vacation. For each island or island group — New Providence, Grand Bahama (Freeport/Lucaya), the Abacos, the Eleuthera chain (including Harbour Island), the Exumas, Bimini, San Salvador, and some of the less-visited islands for escapists — you get the lowdown on hotels, what to expect when you arrive (from landing at the airport to dealing with local taxi drivers), what restaurants to try and, of course, where to go and what to do, including beaching it.

For each island, we include a section called "Fast Facts." These quick tips give you handy information that you may need, including phone numbers to use in an emergency, where to find area hospitals and pharmacies, where to find ATMs, and more. For the bigger islands, you find "Fast Facts" at the end of the "Settling In" chapters. For the smaller islands, you can locate them at the end of the chapters.

Part VII: The Part of Tens

As in every *For Dummies* book, this lighthearted part is just for fun. We share our ten favorite island experiences with you, along with ten common myths about The Bahamas.

Icons Used in This Book

Throughout this book, icons highlight useful information. Here's what each symbol means:

 Keep an eye out for the Bargain Alert icon as you seek out money-saving tips and great deals.

 Best of the Best highlights the best the destination has to offer in all categories — hotels, restaurants, attractions, activities, shopping, and nightlife.

 Watch for the Heads Up icon to identify annoying or potentially dangerous situations, such as tourist traps, unsafe neighborhoods, monetary rip-offs, and other things to beware.

 Look to the Kid Friendly icon for attractions, hotels, restaurants, or activities that are particularly hospitable to children or people traveling with kids.

 When you see the Tip icon, you find useful advice on things to do and ways to schedule your time.

 The Worth the Search icon points out secret discoveries or useful resources that are worth the extra bit of effort to find.

Where to Go from Here

Nothing's like a vacation in the islands — when you plan it with the right advice and inside tips, that is. Whether you're a veteran traveler or a rookie, this book helps you put together just the kind of trip you have in mind. So, start turning these pages, and before you know it, you'll feel that warm island breeze on your face.

Part I
Introducing
The Bahamas

The 5th Wave By Rich Tennant

YEAR 1 - GET RESCUED
YEAR 2 - GET RESCUED!
YEAR 3 - GET RESCUED!! NOW!!
(FOCUS MORE)
YEAR 4 - GET RESCUED
(SCREAM LOUDER!)
YEAR 5 - BUILD GOLF
RESORT

"My thinking has changed a little this year."

In this part . . .

We arm you with everything you need to know about
The Bahamas before you begin making your travel
plans. We tell you about the best the islands have to offer,
and we introduce you to the islands' customs, music, and
cuisine.

After giving you an overview of this sunny archipelago, we
describe the highlights and drawbacks of each island and
help you decide exactly where you want to go. We also give
you an enjoyable quiz that helps you pinpoint the island or
islands that match your preferences. Finally, we help you
choose the best time of year to travel to your island getaway.

Chapter 1

Discovering the Best of The Bahamas

In This Chapter

▶ Finding the best beaches
▶ Scoping out the top hideaways and resorts
▶ Seeking the most exciting watersports
▶ Checking out the best restaurants, nightlife, and shopping

*I*n The Bahamas, you can island hop by boat or scuba dive along what some devotees believe are the remains of the lost continent of Atlantis. But perhaps your idea of a perfect island vacation is to plunk yourself down on a pink sand beach with a frosted drink in hand. Whether you're looking for adventure or relaxation — or a bit of both — this chapter points you to the best The Bahamas has to offer. We also let you know where you can find the details on each location or activity later in this book. Throughout the book, look for the "Best of the Best" icon to highlight our picks.

The Best Beaches

✔ **Cable Beach** (New Providence): This crescent-shaped, sandy 6.5km (4-mile) strip of shoreline is even better than Paradise Island's Cabbage Beach, which is more crowded. The prime beachfront strip of Cable Beach came into prominence during the post-World War II boom on the island, and today the beach is a beehive of activities, ranging from water-skiing to banana-boat rides. Cable Beach isn't always kid-safe, however, because during the winter months waters are sometimes rough. See Chapter 13.

✔ **Cabbage Beach** (Paradise Island): Across the waters from New Providence, the sandy strands of Paradise Island are called Cabbage Beach (no one's quite sure how the beach got its name). Cabbage Beach is a spectacular strip of sand running in front of the swanky Ocean Club Resort, and it's ideal for swimming, sunning, and watersports, such as Jet-skiing and para-sailing. The big drawback to this beach is that it's overcrowded in winter. On the western tip of the island, this beach even charges admission. The showpiece of Paradise Island, Cabbage Beach stretches for 3km (2 miles), rimming the north coast from the Atlantic lagoon all the way to the intimate Snorkeler's Cove. See Chapter 13.

✔ **Xanadu Beach** (Grand Bahama): In Samuel T. Coleridge's *Kubla Khan*, Xanadu is an idyllic, exotic, and luxurious place, and so is this aptly named stretch of white sands. Xanadu Beach is located on the most populated sector of this sprawling island and is convenient to the resorts of Freeport and Lucaya. The surf is most often tranquil, and the white sands stretch for 1.6km (1 mile). During the winter, Xanadu Beach is crowded, but it's a year-round magnet, with kid-friendly waters from spring to fall. You'll find the best watersports on the island here. See Chapter 17.

✔ **Tahiti Beach** (Elbow Cay): Think South Pacific in The Bahamas. Lying at the far southern end of remote Elbow Cay Island in the yachting haven of the Abacos, this relatively undiscovered beach is Paradise Found. After three days on this strip of white sands, you'll lose all sense of time and space, and devote the rest of your life to beachcombing. The sands of Tahiti Beach are set against a backdrop of thick walls of palm trees. See Chapter 19.

✔ **Treasure Cay Beach** (Treasure Cay): Tucked away on a remote island in the Abacos, Treasure Cay Beach is one of the best beaches in The Bahamas or even the Caribbean. Treasure Cay Beach is so large — 5.5km (2½ miles) — that you never feel crowded, even during the high season. Nowhere else in the Abacos (or most anywhere else) can you find sand this soft and white. Unpolluted water in striking shades of blue and green washes up on this peaceful shore. See Chapter 21.

✔ **Pink Sands Beach** (Harbour Island): In our view, no beach in the Out Islands — or even in Nassau, Grand Bahama, or Paradise Island — tops this lovely strip of pink sands that stretches for a whopping 5km (3 miles). Swimming is idyllic year-round because the natural harbor is protected by reefs that break up the turbulent sea's waves. Going sunning in the morning is best because afternoon can be a bit shadowy. See Chapter 22.

✔ **Ten Bay Beach** (Eleuthera): These golden sands, lying just north of Savannah Sound, are waiting for your beach towel. Don't expect watersports kiosks, fast-food stands, and vendors pushing handicrafts. Instead, expect relatively undiscovered sands opening onto generally tranquil waters. In the 1960s, this beach was one of the most fashionable in The Bahamas, but the exclusive clubs that once flourished here are long gone, leaving . . . well, the beach. See Chapter 23.

The Best Places to Get Away from It All

- ✔ **Ocean Club** (Paradise Island; ☎ 800-321-3000 or 242-363-2501): This hideaway is the most exclusive on New Providence and the adjoining Paradise Island. A true pocket of posh, the Ocean Club was once a private club owned by A+P zillionaire Huntington Hartford, but today it's a glitzy sanctuary of elegance and charm. Surrounded by splendid terraced gardens, it offers a country-club ambience, prime beachfront, and gourmet dining. See Chapter 11.

- ✔ **Compass Point** (New Providence; ☎ 800-688-7678 or 242-327-4500): The hip music mogul Chris Blackwell owns this small, charming, casually elegant, and personalized retreat far removed from the bustling activities of mass-market Cable Beach. Compass Point, with its electric color scheme, features one- and two-bedroom cottages set on stilts overlooking the water. The resort is only a 20-minute ride from the center of Nassau, and it opens onto one of the most beautiful sandy coves along the northwest coast. Bahamian "huts" have never been more comfortable than the ones at this bungalow colony! See Chapter 11.

- ✔ **Paradise Cove** (Grand Bahama Island; ☎ 242-349-2677): Away from the hordes at Freeport or Lucaya, this small island inn is only a 20-minute drive east of the bustling West End. But being at Paradise Cove is like being in a world far removed. At this secluded hideaway on the beach, you can rent one-bedroom apartments or two bedroom cottages with full kitchens. You can fill your day with swimming, sunbathing, and kayaking. See Chapter 15.

- ✔ **Green Turtle Club** (Green Turtle Cay; ☎ 800-963-5450 or 242-365-4271): Boasting the most complete yachting facility in its archipelago, this resort is one of the most charming of the "in" spots. Green Turtle Club has some of the best fishing and diving facilities. The villas include kitchens, and standard rooms are decorated in the colonial style. Two small, white sandy beaches are within walking distance. See Chapter 20.

- ✔ **Treasure Cay Hotel Resort & Marina** (Treasure Cay; ☎ 800-327-1584 or 242-365-8535): Boaters, golfers, fishermen, divers, yachties, and just plain escapists retreat to this luxurious resort on remote Treasure Cay. This resort boasts 5.5km (3½ miles) of spectacular sandy beach, and guests stay in privately owned condos when the owners aren't using them. The attraction here is not only a superb 18-hole golf course but also a 150-slip marina. See Chapter 21.

- ✔ **Pink Sands** (Harbour Island; ☎ 800-OUTPOST or 242-333-2030): Posh and sophisticated, this plush hideaway opens onto a 5km (3-mile) stretch of pink sandy beach sheltered by a barrier reef. This luxury resort features a main house and one- and two-bedroom villas spread across 10 hectares (25 acres) of property. This resort serves the best meals in Harbour Island. See Chapter 22.

✔ **Four Seasons Resort Great Exuma at Emerald Bay** (Exuma; ☎ 800-819-5053 or 242-358-4185): The grandest resort to open in the Out Islands, this 183-room resort is waking up this sleepy archipelago, whose tranquil waters are loved by yachties. At the Four Seasons' centerpiece is an 18-hole golf course designed by Greg Norman, and the resort's full-service spa and health club is also the finest in the Out Islands. See Chapter 24.

✔ **Club Med–Columbus Isle** (San Salvador; ☎ 800-CLUB-MED or 242-331-2000): One of the most remote Club Meds in the Western Hemisphere but also one of the most luxurious, this resort opens onto one of the most pristine beaches in the southern Bahamas. This getaway attracts tennis buffs along with scuba divers, honeymooners, and escapists. Other enticements include the lavishly decorated public lounges and the supremely comfortable bedrooms. See Chapter 25.

The Best Honeymoon Resorts

✔ **Sandals Royal Bahamian Hotel** (New Providence; ☎ 800-SANDALS or 242-327-6400): If you're a heterosexual couple, you can receive the most lavish and catered honeymoon in New Providence or Paradise Island. The way to go, of course, is to book one of the 27 secluded honeymoon suites with semiprivate plunge pools. The staff handles on-site wedding celebrations, and you're supplied with everything from the minister to the flowers, not to mention champagne and a wedding cake. See Chapter 11.

✔ **Wyndham Nassau Resort and Crystal Palace Casino** (New Providence; ☎ 800-222-7466 or 242-327-6200): If you and your loved one want glitter and bright lights instead of romantic isolation, this mega-resort is for you. Honeymooners flock here for its wide array of drinking, dining, and gambling options. Of course, when it's time to put up the DO NOT DISTURB sign and retreat to a king-size bed, that's all right, too. Ask about honeymoon package deals. See Chapter 11.

✔ **Compass Point** (New Providence; ☎ 800-688-7678 or 242-327-4500): An alternative to the mega-resorts of Cable Beach, Compass Point is a more isolated and personalized beach colony of flamboyantly painted "huts" that appeals to many young honeymooners. Very little is planned for you, but you have your own cottage on the sea, usually with a kitchenette where you can test the culinary skills of your new bride or groom. The property lies beside an idyllic sandy cove. See Chapter 11.

✔ **Ocean Club** (Paradise Island; ☎ 800-321-3000 or 242-363-2501): On lush acres between the golf course and a white sandy beach, this resort is a chic — though costly — address. Luxury rooms and suites are created from the finest materials. Ocean Club is a haven of tranquility, fine dining, formal gardens, and even reflecting pools that stretch toward a cloister assembled stone by stone from Europe. No staff on the island pampers honeymooners more, but if you want to be left alone with your mate, the staff gently retreats. See Chapter 11.

✔ **Abaco Inn** (Elbow Cay; ☎ **800-468-8799** or 242-366-0133): For barefoot elegance in the sands and romance, this sophisticated little hideaway is one of the gems of the yachting haven known as the Abacos. Luxury villa suites with sunrise and sunset views are the way to go. If you and your loved one find a hammock in the gardens, the day is yours. See Chapter 19.

✔ **The Bluff House Beach Hotel** (Green Turtle Cay; ☎ **800-745-4911** or 242-365-4247): This hotel, located in a romantic spot on a secluded beach, is an escapists' dream. The hotel has a nautical charm with British colonial overtones. The best honeymoon accommodations are the spacious suites, with cathedral ceilings and balconies overlooking the Sea of Abaco and a beach nearby. The 4 hectares (10 acres) on which the hotel sits are some of the most desirable real estate in The Bahamas. See Chapter 20.

✔ **Pink Sands** (Harbour Island; ☎ **800-OUTPOST** or 242-333-2030): This resort is the one place in all The Bahamas where we'd personally go for a honeymoon. Chris Blackwell, who brought reggae star Bob Marley to world attention, created the most sophisticated hideaway in the Out Islands, opening onto the pink sands of one of the country's greatest beaches, stretching for 5km (3 miles). The inn's luxurious accommodations are set on an 11 hectare (28-acre), beautifully landscaped estate. See Chapter 22.

The Best Family Resorts

✔ **Radisson Cable Beach Hotel** (Cable Beach; ☎ **800-333-333** or 242-327-6000): A well-organized kids' camp lures families to this sprawling 691-room resort, which opens onto some of the best sands along Cable Beach right outside Nassau. The resort's children's activities are the best organized on New Providence, but they're nowhere near the equal of Atlantis on Paradise Island. An added plus is that many of the bedrooms contain two double beds, making them suitable for families of four. Dining is no problem here because of the vast array of possibilities. See Chapter 11.

✔ **Atlantis Paradise Island Resort and Casino** (Paradise Island; ☎ **800-ATLANTIS** or 242-363-3000): Imagine yourself and your kids washed up on the shores of the lost continent of Atlantis. The Bahamas don't offer any other choices that are more fun for a family vacation than this sprawling mega-resort, a true fantasy world that's nautical with a vengeance. The children's programs (for ages 4 to 12) are the most spectacular in the country — a "sea world" of underground grottoes sprawls across 5.5 hectares (14 acres) of boundless fun, including aquariums, underwater viewing tunnels, and cascading waterfalls. See Chapter 11.

✔ **Ritz Beach Resort** (Lucaya; ☎ 242-373-9354): Think Disney on Grand Bahama Island. Surrounded by semi-tropical gardens, the Ritz is in the midst of all the fun, next door to a water park and the Pirates of The Bahamas Theme Park (all that's missing is Johnny Depp). Efficiencies, one-bedroom suites, or multi-level studio penthouses with private pools are available to suit the needs of your family. See Chapter 15.

✔ **Lofty Fig Villas** (Marsh Harbour; ☎ 242-367-2681): This family-owned bungalow colony is for self-sufficient types who want more of a Robinson Crusoe holiday. Vacationing families meet like-minded people around the outdoor barbecue or the freshwater pool. Each bungalow comes with a fully equipped kitchen and a private screened-in porch. See Chapter 18.

✔ **Banyan Beach Club Resort** (Treasure Cay; ☎ 888-625-3060 or 242-365-8111): Right on a beach that's widely hailed as one of the world's top ten, this resort offers spacious condos that are well suited for families. All the condos come with complete kitchens, and you can get burgers and hot dogs served at the beach bar and grill. For larger families, two-bedroom accommodations with an additional sleeping area are available. See Chapter 21.

✔ **Four Seasons Resort Great Exuma at Emerald Bay** (Great Exuma; ☎ 800-819-5053 or 242-358-4183): This resort is the only major resort in the Exumas, or in all the southern Bahamas, that caters to families, and it does so exceedingly well with its well-organized children's programs. If your budget allows, book one of the idyllic beachfront properties that has one or two bedrooms. The array of activities, the great beaches, the wide variety of dining options, and the overall comfort make this resort a winning choice. See Chapter 24.

The Best Restaurants

✔ **Chez Willie** (Nassau; ☎ 242-322-5364): One of the most elegant and romantic restaurants in New Providence, Chez Willie recaptures some of the magic of Nassau in the 1940s during the heyday of the Duke and Duchess of Windsor. The host, Willie Armstrong, is the epitome of graciousness, and the French and Bahamian cuisine is elegantly presented and beautifully prepared. See Chapter 12.

✔ **Sun And . . .** (Nassau; ☎ 242-393-1205): This restaurant, which serves Continental (mainly French) cuisine and seafood, is a Nassau classic with an overlay of British charm. The chef uses exceptional products along with a finely honed technique in the kitchen and is known for his to-die-for soufflés. See Chapter 12.

✔ **Sole Mare** (Cable Beach; ☎ 242-327-6200): The most elegant choice for dining on the beachfront strip outside Nassau also serves the finest Northern Italian cuisine on island. Candlelit tables and a guitarist playing soft tunes add to its romantic allure. Even though most of the ingredients are imported, the chefs still work their magic. See Chapter 12.

✔ **Dune** (Paradise Island; ☎ 242-363-2000): Better than any restaurant in Nassau, this elegant dining choice is located on the lobby level of the chic Ocean Club. French-born master chef and restaurant guru, Jean-Georges Vongerichten created this fine dining experience. With its trendy decor and sweeping view of the ocean, Dune is a study in culinary classicism, where flavors, aromas, and textures are perfectly combined. See Chapter 12.

✔ **Bahamian Club** (Paradise Island; ☎ 242-363-3000): A notch down from the superb Dune, this establishment is one of the leading restaurants in The Bahamas and is our favorite at the sprawling mega-resort of Atlantis. Strictly upscale, it presents a superb French and international cuisine nightly against a backdrop that evokes the British Colonial era. The restaurant serves the island's finest cuts of meats. See Chapter 12.

✔ **Rock House Restaurant** (Harbour Island; ☎ 242-333-2053): On the increasingly chic Harbour Island, the restaurant in the Rock House Hotel serves superb international cuisine. Its hip bodega aura evokes Miami, but it's thoroughly grounded on the island. At lunch you can get a rock lobster sandwich, but at night the chefs display their culinary prowess with an array of satisfying dishes. See Chapter 22.

The Best Diving

✔ **New Providence:** Right off the coast of Nassau lies a spectacular underwater world with many stunning dive sites that offer a panorama of rainbow-hued fish, large sponges, and a wide variety of coral reef life along with ocean holes, wrecks, old shipwrecks, caves, and cliffs. One of the greatest dive sites is Shark Wall, which is 16km (10 miles) off the coast of New Providence. Other good dive sites are Southwest Reef, Razorback, Booby Rock Reef, and Rose Island Reef.

The coastline of New Providence, called "the best-kept diving secret in The Bahamas," is home to some fascinating wrecks that you can explore in shallow water, including the *Mahoney* and the *Alcora*. The *Never Say Never Again* wreck was a backdrop for the James Bond film: A 34m (100-ft.) freighter, seized as a drug runner, was sunk by the film crew. Nearby, you can explore the remains of an airplane prop created for another Bond thriller, *Thunderball*. The best outfitter is **Bahama Divers** (☎ 242-393-5644). See Chapter 13.

✔ **Grand Bahama:** On Grand Bahama, you can hook up with **Underwater Explorers Society** (UNEXSO; ☎ 888-365-3483 or 242-373-1250), which is one of the premier dive outfitters in The Bahamas. Its escorted dives are the best, including a series of dramatic reef trips, shark dives, shipwreck dives, and even night dives. See Chapter 17.

✔ **Theo's Wreck** (Grand Bahama): This is one of the most famous wrecks in The Bahamas, and it lies off Freeport. The site is ideal for photo ops. In 1982, the 70m (230-ft.) freighter was deliberately sunk just to attract marine life. It succeeded: The wreck teems with sea turtles, moray eels, eagle rays, and horse-eyed jacks, among other creatures of the deep. For spur and groove coral beds, you can also explore other dive sites, including Gold Rock, Pygmy Caves, and Silver Point Reef. If you're an experienced diver, you can explore these sites independently; otherwise, hook up with the previously recommended UNEXSO. See Chapter 17.

✔ **Marsh Harbour:** You can explore the *Abacos Train Wreck* in 4.5 to 6m (15–20 ft.) of water. This wreck consists of two almost-intact loco-motives lying on their sides. Another wreck in the area, *Adirondack,* also lies in shallow water some 3 to 7.5m (10–25 ft.) deep. Marsh Harbour is also the jumping-off point for the government-protected **Sea Preserve** and **Fowl Cay Land,** both teeming with sea life in shallow reefs. Divers have actually kissed barracudas here (not recommended!). Look for "The Towers," two coral towers rising 22.8m (75 ft.). The best outfitter is **Dive Abaco** (☎ **800-247-5338** or 242-367-2787). See Chapter 18.

✔ **Exuma Cays National Land and Sea Parks:** A major attraction of The Bahamas, this park is the first of its kind in the world. The 35km (22-mile) long, 13km (8-mile) wide natural preserve attracts scuba divers to its 453 sq. km (175 sq. miles) of sea gardens with spectacular reefs, flora, and fauna. Inaugurated in 1958, you can access it only by boat. See Chapter 24.

✔ **San Salvador:** Some of the best diving in the southern Bahamas centers around this remote island, which is the site of Riding Rock, a dive resort, and a Club Med. Some 40 well-preserved dive sites are no more than 45 minutes away by boat from either resort. The scuba diving takes place amidst stunning sea walls — called *wall diving* — at sites where the coral reef drops steeply. The underwater photography is great here, and you can even arrange to night dive. The best outfitter is **Guanahani Dive Ltd.** (☎ **242-331-2631**). See Chapter 25.

The Best Snorkeling

✔ **New Providence/Paradise Island:** Most of the big hotels and resorts at Cable Beach and on Paradise Island lend or rent snorkel-ing equipment. A number of intriguing sights await you, especially at Love Beach on New Providence. Also attracting snorkelers are such areas as Rose Island Reefs, Booby Rock Channel, the Goulding Reef Cays, and Gambier Deep Reef, plus some underwater wrecks lying in shallow water. **Bahamas Divers** (☎ **242-393-8234**) can give you the most helpful advice on snorkeling possibilities. The com-pany's branch on Paradise Island is located at the Shertaon Grand

Resort (☎ 242-393-8724). Also consider **Hartley's Undersea Walk** (☎ 242-393-8234), which allows you to walk through an underwater world. See Chapter 13.

✔ **Grand Bahama:** Resort hotels on island can hook you up with snorkeling excursions, such as the ones offered by **Ocean Motion Water Sports Ltd.** (☎ 242-374-2425), which is the best outfitter for snorkeling. In addition, the outlet can connect you with any number of other watersports, from banana-boating to water-skiing. The clear water around Grand Bahama is wonderful for snorkeling because it has a rich marine life. Snorkelers are fond of exploring Ben's Cave, a stunning cavern that's part of Lucayan Caves, as well as the coral beds at places like Silver Point Reef and Gold Rock. See Chapter 17.

✔ **Elbow Cay:** With its 209km (130-mile) string of beautiful cays and some of the best beaches in The Bahamas, the Abacos are ideal for snorkeling, especially in the waters off Elbow Cay. Visibility is often great because the cay lies close to the cleansing waters of the Gulf Stream. Mermaid Beach, a particularly colorful reef, is a favorite. **Sea Horse Boat Rentals** (☎ 242-367-2513) provides equipment and the best snorkeling advice. See Chapter 19.

✔ **Green Turtle Cay:** Because the Abacos have one of the world's largest barrier reefs, the island chain — and especially Green Turtle Cay — is a snorkeler's delight. Some of the colorful reefs start at depths of just 1.50m (5 ft.). Immerse yourself in a world of schools of fish along with coral caverns, huge tube and barrel sponges, and fields of elk and staghorn coral. Snorkelers can contact **Green Turtle Divers** (☎ 242-365-4271) or **Brendal's Dive Center** (☎ 242-365-4411). See Chapter 20.

✔ **Stocking Island:** George Town is the capital of Exuma, which is celebrated for its crystal clear waters so beloved by yachties. From George Town, Stocking Island lies across Elizabeth Harbour, which is only 1.5km (1 mile) away. Stocking Island is a long, thin, barrier island that attracts snorkelers who explore its blue holes (ocean pools of fresh water floating on heavier saltwater). The island is also ringed with undersea caves and coral gardens in stunning colors. You'll also find that Stocking Island has some of the most gorgeous white sand beaches in the southern Bahamas. See Chapter 24.

✔ **San Salvador:** Following in the footsteps of Columbus, snorkelers find a rich paradise on this relatively undiscovered island, with its unpolluted and unpopulated kilometers and kilometers of beaches that are ideal for swimming, shelling, and close-in snorkeling. A week's stay is enough time to become acquainted only with the possibilities, including Bamboo Point, Fernandez Bay, and Long Bay, which are all within a few kilometers of Cockburn (the main settlement) on the western side of the island. At the southern tip of San Salvador is one of our favorite places for snorkeling, Sandy Point, and its satellite Grotto Bay. See Chapter 25.

The Best Fishing

✔ **New Providence/Paradise Island:** The waters around New Providence are thick with game fish. In-the-know fishermen long ago learned the best months to pursue their catches: November through February for wahoo found in the reefs, June and July for blue marlin, and May through August for the oceanic bonito and blackfin tuna. Nassau is ideal for sportsfishing. Most boat charters allow their passengers to start fishing within 15 minutes after leaving the dock. The best outfitter is **Born Free Charters** (☎ 242-393-4144), where anchoring and bottom-fishing are also options. See Chapter 13.

✔ **Grand Bahama:** Off the coast, the clear waters are good hunting grounds for snapper, grouper, yellowtail, wahoo, barracuda, and kingfish. The tropical waters along Grand Bahama lure anglers in search of "the big one" because the island is home to some of the biggest game fish on earth. Many fishermen catch dolphins (not the Flipper kind, though). And Deep Water Cay is a fishing hot spot. The best outfitter is **Reef Tours, Ltd.** (☎ 242-373-5880).

✔ **Green Turtle Cay:** The deep-sea fishing possibilities off the coast of this cay draw anglers from all over the world. An abundance of giant game fish as well as tropical fish live in these beautful waters. Both dedicated fishermen and more casual sportsfishermen come to the little island, seeking yellowfin tuna, a few dolphinfish, and the big game wahoo, among other catches. Green Turtle Cay boasts some of the best fishing guides in The Bahamas: weather-beaten men who've spent a lifetime fishing the surrounding waters. The best place to hook up with one of these guides is **Green Turtle Club** (☎ 242-365-4070). See Chapter 20.

✔ **Treasure Cay:** In the Abacos, some of the best fishing grounds are in the sea bordering this remote island. At the **Treasure Cay Marina** (☎ 242-365-8250), fishermen from all over the world hire experienced skippers to take them out in their searches for barracuda, grouper, yellowtail, snapper, tuna, marlin, dolphinfish, and wahoo. Deep-sea, sea-bottom, and drift fishing are yours for the asking. The cay's own bonefish flats are just a short boat cruise from the marina. See Chapter 21.

✔ **Exuma:** Anglers from all over America descend on this beautiful archipelago for deep-sea or bottom-fishing. Fishermen hunt down kingfish, wahoo, dolphinfish, tuna, and bonito in the deepest waters off the coastline of the Exumas. Many visitors also fly here just to go bonefishing. Among other outfitters who can hook you up with fishing outings is **Club Peace and Plenty** (☎ 242-345-5555), which rents the necessary equipment and can arrange experienced guides to accompany you. See Chapter 24.

The Best Sailing

✔ **New Providence:** Although sailing in the waters off New Providence isn't the equal of yachting-favorites the Exumas and the Abacos, boaters can still find much to delight in. More organized-boating excursions are offered in New Providence than anywhere else in The Bahamas, especially by outfitters, such as **Barefoot Sailing Cruises** (☎ 242-393-0820) and **Majestic Tours Ltd.** (☎ 242-322-2606). You can also choose from an array of sunset cruises, like the ones **Flying Cloud** (☎ 242-393-4430) offers, which feature its fleet of catamarans. The most popular — and the most scenic — trip is sailing to tranquil Rose Island, which is 13km (8 miles) east of the center of Nassau and is reached after sailing past several small uninhabited cays. In addition, Blue Lagoon Island, 4.8km (3 miles) northeast of Paradise Island, is a magnet for boaters because it offers seven white sand beaches along with seaside hammocks. The drawback to this island, however, is that cruise-ship passengers flock here and many beach buffs come over on day trips. See Chapter 13.

✔ **Grand Bahama:** On the beautiful waters off this large island, you can go sailing aboard *Ocean Wonder* (☎ 242-373-5880), which is supposedly the world's largest twin-diesel engine glass-bottom boat. This boat offers the best and most panoramic view of under-life off the coast of Grand Bahama Island — a view most often reserved for scuba divers. You can also go sailing aboard *Bahama Mama*, a two-deck 22m (72-ft.) catamaran on a Robinson Crusoe Beach Party. The catamaran also sails at sunset on a booze cruise. **Superior Watersports** (☎ 242-373-7863) operates this catamaran. See Chapter 17.

✔ **Marsh Harbour:** One of the finest anchorages in the Out Islands is found in Marsh Harbour, which is called "The Boating Capital of The Bahamas." **The Moorings** (☎ 800-535-7289 or 242-367-4000) is one of the leading charter sailboat outfitters in the world, renting boats to sail the waters of the Abacos. Passengers discover white sand beaches and snug anchorages on uninhabited cays. Sailing here is one of the great experiences of visiting The Bahamas. See Chapter 18.

✔ **Exuma:** Yachties flock to these beautiful sailing waters to see some of the most dramatic coastal scenery in The Bahamas. The National Family Island Regatta, the most popular boating spectacle in The Bahamas, is held here annually. Most recreational boating is in the government-protected Exumas Cays Land and Sea Park, an area of splendid sea gardens and rainbow-hued coral reefs that stretches south from Wax Cay to Conch Cay. You can rent motorboats at **Minns Water Sports** (☎ 242-336-3483) in George Town. See Chapter 24.

The Best Shopping

✔ **Nassau:** Nassau is home to more shops than anyplace else in The Bahamas. If you're seeking anything from a Swiss watch to British-made china, you can find it at one of the shops along Bay Street in the heart of Nassau. Some of the merchandise — but hardly all of it — sells at discounts that range from 30 to 50 percent. You can purchase a lot of the merchandise for the same price or lower in your hometown, so the wise shopper who knows his prices can make off with the bargain merchandise. Surprisingly, goods actually made in The Bahamas are hard to come by. If you're in the market for Bahamian handicrafts, you can stroll by the famous Straw Market in Nassau, but watch which items you pick up — that handicraft may have MADE IN TAIWAN stamped on it. See Chapter 13.

✔ **Grand Bahama:** The only island in The Bahamas to rival the shopping in Nassau is the **Freeport/Lucaya** area. Much of the same merchandise that's sold in New Providence — including international imports of china, perfume, crystal, gemstones, or watches — is also for sale here at virtually the same prices. We're drawn more to the **Port Lucaya Marketplace** these days than to the more famous **International Bazaar** at Freeport. The situation at both markets is very tricky. We've found merchandise 20 to 40 percent lower than Stateside prices displayed along with so-called "discounted" and "duty-free" products that were actually cheaper in our hometown. See Chapter 17.

The Best Nightlife

✔ **Cable Beach:** The partying crowd packs the bars and restaurants at the resorts along this beachfront strip at night. Most of the action is around the **Wyndham Nassau Resort and Crystal Palace Casino** (☎ 242-327-6200) in the center of Cable Beach. This resort and casino obviously evoke Las Vegas and stand up well when compared to other glittering casinos in the Caribbean. If you want to see a Bahamian show, head for **King and Knights** (☎ 242-327-5321), which is like a Junkanoo festival. See Chapter 13.

✔ **Grand Bahama:** Most of the after-dark diversions on this island spin around two major casinos: the Royal Oasis Casino at the Crowne Plaza Golf Resort & Casino (☎ 242-350-7000) and the Isle of Capri Casino at The Westin and Sheraton at Our Lucaya Beach & Golf Resort (☎ 242-373-1333). In winter, gamblers and others can catch periodic stage shows, which pack the house with Las Vegas-style revues. Another popular gathering place is Count Basie Square at the Port Lucaya Marketplace, where musicians perform live three nights a week. And did we mention that it's free? See Chapter 17.

Chapter 2

Digging Deeper into The Bahamas

*F*ollowing in the footsteps of Columbus, Ponce de León arrived in The Bahamas searching for the legendary Fountain of Youth, which led to the discovery of Florida and the Gulf Stream. Chances are your own discoveries won't be quite as legendary. But you'll appreciate the archipelago more if you read the easy-to-digest cultural information in this chapter: historical background, culinary tidbits, local lingo, and some films or books you may want to check out before your trip.

Part of the fun of visiting The Bahamas is for a taste of island life — and that means listening to Junkanoo music, eating conch prepared in countless ways, meeting the friendly locals (who'd rather not be called "natives"), proclaiming guava duff your favorite dessert, finding the bar that makes the best Bahama Mamas and, in general, putting yourself on "island time," which is one slow-moving clock.

History 101: The Main Events

This island nation has an exciting history — a tale of conquistadors, pirates, rumrunners, and post-colonial prosperity. Here's the story.

The early years

Columbus first landed in the New World somewhere in The Bahamas on October 12, 1492. He landed on an island called "Guanahani" by the local inhabitants, who were Arawak Indians known as Lucayans. Over the years, exactly which island Columbus landed on has been much disputed. Recent research places the first landing on Samana

Cay, 105km (65 miles) southeast of Guanahani, which Columbus renamed San Salvador.

The Lucayans Columbus encountered are believed to have come to the islands from the Greater Antilles in the 8th century A.D. They were seeking refuge from the Carib Indians then living in the Lesser Antilles. The Lucayans were peaceful people who welcomed the Spaniards and taught them a skill soon shared with the entire seafaring world: how to make hammocks from heavy cotton cloth.

The Spanish conquistadors who claimed the islands for their king and queen didn't repay the Lucayans kindly. Finding neither gold nor silver mines nor fertile soil, the conquistadors cleared out the population of the islands, taking some 40,000 doomed Lucayans to other islands in the Spanish empire to work in mines or dive for pearls.

Ponce de León voyaged here in 1513 looking for the legendary Fountain of Youth. His journey led to the European discovery of Florida and the Gulf Stream — but not the magic fountain. Ponce de León's historian described the waters of the Little Bahama Bank — just north of Grand Bahama — as *bajamar* (pronounced "bahamar," which is Spanish for "shallow water"). This word seems to be a reasonable source of the name "Bahamas." Other than this mention, however, practically no references were made to the islands first discovered by Columbus for 135 years.

Important dates in Bahamian history

700 Lucayans emigrate to The Bahamas from the Greater Antilles, seeking refuge from the cannibalistic Caribs.

1492 Columbus makes his first landfall in the New World, traditionally said to be at San Salvador, although many historians dispute this theory.

1513 Ponce de León searches for the Fountain of Youth and discovers the Gulf Stream.

1629 England claims The Bahamas, which were then destitute of population.

1640s The first Western settlements are established.

1656 New Providence Island (site of Nassau) is settled.

1717 King George I orders Captain Woodes Rogers, the first royal governor, to chase the pirates out of Nassau.

1776 The fledgling United States Navy captures Nassau but soon departs.

1782 The British Crown Colony surrenders The Bahamas to Spain.

1783 Spain signs the Treaty of Paris, ceding The Bahamas to Britain.

1833 The United Kingdom Emancipation Act frees slaves throughout the British Empire.

1861–65 Blockade-running during the U.S. Civil War brings prosperity to The Bahamas.

1920–33 Rumrunning during Prohibition in the U.S. revives a slumping Bahamian economy. The 1920s are a busy and prosperous time for bootleggers.

1933 The repeal of Prohibition causes an economic collapse on the islands.

1940 The Duke of Windsor, after renouncing the British throne, becomes governor of The Bahamas as war rages in Europe.

1964 Sir Roland Symonette becomes the country's first premier. The Bahamas are granted internal self-government.

1967 Lynden Pindling, named premier in a close election, begins a long, notorious reign.

1968 African-Bahamian rule becomes firmly entrenched.

1972 Bahamians vote for total independence from Britain.

1973 On July 9, the Union Jack in New Providence is lowered for the last time, ending more than three centuries of British rule.

1992 After 25 years, controversial Prime Minister Pindling goes down in defeat. Hubert Ingraham, campaigning against corruption and recession, replaces him.

1994 Hotel mogul and entertainer Merv Griffin sells Paradise Island properties.

1995 Developers of the famed Sun City complex in Swaziland become hotel czars of Paradise Island.

2002 Perry Gladstone Christie becomes the third prime minister in the nation's history.

The coming of the English

England formally claimed The Bahamas — by then unpopulated — in 1629. No settling took place, however, until the 1640s, and it resulted from a religious dispute that arose in Bermuda. Dissident English and Bermudian settlers (known as the Eleutheran Adventurers) sailed to an island called Cigatoo, changed the name to Eleuthera (from the Greek word for freedom), and launched a tough battle for survival. Many settlers became discouraged and went back to Bermuda, but a few hardy souls remained, living on fish and salvage from shipwrecks.

Other people from Bermuda and England eventually followed, and they helped settle New Providence Island in 1656. They planted crops of cotton, tobacco, and sugar cane and established Charles Towne (named in honor of Charles II) at the harbor.

Pirates and privateers

The promising agricultural economy of The Bahamas was short-lived. Several of the governors of The Bahamas during the late 17th century were corrupt, and soon the island became a refuge for English, Dutch, and French buccaneers who plundered Spanish ships. The Spaniards repeatedly attacked New Providence for revenge, and many of the settlers left. Those settlers who remained found supplying the rich pirates to be a good source of income. Privateers, a slightly more respectable type of freebooter (they had their sovereign's permission to prey on enemy ships), also found the many islets, tricky shoals, and secret harbors of the islands to be good hiding places from which they could stage their attacks on ships sailing between the New and Old Worlds.

Late in the 17th century, the settlers changed the name of Charles Towne to Nassau to honor King William III, who also held the title Prince of Nassau. At the time, some 1,000 pirates still called New Providence their home base.

Finally, the appeals of merchants and law-abiding islanders in favor of Crown control were taken seriously, and in 1717 the lord proprietors turned over the government of The Bahamas, both civil and military, to King George I, who commissioned Captain Woodes Rogers as the first royal governor.

Rogers captured hundreds of the lawless pirates. He sent some pirates to England to be tried; eight were hanged, and the king pardoned others after they promised to lead law-abiding lives. Later, Rogers was given the authority to set up a representative assembly, the precursor of today's Parliament. Despite such interruptions as the fledgling U.S. Navy capturing Nassau in 1776 (for only a few days) and the Crown Colony surrendering to Spain in 1782 (which lasted almost a year), the government of The Bahamas since Rogers's time has been conducted in an orderly fashion. In early 1783 under the Treaty of Paris, Spain permanently ceded The Bahamas to Britain, ending some 300 years of disputed ownership.

Loyalists, blockade runners, and bootleggers

After the American Revolution, several thousand Loyalists from the former colonies immigrated to The Bahamas. Some of the immigrants, especially southerners, brought slaves with them and tried their luck at planting sea-island cotton in the Out Islands. Growing cotton was unsuccessful (the plants fell prey to the chenille bug), but the former Deep South planters learned to fish, grow vegetables, and provide for themselves in other ways.

The first white settlers of The Bahamas also brought slaves with them, but when slavery was abolished throughout the British Empire in 1834, they were freed. The settlers achieved a fairly peaceful transition, although many years passed before any real equality between blacks and whites existed.

During the American Civil War, blockade running brought prosperity to The Bahamas. Nassau became a vital base for the Confederacy, with vessels taking manufactured goods to South Carolina and North Carolina and bringing back cotton. The Union victory ended blockade running and plunged Nassau into an economic depression.

The islands' next real economic boom resulted from Prohibition in the U.S. Just like the blockade runners who preceded them — only with faster boats and more of them — rumrunners plied the waters between The Bahamas and the southeastern U.S. From the enforcement of the 18th Amendment in 1920 to the repeal of that law in 1933, bootleggers used Nassau, Bimini, and Grand Bahama as bases for running contraband alcoholic beverages across the Gulf Stream. The U.S. Coast Guard and the bootleggers waged a ceaseless battle on each other. The repeal of Prohibition dealt another shattering blow to the vulnerable Bahamian economy.

The war, the duke, and the woman he loved

On August 17, 1940, the Duke and Duchess of Windsor arrived in Nassau following his appointment as governor of the colony. The duke abdicated his throne as King Edward VIII so he could marry the woman he loved, the divorcée American Wallis Simpson. The people of The Bahamas were shocked that such a once-powerful figure was assigned to govern their impoverished colony, which was viewed then as a backwater of the British Empire. The duke tried to bring self-sufficiency to The Bahamas and provide more employment for its out-of-work population.

World War II healed the wounds left over from the bootlegging days. The Bahamas served as an air and sea station in the Atlantic; as a result, the country inherited two airports built by the U.S. Air Force. The islands also were strategically important when Nazi submarines intruded Atlantic coastal and Caribbean waters. Today, some of the outlying islands still house U.S. missile-tracking stations.

A declaration of independence

In the years after World War II, party politics developed in The Bahamas as independence from Britain seemed more possible, and change came at the ballot box. In 1967, Lynden Pindling won a close election to become prime minister. During the general election of 1972, the Bahamian people voted for total independence. The people of The Bahamas agreed to be a part of the British Commonwealth, presided over by Queen Elizabeth II. Her representative in The Bahamas would be a governor-general, a position with mostly symbolic power. In 1992, after years of corruption under Pindling and countless exposés in the *Miami Herald,* Hubert A. Ingraham became prime minister. In office, he pledged to promote quality tourism for his nation.

In May 2002, Perry Gladstone Christie led the Progressive Liberal Party to victory, becoming the third prime minister to govern the island nation. Public opinion seems divided on Christie's reign. Many voters praise him as a progressive, modern leader; others have attacked him, including scorching editorials in *The Nassau Guardian*. Christie has been accused of receiving a vast amount of campaign money from known drug dealers, an accusation that the prime minister denies.

Building Blocks: Local Architecture

The unique geography and history of The Bahamas contributed to a distinctive architectural feature — the Bahamian clapboard house — that is today one of the most broadly copied styles in the tropics. But this design wasn't perfected and standardized until the early 19th century.

The earliest clapboard-sided houses were usually angled to receive the trade winds. Large window openings and high ceilings increased airflow, and awning-style push-out shutters shaded the windows and helped direct breezes indoors, even during rainstorms. Unlike larger, more impressive houses where foundations were massive edifices of coral, brick, or stone, the first floors of Bahamian cottages were elevated on low stilts or light masonry pilings to allow more air circulation. Raising the building also kept the floor joists, beams, and planks above floodwaters during a hurricane surge.

Ruggedly built of timbers whose ends were often pegged (not nailed) together and pinned to stone pilings several feet above the ground, Bahamian-style clapboard houses survived when many rigid and unyielding stone-built structures collapsed during hurricanes. Modern engineers claim that the flexibility of these structures increases their stability in high winds.

Within The Bahamas, you can check out some of the best-preserved and most charming examples of the Bahamian cottage style in Harbour Island (off the coast of Eleuthera) and, to a lesser extent, in Spanish Wells and Green Turtle Cay.

Living on Island Time

Island clocks aren't wound as tightly as clocks in other parts of the world. Life in The Bahamas moves much more slowly than many visitors are used to. Waiters, salespeople, and hotel desk clerks operate at what some outsiders consider too leisurely a pace. Especially in Nassau and Freeport, you may find some poorly trained, less-than-accommodating staff members here and there. But getting annoyed is a waste of energy. Most travelers soon learn to go with the flow and get in step with island time. If you're going to enjoy your vacation, you have to crank your expectations about time — and sometimes service — down a notch.

Word to the Wise: The Local Language

Bahamian dialect has its own cadence and musical rhythm. Sometimes an educated Bahamian dining with you will speak a lilting Queen's English and then suddenly lapse into Bahamian dialect when he hits on an emotional subject.

Accents in The Bahamas resemble those of the Caribbean region, just south of these Atlantic isles. However, a trained ear can easily pick up the difference. Some Bahamians sound as if they were imported from Brooklyn. For example, *woik* is what you do *fuh* a living, and a waiter will *soive* you.

Sometimes the letters *v* and *w* are interchanged. "So you wisitin', ay?" translates into "So you're visiting, are you?" If a Bahamian tells you he's going "spilligatin'," he means that he's planning to "carry on bad" — he intends to party and have an all-out good time. If he says he wants to "conversate" (a common Bahamian variation on the word converse) with you for a while, he wants to chat.

Some of the Loyalist villages, such as the ones found in Eleuthera, including Spanish Wells, retain certain pronunciations that were in use in the England of Shakespeare's day. For instance, the glass that someone serves your rum punch in may be called a *goblet.*

Taste of The Bahamas: Local Cuisine

When it's time to chow down in The Bahamas, settings range from casual family-run restaurants featuring local treats to elegant candlelit dining rooms offering gourmet international fare. The main source of food is the ocean. The steak you order may be juicy, but it didn't come from an island cattle farm. Instead, it was flown in to the restaurant, along with lamb and other meats, as well as most of the fruits and vegetables on your plate.

You find plenty of good food here and some mediocre eats as well — imported or not. Menus throughout the islands are varied. You may dine on an Indian or Greek appetizer one night, an Italian or Tex-Mex main course another night, and a French dessert the next night.

 Are you traveling with fussy kids? Don't worry. Burgers and fries, pizza, fried chicken, pasta, sandwiches, and other child-friendly fixings are easy to find, especially in Nassau and Freeport/Lucaya, where you find some fast-food chains.

 For the tastiest, most authentic (and least expensive) island cuisine, head to the smaller, locally run restaurants, where the home-style cooking revolves around the sea. Even the so-called island dishes at the larger hotels and restaurants have American and Continental influences.

Eating like a local

Restaurants specializing in island cuisine commonly serve conch, fish (especially grouper), and lobster. Among other local favorites are crab and rice, okra soup, chicken and dough (dumplings), mutton, wild boar, and souse, but these dishes are harder to find outside of people's homes. If you stop by a local restaurant in the morning and see men eating souse or conch salad, chances are they're trying to kill hangovers; locals believe that the hot peppers do the trick.

In the dining sections of the chapters, we sprinkle in a number of local eateries serving authentic and affordable Bahamian cuisine. In Nassau, sample island cuisine at **Shoal Restaurant and Lounge,** the **Bahamian Kitchen,** or the **Palm Tree** (see Chapter 12). On Grand Bahama Island, bite down at **Becky's Restaurant & Lounge** or **Fatman's Nephew** (see Chapter 16). After you reach many of the Out Islands, Bahamian food is all you can order in some of the smaller places, except for a first-class resort here and there, including the ones found on Harbour Island. Other top locations to check out island treats include

- Restaurants on Arawak Cay, between Cable Beach and downtown Nassau on New Providence. Sometimes you can make a special request and then return the next day for your meal.

- Stands on Potter's Cay, the dock beneath the Paradise Island exit bridge on New Providence (see Chapter 12).

- Many restaurants in The Bahamas' Out Islands (see Chapters 22 through 25).

- Kiosks during Bahamian festivals such as Junkanoo (at Christmas and New Year's) and the National Family Island Regatta (in George Town, Exuma, in April).

It's all about conch

The star of the culinary show is *conch* (pronounced "konk"). On every island at the edge of the water near boat docks, you see huge mounds of discarded conch shells — the kind with the shiny pink spiral interior that you put to your ear to hear the waves. Residents claim that conch gives men "strong back" — in other words, this tasty mollusk can raise the roof in the boudoir. No wonder the meat is transformed into so many local favorites, including

- **Conch chowder:** A rich, spicy soup with vegetables and bits of conch.
- **Conch fritters:** Golf ball-sized fried appetizers made with chopped conch, herbs, flour, baking powder, and water.
- **Conch salad:** Minced raw conch, marinated in lime juice, and mixed with chopped onions and peppers.
- **Cracked conch:** Pounded until tender, battered, and deep fried like a breaded veal cutlet.

✔ **Scorched conch:** Raw meat washed with seawater and lime juice, cut into large pieces and scored with a knife, and then rubbed with hot pepper and topped with sliced fresh tomatoes and onions. (You may catch fishermen on docks preparing this delicacy.)

✔ **Steamed conch:** Tenderized by beating or boiling, and then cooked with sautéed onions, bell peppers, hot peppers, thyme, tomatoes, and sometimes okra or carrots.

✔ **Stewed conch:** Made with a seasoned, flour-thickened gravy.

Dining on other Bahamian favorites

Fish, another staple, turns up for dinner, lunch, and even breakfast. Grouper and snapper are the usual suspects. *Boil fish* (cooked with salt pork, onions, and green peppers) is a popular morning eye-opener that comes with grits. Many places also often serve delicately sweet *johnny-cake* (a mildly sweet bread) on the side. Also eaten as the day's first meal is stewed fish that comes in a rich brown gravy. Steamed fish (which may sound bland, but is far from it), however, isn't eaten before noon and is cooked with a tomato base.

Local lobster is a bit tougher than the Maine variety, but it's prepared in lots of tasty ways: steamed, breaded, sautéed in butter, or topped with grated cheese. To make minced lobster — a Bahamian winner served in the shell — chefs shred the meat and cook it with tomatoes, green peppers, and onions.

A limited number of chickens are raised locally in The Bahamas, mostly on Eleuthera. *Chicken souse* is a popular dish made with chicken, onion, sweet peppers, bay leaves, allspice, and other ingredients, as the cook's imagination dictates. This dish simmers in a pot for about an hour, then the cook adds lime juice, and it simmers a little longer. Pig's feet souse is also a favorite dish.

Goats and sheep are also raised on the Out Islands. On a menu, "mutton" can refer to either type of meat and is often curried. Bahamians catch wild boar on some of the islands and hunt game birds, such as ducks and pigeons. They also eat raccoon stew.

Most meats, including pork, veal, and beef, are imported. Even with these meats, however, Bahamian cooks show their ingenuity with interesting variations. For example, at an Out Island inn, we recently enjoyed pork that was marinated with vinegar, garlic, onion, celery tops, cloves, mustard, and Worcestershire sauce and then baked and served with gravy. Even a simple baked ham is given a Bahamian touch — cooked with fresh pineapple, coconut milk, coconut flakes, mustard, honey, and brown sugar.

Many vegetables are grown in The Bahamas; others are imported. If you have a cucumber, you can be almost certain that it's from one of Edison Key's farms in North Abaco. They supply cucumbers to not only their own country, but also to about five percent of the stateside market. Bahamians also grow their own sweet potatoes, corn, cassava, okra, and peppers (both sweet and hot), among other produce. Lunch and dinner come with heaping portions of peas and rice, potato salad, coleslaw, or macaroni and cheese — and sometimes all of them.

Guava duff is the dessert specialty of The Bahamas. This dessert, which resembles a jellyroll, is made with guava pulp that has been run through a food mill or sieve. Nobody seems to agree on the best method of cooking it. One way you can make this dessert is to cream sugar and butter, and then add eggs and spices, such as cinnamon and cloves or nutmeg. Make a stiff dough by adding flour and mix the dough with the guava pulp, which you then place in the top of a double boiler and cook over boiling water for hours. You can also boil or steam the dough, and some cooks insist that you bake it. Guava duff is served with hard sauce (a blend of butter, confectioners' sugar, vanilla, and rum).

Other tasty Bahamian desserts and breads include coconut tarts, benne seedcakes, and potato bread.

Drinking island cocktails

Vacationers and residents alike satisfy their thirst with beer, much of it imported from the U.S., Germany, and The Netherlands.

 These imports have a higher alcohol content than the same brands of foreign beer sold in the U.S. The Bahamas' high-quality brew is called *Kalik,* named for the sound cowbells make in Bahamian Junkanoo music.

If you're not a beer drinker, colorful rum and fruit juice concoctions are the rage. Depending on who makes them, the ingredients and proportions vary; most bartenders won't reveal the secrets of their success. Besides rum punch, the top three tropical island cocktails are:

- ✔ **Bahama Mama:** Vat 19, citrus juice (often pineapple), bitters, a dash of nutmeg, crème de cassis, and a hint of grenadine

- ✔ **Goombay Smash:** Coconut rum, pineapple juice, lemon juice, Triple Sec, Vat 19, and a dash of syrup

- ✔ **Yellowbird:** Crème de banana liqueur, Vat 19, orange juice, pineapple, apricot brandy, and Galliano

Of course, you can find colas and other sodas, bottled (and sometimes freshly squeezed) juices, and bottled water on all islands. Although tap water is safe for brushing your teeth, most people drink bottled or filtered water.

Jumping to Junkanoo

The Bahamas maintain great pride in their original musical idioms, often comparing their vitality to the more famous musical traditions of Jamaica,

Puerto Rico, and Trinidad. Other than spirituals, which share roots with slave music from colonial North America, by far the most famous musical products are Goombay and its closely linked sibling, Junkanoo.

Goombay music is an art form with melodies and body movements that are always accompanied by the beat of goatskin drums and, when available, the liberal consumption of rum. The most outlandish expressions of Goombay occur the day after Christmas (Boxing Day), especially in Nassau on Bay Street. Dancers outfit themselves in masquerade costumes with bizarre accessories and glittering colors that evoke the plumage of jungle birds. Goombay musicians and dancers are almost always male, a custom dating from the days of slavery, and before that, originating in West Africa. However, in the "Jump-In Dance," performers dance around in a circle in which a solo dancer performs. To the rhythm of drums, the star dancer selects another person to take his place. Today this person is likely to be a female, who will then dance in the circle and select a male to replace her.

Junkanoo music is to The Bahamas what reggae is to Jamaica. In other words, you can't miss hearing it. All hotels and resorts, and even some restaurants, offer this music as part of the evening's entertainment. Some musical groups even call themselves "Junkanoo." Hearing it performed by locals in resorts or hotels is a lot safer than wandering the back streets of Nassau at night looking for a local club. The music will probably be just as authentic at the resort.

You can get a taste of Junkanoo at **Café Johnny Canoe** on Cable Beach, where the weekly Friday-night parade turns this New Providence restaurant into a party (Chapter 12). If you want a close-up look at the elaborate costumes, stop by the **Junkanoo Expo at Prince George Dock** in Nassau (see Chapter 13).

Background Check: Recommended Books

The checkered past of the archipelago — from pirates to shipwreckers and rumrunners — comes alive again in Paul Albury's *The Story of The Bahamas* (Macmillan Caribbean). This 294-page book is the best of its kind for a quick overview. Author Robert H. Fuson dug into the archives and came up with *The Log of Christopher Columbus* (International Marine Publishing), dating from 1492, of course. On seeing The Bahamas for the first time, the explorer wrote: "I made sail and saw so many islands that I could not decide where to go first."

For a lighter read, try Ernest Hemingway's *Islands in the Stream* (Charles Scribner & Sons), the classic novel in which "Papa" created the fascinating fictional character of Thomas Hudson, tracing his life from his years as a painter in Bimini in the 1930s through his anti-submarine activities off the Cuban coast during World War II. The character of Hudson is much like Hemingway himself.

Isles of Eden: Life in the Southern Family Islands of The Bahamas by Harvey Lloyd, with a foreword by former Prime Minister Lynden Pindling (Benjamin), chronicles the island people who live in this rarely visited archipelago, which stretches 144km (90 miles) southeast of Nassau all the way to Haiti. Lloyd blends unusual island photographs with social commentary, history, and personal recollections.

If you go to The Bahamas for a close encounter with nature, *The Ephemeral Islands: A Natural History of The Bahamas* by David G. Campbell (Media Publishing Ltd.) is the best fauna and flora book you can find. A well-written survey of the natural history of the island also comes with beautifully illustrated color plates.

The Yachtsman's Guide to The Bahamas (Tropic Isle Publishers, revised annually) is an essential guide for all visitors who are considering boat tours of The Bahamas. This guide is the standard one used by most yachties, but Stephen Pavlidis is cutting in on the market with *The Abaco Guide: A Cruising Guide to the Northern Bahamas including Grand Bahama, the Bight of Abaco, and the Abacos* (Seaworthy Publications). Pavlidas is a veteran of these seas, and his charts are the most accurate ones published. Because he's an active ham-radio operator, yachties in the Abacos often talk to him.

One of the most evocative novels on The Bahamas is *Paradise Overdose: A Novel* by Brian Antoni (Grove Press). Drug-trafficking once again figures into this tale of a young bachelor, Chris Angostura, whose life centers around women and cocaine. The tropical paradise comes alive in the descriptions of beaches and turquoise seas, but the profanity isn't for the faint of heart.

Beach reads

Before heading for the sands, pick up a copy of Desmond Bagley's *Bahama Crisis* (Fontana/Collin). This mystery spins around the character of Tom Mangan, who lures rich guests to his hotel in The Bahamas where disaster strikes in a series of strange accidents.

Barry Estabrook's *Bahama Heat* (St. Martin's Press) is whimsical and a good read, dealing with the usual drug-running schemes in The Bahamas, but with more plot than most. The cast of characters range from a rum-guzzling, charismatic pastor and a crazed lesbian pilot.

Great descriptions of The Bahamas, especially underwater, appear in the fast-paced *Bahamas Blue,* by D.C. Poyer (St. Martin's Press). This action-packed thriller has both a love of the sea combined with contempt for the drug runners who abuse it. Poyer (*Hatteras Blue*) is a well-known writer of sea adventures.

Chapter 3

Choosing Where to Go

● ●

In This Chapter

▶ Getting to know The Bahamas

▶ Picking the right island(s) for you

▶ Rating the islands

● ●

*W*hen measured against any region of the Caribbean, the Bahamian archipelago — which lies entirely in the Atlantic Ocean — is the number-one destination for visitors.

In this chapter, we help you decide which island is best for you by giving you a rundown of the highlights and drawbacks of each of the most popular (and most accessible) islands. If you want casinos and mega-resorts, for example, you may want to head for Paradise Beach, the most expensive area in The Bahamas. But if you seek a remote, tranquil location with pink sandy beaches and quiet inns, then Harbour Island may be for you, although it's also expensive. A fun quiz at the end of this chapter helps you narrow down your island options.

For details on where to stay, where to dine, and where to play on each of the islands covered in this book, check out Parts III through VI.

Introducing The Bahamas

Many people think that The Bahamas are in the Caribbean Sea when, in fact, they're surrounded by the Atlantic Ocean. But culturally, The Bahamas are part of the Caribbean.

The island nation of The Bahamas lies on a submarine platform that's actually an extension of the U.S. continental shelf. For many millions of years, the landmass of The Bahamas was much larger, with most of it above water until it sank during the Mesozoic period.

The Bahamas are an archipelago of some 700 islands (many mere islets) and 2,500 coral reefs. These reefs extend for about 1,290km (800 miles) on a northwest/southeast slant. The archipelago lies between the Atlantic Ocean and the Straits of Florida, with channels separating The Bahamas from Cuba and the island of Hispaniola (jointly owned by the Dominican Republic and Haiti).

In The Bahamas, only about 20 of the islands are inhabited in this landmass of 11,400 square km (4,405 sq. miles), which begins in the north at Little Abaco Island and stretches south to Great Inagua Island, which is famous for its colonies of flamingos.

George Washington called The Bahamas the "isles of perpetual June." They have a warmer climate than their northern latitude would suggest because equatorial sea currents bathe them. And the refreshing trade winds blowing in from the Atlantic rescues them from torrid summer seasons — the effect is kind of like natural air-conditioning.

 The northern locale of these islands means that during winter months, the weather is sometimes cooler than it is in the always-warm Caribbean. We've even seen snowflakes in winter in the northern Bahamas, but it's a rare event. (For more details about the best times to travel, turn to Chapter 4.) Without question, most of these islands have beautiful beaches, superb snorkeling, great scuba diving, and big-time boating and fishing. Each island also boasts its own special character and atmosphere. This variety means that you can easily tailor a trip to almost any desire or budget.

Finding the Right Island for You

The most frequently visited island in The Bahamas is **New Providence,** which includes the resort areas of **Nassau** and **Cable Beach** on its northern shore, and the offshore **Paradise Island.** New Providence is a world of gambling casinos, cruise-ship arrivals, mega-resorts, Las Vegas-like entertainment, and fancy restaurants.

The area's cousin, which offers the same diversions but without so much glitter, is the second-most visited island: **Grand Bahama,** with its vacation "villages" of **Freeport** and **Lucaya.**

New Providence and Grand Bahama are where most of the dry-land sightseeing is concentrated, from forts and museums to aquariums, gardens, and nature reserves. A couple of straw markets plus scores of stores and boutiques are additional attractions.

 Don't be misled by all the hype in Nassau and Freeport about shopping bargains. You do save on tax, but prices on many international goods are list, so you often pay what you would back home.

New Providence and Grand Bahama are the most accessible islands from the United States because of frequent flights and ship or ferry connections.

If the thought of taking an elevator to the beach leaves you cold, you may want to pass on the high-rises and impersonal crowds of Nassau, Paradise Island, and Freeport/Lucaya. If so, head to The Bahamas' **Out Islands,** which are sprinkled across thousands of square miles in the Atlantic Ocean.

 The Out Islands are the most beautiful part of The Bahamas. Miles of empty, golden sand beaches trim the clear waters. Except for scattered small towns — villages, really — and only a few large-scale beach resorts, nature has been left almost intact. Chickens, donkeys, sheep, and goats wander freely through front yards and on roads. In fact, boats, bicycles, golf carts, and feet are more prevalent than cars on some islands.

The most visited of the Out Islands include, in order, the **Abacos** (with Marsh Harbour, on Great Abaco, as its capital), **Eleuthera** (with its major vacation spot of Harbour Island), and the **Exumas** (popular with the boating crowd). Less visited and more alluring to those visitors who seek offbeat locations is **San Salvador,** which is home to a Club Med, the only major resort in the southern Bahamas.

The Out Islands aren't as easy to get to as Nassau, Paradise Island, or Freeport/Lucaya. In some cases, you have to take a plane (or two), a taxi to a dock, a ferry, and then another taxi to your hotel. But the inconvenience of transportation is a small price to pay for the peacefulness of a more secluded part of The Bahamas.

Knowing New Providence

A trio of destinations — **Nassau, Cable Beach,** and **Paradise Island** — are The Bahamas' main vacation areas, outranking its nearest rival, Freeport/Lucaya, in charm, class, and grandeur. Nassau, Cable Beach, and Paradise Island are adjoined, so you can stay in one and play in all three.

An architectural delight of old-world charm, Nassau is also The Bahamas' largest cruise-ship port. When ships are in port, the center of the city is congested, with shops, restaurants, and other businesses overflowing. Some cruise-ship passengers head for the beach, while others shop to seek out duty-free items, such as jewelry, cameras, china, crystal, and liquor.

New Providence is a mix of the ultra-modern and colonial quaint. The majority of The Bahamas' roughly 260,000 residents live on New Providence. **Nassau,** the archipelago's colonial capital, consists of a historic center that stretches for about a dozen blocks and is four blocks wide. Many government buildings have a rather grand neocolonial style of architecture, and even smaller buildings have style with wide balconies, louvered windows, and wood construction. Aging forts, small museums, gardens, and a zoo can amuse you when you're not bouncing along the waves on banana boats and Jet skis or off snorkeling or scuba diving.

New Providence and Paradise Islands

The part of the city that attracts most visitors lies along the waterfront and Bay Street, the main street of Nassau, which is a block away from the water. As you proceed inland from Nassau, the buildings become less grand, and the incomes of the families dwindle. Families on the lower end of the economic ladder live on the fringes of Nassau in clap-trap housing.

Emerging in recent years is New Providence's answer to Miami Beach: **Cable Beach.** Reached by heading west from Nassau along West Bay Street, Cable Beach opens onto a broad strand of golden sands and has a series of mega-resorts lined up one by one. Plenty of casino action and a wide array of watersports facilities are available for fun on the beach.

Cable Beach's major competition is the even glitzier **Paradise Beach,** which lies on **Paradise Island,** reached by a bridge. Although technically part of New Providence, Paradise Beach is a world unto itself. This beach has come a long way since it was called Hog Island.

Paradise Beach boasts the priciest real estate in The Bahamas. Its old-world charm is long gone, and today it's home to a colony of high rises, condos, second homes of the wintering wealthy, and gambling casinos. Its centerpiece is the mammoth Atlantis Paradise Island Resort and Casino (see Chapter 11), which isn't so much a hotel as a "city" in its own right.

Whether you're looking for an old-fashioned guesthouse or a splashy multi-story beach resort, you can find it in New Providence. Restaurants and fast-food eateries cater to a range of tastes, from the burger-on-the-run crowd to romantic couples enjoying a Continental cuisine by candle-light overlooking a lagoon.

Sports lovers can find plenty of golf, tennis, and horseback riding to keep them busy. Only a few nightclubs in Nassau itself are special. But after dark, Cable Beach and Paradise Island light up with elegant bars, dance floors, casinos, and Las Vegas-style stage shows.

Drawing everyone from American college students on spring break to middle-aged gamblers, many hotels offer economical air/land package deals. Nassau has a very limited number of hotels and not much in the way of a beach. Most resorts are clustered along Cable Beach on the North Coast and on Paradise Island. If you're looking for a moderately priced place to stay, you'll find it on Cable Beach — not on Paradise Island.

Bottom line: New Providence isn't the place for a cozy retreat. But if you want plenty of diversions and you don't mind crowds, it sizzles more than anywhere else in The Bahamas. (For more information on New Providence, see Part III.)

New Providence delivers a punch because it offers

✔ **Plenty of sights:** Nassau lures travelers with old forts, impressive colonial buildings, small museums, manicured gardens, and a small zoo.

✔ **A variety of vacation playgrounds:** Choose among action-packed Cable Beach, historic downtown Nassau, and glitzy Paradise Island — or hang out in all three areas.

✔ **Shops galore:** Here you find The Bahamas' largest selection of duty-free stores and designer boutiques, plus the largest straw market.

But New Providence is far from being paradise. Here's a look at the downsides:

✔ **No warm and cuddly hotel service:** With thousands and thousands of visitors arriving in Nassau every day, staffs at restaurants and hotels have grown jaded by tourism. You won't get the kind of service you may get at an Out Island inn, where all the staff knows you by name.

✔ **Crowds and congestion:** If you live in a metropolis and want to escape crowds on your vacation, Nassau isn't for you. It's not New York, but it may seem like it when cruise ships pull in at the same time, with passengers overrunning shops at the Straw Market and in the center of town. Visitors also crowd the golf courses, beaches, and popular restaurants.

✔ **A walk on the wild side:** You can find safer places to be at night than downtown Nassau. It has the highest crime rate in all The Bahamas. Our advice is to take a taxi to where you're going after dark in the center of Nassau. Cable Beach and Paradise Island are safer havens, though you must keep your guard up there, too.

Getting to know Grand Bahama

After New Providence, the second-most popular attraction in The Bahamas is the large island of **Grand Bahama,** which contains **Freeport,** the second-largest city in The Bahamas. When compared to Nassau, Freeport is rather unsophisticated. But its beaches at **Lucaya,** site of the major tourist development, are top-notch, as are its duty-free shopping, glittering casinos, and two national parks. When you want to capture some of the spirit of The Bahamas of yesterday, you can escape from all this modernity by heading to the funky little village of **West End.**

Grand Bahama has a much younger and trimmer look than Nassau. Stately palms and pines border broad, landscaped boulevards. Modern high-rise hotels, apartment buildings, and condominiums overlook beaches and marinas. Smooth lawns sprouting flowering shrubs surround stucco homes topped with terra-cotta tiles. The flip side of this

Grand Bahama Island

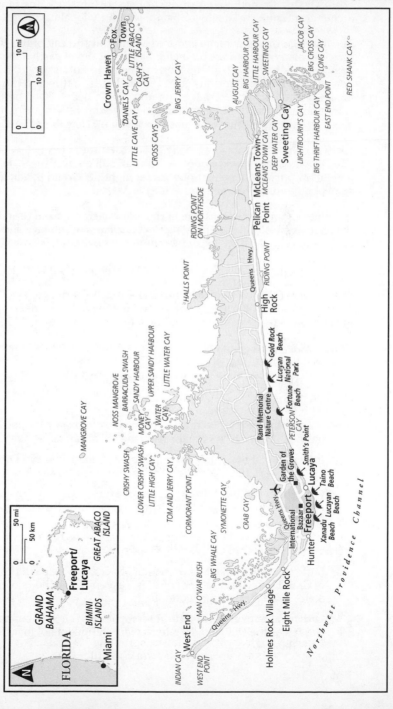

beauty is that Grand Bahama doesn't offer much history. Too much of its architecture is either kitschy or bland, with little local flavor.

The hotels in Grand Bahama endured a slump at the end of the 20th century, but many of them are bouncing back after being vastly restored or completely rebuilt. With all the improvements in hotels, Grand Bahama now offers some winners, although they're hardly a threat to the glittering array of choices on Paradise Island or Cable Beach. Even better news is that hotel rates on the island tend to be moderate — none of the lodgings carry the high price tags that shock you on New Providence.

Likewise, Grand Bahama has many good restaurants but not world-class ones like those in New Providence. You can still eat well, especially if you follow our recommendations. As for nightlife, Grand Bahama has some, but no one ever mistakes it for Las Vegas.

Duty-free shopping remains one of the major attractions of Grand Bahama, especially at the emerging **Port Lucaya Marketplace** and also at the famous but rather tacky **International Bazaar at Freeport.**

Grand Bahama is perfect for the active vacationer. Topping most lists is excellent scuba diving, snorkeling trips by kayak to offshore islets, the chance to pet Flipper's cousins in the **Dolphin Experience** (see Chapter 17), the island's landscaped gardens and nature reserves, deep-sea fishing and, of course, the golden sand beaches.

Bottom line: Grand Bahama is short on island spice but compensates with its diversity of activities, ranging from gambling to watersports. (For more information on Grand Bahama, see Part IV.)

Grand Bahama is a hit with travelers because

- ✔ **It's a baby:** Developed during the 1960s, the ox-jaw shaped island has been called a "mecca for fast-lane vacationers."

- ✔ **International appeal:** Many Americans, Canadians, and Europeans live and work here alongside Bahamians.

- ✔ **Fewer hotels:** The main beach resort area, Lucaya, isn't nearly as crowded with hotels as New Providence's Cable Beach or Paradise Island.

But Grand Bahama has its downsides:

- ✔ **Little history:** Unlike Nassau with its buccaneering past, the history of Grand Bahama is rather colorless, except when the Confederate States used it as a supply depot.

- ✔ **Less local appeal:** The cultural scene here is much blander than in Nassau or the Out Islands, where you can find lots of local flavor and island spice.

🖊 **A jumping-off point for day-trippers:** Unlike New Providence and the Out Islands, Grand Bahama attracts a lot of day-trippers who are on cheap cruises from Florida. In general, Grand Bahama is a venue for less sophisticated travelers.

🖊 **Not many beach hotels:** Not all the best hotels are on the golden sands.

Arriving in the Abacos

Spanning 1,683 square km (650 sq. miles), the **Abaco Islands** form the second-largest landmass in this island nation. The boomerang-shaped chain is at the northernmost tier of The Bahamas, stretching 321km (200 miles) from Walker's Cay in the northwest to Cherokee Sound in the southeast.

A true water world, the Abacos make a prime destination for sailing, scuba diving, snorkeling, fishing, and island hopping. The deserted powdery beaches with frothy waves look just like computer-enhanced photographs, especially in Elbow Cay and Treasure Cay. Green Turtle Cay boasts one of the fanciest hotels in the Out Islands but, for the most part, lodgings in the Abacos are laid back. Travelers arriving in September and October will find many hotels and restaurants closed because of the lack of business.

Unlike the relatively flat and charmless Grand Bahama Island, the Abacos are among the most beautiful islands in the nation. The man-made attractions are appealing as well.

If you want to tee off, you don't have to go to New Providence or Grand Bahama. One of The Bahamas' best golf courses is in the Out Islands at Treasure Cay. And, if you're into history and colonial architecture, you can enjoy the tidy New England-style seaside villages on Elbow Cay, Green Turtle Cay, and Man-O-War Cay.

Here's a rundown of the Abaco Islands:

🖊 **Marsh Harbour:** Marsh Harbour is the capital of the Abacos. But don't expect congestion, even though it contains the only traffic light in the Out Islands. A legendary port among boaters, especially yachties from Florida, Marsh Harbour lies on **Great Abaco Island** and is a shipbuilding center. The town lacks the New England charm of either New Plymouth or Hope Town (see Elbow Cay and Green Turtle Cay in this list) and instead has the feel of a small Florida town.

Everything is relatively new in Marsh Harbour, most of it dating from the middle of the 1980s. The town's growth originally was fueled by drug money; it only recently discovered tourism. To meet the demands of modern tourism, some excellent restaurants have opened, as well as hotels, shops, bars, cafes, and boat outfitters. For more information on Marsh Harbour, see Chapter 18.

The Abaco Islands

WALKER'S CAY

GRAND CAY

STRANGER'S CAY

Carter's Cay

Florida

Grand Bahama

Abaco

Eleuthera

Paradise Island

Cat Island

Andros

San Salvador

Great Exuma

Long Island

Crooked Island

Cuba

Great Inagua

Turks and Caicos

Little Abaco Island

SPANISH CAY

PENSACOLA CAYS

LITTLE CAVE CAY

CROSS CAYS

Cooper's Town

MANJACK CAY

GREEN TURTLE CAY

New Plymouth

Treasure Cay Airport

TREASURE CAY

GREAT GUANA CAY

MAN O' WAR CAY

Marsh Harbour

Tahiti Beach

THE MARIS

Hope Town

Marsh Harbour Airport

Elbow Cay

MOORE'S ISLAND

Great Abaco Island

Pelican Cays Land & Sea Park

Pelican Harbour

Casaurina Point

Little Harbour

Eight Mile Bay

Cherokee

GORDA CAY

Crossing Rocks

Sandy Point

Cross Harbour

Bahamas National Trust Sanctuary

Hole in the Wall

0   15 mi

0   15 km

✈ Airport

Scuba Diving

⚓ Shipwreck

✔ **Elbow Cay:** All motor vehicles are banned from the center of Hope Town, the island's Cape Cod-like village. Along the narrow, paved streets, you find harborside restaurants and saltbox cottages painted in tropical tones, with pink and yellow bougainvillea dripping over stone or picket fences. Many Americans, Canadians, and Europeans, who first arrived as vacationers decades ago, own some of the biggest and most attractive homes.

People get around this small island by golf cart, bicycle, and foot, but the boat is the primary means of locomotion. Gazing down on a bobbing mass of boats, Hope Town's red-and-white striped lighthouse probably has had more photographs taken of it than any other sight on the island. You can hike or bike to isolated **Tahiti Beach,** where shelling at low tide is great fun. For more information on Elbow Cay, see Chapter 19.

✔ **Green Turtle Cay:** The 18th-century New England-style village New Plymouth is idyllic for strolling. You can find out about the Abacos' seafaring past at the **Albert Lowe Museum,** housed in an old cottage. Across the street, the **Memorial Sculpture Garden** honors noteworthy Bahamians.

Boats take people around Green Turtle Cay more than wheels and feet do. Coral colonies starting in relatively shallow water make for some of the best snorkeling in The Bahamas, and diving is exceptional. You can spend a day on a deserted beach on an uninhabited island. You can swim with stingrays, and the captain of your boat can spear some lobster and fish and then grill them for you right on the beach.

With rooms decked out with Oriental rugs and Queen-Anne chairs, **Green Turtle Club and Marina** is among the most upscale places to stay in the Out Islands. Tiny Green Turtle Cay doesn't have fairways, but if you're a golfer, you can take the ferry and a taxi (or charter a boat) to the championship golf course at Treasure Cay. For more information on Green Turtle Cay, see Chapter 20.

✔ **Treasure Cay:** A little sterile for our tastes, Treasure Cay feels too much like a playground designed exclusively for visitors. Not much of a local settlement was here before this resort developed during the 1960s, so you won't find any historic sites or old island communities. If not for the golden crescent beach and the rich blues of the water, you might forget that you're in The Bahamas.

This lack of local color doesn't seem to bother the vacationers who come to fish and play golf on one of the country's best courses. They stay in the attractive hotels, condos, and villas on the marina and beach. Treasure Cay is close to the dock where you can catch the ferry to Green Turtle Cay, and you can easily rent a boat to sail to Elbow Cay, Man-O-War Cay, and other nearby islands. Rooms are hard to come by in May during the **Treasure Cay Billfish Championship.** For more information on Treasure Cay, turn to Chapter 21.

Bottom line: Nirvana for divers, snorkelers, and anglers, the Abacos offer many opportunities to sail off to different islands, each with its own special allure. Many islands are uninhabited while others have man-made attractions that run a distant second to natural beauty.

The Abacos are a good choice if you're hoping for

- ✔ **An underwater wonderland, fish tales, and great greens:** The Abacos have some of the most alluring scuba diving, snorkeling, and fishing around and, in Treasure Cay, you'll find a championship golf course.

- ✔ **Scenic villages:** Historic seaside settlements on Elbow Cay, Green Turtle Cay, and Man-O-War Cay are filled with pretty clapboard cottages surrounded by white-picket fences set off by tropical flowers.

- ✔ **Spectacular sailing:** With so many appealing islands clustered together, the Abacos are called "the Sailing Capital of the World."

Locals who love their islands claim that the Abacos are Paradise Found and that they have no downsides. Even so, you may not like

- ✔ **The travel time:** Getting to these islands can take a while. Sometimes you need at least three means of transportation — planes, ferries, and taxis — and you may experience long waits and delays.

- ✔ **Potential seasickness:** If you're that rare landlubber who gets seasick when faced with lapping waves, the Abacos may not be for you. Almost everybody in the Abacos uses boats to travel more than they rely on wheels.

- ✔ **Hardly any hotels:** You don't have many choices for lodging, and most options are small and low-key.

Hanging out on Harbour Island

Harbour Island is small — barely 5 sq. km (2 sq. miles) — but it's one of the most beautiful islands in The Bahamas. Its major attraction is a long, broad, pink beach, tinted by pulverized coral and shells. The snorkeling and scuba diving are first rate. You can even reach shipwrecks on a scuba outing. Perched on a bluff overlooking the water are several of the country's prime — and most expensive — inns and small hotels. (Many accommodations and restaurants close here during the fall.) Wander into **Dunmore Town,** and you stroll past historic churches, 18th-century cottages with lacy gingerbread trim, and tropical flowers nuzzling picket fences.

Harbour Island is affectionately known to residents as *Briland.* Briland lures mainly American and Canadian vacationers, and more than a few of them have snapped up prime real estate here. However, the island maintains a distinct Bahamian look and feel. At the harbor's edge, old men shoot the breeze while slapping dominos onto card tables.

Harbour Island

Chickens and horses wander through front yards. Women trade gossip while selling straw goods and shell jewelry from outdoor stalls. If those wares aren't upscale enough for you, go boutique browsing for Haitian paintings, Balinese silver, and French wine vinegar.

In Harbour Island, you can don your drop-dead duds for candlelit cocktails one night and cool out over *Kaliks* (the local brew) in a smoky pool hall the next. However, hipbones don't usually start slipping until the weekend, when anything from waterside hotel decks to cavelike local bars morph into dance clubs. Mom-and-pop kitchens whip up Bahamian favorites, such as cracked conch (pounded, battered, and fried) and peas and rice. Hotels lure diners with gourmet creations. And don't be surprised if your waiter knows you went sailing before you tell him — folks are friendly, and word travels fast. But don't worry: With quiet roads, romantic lookout points, and empty sandy strands, you can find plenty of places to keep your privacy intact. For more information on Harbour Island, see Chapter 22.

Bottom line: With some of The Bahamas' finest small beach hotels, a time-warp waterfront village, and a pink sand beach, you can't go wrong with Harbour Island — if you can afford it.

Harbour Island's highlights include

- ✔ **Pink sand:** The hue of this stunning 5km (3-mile) beach is rosy, and it runs the whole length of the eastern side of the island.

- ✔ **Eye candy:** Picture this scene: New England meets the tropics with white picket fences around colonial clapboard houses that are shaded by palm trees.

- ✔ **Small-town hospitality:** Briland is so petite and friendly that residents may start greeting you by name before you can say "cracked conch."

Before you decide on Harbour Island, however, consider the following:

- ✔ **Cost:** Harbour Island is one of the most expensive islands in The Bahamas.

- ✔ **Travel fatigue:** A trip here from the U.S. requires a plane or two, a taxi, a ferry, and another taxi.

- ✔ **Quiet nights:** What little nightlife there is wakes up mainly on the weekends.

Eloping to Eleuthera

Eleuthera is a wisp of an island chain that stretches for a distance of 161km (100 miles) from north to south. It lies only 81km (50 miles) east of Nassau, but it's 1,000 miles removed from that busy scene.

Even though the atmosphere is relatively quiet, Eleuthera remains one of the most developed of the Out Islands when stacked against the Exumas or the southern Bahamas.

However, Eleuthera's heyday is long gone. The chic social scene is now but a memory with the closing of such ritzy resorts as the Cotton Club and the Winderemere Club in South Eleuthera. Today, the rich and famous head for Harbour Island because the entire mainland of Eleuthera doesn't really have a state-of-the-art hotel.

At no point is Eleuthera more than 6km (4 miles) wide. Despite the island's size, some 10,000 people eke out a living on Eleuthera, which hasn't always been a friendly place to do so. What Eleuthera offers in great abundance is a galaxy of beaches, an "endless summer," and multi-hued seas ranging from deep blue to aquamarine.

On Eleuthera, you don't have to bother with historical sites or museums because none exist. What we like to do is drive the Queens Highway for the whole length of the island. We know of no more dramatic drive in all

Eleuthera

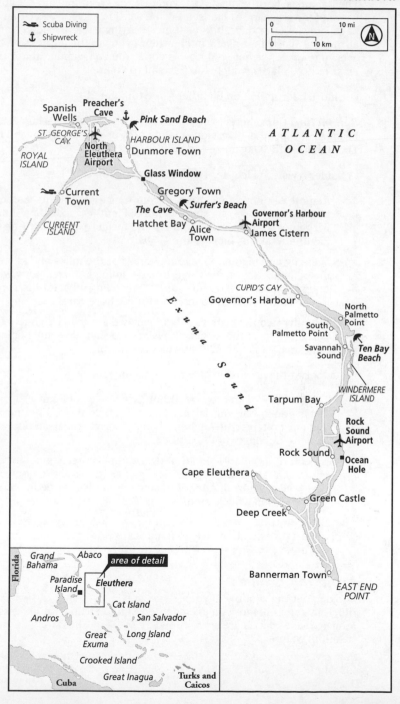

Scuba Diving
Shipwreck

0   10 mi
0   10 km

Spanish
Wells
ST. GEORGE'S
CAY
ROYAL
ISLAND

Preacher's
Cave
Pink Sand Beach
North
Eleuthera
Airport
HARBOUR ISLAND
Dunmore Town

**ATLANTIC
OCEAN**

Glass Window

Current
Town
CURRENT
ISLAND

Gregory Town
The Cave *Surfer's Beach*
Hatchet Bay
Alice
Town

Governor's Harbour
Airport
James Cistern

CUPID'S CAY
Governor's Harbour

North
Palmetto
Point
South
Palmetto Point

Savannah
Sound

*Ten Bay
Beach*

*WINDERMERE
ISLAND*

Tarpum Bay

Rock
Sound
Airport
Rock Sound
Ocean
Hole

Cape Eleuthera

Green Castle

Deep Creek

Bannerman Town

*EAST END
POINT*

Florida
Grand
Bahama
Abaco
area of detail
Paradise
Island
Eleuthera
Andros
Cat Island
San Salvador
Great
Exuma
Long Island
Crooked Island
Great Inagua
Turks and
Caicos
Cuba

The Bahamas. For the most part, you hug the coastline and get stunning views of the seascape or landscape. The seaside villages you come across have known better days, but it's their decaying gingerbread charm that attracts us in the first place. In Eleuthera, you get the impression that everyone was once here but now is gone. You can wander about the most remote places, which you have all to yourself.

For more information on Eleuthera, see Chapter 23.

Bottom line: Come here if you're the ultimate escapist, seeking unspoiled beaches, few people, diversions mainly of your own creation, and life in The Bahamas the way it used to be.

Consider a visit to Eleuthera if you're hoping for

- ✔ **Remote seaports and villages from long ago:** With its fashionable heyday long gone, the settlements of Eleuthera exist in a time warp. Far removed from casino wheels and mega-resorts, the little inns of Eleuthera take us back to the 1950s.

- ✔ **Scenery and sights:** Why come here? For the miles and miles of unspoiled beaches, for gingerbread-trimmed houses hung with bougainvillea, for bargains galore, for rolling hills, for lush green forests, for sheltered coves, and for offshore coral reefs.

- ✔ **Friendly people:** Instead of being locked away in a high-rise hotel, you get to meet the locals. The island doesn't have any big towns — only small settlements that welcome visitors.

For a look at the downside of Eleuthera, consider

- ✔ **The absence of any top-rated hotels:** If you want luxury, Eleuthera sends you to Harbour Island. To live on "mainland" Eleuthera, you most often settle for "rental units," which are clean but rather basic — definitely not luxurious.

- ✔ **No catering:** Visitors find that everything is pretty much of a do-it-yourself affair on Eleuthera. "Things," as they're called here, aren't very well organized. A lot of personal initiative is needed to make your vacation wheels spin.

- ✔ **Difficult transportation:** Except for the main highway, roads are often a disaster. Because no major car-rental companies exist, you often have to negotiate with a local for a rental.

Exploring Exuma

Looking out the window of your plane, you can see that the water is different colors before you even get to **Exuma.** Strung out like stepping stones, these islands are surrounded by some of The Bahamas' most beautiful waters.

Exuma

With a cay for every day of the year — and most of them uninhabited — Exuma is prime sailing territory. A bridge joins **Great Exuma** and **Little Exuma,** the two largest islands in the chain. Hotels and island action are concentrated in and around **George Town,** Exuma's pretty capital on Great Exuma. If you happen to vacation here in April, you can catch the festivities of the **National Family Island Regatta.** Far up north — and accessible only by chartered boat — the gorgeous **Exuma Cays Land and Sea Park** covers 160 sq. km (177 sq. miles) of islands and marine life. See Chapter 24 for more on Exuma's attractions.

You can make arrangements for sailing, snorkeling, diving, and fishing through your hotel. Be forewarned, though, that George Town's few hotels aren't located on the best beaches. For the best sandy stretches, you have to take a ferry to undeveloped **Stocking Island,** which has a sole hotel just across the harbor.

Bottom line: Exuma is a fine choice if sailing, R&R, and absorbing natural beauty are more important to you than man-made sights and late-night entertainment.

Exuma has many idyllic qualities, including

✔ **Water colors:** Bring your camera, or no one at home will believe you when you describe the range of aquatic hues.

✔ **Small size:** Petite hotels — a couple of hotels are on their own islands — and friendly residents quickly make you feel at home.

✔ **Parties:** Well, sometimes, at least. On most Saturday nights, everyone heads to Club Peace and Plenty's dance party, and in April, the festivities of the National Family Island Regatta bring many a far-flung Bahamian home to Exuma.

But Exuma isn't always convenient because

✔ **The marine park isn't nearby:** You may hear talk of the Exuma Cays Land and Sea Park, but unless you charter a boat (or both a boat and a small plane), you can't get there from George Town, where most vacationers stay.

✔ **You may have to take a boat to the beach:** George Town, where most hotels reside, isn't known for its beaches, and not all hotels are on the sand. Better beaches surround Stocking Island, which is a short ferry ride across the harbor.

✔ **April crowds:** During the National Family Island Regatta each spring, George Town can get as packed as Cable Beach in February.

Savoring San Salvador

Lying 322km (200 miles) southeast of Nassau is the Bahamian island of **San Salvador,** which is often confused with the Central American country of the same name. Some folks say that this scuba-diving mecca is the first place that Christopher Columbus stepped ashore in the "New" World (the world that wasn't new at all, of course, to the Native Americans living there for at least five centuries). Historians bitterly debate whether the famed explorer ever came here, however, with some experts believing his first landfall was actually at Samana Cay, another Bahamian island 105km (65 miles) to the south. But don't tell that to residents of San Salvador. They point you with pride to all the island's monuments that commemorate the world-changing event.

Columbus's visit, if it happened at all, didn't change San Salvador very much. Most of this island is nearly as undeveloped as it was back in the days when Lucayan Indians called it home. The interior is still interlaced with a network of quiet lakes, and the main village, **Cockburn Town,** couldn't be much drowsier. Climb to the top of **Dixon Hill Lighthouse,** and you get a sweeping view of the island and its pristine coastline. Bicycling is another good way to see San Salvador.

San Salvador

Today, many visitors are avid divers who wax poetic about the variety and bright colors of the coral and other marine life. Visitors don't frequent the best dive sites as much as the ones around New Providence because San Salvador has only a couple of hotels. True, one hotel is the sprawling **Club Med,** but not all the guests here are interested in scuba. Although the other hotel, the locally run **Riding Rock Inn Resort and Marina,** has long been a favorite among serious divers, it's not large enough to cause scuba gridlock at any diving sites.

The island's two main beach hotels give vacationers a choice: Do you want a small, unassuming scuba-lover's hangout that's dead-quiet during the day (Riding Rock), or do you want a huge low-rise resort decorated with an impressive collection of international folk art that's like a playground for adults (Club Med)? The bar at Riding Rock is the island's social center, and it hosts parties once or twice a week where vacationers hang out with locals. Although something's happening every night at Club Med, you can forget that you're in The Bahamas after dark because most people here aren't locals. For more information on San Salvador, check out Chapter 25.

Bottom line: Since Club Med hit the scene, San Salvador isn't just for divers anymore, but the underwater sights are still the main draw beyond cooling out amid pristine surroundings.

San Salvador may be a good choice if you find the following activities enticing:

✔ **Serene scuba:** More than three dozen unspoiled dive sites are less than 45 minutes from shore.

✔ **Fabulous digs:** A great all-inclusive resort — one of the top of Club Med's line — sits along an excellent sandy stretch.

✔ **Striking beaches:** Finding shores that are more naturally stunning is hard to do.

But, consider these downsides:

✔ **Few hotels:** Your choice of accommodations is basically between an upscale Club Med and a modest diving-oriented resort.

✔ **Where's the town?** Cockburn Town is more like a sleepy residential neighborhood.

✔ **Little island action:** Don't come here looking for any activities other than what Club Med offers.

Visiting More than One Island

One island is certainly enough for most visitors, especially if you stay in Nassau on New Providence or Freeport/Lucaya on Grand Bahama, where you can find sights and activities to keep you busy beyond the waves.

If you need variety to spice up your life, consider an island that makes a good home base for exploring other landfalls by boat, such as an island in the Abacos or the Exumas. From many islands, checking out a second island (or third or fourth) is as easy as hopping in a water taxi, a ferry, or taking a snorkeling cruise.

For example, on a visit to New Providence, based at either Cable Beach or Nassau, all you have to do is cross a bridge to enter another world — Paradise Island. From New Providence, you can also take boats to off-shore cays. If you have the time, you can plan three nights in cosmopolitan New Providence and then spend the rest of your vacation week in, say, Harbour Island near Eleuthera.

Keep in mind that getting from some islands to others can be tricky, especially when you need to fly. Visiting more than one Out Island by air usually means that you have to return to Nassau between islands because most remote islands don't have air links, except by expensive charter planes. Therefore, you may spend a lot of time sitting around Nassau International Airport because some flights are once a day (or even once every few days) and delays are common. See Chapter 6 for more information.

Narrowing Your Island Choices

The following quiz helps you determine which islands are best suited to your vacation style and interests.

Step 1: Get to know your "Rate the Islands" scorecard.

The scorecard at the end of the quiz has a column for each island and a row for each of the categories in our island-rating system. Use this scorecard to compile a rating for each island, based on the special-interest categories that follow.

On a scale of 1 to 4 points, the top vacation destinations are rated in various categories, such as dining, nightlife, price, sights, diving, and more. The lowest rating is 1, and the highest is 4. When an island isn't listed, it flunked completely. For example, golfers don't go to Harbour Island because it has no greens.

Step 2: Score islands based on what interests you.

Rate islands only in categories of interest to you. For example, if you don't play golf, skip that one. Write the scores for each island in the appropriate row under each column in your scorecard. For example, if you're looking for luxury, go across row 1 of your scorecard and put 4 under New Providence, 3 under Harbour Island, 2 under San Salvador, and 1 under Grand Bahama.

Keep racking up points until you review all the categories and give each island a score for every category of interest to you.

1) If you want to be in the lap of luxury . . .

Rating	Island	Why?
4	New Providence	Cable Beach and Paradise Island are graced with the most elegant pockets of posh in The Bahamas, with the Atlantis Paradise Island Resort & Casino being the country's most spectacular hotel.
3	Harbour Island	Some of The Bahamas' most distinctive small hotels overlook the pink sand beach.
2	San Salvador	Home of one of Club Med's snazziest resorts and the only first-class hotel in the southern Bahamas.
1	Grand Bahama	The Our Lucaya resort is more affordable than comparable beach resorts on New Providence.

2) If you're watching your wallet but still want to stay on the sand . . .

Rating	Island	Why?
4	Grand Bahama	Beach resorts may not be as plentiful here as they are on New Providence, but they're easier on your pocketbook.
3	New Providence	With a good choice of affordable shoreline hotels, Cable Beach is a better bet than pricier Paradise Island.
2	Elbow Cay	Several small hotels on this tiny cay hug near-empty beaches of golden sand — if you don't mind getting here by plane, taxi, and ferry.
1	Eleuthera	This narrow island, or series of islands, has virtually no expensive hotel — at least since the luxury resorts went belly up and a hurricane blew away Club Med. You're housed at a lot of mom-and-pop inns on local beaches.

3) If you want an island (almost) all to yourself . . .

Rating	Island	Why?
4	Exuma	Hotel Higgins Landing on Stocking Island and Latitude Exuma Resort on Rolle Cay are true getaways.
3	Elbow Cay	On this petite island that has more boats than cars, you can stay in small, isolated beach hotels that are really intimate inns.
2	Green Turtle Cay	Coco Bay Cottages are tucked away in a quiet corner of this sleepy island on a near-empty beach.
1	Harbour Island	You may not have your own island, but staying at the intimate Landing, an historic seven-room harborfront inn, may make you think the panoramic sunset is for your eyes only.

4) If you want to party the night away . . .

Rating	Island	Why?
4	New Providence	Here you find plenty of dance clubs, bars, island musical revues, and Las Vegas-style casinos. Atlantis Paradise Island Resort & Casino alone can keep you entertained for weeks!
3	Grand Bahama	This island doesn't offer as much after-dark action as New Providence does, but you can still choose from some good selections, including gambling.
2	Green Turtle Cay	Here you're down to mainly midweek and weekend partying, with dance bands at the hotels.
1	Exuma	Club Peace & Plenty is the place to be on Saturday night if you like to shake it up to a poolside calypso band. Also, you can check out the weekly rake and scrape at Eddie's Edgewater, a local dive.

5) If you like dining really well . . .

Rating	Island	Why?
4	New Providence	This island offers plenty of first-rate restaurants, plus a good selection of local eateries.
3	Harbour Island	The Bahamas' best collection of small beach hotels — plus the historic Landing, a harborside dining spot — offer some of the country's most creative cooking.
2	Green Turtle Cay	Bluff House, New Plymouth Club & Inn, and Green Turtle Club & Marina create a culinary buzz.
1	Grand Bahama	From steak in an elegant dining room to oceanfront seafood, it's all here.

6) If you're looking for the most unspoiled beaches . . .

Rating	Island	Why?
4	Harbour Island	The broad beach is 5km (3 miles) long, almost deserted, and the sand is actually pink. For once, you can believe all that tourist stuff.
3	Elbow Cay or Green Turtle Cay	Many empty sandy stretches encircle uninhabited islands offshore or border populated-but-low-key locales on the cays themselves.
2	Exuma	For a drop-dead gorgeous white sand beach, ferry over to Stocking Island from George Town.
1	San Salvador	Club Med–Columbus Isle hugs one of The Bahamas' most striking golden strands.

7) If you want to experience island spice . . .

Rating	Island	Why?
4	New Providence	Funky Nassau is The Bahamas' political (and cultural) capital and is the place to be during the Christmas/New Year's Junkanoo festival.
3	Exuma	You can visit here during the National Family Island Regatta every April for a real island vibe. Any time of year is fine because cute little George Town is never overrun with visitors.
2	Harbour Island	Chickens and horses wander in front yards, and residents soon call you by name.
1	Green Turtle Cay	This place is home to friendly folks who enjoy showing off their little gem of an island.

8) If you want to tee off . . .

Rating	Island	Why?
4	Grand Bahama	The island boasts more golf courses than any other in The Bahamas. The first golf course ever to open in The Bahamas, The Reef Course, made its debut here back in 1969.
3	Treasure Cay	The desert-type, windy Dick Wilson course at the Treasure Cay Golf Club is a winner.
2	New Providence	This island offers a trio of good courses, plus plenty of hotels and activities, both wet and dry.
1	Green Turtle Cay	You can take the ferry and a taxi (or a chartered boat) to the championship Treasure Cay golf course.

9) If you like sightseeing . . .

Rating	Island	Why?
4	New Providence	It's the home of Nassau, The Bahamas' stately colonial capital, with historic forts, gardens, museums, and horse-drawn carriages galore.
3	Green Turtle Cay	New Plymouth looks like an 18th-century New England seaside village. It lives in a time capsule, and its museum evokes the days of the Loyalists who escaped here instead of becoming part of the new American Republic.
2	Elbow Cay	Elbow Cay is another Loyalist Cay, settled by blond, blue-eyed people whose descendants are still here. It's like Lilliput, and its red-and-white striped lighthouse is the most photographed sight in the Abacos.
1	Harbour Island	Harborside Dunmore Town boasts 18th-century gingerbread cottages and The Bahamas' oldest Anglican church.

10) If you want the best scuba diving or snorkeling . . .

Rating	Island	Why?
4	San Salvador	Scuba divers in the Columbus spirit go exploring here, finding more than a dozen shipwrecks, including the most famous, the Frascate, along with canyons and reefs to the southwest that are spectacular.
3	Green Turtle Cay	Excellent reefs teeming with a varied marine life line its Atlantic shores. Loggerhead turtles still crawl ashore to nest. Snorkelers have great visibility in these waters.
2	Harbour Island	Certified divers ride in underwater scooters, and rushing waters make Current Cut an exhilarating scuba site.
1	Exuma	Many excellent reefs are just 20 or 25 minutes away from the George Town area, so long boat rides don't cut into your underwater time.

11) If you want the best sport fishing . . .

Rating	Island	Why?
4	Treasure Cay	Anglers snag wahoo, billfish, and other big game all over the Abacos, where the Treasure Cay Billfish Championship is one of The Bahamas' most popular fishing tournaments.
3	Green Turtle Cay	The Green Turtle Club & Marina hosts a major fishing tournament each spring.
2	Exuma	Just outside George Town, try bonefishing right from the shore. Deep-sea fishing is excellent as well.
1	Grand Bahama	Waters off Grand Bahama turn up impressive catches in barracuda, snapper, grouper, yellowtail, wahoo, and kingfish. Some of the best deep-sea fishing charters in The Bahamas are found here.

12) If you want to island hop . . .

Rating	Island	Why?
4	Elbow Cay	Frequent ferries connect Marsh Harbour with Elbow Cay and Man-O-War Cay, and you can charter a boat to Treasure Cay for golf or Green Turtle Cay for more quaint beauty.
3	New Providence	A bridge links you to Paradise Island, boats cruise to various beach-rimmed uninhabited islets, and planes fly to Grand Bahama and all Out Islands.
2	Eleuthera	Eleuthera itself is like a string of little islands, but in the north, you can take the ferry to remote, isolated Spanish Wells or chic Harbour Island.
1	Exuma	Wherever you go in the Exumas, you seem to land on another island in about 15 minutes of boating. These islands are the sailing capital of The Bahamas.

13) If you're craving peace and quiet . . .

Rating	Island	Why?
4	Exuma	Check out the gorgeous surrounding waters stocked with serene, uninhabited islets.
3	Green Turtle Cay	Historic seaside New Plymouth village enhances Mother Nature's handiwork on this tranquil island.
2	Elbow Cay	The quaintest of all Bahamian villages, this place seems more like a Hollywood set than reality. The population is scarce, and you have much of the place to yourself, except for some feral cats, curly-tailed lizards, and cooing doves.
1	Eleuthera	The celebrities of yesteryear have long since departed, leaving this island asleep in the sun. You not only get sun but also sands and only a few other people.

14) If you're traveling with children . . .

Rating	Island	Why?
4	New Providence	You can visit an aquarium, zoo, and dolphin encounter program, as well as enjoy children's camps at Atlantis, the Radisson, and elsewhere.
3	Grand Bahama	Our Lucaya's children's program and the Dolphin Experience make a kid's stay enjoyable.
2	Elbow Cay	Here you can find family-friendly villas, but you won't find much to do beyond the beach.
1	Exuma	The cottages of Latitude Exuma Resort, the only place to stay on peaceful, undeveloped Rolle Cay off George Town, are kid-friendly.

15) If you want to get there quickly and easily . . .

Rating	Island	Why?
4	New Providence	Airlines offer plenty of daily flights (a little more than three hours from New York or 50 minutes from Miami).
3	Grand Bahama	Not as many daily flights are available here, but the trip is shorter (a 40-minute flight from Miami).
2	Exuma	You can catch just one or two flights a day to this island, but travel time from Miami is a comfortable hour and 40 minutes.
1	San Salvador	Weekly charters take three hours and 15 minutes from New York or an hour and 45 minutes from Miami. Small airlines also connect San Salvador with Florida twice a week and with Nassau daily.

Step 3: Tally the scores to determine your final favorite(s)

After you review all the categories and plug scores into your scorecard for all islands in the categories that matter to you, add up each of the results.

And the winner is . . . the island with the highest total score. Chances are this island is the one that most caters to your vacation needs. If a second island scores high, consider dividing your time between the two islands — that is, if they're close or accessible enough. If a third island scores high as well, you have an excuse to plan your next vacation there.

"Rate the Islands" Scorecard

POINTS FOR:	Elbow Cay	Eleuthera	Exuma	Grand Bahama	Green Turtle Cay	Harbour Island	New Providence	San Salvador	Treasure Cay
1) Luxury									
2) Beach bargains									
3) Solitude									
4) Nightlife									
5) Great food									
6) Best beaches									
7) Island spice									
8) Golf									
9) Sightseeing									
10) Diving/snorkeling									
11) Fishing									
12) Island-hopping									
13) Peace & quiet									
14) Families									
15) Easy access									
TOTAL SCORE:									

Chapter 4

Deciding When to Go

● ●

In This Chapter

▶ Evaluating the seasons
▶ Charting the weather
▶ Planning your trip around special events

● ●

The Bahamas have their high season in winter and their low season in summer, but any time of the year can be a good time for a visit — that is, if the weather holds. Off-season can bring hurricanes, but you receive plenty of warnings before these storms arrive.

This chapter highlights not only the weather but also the best year-round happenings, from Junkanoo parades to sailing regattas.

Revealing the Secrets of the Seasons

Bahamian weather falls into two main seasons: winter (high season) and summer (low season). Especially in the northern Bahamas, high season can also mean surprisingly cool weather. But cool spells, if they descend at all, blow away rather quickly, and you're back on the beach after a day or two. The southern Bahamian islands, on the other hand, truly live up to their reputation of being "June all year-round."

The Bahamas are in the Atlantic Ocean, just north of the warmer Caribbean region. Their location is why winter in the subtropical Bahamas can be spring-like, even though their Caribbean neighbors boast year-round beach weather.

Visiting during high season

High season is roughly November through April, which is the cooler, drier, and more expensive time of year to visit. Although average temperatures in The Bahamas may vary only about 12°F throughout the year, winter temperatures can sink into the 60s (about 18°C). Especially during winter months, early morning and evening temperatures are often cool enough to require sweaters or jackets, even when you wear beach gear during the day. See Tables 4-1 and 4-2 for more info on the weather.

If you're not willing to risk a few days that are better suited to golf and tennis than to sand and surf, you may not want to book your vacation during January or February.

 Spring break occurs during the high season (from late February to mid-April). This time of year is when many hotels, restaurants, and beaches are packed with vacationing American college students who have clearly checked their inhibitions at the airport. If you're not looking to party, you may want to avoid the area. But if you're here during these festive weeks, you can treat yourself to an extra dose of entertainment, including sporting events, beach parties, and musical performances.

Table 4-1			Average Monthly Temperatures								
Jan	*Feb*	*Mar*	*April*	*May*	*June*	*July*	*Aug*	*Sep*	*Oct*	*Nov*	*Dec*
70°F	70°F	72°F	75°F	77°F	80°F	81°F	82°F	81°F	78°F	74°F	71°F
21°C	21°C	22°C	24°C	25°C	27°C	27°C	28°C	27°C	26°C	23°C	22°C

Table 4-2			Average Monthly Rainfall								
Jan	*Feb*	*Mar*	*April*	*May*	*June*	*July*	*Aug*	*Sep*	*Oct*	*Nov*	*Dec*
1.9"	1.6"	1.4"	1.9"	4.8"	9.2"	6.1"	6.3"	7.5"	8.3"	2.3"	1.5"
(4.1 cm)	(3.6 cm)	(5 cm)	(12.2 cm)	(23.4 cm)	(5 cm)	(15.5 cm)	(16 cm)	(19.1 cm)	(21.1 cm)	(5.8 cm)	(3.8 cm)

In-season advantages

If you live in the northern climates that are swept with wintry blizzards, nothing is more appealing than a white sandy beach under a summer-like sun on a palm tree-studded Bahamian island in February.

✔ The winter weather in The Bahamas has been called "a perpetual June." The daytime temperature usually doesn't dip below 70°F (21°C).

✔ All restaurants, services, sports activities, entertainment, shops, and facilities operate at full blast from mid-December to mid-April.

✔ The in-season is ideal for singles and honeymooners because families with children are gone and a more romantic atmosphere prevails.

✔ Both the rainy season and the hurricane season are over. Except for a rare cloudy day, you mostly have sand, sea, and sunshine. Some visitors add an extra "s" to that allure — sex.

✔ The cuisine at resorts is better than ever. The resorts bring in top chefs from both Europe and America during the winter months to tease your taste buds.

In-season disadvantages

Of course, the greatest allure is enjoying sun and sand when much of the United States and Canada is in a deep freeze. But here are the downsides:

✔ You find lots of people crowding around you in airport lounges, on the most popular beaches, at the resorts' buffet tables, at the best restaurants (the lucky stiffs reserved the best tables before you called), and in the casinos.

✔ Reservations become extremely important at resorts, car-rental agencies, nightclubs, the best restaurants, and even for sports activities, such as scuba-diving courses.

✔ You pay top dollar for everything from your hotel room to your car rental. Hotel rates skyrocket, especially around the Christmas holidays. Nothing, including the merchandise in shops, is discounted in winter.

✔ Expect a more frantic pace at the resorts when the guest count reaches maximum capacity. Personalized service goes the way of the trade winds.

Checking out the islands during low season

Low season — May through October — is warmer and wetter and, therefore, is a less expensive time to travel to The Bahamas. Most rain falls between June and October. Showers are usually brief, often coming in the late afternoon, and sometimes the sun doesn't even bother to stop shining during downpours.

 As pleasant as you may find the balmy subtropical summer, the low season is also hurricane season. Officially, hurricane season lasts from June to November, but these storms are most likely to arrive during late August, September, or October. Although summer or fall travel can save you a few bucks, it can also cancel your trip. You can, of course, insure yourself in case you're forced to cancel your Bahamian vacation because of a hurricane (see Chapter 9).

The good news is that hurricanes aren't all that common in The Bahamas. Even if one is predicted to hit during your vacation, you usually have enough warning (with the help of satellite forecasts) to rearrange your plans. If you choose to travel during this time of year, you can keep an eye on weather patterns by visiting the National Weather Service Web site at www.nws.noaa.gov.

Off-season advantages

Although The Bahamas may seem more inviting during the winter, here are the many reasons why your trip may be much more enjoyable if you go during the off-season:

- ✔ A less-hurried way of life prevails. You have a better chance to savor the food, culture, and customs.

- ✔ Swimming pools and beaches are less crowded — and perhaps aren't crowded at all.

- ✔ Resorts offer year-round activities, like snorkeling, boating, and scuba diving, often at reduced rates.

- ✔ Resort boutiques often feature summer sales, hoping to clear excess merchandise.

- ✔ You frequently can get a table at a top restaurant without a reservation.

- ✔ The endless waiting game is over: You don't have to wait for a rental car, tee time, or an open tennis court.

- ✔ Some package-tour prices are as much as 20 percent lower, and individual excursion fares are also reduced between 5 and 10 percent.

- ✔ You may have an easier time booking accommodations and flights.

- ✔ The very best of attractions — sea, sand, and surf, and plenty of sunshine — remain undiminished in the off-season.

Off-season disadvantages

We don't want to paint too rosy a picture, though. Although the advantages of off-season travel outweigh the disadvantages, here are some drawbacks to summer travel:

- ✔ You may end up staying at a construction site: Caribbean hoteliers save their serious repairs and major renovations until the off-season.

- ✔ Hotels often reduce their services and staff.

- ✔ Not all resort restaurants and bars are fully operational.

Perusing a Calendar of Events

The following are some special events that you may want to keep in mind when you plan your vacation.

 Bahamians celebrate familiar holidays, such as New Year's Day, Good Friday, Easter, and Christmas, but you should also prepare for closed businesses, shorter hours, or wild partying on Easter Monday, Whitmonday (seven weeks after Easter), Labour Day (the first Friday in June), Independence Day (July 10), Emancipation Day (the first Monday in August), Discovery Day (October 12), and Boxing Day (December 26).

January

New Year's Day Junkanoo Parades: These parades are held throughout The Bahamas, but the most spectacular one is on Bay Street in downtown Nassau, New Providence. The annual Junkanoo Parade begins in the wee hours (around 1 a.m.). People dance down the street to the sound of cowbells, goatskin drums, and whistles while wearing elaborate masks and costumes (ranging from giant conch shells to overgrown silk cotton trees) that they've taken months to create. With roots in Africa, this festival (also held on Boxing Day, December 26) is the Bahamian version of Rio de Janeiro's Carnival and New Orleans's Mardi Gras. A traditional breakfast of *boil fish* and *johnnycake* (see Chapter 2) caps off the parade. For more details about the Nassau parade, contact the **Ministry of Youth, Sports and Culture** at ☎ 242-325-9370. For information about the **Grand Bahama Parade**, call ☎ 242-352-8044.

 Want to jump up with the Nassau crowd? Visitors are welcome to participate. Call **X-plorers Junkanoo** to make arrangements at ☎ 242-361-0907 or 242-325-3567.

Annual New Year's Day Sailing Regatta: Some 40 locally built sailing sloops duke it out for the championship during the Annual New Year's Day Sailing Regatta (Nassau and Paradise Island), organized by The Bahamas Boat Owners Association. For details, contact the Rev. Phillip McPhee of the **Ministry of Youth, Sports and Culture** at ☎ 242-325-9370.

Polar Bear Swim: On New Year's Day, with beach party spectators cheering them on, daring (crazy) swimmers plunge into Cable Beach waters, cooled by huge blocks of ice, during the Polar Bear Swim in Nassau. For details, call Tom Muir of the **Canadian Men's Club** at ☎ 242-323-1048.

February

Farmer's Cay Festival: This festival is a rendezvous for yachtsmen cruising the Exumas and a homecoming for the people of Farmer's Cay. Boat excursions depart Nassau for the festival at 8 p.m. from Potter's Cay on the first Friday in February and return to Nassau the next day. For information, contact Terry Bain in **Little Farmer's Cay** at ☎ 242-355-4006 or 242-355-2093, or the **Exuma Tourist Office** at ☎ 242-336-2430.

Annual Georgetown Cruising Regatta: More than 500 visiting yachts flock to Exuma for a splashy week of fun and competition during the Annual Georgetown Cruising Regatta. The regatta occurs during late February to March. For details, call the **Exuma Tourist Office** at ☎ 242-336-2430.

March

Annual Garden of the Groves Art Festival: The daylong festival takes place at the flourishing Garden of the Groves in Grand Bahama. Bring the kids for the local arts and crafts, music, food, and pony rides, as well as a skydiving exhibition. This event occurs in early March. For more information, call ☎ 242-352-8044.

Annual Art Exhibition: Hope Town, Elbow Cay, shows off its creativity with a display of watercolors, oils, wood-carvings, and sculpture during this mid-March art exhibition. Call **Abaco Inn** at ☎ 242-366-0133.

Bacardi Rum Billfish Tournament: The prestigious week-long tournament attracts the who's who of deep-sea fishing. The Port Lucaya Marina in Grand Bahama is the headquarters for the event. The tournament takes place in mid- to late March. For more information, call ☎ 242-373-9090.

Easter Junkanoo Parade: If you can't get to The Bahamas on Boxing Day (December 26) or New Year's Day, you can still catch Junkanoo festivities at Marsh Harbour during the Easter Junkanoo Parade (late March or April). Contact the **Abaco Tourist Office** at ☎ 242-367-3067.

April

Annual Abaco Anglers Fishing Tournament: Men, women, and children can compete in the popular **Annual Abaco Anglers Fishing Tournament,** which takes place in late April. Contact the **Abaco Tourist Office** at ☎ 242-367-3067.

The **National Family Island Regatta:** Every single Bahamian living abroad seems to come home for this event. If you're planning to visit George Town, Exuma, during this week-long event, book your room months in advance. As the handcrafted sloops, owned and sailed by Bahamians, compete in Elizabeth Harbour, you can eat, drink, and socialize nonstop. Food stands, set up along the waterfront, tempt you with fresh pineapple, grilled chicken, peas and rice, and conch in all its incarnations. Events include a parade, Junkanoo and police bands, and nightly parties. If you're in Nassau but want to hop over for the festivities, you can get special excursions that are set up to get you here by motor boat or plane. The regatta takes place in late April. Contact the **Exuma Tourist Office** at ☎ 242-336-2430 or 242-336-2457.

May

Treasure Cay Billfish Championship: Taking place in the waters off beautiful Treasure Cay in the Abacos, the popular, challenging Treasure Cay Billfish Championship draws serious anglers, but amateurs can also participate. Entertainment and other festivities surround the tournament. Contact the **Abaco Beach Resort & Boat Harbour** at ☎ 800-468-4799. Dates vary, so call for information.

Long Island Regatta: This regatta in the Out Islands sees some 40 to 50 sailing sloops from throughout The Bahamas compete in three classes for trophies and cash prizes. Onshore, you find sporting events, dancing to indigenous "rake 'n' scrape" music, and local food specialties, all of which make for a carnival-like atmosphere. This event takes place in late May. For more information, call ☎ 242-394-1535.

June

Eleuthera Pineapple Festival: This festival is held in Gregory Town, Eleuthera, and is a celebration devoted to the island's succulent pineapple. It features a Junkanoo parade, craft displays, dancing, a pineapple-recipe contest, tours of pineapple farms, and a "pineathalon" — a half-kilometer (¼-mile) swim, a 5.5km (3½-mile) run, and a 6.5km (4-mile) bike ride. This festival occurs in early June. For more information, call ☎ 242-332-2142.

July

Independence Week: Festivities, parades, and fireworks mark Independence Week throughout the islands. The celebrations culminate on Independence Day, which is July 10.

Regatta Time in Abaco: This event is an eight-day series of five boat races at Marsh Harbour. The event lures plenty of sailors during The Bahamas' Independence Week. Beach parties, dances, and live music accompany the races. Contact the **Abaco Tourist Office** at ☎ 242-367-3067.

August

Emancipation Day: The first Monday in August commemorates the emancipation of slaves in 1834. A highlight of this holiday is an early morning "Junkanoo Rushout" starting at 4 a.m. in Fox Hill Village in Nassau, followed by an afternoon of cookouts and fun events, such as climbing a greased pole and the plaiting of the maypole.

Fox Hill Day: This day is a big blast, celebrating the abolition of slavery. A daylong series of entertaining events is planned along with a giant food fest, serving Bahamian specialties. The celebration takes place on the second Tuesday in August in the Fox Hill area about 8km (5 miles) from the center of Nassau.

September

The Grand Bahama Jazz and Rhythm Blues Festival: Jazz, R&B, reggae, and calypso musicians from around the globe descend on Grand Bahama for this four-day festival during the third week in September. There is music in the morning, music in the afternoon, and most definitely at night — much of it extraordinary. For more information, visit www. grand-bahama.com.

October

Annual McLean's Town Conch Cracking Championship and Festival:
Visit the small fishing village of McClean's Town in Grand Bahama to
watch fast-fingered contestants race each other to extract the greatest
number of conchs from shells in the shortest amount of time. The festival takes place on Discovery Day (in commemoration of Columbus' first
landing in the New World), celebrated on the second Monday in October.
For details, call the **Grand Bahama Island Tourism Board** at ☎ 242-352-
8044, or fax 242-352-7840.

November

Guy Fawkes Day: The best celebrations of Guy Fawkes Day occur in
Nassau. On many islands, Bahamians hold nighttime parades throughout
the streets, culminating in the hanging and burning of Guy Fawkes, an
effigy of the British malefactor who was involved in the Gunpowder Plot
of 1605 in London. This celebration occurs in early November. For more
details, call ☎ **242-356-5216.**

Bahamas Wahoo Championship: Test your skill at snagging one of the
ocean's fastest fish, wahoo, which can cut through the waves at speeds up
to 113km (70 miles) per hour. The annual Bahamas Wahoo Championship
is held in three different legs in November, January, and February. The
first leg usually kicks off in early to mid-November. For complete details,
call ☎ **800-32-SPORT** (800-327-7678) or check out the Web site at www.
bahamaswahoo.com.

Bimini Big Game Fishing Club All Wahoo Tournament: During this
tournament, anglers try to bait one of the fastest fish in the ocean. The
Port Lucaya Resort and Yacht Club is the headquarters for this event,
which usually occurs over four days during the third week of November.
For information, call ☎ **800-737-1007** or 242-373-6618, or visit www.
bahamaswahoo.com.

Annual One Bahamas Music and Heritage Festival: The three-day
Annual One Bahamas Music and Heritage Festival is staged at both
Nassau and Paradise Island to celebrate national unity. Highlights
include concerts featuring top Bahamian performing artists, as well
as island walks and other activities. This three-day festival takes place
during the last week of November. For more information, contact the
Nassau/Paradise Island Tourist Office at ☎ 242-356-5216, ext. 4100.

December

Boxing Day: The famed Junkanoo Parade kicks off on Boxing Day,
December 26 (see the January events for more info on the parade).
Bahamians inherited this holiday from England's Queen Victoria's Day,
when the upper class would give gifts of cash or presents — in boxes,
of course — to the lower class, usually servants.

Part II
Planning Your Trip to The Bahamas

By Rich Tennant

WHILE TRYING TO FIND THE RENTAL RETURN AREA AT MIAMI INTERNATIONAL AIRPORT, FRANK AND MONA DISCOVER THE BAHAMAS.

©RICHTENNANT

In this part . . .

In this part, we help you book your ideal vacation in The Bahamas. We tell you the fastest and most economical ways to reach your chosen island. We also explain how to estimate your trip's price tag and how to stay within your budget.

We also offer tips for getting married or honeymooning in The Bahamas, as well as special advice for families, seniors, and travelers who are single, gay or lesbian, or disabled. Finally, we help you tie up loose ends to ensure a hassle-free vacation, with details about getting a passport, considering travel insurance, and staying safe.

Chapter 5

Managing Your Money

• •

In This Chapter

▶ Figuring out your budget

▶ Saving money without skimping on fun

▶ Choosing between paper and plastic

▶ Knowing what to do when you lose your wallet

• •

A fabulous vacation in The Bahamas doesn't have to put you in the poor house. Taking a few moments to figure out your expenses in advance, deciding how to carry your money, and finding out what to do if your wallet is lost or stolen can ensure a trouble-free vacation without a financial hangover.

Planning Your Budget

To get an idea of your expenses, try taking a mental stroll through your entire trip. Start with the cost of transportation from your home to the airport, your airline tickets, and transfers to your accommodations. Add your daily hotel rate, meals, activities and entertainment, and your return to the airport. Then add in your transportation home from the airport. And finally, just to be on the safe side, add another 15 to 20 percent for other costs that may crop up. Table 5-1, "What Things Cost in The Bahamas," contains a few representative examples of prices you'll find.

The lowest airfares and the cheapest resort rates are in effect from April 15 to December 15. If you must go during the Christmas and New Year's holidays, expect the steepest airfares and hotel rates. Resort prices tend to fall right after New Year's and then pick up again in February.

In general, you'll pay more for your hotel room than your other expenses. Unless you're at an all-inclusive hotel, you can escape your resort's usually expensive dining tabs by sneaking away to a little Bahamian kitchen where you can dine reasonably well on authentic island fare.

Special deals come and go in The Bahamas, even in the peak winter season. Always check for last-minute deals; otherwise, you may end up staying in a $275 double room on Paradise Island next door to a couple who got a room with an even better view for less than $190.

Table 5-1	What Things Cost in The Bahamas		
Travel Expense	*U.S. or Bahamian $*	*U.K. £*	*Canadian $*
Taxi from airport to Nassau's center	$20.00	£12.00	$26.00
Local phone call	25¢	15p	33¢
Double room at Atlantis Resort (expensive)	$346.00	£207.60	$449.80
Double room at Holiday Inn Junkanoo Beach (moderate)	$154.00	£92.40	$200.20
Dinner for one at Chez Willie (expensive)	$60.00	£36.00	$78.00
Dinner for one at Bahamian Kitchen (inexpensive)	$22.00	£13.20	$28.60
Bottle of beer in a bar/hotel	$3.00–$3.95	£1.80–£2.40	$3.90–$5.14
Rolls of ASA 100 Color Film (36 exposures)	$6.00	£3.60	$7.80
Movie ticket	$6.00	£3.60	$7.80

Lodging

The biggest chunk of your budget goes to your accommodations. As you flip through the island chapters, dollar signs ($ to $$$$$) indicate the price category of each hotel. For an explanation of these price categories, turn to the Introduction at the beginning of this book. Notice that hotel rates are all over the map and may include more than just your room. Some rates cover breakfast or breakfast and dinner. Also, some rates include taxes and gratuities but others don't. The highest-priced properties we list are *all-inclusive* resorts, which means that you can't compare their rates to the ones of other hotels without taking into account that one price includes all meals, beverages, and most activities.

The prices of rooms within a single resort can vary as much as the prices of hotels. Should you shell out top dollar to stay in an oceanfront suite? Your answer depends on your budget and desire to fall asleep to the sound of the surf or wake up to the sun shimmering on the water. But if you find a garden room steps away from the shore just as attractive and comfortable, you can save the extra cash for something else.

The least you can expect to pay for a double room is about $85 (in the low season) or $140 (in high season) per night at a small hotel — that is, on a *rack rate,* or the top price a hotel charges for a room. See Chapter 7 for a discussion of rack rates and how to avoid paying them.

Transportation

Because The Bahamas lie right off the coast of Florida, getting here for a beach holiday is most often cheaper than flying farther south to the Caribbean. For specifics on saving money on flights, see Chapter 6.

After you pay for airfare, your transportation costs should be low. Taxis, hotel shuttles, and public buses are readily available on some islands. Many vacationers don't rent cars for good reason: Gas on some islands can cost as much or more than $3.50 per gallon.

Most package deals include transfers between the airport and your hotel. Ferries to Harbour Island, Green Turtle Cay, Elbow Cay, and Man-O-War Cay run $8 to $16 round-trip.

On New Providence (Nassau, Cable Beach, and Paradise Island), you can get to most sights and attractions on foot or by public bus. Cab fares to and from sights can add up fast, but you can always take a taxi tour of several attractions. Half-day taxi tours begin at about $35 for adults. Most taxi expenses are for transportation to and from restaurants.

 Take advantage of the free shuttle buses that some resorts offer. You can find such shuttles on Paradise Island and Cable Beach on New Providence as well as in George Town, Exuma.

Dining

In each island chapter in Parts III through VI, we recommend our favorite restaurants. Dollar signs ($ to $$$$$) indicate whether the restaurant is cheap, expensive, or somewhere in between (see the Introduction for an explanation of these price categories).

The prices we quote are for main courses at dinner, unless we state otherwise. When a restaurant has $$, for example, these signs mean that most of the dinner courses are in that price range, but some may be more or less expensive. To get a picture of your total expenses, remember to estimate your beverage, appetizer, dessert, and tip as well.

À la carte hotel breakfast buffets can be expensive, but they're often elaborate. With everything from made-to-order omelets and waffles to carved meats, an array of fresh fruit, and a variety of bread and cereal, you often don't need to eat again until dinner.

On the larger islands (New Providence or Grand Bahama), you can sample some top-rate cuisine. But dinner for two at a top-drawer restaurant can easily run more than $100 — before the tip. Costs for these meals are high because much of the food is imported. Quite a few chefs are from Europe, however, so you're treated to the imaginative creations of some of the Continent's best. Some of the best food comes from the marriage of European and island cuisine.

 Check out local restaurants outside the hotels and away from resort areas. Not only do you come across savory home-style food, but you also save money. Many of these local establishments aren't much on decor, and you may sit in metal chairs and dine on plastic tablecloths, but the atmosphere is friendly and the price is usually right.

Staying in a rental unit with a kitchen or kitchenette can help you cut costs. Even if you don't feel like cooking every meal, you can save plenty of money by not eating out for every breakfast or lunch. Likewise, if your room has only a refrigerator, fill it with drinks, snacks, and fruit from the local grocery store.

Sightseeing and outdoor fun

Of course, the two main activities in The Bahamas — swimming in that beautiful, impossibly blue sea and basking on those sandy beaches — are absolutely free. However, if you're interested in activities like sightseeing attractions, scuba diving, snorkeling, windsurfing, and waterskiing, they usually cost extra.

 In recent years, more and more of the all-inclusives are offering terrific freebies like scuba and windsurfing lessons, free water-skiing, and free snorkeling gear for the week. Some all-inclusive resorts even toss in a free round of golf.

The costs for activities and attractions can differ greatly from resort to resort and from island to island. The following are some popular activities and what you can expect to pay for them:

> ✔ **Golfing on the go:** Greens' fees run $85 to $140 at most courses for 18 holes, including a shared cart, plus about $25 to $35 for club rentals. If that price range isn't expensive enough for you, try the course at the **Ocean Club** on Paradise Island, where greens' fees run around $245. Some courses offer reduced fees for 9 holes in the afternoon, and rates for both 9 and 18 holes drop during the

off-season (roughly May through October). Arrange tee times as far ahead of time as you can.

✔ **Indulging in watersports:** Even at all-inclusive resorts, you have to pay extra for scuba diving, which starts at $80 for a two-tank dive. To sail off to a reef for snorkeling, expect to spend at least $30. If you want to rent snorkel gear at the beach, you pay about $15. For deep-sea fishing, expect to spend at least $75 per person. For details on boat rentals, windsurfing, water-skiing, and golf (on New Providence, Grand Bahama, and the Abacos), turn to the island-specific chapters.

✔ **Taking a tour:** Save a day to take an island tour, especially if you aren't renting a car. Even though taking an island tour may seem very touristy, it's cheaper and more convenient to take an organized tour than to take taxis, especially on Grand Bahama, where the major attractions are spread out across the island. Island tours begin at $25. See the individual island chapters in Parts III through VI for information on destination-specific tours.

Shopping

In 1992, the government abolished all import duties on a variety of items, making for duty-free shopping. You save tax on perfumes, crystal, leather goods, watches and clocks, jewelry, fine linens and tablecloths, china, camera equipment, and binoculars and telescopes. If you're in the market for any of these goods, you can pay anywhere from 25 to 50 percent less in The Bahamas than in the U.S. You can also take home up to two liters of liquor duty-free, as long as you're of legal drinking age in your country of citizenship.

Save your most serious purchases for Nassau and Freeport/Lucaya, which have the most variety of merchandise and the best discounts. Stores on Cable Beach and Paradise Island charge more for their merchandise because of higher rents, and shops in the Out Islands can't afford to be as generous in their discounting.

Nightlife

The center of Nassau is rather dead and dull at night, although Cable Beach and Paradise Island are jumping, as is the Freeport/Lucaya area. In the Out Islands, a drink in a pub or bar suffices for entertainment.

Because The Bahamas don't have much spectacular nightlife, you're not likely to spend a great deal on it — and, in fact, you can bring your budget under control by not doing so. That is, unless you gamble. Then the sky's the limit.

In general, cover charges for clubs range from $10 to $25. You can find a lot of cheap entertainment because the lounges of the big resorts often have live Bahamian bands entertaining you after dark. The price of admission is the price of a drink.

Taxes

On your hotel bill, you pay resort taxes, gratuities, and sometimes an energy surcharge. Some hotels include these extras in the quoted rates, while others add them on to your bill. Make sure that you're aware of any extra charges that you'll have to pay, because they can easily inflate your hotel bill by $20, $30, or even $60 or more per night, depending on the cost of your room.

Total charges vary from hotel to hotel, but you can roughly expect to pay a 12 percent resort tax and about $8 per day per guest (over age 12) for housekeeping gratuity and energy surcharges for use of electricity.

 Don't gamble away your last few dollars in cash because you need extra cash to leave the country. The airports collect a **departure tax** from all passengers over age 12. You pay $15 if you're leaving from New Providence (Nassau) or Out Islands and $18 from Grand Bahama.

Cutting Costs — But Not the Fun

You can save money without shortchanging yourself of a good time. Here are a few ways:

- ✔ **Go during the off-season.** If you can travel at non-peak times (from mid-April to mid-December, for example), you find hotel prices are almost half the price they are during peak months.

- ✔ **Look for a package deal.** For many destinations, you can book airfare, hotel, ground transportation, and even some sightseeing just by making one call to a travel agent or packager, for a price much less than if you put the trip together yourself. (Chapter 6 is your source for more on package deals.)

- ✔ **Reserve a room with a refrigerator and coffeemaker.** You don't have to slave over a hot stove to cut a few costs; several hotels have minifridges and coffeemakers. Buying supplies for breakfast saves you money — and probably calories, too.

- ✔ **Always ask for discount rates.** Membership in AAA, frequent-flier plans, trade unions, professional organizations, AARP, or other groups may qualify you for savings on car rentals, plane tickets, hotel rooms, and even meals. Ask about everything; you may be pleasantly surprised.

- ✔ **Get a room off the beach.** Accommodations within walking distance of the shore can be much cheaper than accommodations right on the beach. Beaches are public, so you don't need to stay in a hotel that's on the sand to spend most of your vacation at the beach.

- ✔ **Ask if your kids can stay in the room with you.** A room with two double beds usually doesn't cost any more than a room with a queen-size bed. And many hotels don't charge you the additional person rate if the additional person is pint-sized and related to you. Even if you have to pay $10 or $15 extra for a rollaway bed, you can save hundreds by not taking two rooms.

✔ **Use a pay phone to call home.** Avoid using the phone in your hotel room to call outside the hotel. Charges can be astronomical, even for local calls, which are sometimes at least $1 a pop (instead of 25¢ at a pay phone). When you call long distance, you may think that you're saving money by using the toll-free number of your calling card instead of dialing direct. However, most hotels charge you at least $1 to connect you to an outside line for the toll-free call. On top of whatever your calling card bills you, the hotel also charges you just for picking up the phone — whether or not you reach the person you wanted.

✔ **Try expensive restaurants at lunch instead of dinner.** Lunch tabs are usually a fraction of what dinner costs at a top restaurant, and the menu often boasts many of the same specialties.

✔ **Walk a lot.** A good pair of walking shoes can save you lots of money on taxis and other local transportation. As a bonus, you get to know your destination more intimately, as you explore at a slower pace.

✔ **Steer clear of the casinos.** If you can't resist gambling, head to an island without casinos. Only New Providence and Grand Bahama offer casinos.

Handling Money

In The Bahamas, you can use U.S. dollars interchangeably with the local Bahamian dollar — they have the same value. So you don't have to worry about exchanging your U.S. cash, and you don't have to exchange a small amount of money before you go, either. (If you're carrying a currency other than greenbacks, check out the "Converting currency" section later in this chapter.)

As you near the end of your trip, ask for your change in only American dollars if you're headed back to the States. Otherwise, you can end up with unwanted Bahamian currency that you need either to spend or exchange at the airport, and, if you exchange it there, you lose some of it to service charges.

Carrying cash, traveler's checks, or credit cards?

You're the best judge of how much cash you feel comfortable carrying or what alternative form of currency is your favorite. Credit and debit cards, traveler's checks, and cash are all welcome in The Bahamas, but some forms of payment are more convenient (or cheaper) than others.

Using ATMs

Nassau and Freeport have handy 24-hour ATMs linked to an international network that almost always includes your bank at home. For the most part, the Out Islands lack this convenience. **Cirrus** (☎ 800-424-7787; www.mastercard.com) and **Plus** (☎ 800-843-7587; www.visa.com) are the two most popular networks. Check the back of your ATM card to see which network your bank belongs to. The networks' toll-free numbers and Web sites give specific locations of ATMs where you can withdraw money while on vacation. You can use them to withdraw just the amount that you need every couple of days, which eliminates having to carry around a large green stash.

 Of course, many ATMs are little money managers (or dictators, depending on how you look at it) that may allow you to withdraw only a certain amount of money — a maximum of $200, say — per day. Check with your bank about withdrawal limits before you set off on your vacation.

Another important reminder before you go ATM crazy: Many banks now charge a fee ranging from 50¢ to $3 whenever a nonaccount holder uses their ATMs. Your own bank may also assess a fee for using an ATM that isn't one of their branch locations. In some cases, you get charged twice just for using your bankcard when you're on vacation. Reverting to traveler's checks may be cheaper (although certainly less convenient to obtain and use).

The most common bank branches in The Bahamas are offices of First Caribbean International Bank. All these branches assess small fees for their transactions.

Toting traveler's checks

Traveler's checks are a holdover from the days when people wrote personal checks instead of going to an ATM. On New Providence (Nassau, Cable Beach, and Paradise Island) or Grand Bahama (Freeport/Lucaya), finding a 24-hour ATM is easy, so you don't need to carry traveler's checks or a wad of cash. On smaller islands, such as Eleuthera or the Abacos, ATMs are few and far between, if not nonexistent, so carrying traveler's checks may be a good idea. Be aware, however, that in The Bahamas, some restaurants tack on an additional service charge when you pay with a traveler's check.

You can get traveler's checks at almost any bank, most often in denominations of $20, $50, $100, $500, and $1,000. For **American Express** traveler's checks, you pay a service charge ranging from 1 to 4 percent. You can get American Express traveler's checks at the bank or over the phone by calling ☎ 800-221-7282. Amex gold and platinum cardholders who use this number are exempt from the 1 percent fee.

Visa also offers traveler's checks, available at Citibank locations nationwide and at several other banks. The service charge ranges from 1.5 to 2 percent. Call ☎ 800-732-1322 for information. AAA members can obtain

Visa traveler's checks without a fee at most AAA offices or by calling
☎ 866-339-3378. MasterCard has its hand in the traveler's check market,
too; call ☎ 800-223-9920 for details.

 If you choose to carry traveler's checks, keep a record of their serial
numbers separate from your checks, just in case someone steals them
or you lose them. If you know the serial numbers of your checks, you get
a refund faster.

Charging ahead with credit cards

Credit cards are a safe way to carry money. They also provide a convenient record of all your expenses, and they generally offer relatively good
exchange rates. You can also withdraw cash advances from your credit
cards at banks or ATMs, provided you know your personal identification
number (PIN). If you've forgotten your PIN or didn't even know that you
had one, call the number on the back of your credit card and ask the
bank to send it to you by mail. It usually takes five to seven business
days to arrive.

Never get a cash advance from your credit card *except* in emergencies.
Interest rates for cash advances are often significantly higher than the
rates for credit-card purchases. More importantly, you start paying interest on the advance the moment you receive the cash. On airline-affiliated
credit cards, a cash advance doesn't earn frequent-flier miles.

 Even though the Bahamian dollar is equivalent to the U.S. dollar, the two
currencies are still different. If you use a credit or debit card, when you
receive your monthly statement, you'll likely find that the bank or credit-
card company added a currency conversion fee (usually about 2 percent) to your charges.

Some credit-card companies recommend that you notify them of any
impending trip abroad so that they don't become suspicious when the
card is used numerous times in an unusual location. If the company
becomes suspicious, it may block your charges. Even if you don't call
your credit-card company in advance, you can always call the card's
emergency number if a charge is refused.

Converting currency

Conversion ratios between the U.S. or Bahamian dollar and other currencies fluctuate, and their differences could affect the relative costs of your
holiday. The figures in Table 5-2 were valid at the time of this writing, but
they may not be valid by the time you depart. This table would still be
useful for conversions of small amounts of money, but if you're planning
on any major transactions, check for more updated rates prior to making
any serious commitments.

Table 5-2		Foreign Currencies versus the U.S./ Bahamian Dollar					
$U.S./$B	*U.K. £*	*Canadian $*	*E.U. €*	*$U.S./$B*	*U.K. £*	*Canadian $*	*E.U. €*
1	0.60	1.35	1.15	10	6.00	13.50	11.50
2	1.20	2.70	2.30	15	9.00	20.25	17.25
3	1.80	4.05	3.45	25	15.00	33.75	28.75
5	3.00	6.75	5.75	100	60.00	135.00	115.00

Dealing with a Lost or Stolen Wallet

Be sure to contact all your credit-card companies the minute you discover that your wallet's been lost or stolen. Then file a report at the nearest police precinct. Your credit-card company or insurer may require a police report number or a record of the loss. Most credit-card companies have an emergency number to call if you lose your card or it gets stolen; they may be able to wire you a cash advance immediately or deliver an emergency credit card in a day or two. Call the following emergency numbers:

 ✔ **American Express:** ☎ **336-393-1111** collect

 ✔ **MasterCard:** ☎ **800-307-7309** or 636-722-7111 collect

 ✔ **Visa:** ☎ **800-847-2911** or 410-581-9994 collect

If you need emergency cash over the weekend when all banks and American Express offices are closed, you can have **Western Union** wire money to you (☎ **800-325-6000**; www.westernunion.com).

Identity theft and fraud are potential complications of losing your wallet, especially if you lose your driver's license along with your cash and credit cards. Notify the major credit-reporting bureaus immediately; placing a fraud alert on your records may protect you against liability for criminal activity. The three major U.S. credit-reporting agencies are

 ✔ **Equifax:** ☎ **800-766-0008**; www.equifax.com

 ✔ **Experian:** ☎ **888-397-3742**; www.experian.com

 ✔ **TransUnion:** ☎ **800-680-7289**; www.transunion.com

Finally, if you lose all forms of photo ID, call your airline and explain the situation. The airline may allow you to board the plane if you have a copy of your passport or birth certificate and a copy of the police report that you filed.

Chapter 6

Getting to The Bahamas

• •

In This Chapter

▶ Securing a great deal on a flight
▶ Cruising to The Bahamas
▶ Deciding if packages are right for you

• •

*U*nless you're a long-distance swimmer who enjoys swimming through shark-infested waters, you have to get to The Bahamas by air (commercial, chartered, or private plane) or by sea (cruise ship or ferry). Of course, the quickest, easiest, and most convenient way to reach The Bahamas is by plane. Many people enjoy cruising to The Bahamas, although these trips mean spending a lot more time on the surf than on the turf.

Flying to The Bahamas

New York and Miami are the most popular gateway cities to fly from the United States to Nassau (New Providence and Paradise Islands) and to Freeport/Lucaya (Grand Bahama Island). Several other U.S. cities, including Philadelphia and Atlanta, also offer direct service.

Nassau is the busiest and most popular entry point. From here, you can make travel arrangements to many of the remote Out Islands. Freeport, on Grand Bahama, also has its own airport, which serves flights from the U.S. mainland, too.

Flight time to Nassau from Miami is about 35 minutes; from New York, two hours and 30 minutes; from Atlanta, two hours and 5 minutes; from Philadelphia, two hours and 45 minutes; from Charlotte, two hours and 10 minutes; from central Florida, one hour and 10 minutes; and from Toronto, three hours.

Connecting airlines and islands

To help you get started making your travel arrangements, we break this section down island by island so that you can tell how easy — or how difficult — it is to reach the vacation spot you have in mind.

We list information about only nonstop flights and direct flights (where you may touch down once, but you don't have to change planes). Therefore, if you're not starting from one of the cities mentioned in the preceding section, you'll probably have to change planes or even airlines to get to the island of your choice. Keep in mind that no matter where you start, to get to some of the smaller cays, you have to fly to one island and then take a ferry or switch to a small airline (see the individual island chapters for complete details). Planes flying from Florida to The Bahamas and from Nassau (New Providence) to other Bahamian islands often carry fewer than 30 or 40 passengers.

Also, remember that flight schedules always change, so use the information in this section to get a rough idea of what's available. Some routes are seasonal, with fewer flights or no flights at all, at various times of the year. For up-to-the-minute details, call the airlines directly or check their Web sites.

Flying to Nassau, New Providence (for Nassau, Cable Beach, and Paradise Island): American Eagle (☎ 800-433-7300; www.aa.com) offers about 12 flights each day from Miami to Nassau, as well as less frequent service from Ft. Lauderdale, Orlando, and Tampa. **Bahamasair** (☎ 800-222-4262; www.bahamasair.com) flies from West Palm Beach, Miami, Ft. Lauderdale, and Orlando to Nassau. **Continental Airlines** (☎ 800-321-0856; www.continental.com) offers daily flights to Nassau from Newark, Miami, Ft. Lauderdale, and West Palm Beach. **Delta** (☎ 800-221-1212; www.delta.com) has several flights to Nassau, providing service from Atlanta, Orlando, and New York's LaGuardia Airport. **U.S. Airways** (☎ 800-428-4322; www.usairways.com) offers daily flights to Nassau from West Palm Beach, Philadelphia, and Charlotte, North Carolina. **Air Canada** (☎ 888-247-2262 in the U.S. or 800-268-7240 in Canada; www.aircanada.com) is the only carrier that offers service to Nassau from Canada.

British Airways (☎ 800-247-9297 in the U.S. or 0870-850-9850 in the United Kingdom; www.britishairways.com) flies directly only to Nassau, offering four weekly flights from London. The airline also has at least one flight daily to Miami, where a staggering number of connections are available to Nassau and many other points within the archipelago on several carriers. Prospective visitors from Australia or New Zealand usually fly to London, where they take a connecting flight across the Atlantic to Nassau on British Airways.

Flying to Paradise Island: Most visitors to Paradise Island arrive in Nassau and commute to Paradise Island by ground transport. However, **Chalk's International Airlines** (☎ 800-424-2557 or 242-363-1687; www.chalksoceanairways.com) flies daily from Ft. Lauderdale International Airport directly to Paradise Island. This airline offers about five flights on weekdays and around eight flights on Saturdays and Sundays. The airplanes are Grumman G-73T; each aircraft carries up to 17 passengers.

Flying to Freeport, Grand Bahama (for Freeport and Lucaya): A number of airlines fly to Grand Bahama International Airport from the continental

U.S., including **American Eagle** (☎ 800-433-7300; www.aa.com) and **Bahamasair** (☎ 800-222-4262; www.bahamasair.com). Both airlines have daily flights from Miami. **GulfStream Continental Connection** (☎ 800-231-0856; www.gulfstreamair.com) flies to Freeport from both Ft. Lauderdale and Miami. **U.S. Airways** (☎ 800-428-4322; www.usairways.com) flies daily from New York's LaGuardia Airport, Charlotte, North Carolina, and Philadelphia. And **U.S. Airways Express** (☎ 800-428-4322; www.usairways.com) wings in from West Palm Beach to Freeport.

Many visitors arrive in Nassau and then hop a **Bahamasair** flight to Freeport. These 35-minute hops run $154 round-trip.

Flying to Marsh Harbour, The Abacos (for Elbow Cay): Air Sunshine (☎ 800-327-8900; www.airsunshine.com), a small commuter airline, offers daily flights from Ft. Lauderdale to Marsh Harbour, where you can catch the ferry to Elbow Cay. **Bahamasair** (☎ 800-222-4262; www.bahamasair.com) flies to Marsh Harbour from West Palm Beach or Nassau. You can find other connections aboard **American Eagle** (☎ 800-433-7300 or 242-367-2231; www.aa.com) with flights from Miami to Marsh Harbour. **Continental Connections** (☎ 800-231-0856; www.continental.com) flies into Marsh Harbour from several locales in Florida. **U.S. Airways Express** (☎ 800-428-4322; www.usairways.com) flies from West Palm Beach to Marsh Harbour.

Flying to Treasure Cay, The Abacos (for Green Turtle Cay and Treasure Cay): Air Sunshine (☎ 242-365-8900; www.airsunshine.com) offers daily flights from Ft. Lauderdale to Treasure Cay (you can take a ferry from Treasure Cay to Green Turtle Cay). **Bahamasair** (☎ 800-222-4262; www.bahamasair.com) flies in daily from Nassau and West Palm Beach. You can find other connections aboard **Twin Air** (☎ 954-359-8266; www.flytwinair.com), which wings in from Ft. Lauderdale. **Continental Connection** (☎ 800-321-0856; www.continental.com) flies to Treasure Cay from several Florida locales.

Getting to Eleuthera and Harbor Island: Bahamasair (☎ 800-222-4262; www.bahamasair.com) flies daily from Nassau to North Eleuthera, where you catch the ferry to Harbour Island. **U.S. Airways Express** (☎ 800-428-4322; www.usairways.com) flies daily from Miami and West Palm Beach to North Eleuthera.

Flying to George Town, Exuma: The most popular way to visit the Exumas is to fly aboard **Bahamasair** (☎ 800-222-4262; www.bahamasair.com), which offers twice-daily service from Nassau to George Town. Flights usually begin leaving Nassau sometime around 6:30 a.m., depending on the day. Be sure to call ahead, because flight schedules can change. **American Eagle** (☎ 800-433-7300; www.aa.com) serves Exuma from Miami daily. Other minor carriers that serve the archipelago include **Lynx Air International** (☎ 888-596-9247; www.lynxair.com), which has flights on Fridays, Saturdays, and Sundays, with links from Ft. Lauderdale. **Air Sunshine** (☎ 800-327-8900 or 954-434-8900; www.airsunshine.com)

flies from Ft. Lauderdale, but only on Mondays and Thursdays. You can return to Ft. Lauderdale aboard this airline on Mondays and Fridays.

Flying to San Salvador: Bahamasair (☎ 800-222-4262; www.bahamas air.com) offers flights six days a week from Nassau. Flight times constantly change. The island's most popular hotel, **Club Med** (☎ 800-CLUBMED [800-258-2633] or 242-331-2000) flies guests in on weekly charter flights from Miami. In winter, charter flights from New York are available once a week.

Getting the best deal on your airfare

Competition among the major U.S. airlines is unlike that of any other industry. Every airline offers virtually the same product (basically, a coach seat is a coach seat is a . . .), yet prices can vary by hundreds of dollars.

Business travelers who need the flexibility of buying their tickets at the last minute and changing their itineraries at a moment's notice — and who want to get home before the weekend — pay (or at least their companies pay) the premium rate, known as the *full fare*. But if you can book your ticket far in advance, stay over Saturday night, and travel midweek (Tuesday, Wednesday, or Thursday), you can qualify for the least expensive price — usually a fraction of the full fare. On most flights — even the shortest hops within the U.S. — the full fare is close to $1,000 or more, but a 7- or 14-day advance-purchase ticket may cost you less than half of that amount. Obviously, planning ahead pays.

Periodically, the airlines hold sales in which they lower the prices on their most popular routes. These fares have advance-purchase requirements and date-of-travel restrictions, but you can't beat the prices. As you plan your vacation, keep your eyes open for these sales, which tend to take place in seasons that have low travel volume — from May to October for The Bahamas.

Consolidators, also known as "bucket shops," are great sources for international tickets, although they usually can't beat the Internet on fares within North America. Start by looking in travel sections in the Sunday newspaper; U.S. travelers should focus on *The New York Times, Los Angeles Times,* and *The Miami Herald.*

Bucket-shop tickets are usually nonrefundable or are rigged with stiff cancellation penalties, often as high as 50 to 75 percent of the ticket price. And some bucket shops put you on charter airlines with questionable safety records. Ask plenty of questions before you fork over your money.

Several reliable consolidators are worldwide and available on the Net. **STA Travel** (☎ 800-781-4040; www.statravel.com), the world's leader in student travel, offers good fares for travelers of all ages. **FlyCheap** (☎ 800-FLY-CHEAP [800-359-24327]; www.1800flycheap.com) has especially good access to fares for sunny destinations because it's owned by package-holiday megalith MyTravel. **Air Tickets Direct** (☎ 800-778-3447; www.airticketsdirect.com) is based in Montreal and leverages the currently weak Canadian dollar for low fares; it also books trips to places that U.S. travel agents won't touch, such as Cuba.

Another good outfit, **Nassau-Paradise Island Express** (☎ 800-722-4262), specializes in selling bulk seats to Nassau (New Providence) from Newark, New Jersey, on Continental Airlines. All these flights are not only nonstop, but you also pay a lot less than you would if you booked your flight directly through the airline. Flights are daily to Nassau from Newark. You can also book your hotel through this company.

Booking your flight online

The big three online travel agencies, **Expedia** (www.expedia.com), **Travelocity** (www.travelocity.com), and **Orbitz** (www.orbitz.com), sell most of the air tickets that are bought on the Internet. (Canadian travelers can try www.expedia.ca and www.travelocity.ca; U.K. residents can go for www.expedia.co.uk and www.opodo.co.uk.) Each site has different business deals with the airlines and may offer different fares on the same flights, so shopping around is wise.

Expedia and Travelocity also send you an **e-mail notification** when a cheap fare to your favorite destination becomes available. Of the smaller travel-agency Web sites, **SideStep** (www.sidestep.com) receives good reviews from users. SideStep is a browser add-on that claims to "search 140 sites at once," but in reality, it beats competitors' fares only as often as other sites do.

You can find great last-minute deals when you sign up to receive free weekly e-mails from the airlines. Airlines announce most of these deals on Tuesday or Wednesday, and you must purchase these tickets online. Most tickets are only valid for travel that weekend, but you can book some tickets weeks or months in advance. Sign up for weekly e-mail alerts at airline Web sites or check mega-sites that compile comprehensive lists of last-minute specials, such as **Smarter Living** (smarterliving.com). For last-minute trips, **Site59** (www.site59.com) in the U.S. and **Lastminute.com** (www.lastminute.com) in Europe often have better deals than the major-label sites.

If you're willing to give up some control over your flight details, use a service like **Priceline** (www.priceline.com; www.priceline.co.uk for Europeans) or **Hotwire** (www.hotwire.com). Both companies offer rock-bottom prices in exchange for traveling on a "mystery airline" at a mysterious time of day, often with a mysterious change of planes en route. The mystery airlines are all major, well-known carriers, and the airlines' routing computers are a lot better than they used to be. But your chances of getting a 6 a.m. or 11 p.m. flight are pretty high. Hotwire tells you the flight prices before you buy; Priceline usually has better deals than Hotwire, and you now also have the option to pick your flights, times, and airlines from a list of low prices that Priceline offers.

Just a ferry ride away

A great way to get from the Florida coast to Freeport is aboard a modern ferryboat, the sleek **Cloud X,** which transports you there in three hours. Launched in 2004, the ferry sets sail from the port of Palm Beach Wednesday through Monday at 9 a.m., with a return voyage from Freeport at 6:30 p.m. The round-trip fare is $99 for adults, $49 for children ages 6 to 12, and free for kids 5 and under. A $34 port charge is levied on passengers of all ages. A trio of comfortable lounges, two bars, and a casino are on board to entertain. This 367-passenger vessel sails under a U.S. flag. For more information, call ☎ **866-GO-FERRY** (866-463-3779) or visit www.bahamasferry.com.

Unfortunately, **The Cat,** a cheap, speedy ferry service between Ft. Lauderdale and Nassau, has stopped running. According to Bahamas Florida Express and *The Nassau Guardian* newspaper, the company is locked in a political battle with the Bahamanian government over starting a new route to Nassau. Keep an eye on www.ferry bahamas.com to see when the Cat's coming back.

Cruising to The Bahamas

Cruises to The Bahamas are usually either three- or four-day weekend getaways or week-long itineraries. If you go on a week-long cruise, the ship may stop at Nassau, Freeport, and/or one of several privately owned Bahamian islands for a day at the beach en route to Caribbean ports farther south.

 If you've never been to The Bahamas, consider taking a cruise to Nassau, where you can also enjoy Paradise Island and Cable Beach on the same visit. Nassau has better shopping possibilities, better restaurants, and more entertainment than any other site in The Bahamas, including Freeport/Lucaya on Grand Bahama Island.

We provide a summary of cruise lines that offer diversions in The Bahamas in the upcoming section, but for detailed information and reviews of each of the ships spending significant time in either the Caribbean or The Bahamas, consider picking up a copy of *Cruise Vacations For Dummies* or *Frommer's Caribbean Cruises & Ports of Call.*

Regardless of the ship you choose, your cruise will most likely depart from the cruise capital of the world, **Miami.** A handful of vessels also depart for Bahamian waters from Port Everglades (adjacent to Ft. Lauderdale), Port Canaveral, and, in very rare instances, New York. Many cruise-ship passengers combine a three- or four-day cruise with visits to Orlando's theme parks, Miami's South Beach, the Florida Everglades, or the Florida Keys and Key West.

Nearly all cabins aboard ships today have two twin beds that you can push together, plus storage space (of varying size), a shower and a toilet (ditto), and sometimes a TV showing a rotating stock of programs. If you want to keep costs to a minimum when booking, ask for one of the smaller, inside cabins (one without windows). If you're the type who likes being active all day and staying out late to enjoy the ship's bars and nightclubs, you won't miss the sunshine anyway. On the other hand, passengers of means can get suites that have an amazing array of pampering options (including hot tubs on their own private verandas!).

Because cruise lines buy in bulk, they typically offer some of the best deals on airfare to your port of embarkation. They also typically offer extension packages that allow pre- or post-cruise stays at a hotel or resort.

Getting around Freeport/Lucaya or Nassau is relatively easy, and the official shore excursions that most ships offer are dull and sometimes restrictive, so decide what you want to do (shopping, swimming, snorkeling, or gambling) and head off on your own during your stop at each port of call. You certainly have time to relax at the beach or to enjoy watersports (the chapters that follow give you details on what companies or outfitters to contact for equipment, so don't feel dependent on the cruise line for everything).

In Nassau, cruise ships anchor at piers along **Prince George Wharf.** Taxi drivers meet all arrivals and can transport you into the heart of Nassau — the center of most shopping and sightseeing activities. Duty-free shops also lie just outside the dock area, but for shopping, you're better off going inside the city's commercial and historic core.

As you disembark, you'll find a tourist information office in a tall pink tower, where you can pick up maps of New Providence Island or of Nassau itself. The tourist information office conducts one-hour walking tours from here if you'd like an overview of the city, with a guide pointing out historic monuments. Outside this office, an ATM can supply you with U.S. dollars if your cash is running low (for more information on money issues, see Chapter 5).

On Grand Bahama Island, your cruise ship will dock at a dull industrial-looking wasteland on the western part of the island, far removed from the center of all the action at Freeport or Lucaya. For shopping, sightseeing, the best beaches, or gambling, you must take a $10 taxi ride to the resort areas. Taxis await all arriving cruise ships.

Reviewing the major cruise lines

Here's a rundown of the major cruise lines that serve The Bahamas. Most of them focus on either Nassau or Freeport (or both).

- ✔ **Carnival Cruise Line** (☎ **800-327-9501** or 305-599-2200; www.carnival.com): The cruise line that everyone's heard of offers a big, loud, flashy cruise party with lots of gambling, glitz, and crowds, so if you're looking for some quiet, reflective time, this

cruise may not be your cup of rum. Carnival's best bet for The
Bahamas is aboard the *Fantasy,* which sails on three-night loops
to Nassau and four-night excursions to both Freeport and Nassau.
Similar in appeal is the *Fascination,* which visits Nassau and attracts
passengers seeking a "long weekend" at sea and in port.

✔ **Celebrity Cruises** (☎ **800-327-3111** or 305-539-6000; www.celebrity
cruises.com): Celebrity Cruises, a more upscale sibling company to
Royal Caribbean, offers Caribbean cruises (with a Nassau stopover)
that last between seven and eleven nights. This line is unpretentious
but classy and is several notches above mass-market, but with pretty
competitive pricing. Cabins are roomy and comfortable, and the
cuisine is among the best of any of the cruise lines.

✔ **Costa Cruise Lines** (☎ **800-462-6782** or 954-266-5600; www.costa
cruises.com): Similar to Celebrity Cruises, Costa Cruises features
a stopover in Nassau on some of its cruises. This old Italian cruise
outfit offers seven-night jaunts through the western and eastern
Caribbean on *CostaAtlantica* and *CostaMediterranea,* departing
from Ft. Lauderdale. This line attracts passengers who want to
pay a reasonable price and who avoid all-American mega-ships
like those of Carnival. Costa passengers are impressed with Italian
style, appreciate a sense of cultural adventure and fun, and like the
atmosphere of casual elegance. The ship features tame versions of
ancient Roman Bacchanalia, as well as such celebrations as toga
nights and focaccia and pizza parties by the pool.

✔ **Disney Cruise Line** (☎ **800-951-3532** or 888-325-2500; www.disney
cruise.com): Launched with lots of publicity in 1999, the *Disney
Wonder* is saturated with the total Disney vibe and is specifically
marketed to families. It succeeds in mingling state-of-the-art tech-
nology and audio-visuals with lots of Disney razzle-dazzle. Disney
also offers the best-designed family cabins of any cruise ship, the
biggest children's facilities, and even a number of adults-only areas,
including one swimming pool, a piano bar, a comedy club, and various social venues. The three- and four-night Bahamian cruises
depart from Port Canaveral, Florida.

✔ **Holland America Line** (☎ **877-724-5425** or 206-281-3535; www.
hollandamerica.com): Holland America Line is the most high-
toned of the mass-market cruise lines, with nine respectably hefty
and good-looking ships serving a clientele of generally mature travelers. Late-night revelers and serious party people may want to book
cruises on other lines, such as Carnival. Throughout the winter, at
least three of these vessels include day-long stopovers in Nassau
and/or full-day stopovers at the line's privately owned island
(Half Moon Cay, in the Exumas) as part of a seven-night cruise to
Caribbean ports. For the ships that stop in The Bahamas, you
embark at Ft. Lauderdale, Tampa, or Port Canaveral.

✔ **Norwegian Cruise Line** (☎ **800-327-7030** or 305-436-4000; www.
ncl.com): Noweigian Cruise Line offers seven-night Florida-Bahamas

transits aboard the *Norwegian Dawn,* visiting Nassau and Great Stirrup Cay (the cruise lines's private island). Generally inexpensive and emphasizing sports, these ships attract a lot of active travelers in the 24 to 45 age bracket. Activities and cuisine are routine but adequate. Passengers who book on this cruise line want to travel to a hot-weather destination in winter but don't want to spend lavish sums for the experience. A wide variety of cabins are available at a range of prices to cater to a more diverse clientele than those usually found aboard Holland America or Celebrity ships.

✔ **Caribbean International** (☎ 800-327-6700 or 305-539-6000; www. royalcaribbean.com): This is another cruise line that offers The Bahamas (Nassau and Freeport) as a specific destination instead of including the archipelago as a one-night stopover. Things run smoothly on this middle-of-the-road cruise line, which has a less frenetic atmosphere than Carnival's mega-ships but a livelier one than Celebrity or Holland America. The company is well run, and it offers enough on-board activities to suit virtually any taste and age level. Although accommodations and facilities are more than adequate, they're not upscale, and cabins aboard some of the line's older vessels tend to be a bit more cramped than the industry norm.

Getting the best deal on your cruise

Cruise lines operate like airlines, setting rates for their cruises and then selling them in a rapid-fire series of discounts, offering almost whatever it takes to fill their ships. For this reason, great deals come and go in the blink of an eye, and most deals are available only through travel agents.

If you have a travel agent who you trust, leave the details to her. If not, try contacting a travel agent who specializes in booking cruises. Some of the most likely contenders include the following:

✔ **Cruises, Inc.,** 1415 NW 62 St., Ft. Lauderdale, FL 33009 (☎ 800-854-0500 or 954-958-3681; www.cruisesinc.com)

✔ **Cruises Only,** 1011 E. Colonial Dr., Orlando, FL 32803 (☎ 800-242-9000 or 407-898-5353; www.cruisesonly.com)

✔ **The Cruise Company,** 10760 Q St., Omaha, NE 68127 (☎ 800-289-5505 or 402-339-6800; www.thecruisecompany.com)

✔ **Kelly Cruises,** 1315 W. 22nd St., Ste. 105, Oak Brook, IL 60523 (☎ 800-837-7447; www.kellycruises.com)

✔ **Hartford Holidays Travel,** 129 Hillside Ave., Williston Park, NY 11596 (☎ 800-828-4813 or 516-746-6670; www.hartfordholidays.com)

✔ **Mann Travel and Cruises,** 4400 Park Rd., Charlotte, NC 28209 (☎ 800-849-2301 or 704-556-8311; www.manntravelandcruises.com)

Choosing a Package Deal

For The Bahamas, package deals can be a smart way to go. In many cases, a package that includes airfare, hotel, and transportation to and from the airport costs less than the hotel alone that you book yourself. The reason is because tour operators buy packages in bulk and then resell them to the public. It's kind of like buying your vacation at a buy-in-bulk store — except the tour operator is the one who buys the 1,000-count box of garbage bags and resells them ten at a time at a cost that undercuts the local supermarket.

Package tours can vary as much as those garbage bags, too. Some package tours offer better classes of hotel than others; others provide the same hotels for lower prices. Some packages book flights on scheduled airlines; others sell charters. In some packages, your choice of accommodations and travel days may be limited. Some packages let you choose between escorted vacations and independent vacations; others allow you to add just a few excursions or escorted day trips (also at discounted prices) without booking an entirely escorted tour.

If you're dreaming of getting away from it all on one of The Bahamas' undeveloped Out Islands, finding good package deals may be hard. Most packagers concentrate on the larger hotels on the more popular islands, such as New Providence or Grand Bahama.

To find package tours, check out the travel section of your local Sunday newspaper or the ads in the back of national travel magazines, such as *Travel & Leisure, National Geographic Traveler,* and *Condé Nast Traveler.* **Liberty Travel** (call ☎ **888-271-1584** to find the store nearest you; www.libertytravel.com) is one of the biggest packagers in the Northeast and usually boasts a full-page ad in Sunday papers.

Some packagers specialize in types of trips, such as scuba-diving adventures, golf getaways, or casino excursions. Likewise, a few of the larger hotels, such as the all-inclusive Club Med on San Salvador, offer money-saving hotel packages that include charter flights. If you already know where you want to stay, call that resort and ask whether it offers land/air packages.

Another good source of package deals is the airlines themselves. Most major airlines offer air/land packages. Several big online travel agencies — Expedia (www.expedia.com), Travelocity (www.travelocity.com), Orbitz (www.orbitz.com), Site59 (www.site59.com), and Lastminute. com (www.lastminute.com) — also do a brisk business in packages. If you're unsure about the pedigree of a smaller packager, check with the Better Business Bureau in the city where the company is based or go online to www.bbb.org. If a packager won't tell you where it's based, don't book with it.

Here are some of the packagers that we prefer:

✔ **American Airlines Vacations** (☎ 800-321-2121; www.aavacations. com) can arrange packages to Nassau, Cable Beach, and Paradise Island (New Providence); Freeport/Lucaya (Grand Bahama); and Exuma. These economical deals include discounted airfare, hotel, and, if you like, a rental car, as well as meals (at certain accommodations). Flights from Florida are nonstop. You need to stay in The Bahamas for at least three nights, but doing so is hardly difficult because even the most hurried traveler to The Bahamas spends that amount of time in the sun and on the sand.

✔ **American Express Vacations** (☎ 800-941-2639; www.travel impressions.com) books trips to a couple of the smaller Bahamian islands that many packagers ignore: Green Turtle Cay in the Abacos and Harbour Island off the coast of Eleuthera. Of course, the company also sets up air/land packages to the most popular resort areas: Nassau, Cable Beach, and Paradise Island (New Providence); and Freeport/Lucaya (Grand Bahama). Nonstop charter flights from Newark, New York, and Miami can take you to Nassau or Freeport. The minimum stay is two or three nights.

✔ **British Airways** (☎ 0870/850-9850 in the U.K., 800-247-9297 in the U.S.; www.britishairways.com) offers travelers direct flights from Gatwick Airport outside London to Nassau. Call the airline or visit the Web site for information on package deals.

✔ **Caribbean Dive Tours** (☎ 800-404-3483; www.worlddive.com) makes one-stop shopping especially attractive, because this company arranges scuba-diving trips for individuals or groups that include airfare, hotel, meals (in some cases), and all dives and gear.

✔ **Club Med** (☎ 800-258-2633; www.clubmed.com) features all-inclusive options on Paradise Island and San Salvador.

✔ **Continental Airlines Vacations** (☎ 800-301-3800; www.cool vacations.com) customizes hotel and air packages to Nassau, Cable Beach, and Paradise Island that include transfers to and from the airport. Depending on what hotel you choose, you can throw in breakfast or both breakfast and dinner. No matter where you're starting from, you connect to a plane in Florida to get to the islands. Continental's packages require a two-night stay.

✔ **Delta Vacations** (☎ 800-221-6666; www.deltavacations.com) coordinates packages from New York or Atlanta to Nassau, Cable Beach, and Paradise Island that include air, hotel, and transfers between your accommodation and the airport. Flights are nonstop from New York or Atlanta.

✔ **Frontiers International** (☎ 800-245-1950 or 724-935-1577; www. frontierstrvl.com) features fly- and spin-fishing tours of The Bahamas and specializes in saltwater-fishing destinations.

✔ **Grand Bahama Vacations** (☎ **800-545-1300**; www.gbvac.com) books charter flights with Laker Airways to Freeport/Lucaya (Grand Bahama) twice a week from Ft. Lauderdale, Baltimore, Cleveland, Cincinnati, Hartford, Memphis, Nashville, Raleigh, Richmond, and Pittsburgh, as well as every other Saturday from West Palm Beach. When you reserve your flight, you can also book a bed at one of more than a dozen Grand Bahama hotels.

✔ **Harlequin Worldwide Connoisseurs Collection** (☎ **01708/850-300**; www.harlequinholidays.com) is a consideration for British travelers, in addition to the packages offered by British Airways. This agency offers both air and hotel packages not only to Nassau, but also to most of the Out Islands. The company also specializes in scuba diving and golf holidays.

✔ **Just-A-Vacation, Inc.** (☎ **800-683-6313**; www.justavacation.com) specializes in all-inclusive resorts on the islands of The Bahamas, mainly Nassau/Paradise Island and Grand Bahama Island.

✔ **Kuoni Travel** (☎ **01306/744-442**; www.kuoni.co.uk) is another British specialist that offers both land and air packages to The Bahamas, including such destinations as Nassau and Freeport, and to some places in the Out Islands. They also offer packages for self-catering villas on Paradise Island.

✔ **Maduro Dive Fanta-Seas** (☎ **800-327-6709**; www.maduro.com) can set up a complete dive trip with one phone call. Packages for individuals or groups include airfare, hotel, meals (if you want them), and all dives and gear.

✔ **US Airways Vacations** (☎ **800-455-0123**; www.usairways vacations.com) arranges air/hotel packages, with nonstop service to Nassau from Philadelphia or Charlotte, North Carolina. US Airways requires a two-night minimum stay.

Chapter 7

Booking Your Accommodations

• •

In This Chapter

▶ Checking out the options
▶ Deciding whether you want a meal plan
▶ Choosing the right resort or hotel for you
▶ Getting the best room for your money

• •

*W*hen visiting an archipelago as vast and, in some cases, as difficult to reach as parts of The Bahamas are, choosing where to hang your hat becomes all-important. Visiting The Bahamas isn't like visiting a city where you can check out of a hotel you don't like the next morning and take a taxi to another one.

Throughout this guide, we give you honest and candid descriptions about what to expect from a hotel. Working like a marriage broker, we hope to match you up with the right mate for your island fantasy. If you land in the wrong place, especially if you've already prepaid, your vacation might be disappointing. This chapter tells you what you need to know about the types of accommodations awaiting you on each island. In Grand Bahama and New Providence, you have plenty of choices. In the Out Islands, the lack of accommodations greatly restricts you.

Getting to Know Your Options

The Bahamas offer a wide selection of accommodations, ranging from small private guesthouses to large luxury resorts. Hotels vary in size and facilities, from deluxe (offering room service, sports, swimming pools, entertainment, and so on) to fairly simple Out Island inns.

Hotel properties in the islands aren't rated according to any rigid classification system or "star system." The word "deluxe" is often used (or misused) when "first class" may be the more appropriate term. "First class" itself often isn't first class. For those reasons and others, we present fairly detailed descriptions of the properties in destination-specific chapters throughout the book to give you an idea of what to expect. However, even in the deluxe and first-class resorts and hotels, don't expect top-rate service and efficiency. "Things," as they're called in the islands, don't seem to work as well here as they do in certain fancy resorts of California, Florida, and Europe.

Travelers to The Bahamas have the following options:

- ✔ Hotels, resorts, and inns
- ✔ All-inclusive resorts
- ✔ Villas, condos, and timeshares
- ✔ Guesthouses

No matter which option you choose, our accommodations' price ranges apply throughout the book. Check out Table 7-1 for an explanation of the dollar sign symbols and the amenities you can expect at each price level.

Table 7-1	Key to Hotel Dollar Signs	
Dollar Sign(s)	*Price Range*	*What to Expect*
$	Less than $100	These accommodations are relatively simple and inexpensive. Rooms are likely to be small, and you may not have a TV in your room. In some cases, you may not have a phone in your room.
$$	$101–$200	These mid-range accommodations are a bit classier and offer more room, more extras (such as irons, hair dryers, or microwaves), and a more convenient location — perhaps on the beach — than the preceding category.
$$$	$201–$300	Higher-class still, these accommodations begin looking plush. Think chocolates on your pillow, a classy restaurant, underground parking garages, maybe even expansive views of a white sandy beachfront.
$$$$	$301 and up	These top-rate, most often beachfront, accommodations come with luxurious amenities, such as valet parking, on-premise spas, and in-room hot tubs and CD players — but you pay through the nose for 'em.

Hotels, resorts, and inns: Enjoying your stay

If you want to live in luxury, your best and sometimes only bets are found on New Providence, with its array of hotels and resorts spread from Cable Beach to Nassau to Paradise Island. The second-largest concentration of hotels and resorts is on Grand Bahama Island, mainly around Freeport or Lucaya.

Except for certain pockets of luxury, such as Harbour Island off the coast of Eleuthera, resort pickings grow slim as you explore the Out Islands. Hotels are small except Club Med on San Salvador and the Four Seasons Resort in the Exumas. Most of the Out Islands have inns rather than large hotels. Some inns are very basic, often in dull concrete blocks, but our recommendations have style and a bit of class.

We recommend mainstream hotels, resorts, and inns for

✔ Families that want plenty of amusements for their kids and sitters close at hand

✔ Sports lovers who seek golf or watersports facilities

✔ Honeymooners or couples who want to focus on each other

✔ First-time visitors to The Bahamas

✔ Travelers with disabilities

Hotels and resorts also have a downside:

✔ Authentic island flavor doesn't exist in most of these places.

✔ Guests tend to be resort-bound and don't get to sample an island's offerings or charms.

✔ All the extra expenses add up quickly. You may get a shock when it's time to pay up.

All-inclusives: Simplifying your vacation

The all-inclusive resort concept finally has a foothold in The Bahamas. At such resorts, one price includes everything — your room, all meals, entertainment, and many watersports (although some cost extra), and sometimes even drinks. Some people find that the cost of all-inclusive holidays is cheaper than paying individually for each item, and others appreciate knowing in advance what their final bill will be.

The first all-inclusive resort hotel in The Bahamas was **Club Med** (☎ 800-258-2633), with its property on Paradise Island. This resort isn't a swinging-singles kind of place; it's popular with everybody from honeymooners to families. Another Club Med is on San Salvador, located in the southern Bahamas, which has more of a luxurious hideaway atmosphere.

The biggest all-inclusive resort of them all, **Sandals** (☎ 800-SANDALS; www.sandals.com), came to Cable Beach in 1995. This Jamaican company is now walking its sandals across the Caribbean. The most famous of the all-inclusives (but not necessarily the best), it caters only to male-female couples, having long ago rescinded its initial policy of "Any two people in love."

Good candidates for all-inclusive resorts are

- ✔ Honeymooners
- ✔ Families
- ✔ Inexperienced travelers
- ✔ The budget-conscious
- ✔ The super-stressed

What are the downsides?

- ✔ Because you pay for everything in advance, you may feel obligated to spend all your time at the resort and not venture out to see what's happening beyond the compound.

- ✔ At an all-inclusive resort, you live in a cocoon and miss what makes your island special.

- ✔ Exuberant activity coordinators feel their job is to keep you occupied day and night. This "organized fun" may not be for you.

Villas: Vacationing with the comforts of home

You may want to rent a villa, a good-sized apartment in someone's condo or timeshare, or even a small beach cottage (more accurately called a *cabaña*).

Private apartments come with or without maid service, so ask upfront exactly what to expect. This option is more no-frills than a villa or condo. The apartments may not be in buildings with swimming pools, and they may not have a front desk to help you.

Many cottages or cabañas open onto a beach, although others cluster around a communal swimming pool. Most cottages are fairly simple, containing no more than a plain bedroom plus a small kitchen and bathroom. In the peak winter season, make reservations at least five or six months in advance.

VHR Worldwide (☎ 800-633-3284 or 201-767-9393) offers the most comprehensive portfolio of luxury villas, condominiums, resort suites, and apartments for rent not only in The Bahamas, but also in the Caribbean. **Hideaways International** (☎ 800-843-4433 in the U.S. or 603-430-4433; www.hideaways.com), a travel club, publishes *Hideaways Guide,* a 148-page pictorial directory of home rentals throughout the world with full descriptions so you know what you're renting. Rentals range from cottages to staffed villas to whole islands. Annual membership in Hideaways International costs $145 and includes perks such as discounts on condos and resorts and services such as airline ticketing and car rentals.

Sometimes local tourist offices will also advise you on vacation-home rentals if you write or call them directly.

We recommend villas for

- ✔ Families

- ✔ Groups of friends

- ✔ Honeymooners or couples craving privacy

- ✔ Independent travelers who want to connect with the island

But staying at a home-away-from-home also has its downsides:

- ✔ You don't get the extensive dining facilities and other amenities of a resort.

- ✔ A villa may not offer daily maid service and other niceties (like a pool or Jacuzzi) that you consider vital to your relaxation.

- ✔ Few villas are located right on the beach; resorts usually snag the prime real estate.

- ✔ You definitely won't get (or be subjected to, depending on your point of view) the nightly entertainment that almost every Bahamian hotel trumpets.

- ✔ You're more isolated, so you'd better really like your traveling companion (if you have one).

- ✔ Of all the travel options, villas are the least likely to live up to their brochure promises.

We recommend condos and cabañas for

- ✔ Families. You can feed your kids what you want and not suffer disapproving looks from the honeymooners at the next table when junior flips his soggy cereal on the floor.

- ✔ Groups of friends.

- ✔ Older couples looking for quiet.

- ✔ Long-term vacationers. Cooking your own meals is a great money-saving tactic for an extended stay on an island.

- ✔ Independent travelers who want to connect with the island and its people.

What are some drawbacks to staying at a condo or cabaña?

- ✔ All the comforts of home, plus all the work.

- ✔ Limited amenities.

- ✔ You're trusting your tropical dream to someone else's decorating taste.

- ✔ When dinner time comes, you're the staff as well as the diner.

Guesthouses: Living like a Bahamian

The B&B-style guesthouse is where many Bahamians stay when they're traveling in their own islands. In The Bahamas, however, the term "guesthouse" can mean anything. Sometimes so-called guesthouses are really simple motels built around swimming pools. Others are small individual cottages with their own kitchenettes, constructed around a main building in which you often find a bar and restaurant serving local food.

In the Out Islands, the guesthouses are no-frills. The ones we recommend are clean and decent for families or single women. Many of these guesthouses are very basic. Salt spray takes a serious toll on metal or fabric, and chipped paint is commonplace. Bathrooms can fall into the vintage category, and sometimes the water isn't heated — but when the weather is 85°F to 92°F outside, you don't need hot water anyway.

On the other hand, some of these places are quite comfortable. A few guesthouses are almost luxurious; and, in addition to giving you the opportunity to live with a local family, they boast swimming pools, private bathrooms in all rooms, and air-conditioning.

We recommend guesthouses for

- ✔ Older couples who like the bed-and-breakfast concept

- ✔ Long-term vacationers on tight budgets

- ✔ The independent traveler who needs a home base

Here are some of the drawbacks to staying at a guesthouse:

- ✔ You may be far from the beach, without a pool.

- ✔ The digs may not be glamorous.

- ✔ You may not get along with your host.

- ✔ Housekeeping standards vary widely.

- ✔ If a problem occurs, you're stuck dealing one-on-one with the home owner.

Locating Lodging that Suits You

Where you want to sleep often determines your choice of island. The type of accommodation you have in mind means that you should consider some islands and write off others. For example, perhaps you're dreaming of napping in your personal hammock at the edge of a secluded beach right in front of your individually decorated bungalow. Your choices are very limited on New Providence and Grand Bahama. However, The Bahamas' Out Islands offer lots of small, peaceful, beachfront lodgings.

If your ideal vacation includes a hotel with a wide variety of restaurants, Las Vegas-style extravaganzas, and nightly dancing, steer clear of The Bahamas' Out Islands and head to Cable Beach on New Providence, Paradise Island, or Grand Bahama.

Certain hotels allow children under a set age to stay free or at reduced rates in a room with an adult. Many dining rooms offer children's menus with lower prices and smaller portions than the regular fare.

Rooming on the main islands

Rooms in the larger hotels on New Providence, Paradise Island, and Grand Bahama are air-conditioned (some also have ceiling fans) and come with satellite TV and direct-dial telephones. Most rooms have two double beds or one king-size bed, plus a balcony or patio. Many rooms are also equipped with irons and ironing boards, coffeemakers, mini-bars or refrigerators, hair dryers, and in-room safes. Some rooms have Internet access and sometimes even CD players. Hotels have U.S. newspapers — usually from Miami or New York — available. Expect to find plenty of activities, along with restaurants, shops, salons, and (on the premises or nearby) watersports operators. Many hotels also have wheelchair-accessible rooms. Likewise, some hotels offer supervised children's programs.

In some cases, you're on your own, without on-premises restaurants or activities' desks to provide information, help you set up excursions, call taxis, or assist with other arrangements.

Bahamian landlords offer plenty of villas and condos for rent on the main islands, but first-time visitors may want to skip them because you should be familiar with the island and getting around by car.

The more elegant and expensive villa rentals offer maid service, and in some cases, even your own cook — for an extra fee, of course. At cheaper rentals, you may have to do your own cleaning and cooking.

Choosing the less-developed islands

You won't find high-rise hotels in the Out Islands. A few islands offer posh digs with rooms and facilities as snazzy as the ones on busier islands — for example, Pink Sands on Harbour Island (see Chapter 22) or

Green Turtle Club & Marina on Green Turtle Cay in the Abacos (see Chapter 20). Still, these low-rise lodgings are far less formal than upscale hotels on New Providence, Paradise Island, or Grand Bahama.

Accommodations on the less-developed islands may or may not have air-conditioning, but ceiling fans or good cross-ventilation does the trick if they don't. Some rooms have two double beds, and others have only one. In rare cases, some rooms offer only twin beds. In the Out Islands, many hotel rooms don't have telephones, TVs, or radios. In hotels that do have TVs in the rooms, the channels are centrally controlled (usually at the bar), so don't be surprised if the mystery you're watching suddenly turns into a soccer game just before the murderer's identity is revealed. If any of these amenities are important to you, ask about them before you make your reservation.

In many cases in the Out Islands, you don't have to worry about losing your room key because you don't get one in the first place. (No one locks his doors.) Forgot your beach reading? You're likely to find a selection of dog-eared paperbacks that previous vacationers left in your room. You can even take one of those books home with you — as long as you leave one of yours in its place.

You may be surprised to know that quite a few hotels have *honor bars,* where no bartender is on duty. Guests simply take or mix their own drinks, write them down, and pay for them when they check out. With this trusting attitude, it's no wonder that staff members at these small, easygoing hotels quickly get to know guests. Staff members aren't shy about sharing tips about their favorite parts of the islands, either.

Independent families or groups of friends traveling together find villas, condos, and hotel rooms with kitchens convenient places to stay on the quieter, less-developed islands. On less-developed islands, hotels are small enough that managers themselves are usually willing to help you make arrangements for watersports, dining, transportation, and other activities that may or may not be on the premises.

 If you or someone in your group is in a wheelchair, ask about the specifics of the landscape and the facilities at hotels on the less-developed islands. Some hotels, such as a few on Harbour Island and Green Turtle Cay in the Abacos, have hilly grounds or lots of steps.

Understanding the Meal Plans

As you're shopping around for your accommodations (whether while consulting this guide or other sources like hotel Web sites), you'll see prices listed according to meal-plan options.

Many Bahamian resorts offer a **European Plan** (EP) rate, which means that you pay only for the price of a room, and most of our listings are the

EP rate. If you choose this option, you're free to dine at other resorts or restaurants. Another plan is the **Continental Plan** (CP), which means that your room and a continental breakfast of juice, coffee, bread, jam, and so on is included in a set price. A variation of this plan is the **Breakfast Plan** (BP), which is a full traditional American-style breakfast — eggs, bacon, pancakes, French toast, and hash browns. Guests who don't want to "dine around" at breakfast time prefer the Continental and Breakfast plans.

Another major option is the **Modified American Plan** (MAP), which includes breakfast and one main meal of the day, either lunch or dinner. The final choice is the **American Plan** (AP), which includes breakfast, lunch, and dinner. At certain resorts, you can save money by booking either MAP or AP because the per-meal cost may be cheaper. If you dine à la carte for lunch and dinner at various restaurants, your final dining bill is likely to be much higher than if you stayed on the MAP or AP.

Aside from the savings in cost, meal plans have drawbacks if you like to eat in a variety of places as a part of your holiday. You face the same dining room every night, unless the resort you're staying in has many different restaurants on the dining plan. Many resorts have specialty restaurants that serve a variety of cuisines, but these more expensive restaurants aren't included in MAP or AP and charge à la carte prices.

Dining at your hotel cuts down on transportation costs because taxis are especially expensive. Nonetheless, if dining out and having many different culinary experiences is your idea of a vacation and you're willing to pay the higher price, avoid AP plans or at least make sure that the hotel where you're staying has more than one dining room.

Before booking a room, investigate what you're likely to save by booking a dining plan. The meal-plan options may have a significant impact on your choice of accommodations.

Finding the Best Room at the Best Rate

The *rack rate* is the maximum rate a hotel charges for a room. This rate is the one you get when you walk in off the street and ask for a room for the night. Hotel managers are happy to charge you the rack rate, but you can almost always do better. Perhaps the best way to avoid paying the rack rate is surprisingly simple: Just ask whether they can quote you a better price. You may be pleasantly surprised.

In all but the smallest accommodations, a room's price depends on how you make your reservation. A travel agent may be able to negotiate a better price with certain hotels than you can get by yourself. (The hotel gives the agent a discount in exchange for steering her business toward that hotel.) Making a reservation online through a hotel or airline Web site often allows you to take advantage of special discounts. Reserving a room through a hotel chain's central toll-free number may not yield the best rate because the representative may not be aware of local discounts. Your best bet is to call both the local number and the toll-free number to see which one gives you a better deal.

Package deals abound, and they're always cheaper than rack rates. Going to a reliable travel agent to find out what, if anything, is available in the way of a land-and-air package before booking a particular accommodation is sometimes a good idea. For more on package deals, see Chapter 6.

To save money on accommodations, timing is also vital. The winter season in The Bahamas runs roughly from the middle of December to the middle of April, and hotels charge their highest prices during this peak period. During the winter months, make reservations two months in advance if you can. You can't book early enough if you want to travel over Christmas or in February.

The off-season in The Bahamas — roughly from mid-April to mid-December (although the off-season varies from hotel to hotel) — amounts to a sale. In most cases, hotels slash their rates by a startling 20 to 60 percent. This deal is a bonanza for cost-conscious travelers, especially for families who can travel in the summer. For more tips on helping you decide when to take your vacation in The Bahamas, see Chapter 4.

Ask whether you can get an upgrade or a free night's stay if you stay an extra few days. If you travel during the marginal periods between low and high season, you can sometimes delay your travel plans by a week or ten days and get a substantial rate reduction. For example, if you book a $300 room on April 12, the price may lower to $180 by April 17 because mid-April marks the beginning of the low season in The Bahamas.

Surfing the Web for hotel deals

You can shop online for hotels in one of two ways: by booking through the hotel's Web site or through an independent booking agency's Web site. These independent Internet hotel agencies have multiplied in mind-boggling numbers recently, competing for the business of millions of travelers surfing for accommodations around the world. This competitiveness can be a boon to those people who have the patience and time to shop and compare the online sites for good deals — but shop you must, because prices can vary considerably from site to site. And keep in mind that hotels at the top of a site's listing may be there for no other reason than that they paid money to get the placement.

Of the "big three" sites, **Expedia** (www.expedia.com) offers a long list of special deals and *virtual tours,* or photos of available rooms, so you can see what you're paying for. **Travelocity** (www.travelocity.com) posts unvarnished customer reviews and ranks its properties according to the AAA rating system. **Hotels.com** (www.hotels.com) and **Quikbook.com** (www.quikbook.com) are also reliable sites. An excellent free program, **TravelAxe** (www.travelaxe.net), helps you search multiple hotel sites at once, even ones that you've never heard of — and conveniently lists the total price of the room, including the taxes and service charges. Another booking site, **Travelweb** (www.travelweb.com), is partly owned by the hotels it represents (including the Hilton, Hyatt, and Starwood chains) and, therefore, plugs directly into the hotels' reservations systems.

Travelweb's direct link to the hotels gives it a leg up on independent online agencies, which have to fax or e-mail reservation requests to the hotel, a good portion of which get misplaced in the shuffle. More than once, travelers have arrived at the hotel, only to be told that they have no reservation. Getting a confirmation number and making a printout of any online booking transaction is a good idea.

Two other hotel sites worth checking out are **hoteldiscount.com** (☎ 800-364-0801; www.180096hotel.com), which lists bargain room rates at hotels in more than 50 U.S. and international cities, including Nassau and Freeport/Lucaya; and **InnSite** (www.innsite.com), which features B&B listings in more than 50 countries around the globe, including The Bahamas.

Reserving the best room

Somebody has to get the best room at a hotel or a resort, so it may as well be you. Here's how to go about getting the best room:

- ✔ Inquire about ceiling fans, air-conditioning, and whether the windows open.

- ✔ Find out whether the room faces the water or the garage in back. If you're not going to spend a lot of time in your room, getting the back view makes sense because it's cheaper. Upper-floor rooms with views cost more, too.

- ✔ Ask for a room, floor, or annex that was recently renovated.

- ✔ Ask about nonsmoking rooms.

- ✔ Avoid rooms overlooking outdoor nighttime entertainment or the bar or lounge, if you're a light sleeper.

Most Bahamian hoteliers wait until the slow season (summer) to do major renovations. If you're traveling other than in the winter months, check to see whether your hotel is in the midst of renovating. If it is, request a room away from the work site. Those construction workers are early risers.

Chapter 8

Catering to Special Travel Needs or Interests

● ●

In This Chapter

▶ Bringing the kids along

▶ Honeymooning or getting hitched on the islands

▶ Traveling if you're single, gay or lesbian, a senior, or physically challenged

● ●

*O*ne-size-fits-all doesn't pertain to vacations in The Bahamas. Individual travelers or even people traveling with companions or children often have special needs.

Some questions immediately come to mind. Where can couples honeymoon or even tie the knot? What discounts or privileges can people who've reached the golden age get? How wheelchair accessible are the islands? Or are the islands gay friendly? In this chapter, we discuss the challenges and opportunities that some travelers may encounter in The Bahamas.

Traveling with the Brood: Advice for Families

If you have enough trouble getting your kids out of the house in the morning, dragging them hundreds of miles away may seem like an insurmountable challenge. But family travel is immensely rewarding, giving you new ways of seeing the world through smaller pairs of eyes.

A traveling brood plays a big part in your choices of accommodations, dining, and activities. To help make matters easier, remember to look for the Kid Friendly icon we use throughout this book. This icon calls attention to hotels and resorts, restaurants, or attractions that are especially family friendly.

Kids vacationing at some beach resorts need not settle for just a sandy shore. They're treated to organized programs so comprehensive that they rival summer camp. Some larger accommodations offer children's programs year-round.

 Some programs are no more than a bored baby-sitter in a room full of toys or video games. Other programs have enthusiastic, well-trained staff members who engage children in age-appropriate diversions, from face painting and storytelling to beach Olympics and computer-assisted science projects. Some resorts charge an additional fee for their programs, but others are free to guests. Most resorts usually offer morning and afternoon sessions, and meals and night sessions may also be available. Most programs take children from around age 5 up to about age 12.

 The best kids' programs are at **Atlantis Paradise Island Resort & Casino** (Chapter 11) on Paradise Island, New Providence; **Radisson Cable Beach** (see Chapter 11) on New Providence; and **The Westin and Sheraton at Our Lucaya** (see Chapter 13) on Grand Bahama.

Here are some questions to ask when you're evaluating a children's program:

✔ What is the ratio of caretakers/counselors to children?

✔ Are kids divided into age groups?

✔ Exactly what activities do they engage in?

✔ How much time do the kids spend at the pool or beach, and what kind of expert supervision do they have nearby or in the water?

✔ Are meals included?

✔ Do the children leave the drop-off area, and if so, where else do they go?

Flying with children

If you're traveling with an infant, bring along a car seat to use on the plane. Because many airlines allow children under age 2 to fly free when sitting on an adult's lap, you may be tempted not to purchase a seat for your child. Doing so really isn't safe, however, because turbulence can easily injure a child. You may wonder why you should bother buying a ticket for your child when empty seats are often available. The problem is that if the plane is full, you're out of luck.

Don't forget gum or lollipops for kids to chew or suck during take-off and landing to combat ear-pressure pain. And pack a deck of cards or some favorite toys to keep them entertained. You may be used to hearing their mantra of "Are we there yet?," but the whines of bored children can drive other passengers crazy. Flight attendants are quite accommodating if you need to refrigerate baby bottles or if you have other child-related requests.

Remember to specify any food allergies, to slather your younger editions with sunscreen and, of course, to make sure that the caretakers know where to find you in case of an emergency.

If you need a baby-sitter for your smallest tots, you can hire one through your hotel. Expect to pay around $12 to $15 an hour, plus $3 for each additional child. Also refer to "Baby-sitting" in the Fast Facts section of the Appendix.

You can find good family-oriented vacation advice on the Internet from sites like the **Family Travel Network** (www.familytravelnetwork.com), which features excellent articles; **Traveling Internationally with Your Kids** (www.travelwithyourkids.com), a comprehensive site that offers sound advice for long-distance and international travel with children; and **Family Travel Files** (www.thefamilytravelfiles.com), which offers an online magazine and a directory of off-the-beaten-path tours and tour operators for families.

Making Age Work for You: Tips for Seniors

Senior travelers to The Bahamas tend to gravitate toward New Providence and Grand Bahama. For example, the **Nassau Beach Hotel** on Cable Beach receives many repeat guests who've visited for decades, and the **British Colonial Hilton** in downtown Nassau gets plenty of older vacationers as well.

Although all the major U.S. airlines flying to The Bahamas canceled their senior-discount and coupon-book programs, many hotels still offer discounts for seniors. For the most part, The Bahamas charge the same admission for all adults attending museums, theaters, and other attractions. Of course, asking about senior discounts doesn't hurt. You may be pleasantly surprised.

Members of **AARP** (formerly known as the American Association of Retired Persons), 601 E St. NW, Washington, DC 20049 (☎ **888-687-2277** or 202-434-2277; www.aarp.org), get discounts on hotels, airfares, and car rentals. AARP offers its members a wide range of benefits, including *AARP: The Magazine* and a monthly newsletter. Anyone over 50 can join.

A recommended publication offering travel advice for seniors is *Travel 50 & Beyond,* a quarterly magazine (www.travel50andbeyond.com).

Accessing The Bahamas: Advice for Travelers with Disabilities

Travelers with disabilities have an easier time getting around on some islands in The Bahamas than others. Many of the larger hotels on New

Providence, Paradise Island, and Grand Bahama offer ground-floor guestrooms, wide bathrooms, and elevators that make wheelchair accessibility relatively easy. These islands also have plenty of sidewalks, marina boardwalks, and paved pathways.

On the other hand, most hotels on the smaller islands have hilly grounds, narrow, unpaved pathways, and steps leading to guest rooms or dining areas. Several accommodations on Harbour Island, for example, sit at the top of a bluff with long staircases that lead down to the beach. Therefore, if you find a hotel that sounds good, call to ask about the specifics of accessibility. If you're in a wheelchair or you have trouble walking but you want to get as close to the sand as possible, look for hotels with accessible beachfront pool patios.

 The Out Islands are more difficult to reach. The planes that service these islands are usually small, and passengers board and disembark on narrow, somewhat rickety staircases. In some instances, you need to change planes once or twice and catch a ferry, as well as take a taxi or two.

If you're a wheelchair-bound traveler heading to New Providence, you can contact **The Bahamas Association for the Physically Disabled** (☎ 242-322-2393) to rent a specially equipped van for airport pickup or to arrange for transportation around the island. Make reservations as far in advance of your trip as possible. You can get temporary ramps and other portable aids through this association, too.

Organizations that assist travelers with disabilities include the **Moss Rehab Hospital** (www.mossresourcenet.org), which provides a library of accessible-travel resources online; the **Society for Accessible Travel and Hospitality, also known as SATH,** (☎ 212-447-7284; www.sath.org; annual membership fees: $45 for adults, $30 for seniors and students), which offers a wealth of travel resources for all types of disabilities and gives informed recommendations on destinations, access guides, travel agents, tour operators, vehicle rentals, and companion services; and the **American Foundation for the Blind** (☎ 800-232-5463; www.afb.org), which provides information on traveling with Seeing Eye dogs.

Following the Rainbow: Resources for Gay and Lesbian Travelers

If you're gay or lesbian, how comfortable will you feel in The Bahamas? The official word is that everyone is welcome, but the reality is somewhat different, depending on where you go and what you do when you get there. At least one resort (couples-only and all-inclusive Sandals Royal Bahamian on New Providence) unapologetically excludes gay couples altogether.

Homosexuality isn't necessarily illegal, but gay sex acts performed in public can carry a jail sentence of up to 20 years. This law is rarely enforced any more, but as long as it remains on the books, one has to exercise extreme caution.

In The Bahamas, many residents are uncomfortable with public displays of affection between same-sex couples. In fact, "Don't ask, don't tell" reigns. Therefore, if you can't imagine a vacation that doesn't include strolling down the beach hand in hand with your main squeeze, The Bahamas may not be for you. Head for Key West or South Miami Beach, which will welcome you with open arms.

Nevertheless, The Bahamas can be a great vacation choice if you're discreet in public about your sexuality. On the most popular islands (New Providence, Paradise Island, and Grand Bahama), not only can you get lost in the crowds, but also you're also more likely to run into other gay vacationers and residents. Quietly ask around and folks can direct you to other small hangouts, some of which are open only every other weekend.

The **International Gay & Lesbian Travel Association (IGLTA)** (☎ 800-448-8550 or 954-776-2626; www.iglta.org) is the trade association for the gay and lesbian travel industry and offers an online directory of gay- and lesbian-friendly travel businesses; go to its Web site and click on "Members."

Many agencies offer tours and travel itineraries specifically for gay and lesbian travelers. Each of the following includes The Bahamas in their offerings. **Above and Beyond Tours** (☎ 800-397-2681; www.above beyondtours.com) is the exclusive gay and lesbian tour operator for United Airlines. **Now, Voyager** (☎ 800-255-6951; www.nowvoyager.com) is a well-known San Francisco-based gay-owned and operated travel service. **Olivia Cruises & Resorts** (☎ 800-631-6277 or 510-655-0364; www.olivia.com) charters entire resorts and ships for exclusive lesbian vacations and offers smaller group experiences for both gay and lesbian travelers.

Planning the Perfect Getaway: Tips for Honeymooners

The Bahamas offer so many different types of hotels and resorts that you're certain to find just the right honeymoon retreat to jump-start your new lives together. Of course, you don't have to be hitched to indulge in these hideaways.

All-inclusive resorts — where one price covers your room, meals, beverages, entertainment, most activities, tips, taxes, and airfare — are popular among newlyweds. To stay busy day and night, you need never leave these self-contained vacation playgrounds until you have to go home. Check out Chapter 11 for the descriptions of elegant, couples-only **Sandals Royal Bahamian** and the more moderately priced **Breezes;** both resorts are located on New Providence. On Grand Bahama, think about **Club Viva Fortuna** (see Chapter 15). On San Salvador, consider **Club Med–Columbus Isle** (see Chapter 25).

If you don't necessarily want an all-inclusive resort but you want a blizzard of action, check into **Atlantis Paradise Island Resort & Casino** (see Chapter 11) off New Providence. You can also find plenty to see and do in and around **The Westin and Sheraton at Our Lucaya** on Grand Bahama (see Chapter 15).

Some couples prefer quieter, more remote resorts, where the sun, the sand, and each other's company are the main draws. If you prefer this scenario, the elegant **Ocean Club Golf & Tennis Resort** and the funky, startlingly colorful **Compass Point Beach Resort** are excellent honeymoon haunts on New Providence (see Chapter 11). Small is beautiful at cozy resorts like **Green Turtle Club** and **Bluff House** on Green Turtle Cay in the Abacos (see Chapter 20), as well as **Pink Sands** and **Runaway Hill Club** on Harbour Island (see Chapter 22).

 Quite a few accommodations, particularly the larger ones, feature honeymoon packages. These packages aren't usually money-savers, but they do include special extras, such as a corner room, king-size bed, champagne, maybe a first-rate meal or two, and transportation in limousines between your hotel and the airport. Each hotel boasts a somewhat different set of perks, so when you make your reservation, you have to ask exactly what your package includes.

Saying "I Do" Bahamian Style

The Bahamas are popular honeymoon destinations for just-married spouses, but plenty of couples save the wedding for the island as well. Romantic settings, ranging from the beach at sunset to a harborside gazebo to a poolside patio or an elegant yacht, make tying the knot here tempting. With colorful coral and tropical fish as a backdrop, couples have even signaled "I do" underwater while decked out in scuba gear. Many of the larger hotels (and some of the smaller ones, too) provide a wedding coordinator to help you secure all your paperwork, find an official to perform the ceremony, and hire photographers — both still and video — and the florist. Coordinators also organize the reception and make any other arrangements that you need.

Reviewing the marriage requirements in The Bahamas

You and your intended must both be in The Bahamas for at least 24 hours before you can apply for a marriage license. You can fill out applications Monday through Friday.

For details, contact the office of the **Registrar General** (☎ 242-322-3316 in Nassau or ☎ 242-352-4934 on Grand Bahama). If you plan to marry in one of the Out Islands, call the **Bahamas Out Islands Promotions Board** (☎ 800-688-4752).

If you and your partner are U.S. citizens, you need to get an affidavit to confirm this — and the fact that you're both single — from the American Embassy in Nassau. *Note:* The U.S. Embassy is closed on both American and Bahamian holidays. You must present proof of identity, such as a passport and, if necessary, proof of divorce. You don't need to take any blood tests, however. The **Weddings and Honeymoon Unit of The Bahamas Ministry of Tourism** (call ☎ 888-687-8425 or 242-302-2034 for a brochure) can also provide you with information.

For assistance with planning your nuptials in The Bahamas, call your hotel or one of the following tourist offices:

- ✔ Nassau, New Providence (☎ 242-302-2000)
- ✔ Freeport/Lucaya, Grand Bahama (☎ 242-352-8044)
- ✔ The Abacos (☎ 242-367-3067)
- ✔ Andros (☎ 242-368-2286)
- ✔ Bimini (☎ 242-347-3529)
- ✔ Eleuthera (☎ 242-333-2621)
- ✔ Harbour Island (☎ 242-333-2621)
- ✔ Exuma (☎ 242-336-2430)
- ✔ San Salvador (☎ 242-356-0435)

Working out the wedding costs

An island wedding in a stunning setting can cost thousands of dollars less than a traditional wedding at home. Table 8-1 gives you a general idea of how much money you can expect to spend on the ceremony:

Table 8-1	The Cost of a Bahamian Wedding
Marriage license	$100
Affidavit (per person)	$55 and up (U.S. Embassy or Notary Public)
Marriage officer	Weekdays: $160 Weekends: $195
Florist	Bouquet: $30 and up Boutonniere: $10
Limousine	$85 an hour

Tuxedo rental	$85 and up
Video	$350 and up
Photographer	$300 and up
Music	Steel drum band: $550 an hour Organ music in church: $150 an hour Violinist or vocalist: $100 an hour Violin and flute: $200 an hour

Traveling Solo

You don't need kids or a partner to have a great vacation on these islands, especially in Nassau or Freeport/Lucaya. Plenty of couples stay at the smaller, quieter hotels on these islands, so you don't have nearly as many opportunities to meet other single visitors as you may at larger accommodations. However, you can find groups of unattached friends vacationing together. Because hotels in the Out Islands are so much smaller and more intimate than on the busier islands, meeting people in these locations is easier.

If you're shy, join a snorkeling sail, a scuba trip, or an excursion to an uninhabited island for a beach picnic. Before you can say "Goombay Smash," you'll be chatting with new friends.

On the downside, you pay more for a hotel room or an air/hotel package if you go it alone than if you travel with a friend because single rates are higher than double rates divided by two. But the good news is that you can find many affordable hotels on New Providence (particularly in downtown Nassau and some on Cable Beach), so you shouldn't have trouble finding a place that suits your wallet.

Club Med–Columbus Isle (see Chapter 25) on San Salvador attracts plenty of singles. This all-inclusive beach resort offers many diversions designed to get people together. In addition, this place is perfect for two single friends who travel together but like their privacy. (The hotel offers single rooms joined by a shared bathroom.)

If you're a socially minded single, Nassau is a good choice — you can be as busy or as lazy as you want. **Breezes,** a moderately priced all-inclusive resort on Cable Beach (see Chapter 11), is a popular choice because it offers a medley of group activities.

 During March and April, droves of U.S. college students on spring break descend on New Providence. So if you've outgrown toga parties and drinking contests, you may want to skip this scene.

Chapter 9

Taking Care of the Remaining Details

● ●

In This Chapter

▶ Getting your entry and departure documents in order

▶ Deciding whether to rent a car

▶ When to get travel and medical insurance

▶ Opening the lines of overseas communication

▶ Ensuring a safe vacation

● ●

*B*efore you can start wiggling your toes in the sand, you need to handle a few details. In this chapter, we deal with all the nitty-gritty details of your travel plans, such as insurance and car rentals.

Preparing for Arrival and Departure

If you're a U.S., Canadian, or British citizen, you don't *need* a passport to enter The Bahamas, as long as you have two other acceptable forms of identification. However, we strongly recommend taking one with you anyway; in these times of tightened security, there is no guarantee that you'll be able to re-enter your home country without a passport. If you don't have a passport, you must take the following papers with you:

▸ A certified or original copy of your birth certificate (it must have a raised seal)

▸ An official photo ID, such as a valid driver's license

▸ A return or ongoing airplane ticket

 You may enter The Bahamas with an expired passport, as long as it has expired within the last five years. (Again, you may encounter difficulty returning to your home country without a current, valid passport.) Whether your passport is current or not, make photocopies of the inside page — the one with your photo — before you leave home. Also copy any other important documents, such as your driver's license, airline tickets, and hotel vouchers. Of course, keep the copies separate from the originals.

Citizens of Ireland, Australia, and New Zealand are required to present a passport upon entry to The Bahamas.

U.S. citizens under age 17 need only a birth certificate to enter The Bahamas, but our advice about passports applies here as well — apply for one anyway. Minor children from other countries, including Canada, can travel on their parent's passport.

When you enter the country, you receive an Immigration Arrival/ Departure Card to fill out and sign. Do this paperwork before it's your turn with the Customs official. Be sure to keep your carbon copy in a safe place because an official will collect it when you leave The Bahamas.

 Save enough cash for the departure tax that you have to pay when you exit the country. The tax is $15 from New Providence or any Out Island and $18 from Grand Bahama.

Getting a Passport

A valid passport is the only legal form of identification accepted around the world. Getting a passport is easy, but the process takes some time. For an up-to-date country-by-country listing of passport requirements, go to the "Foreign Entry Requirement" Web page of the U.S. State Department at http://travel.state.gov/foreignentryreqs.html.

Applying for a U.S. passport

If you're applying for a first-time passport, follow these steps:

1. **Complete a passport application in person at a U.S. passport office (a federal, state, or probate court or a major post office).** To find your regional passport office, either check the **U.S. State Department Web site,** http://travel.state.gov/passport_services.html, or call the **National Passport Information Center** (☎ 877-487-2778) for automated information.

2. **Present a certified birth certificate as proof of citizenship.** Bringing along your driver's license, state or military ID, or social security card is also a good idea.

3. **Submit two identical passport-sized photos, measuring 2 inches by 2 inches in size.** You often find businesses that take these photos near a passport office. *Note:* You can't use a strip from a photo-vending machine because the pictures aren't identical.

4. **Pay a fee.** For people 16 and over, a passport is valid for ten years and costs $85. For those 15 and under, a passport is valid for five years and costs $70.

When applying for a passport, allow plenty of time before your trip; processing normally takes three weeks but can take longer during busy periods (especially spring).

If your passport is in your current name and was issued within the past 15 years (and you were over age 16 when it was issued), you can renew your passport by mail for $55. Whether you're applying in person or by mail, you can download passport applications from the U.S. State Department Web site at http://travel.state.gov/passport_services.html. For general information, call the **National Passport Agency** (☎ 202-647-0518).

Applying for other passports

If you're a citizen of Australia, Canada, New Zealand, or the United Kingdom, the following lists information on applying for a passport:

✔ **Australians** can visit a local post office or passport office, call the **Australia Passport Information Service** (☎ 131-232 toll-free from Australia), or log on to www.passports.gov.au for details on how and where to apply.

✔ **Canadians** can pick up applications at passport offices throughout Canada, post offices, or from the central **Passport Office, Department of Foreign Affairs and International Trade,** Ottawa, Ontario K1A 0G3 (☎ 800-567-6868; www.ppt.gc.ca). You must send two identical passport-sized photos and proof of Canadian citizenship along with your application. Processing takes five to ten days if you apply in person or about three weeks by mail.

✔ **New Zealanders** can pick up a passport application at any **New Zealand Passports Office** or download it from the office's Web site (www.passports.govt.nz). Contact the Passports Office at ☎ 0800-225-050 in New Zealand or 04-474-8100.

✔ **United Kingdom** residents can pick up applications for a standard ten-year passport (five-year passport for children under 16) at passport offices, major post offices, or a travel agency. For information, contact the **United Kingdom Passport Service** (☎ 0870-521-0410; www.ukpa.gov.uk).

Renting a Car — or Not

Whether or not you need a car depends on which island you're visiting. Many visitors to New Providence, Paradise Island, Freeport/Lucaya, or one of the Out Islands don't bother renting a car. Here are five reasons why you may not want to rent a car, either:

✔ **You don't truly need it.** In New Providence/Paradise Island, a car is more of a burden than a help. Driving around congested Nassau is difficult; parking is limited, and you can walk to most attractions and shops. If you're on Cable Beach, taking a few limited taxi rides is probably cheaper in the long run than renting a car. On Paradise Island, you can generally walk to where you want to go. Grand Bahama Island is spread out, and most locals need a car to get around. But most places of interest are centered around Freeport/ Lucaya, which you can easily traverse with public transportation or taxi. You can also easily explore the vast part of Grand Bahama Island on an organized day tour (far cheaper than renting a car). On Harbour Island you don't need a car, but on "mainland" Eleuthera you may want to rent a car for a day just to tour the entire length of the island.

✔ **Driving is on the left.** If you're unfamiliar with this form of driving, you're more likely to have an accident.

✔ **Reservations may not be honored.** Unless you deal with a major car-rental company, you may arrive on an island and find that the car you reserved was rented to someone else. Many car-rental entrepreneurs figure that a "bird in hand is better than one in the bush," as one staff member recently told us at Marsh Harbour, meaning that he'd rather rent a car to someone who walked in and wanted one than to a couple who may or may not arrive from Chicago on the day they'd reserved. Angry potential motorists at car-rental desks is a common sight in The Bahamas, especially during the overbooked winter months.

✔ **Cars aren't plentiful in the Out Islands.** When you leave Nassau or Freeport/Lucaya and venture to the Out Islands, car rentals become more difficult to acquire and may not be available at all during winter unless you reserve well in advance. The salt air and bad roads take their toll on Out Island cars, so don't expect state-of-the-art maintenance.

✔ **Insurance hassles and accidents.** On Grand Bahama Island and on New Providence Island, you can deal with the big U.S.-based chains, such as Hertz and Avis. If you have an accident, you may have the same problems with insurance companies that you encounter in the U.S.

But driving around in the Out Islands and dealing with relativly unknown car-rental companies or parties could lead to anything. Settling claims may be extremely difficult, especially if you're at fault for causing property damage or bodily injury. You may not want to take these risks because you can rent a taxi for a day tour on every island. Or, for example, if you're in George Town in the Exumas, you can often walk to where you want to go.

Getting the best deal

If you decide to rent a car, be aware that car-rental rates vary even more than airline fares. The price for a rental car depends on the size of the car, the length of time that you keep it, where and when you pick it up and drop it off, where you take it, and a host of other factors. Asking a few key questions may save you hundreds of dollars:

- ✔ Weekend rates may be lower than weekday rates. If you're keeping the car five or more days, a weekly rate may be cheaper than the daily rate. Ask whether the rate is the same for pickup Friday morning as it is Thursday night.

- ✔ Check whether the rate is cheaper if you pick up the car at a location in town rather than at the airport.

- ✔ Ask whether age is an issue. Many car-rental companies add on a fee for drivers under 25, and some companies don't rent to them at all.

- ✔ If you see an advertised price, be sure to ask for that specific rate; otherwise the company may charge you the standard (higher) rate. Don't forget to mention membership in AAA, AARP, professional organizations, and trade unions. These memberships usually entitle you to discounts ranging from 5 percent to 30 percent.

- ✔ Check your frequent-flier accounts. Not only are your favorite (or at least, most-used) airlines likely to have sent you discount coupons, but also most car rentals add at least 500 miles to your account.

- ✔ As with other aspects of planning your trip, using the Internet can make comparison shopping for a car rental much easier. You can check rates at most of the major agencies' Web sites. Plus, all the major travel sites — **Travelocity** (www.travelocity.com), **Expedia** (www.expedia.com), **Orbitz** (www.orbitz.com), and **Smarter Living** (www.smarterliving.com), for example — have search engines that can dig up discounted car-rental rates. Just enter the car size you want, the pick-up and return dates, and location, and the server returns a price. You can even make the car reservation through any of these sites.

Adding up the charges

In addition to the standard rental prices, other optional charges apply to most car rentals (and some not-so-optional charges, such as taxes). Many credit-card companies cover the *Collision Damage Waiver* (CDW), which requires you to pay for damage to the car in a collision. Check with your credit-card company before you leave so you can avoid paying this hefty fee (as much as $20 a day).

The car-rental companies also offer additional *liability insurance* (if you harm others in an accident), *personal accident insurance* (if you harm yourself or your passengers), and *personal effects insurance* (if someone steals your luggage from your car). Your insurance policy on your car at home probably covers most of these unlikely occurrences. However, if your own insurance doesn't cover you for rentals or if you don't have auto insurance, definitely consider the additional coverage (ask your car-rental agent for more information). Unless you're toting around the

Hope diamond — and you don't want to leave that in the trunk of your car anyway — you can probably skip the personal effects insurance, but driving around without liability or personal accident coverage is never a good idea. Even if you're a good driver, other people may not be, and liability claims can be complicated.

Some companies also offer *refueling packages,* in which you pay upfront for your initial full tank of gas and can return the car with an empty gas tank. The prices can be competitive with local gas prices, but you don't get credit for any gas remaining in the tank. If you reject this option, you pay only for the gas you use, but you have to return the car with a full tank or face charges of $3 to $4 a gallon for any shortfall. If you usually run late and a fueling stop may make you miss your plane, you're a perfect candidate for the fuel-purchase option.

Playing It Safe with Travel and Medical Insurance

Three kinds of travel insurance are available: trip-cancellation insurance, medical insurance, and lost luggage insurance. The cost of travel insurance varies widely, depending on the cost and length of your trip, your age and health, and the type of trip you're taking, but expect to pay between 5 percent and 8 percent of the vacation itself. Here's our advice on all three.

- ✔ **Trip-cancellation insurance:** This type of insurance helps you get your money back if you have to back out of a trip, go home early, or if your travel supplier goes bankrupt. The allowed reasons for cancellation range from sickness to natural disasters to the State Department declaring your destination unsafe for travel. (Insurers usually don't cover vague fears, though, as many travelers discovered when they tried to cancel their trips in October 2001 because they were wary of flying.)

  A good resource is **"Travel Guard Alerts,"** which is a list of travel-related companies that Travel Guard International (www.travel insured.com) considers high-risk. You can protect yourself further by paying for the insurance with a credit card; by law, consumers can get their money back on goods and services they don't receive if they report the loss within 60 days after the charge is listed on their credit-card statement.

- ✔ **Travel medical insurance:** This insurance can be a safety net, particularly if you're traveling to a remote or high-risk area where emergency evacuation is a possible scenario. For travel abroad, most health plans (including Medicare and Medicaid) don't provide insurance coverage, and the ones that do often require you to pay for services upfront and reimburse you only after you return home. Even if your plan covers overseas treatment, most out-of-country hospitals make you pay your bills upfront and only send you a refund after you return home and file the necessary paperwork with your insurance company. If you require additional medical insurance, try **MEDEX Assistance** (☎ 410-453-6300; www.medexassist. com) or **Travel Assistance International** (☎ 800-821-2828; www. travelassistance.com; for general information on services, call the company's Worldwide Assistance Services, Inc., at ☎ 800-777-8710).

✔ **Lost luggage insurance:** Most travelers don't need this insurance. Your homeowner's or renter's insurance should cover stolen luggage if you have off-premises theft coverage. Check your existing policies before you buy any additional coverage.

If you lose your luggage, immediately file a lost-luggage claim at the airport, detailing the luggage contents. On international flights, (including U.S. portions of international trips), airline baggage coverage is limited to approximately $9.07 per pound, up to approximately $635 per checked bag. For most airlines, you must report delayed, damaged, or lost baggage within four hours of arrival. The airlines are required to deliver luggage, once found, directly to your house or destination free of charge.

You can get additional baggage insurance as part of your comprehensive travel-insurance package or buy Travel Guard's "BagTrak" product. Don't buy insurance at the airport; it's usually overpriced. Be sure to take any valuables or irreplaceable items with you in your carry-on luggage, because many valuables (including books, money, and electronics) aren't covered by airline policies.

For more information, contact one of the following recommended insurers: **Access America** (☎ 866-807-3982; www.accessamerica. com); **Travel Guard International** (☎ 800-826-4919; www.travel guard.com); **Travel Insured International** (☎ 800-243-3174; www. travelinsured.com); and **Travelex Insurance Services** (☎ 888-457-4602; www.travelex-insurance.com).

Staying Healthy When You Travel

You can get over-the-counter medications — aspirin, cold remedies, antacids, and so on — at pharmacies and hotels on New Providence and Grand Bahama and in many hotels on other islands. If you need to refill a prescription, bring the generic name of your medication because local pharmacists may know only the generic name. Most hotel shops and pharmacies aren't open at night, so travel with any basics that you may need, such as medicine for diarrhea or upset stomach, sunburn remedies, anti-itch cream to soothe insect bites, and children's aspirin if you're traveling with little ones. Don't forget any prescription drugs that you're taking, and if you think that you may run out, plan ahead to refill your prescription. If you wear contact lenses, pack an extra pair in the event that you lose one.

Before you go

If you have a serious or chronic illness, talk to your doctor before you leave. If you have a condition such as epilepsy, diabetes, or heart problems, wear a **MedicAlert identification tag** (☎ 888-633-4298; www.medicalert.org), which immediately alerts doctors to your condition and gives them access to your records through Medic Alert's 24-hour hot line. Contact the **International Association for Medical Assistance to Travelers (IAMAT)** (☎ 716-754-4883 or, in Canada, 416-652-0137; www.iamat.org) for tips on travel and health concerns and lists of local English-speaking doctors. The U.S. **Centers for Disease Control and Prevention** (☎ 800-311-3435; www.cdc.gov) provides up-to-date information on health hazards by region or country and offers tips on food safety.

Emergencies and medical care

If you get sick, ask a staff member at your hotel to recommend a local doctor — even his own doctor, if necessary. If you can't find a doctor to help you right away, try the emergency room at the local hospital or clinic. Many hospital emergency rooms have walk-in clinics for cases that aren't life-threatening. You may not get immediate attention, but you won't pay the high price of an emergency-room visit.

 If you have health insurance, carry your insurance card in your wallet, but you may have to pay all medical costs upfront and be reimbursed for them later. For information on purchasing additional medical insurance for your trip, see the previous section.

 ## Addressing other potential hazards

Here are some ways you can prevent common vacation disasters:

- ✔ **Drinking the water:** Drinking water from the tap is safe, but you may not like the unfamiliar taste. Many hotels supply bottled or filtered water for guests. Before you take a swig from a bottle, though, check whether the hotel gives you the water free. Some resorts charge $5 or more per bottle. Stocking up on bottled water at a nearby drugstore or grocery store is always cheaper than buying it at your hotel or taking it from your minibar.

- ✔ **Sunbathing:** As all visitors to the islands know, you can get a wicked sunburn even on hazy days if you don't wear sunscreen. Reapply the sunscreen every time you come out of the water, even if your sunscreen is waterproof. Reapply the cream periodically throughout the day, whether you go into the water or not. If you get your hair cornrowed and you're not used to wearing it that way, put some sunscreen on the delicate skin of your newly exposed scalp. Wide-brimmed hats also come in handy, of course.

- ✔ **Repelling bugs:** Use insect repellent, particularly at dusk, when the mosquitoes and gnats are at their most treacherous.

✔ **Taking a scuba dive:** If scuba diving is part of your vacation, plan your trip so that you don't fly within 24 hours of diving. Your body needs time to recover from being at a high altitude before it hits the lower depths and vice versa.

When you're in the water, the stunning shapes and colors of fish, coral, and sea plants may make you want to reach out and touch. *Don't.* Not only can you destroy delicate marine life by doing so, but you can also put yourself in danger. Even innocuous-looking coral can be razor sharp, and a variety aptly known as *fire coral* can burn your skin. Also be warned that shiny jewelry in the water can attract barracudas and sharks.

✔ **Keeping safe:** Even though you're relaxing on a vacation, keep up your guard. For example, especially in Nassau, don't venture into unknown neighborhoods alone at night. Don't wear flashy jewelry or leave your valuables lying around, even in your locked hotel room. Many larger hotels have in-room safes or front-desk safety deposit boxes.

Staying Connected by Cellphone or E-mail

Travelers have a number of ways to stay in touch while on the road. Of course, using your own laptop, personal digital assistant (PDA), or cellphone gives you the most flexibility. But even if you don't already own these devices or prefer not to travel with them, you can still stay connected.

Accessing the Internet away from home

Although most cities have cybercafes, you'll only find a few in The Bahamas. Check www.cybercafe.com for locations. Otherwise, you may be at the mercy of your hotel's facilities — but beware of exorbitant rates.

To retrieve your e-mail, find out whether your Internet Service Provider (ISP) has a Web-based interface tied to your existing e-mail account. If it does, follow its instructions for accessing your e-mail. If your ISP doesn't have such an interface, you can use the free **mail2web** service (www.mail2web.com) to view and reply to your home e-mail. Or, for more flexibility, you can open a free, Web-based e-mail account with **Yahoo! Mail** (www.yahoo.com). Your home ISP may be able to automatically forward your e-mail to the Web-based account.

If you need to access files on your office computer, look into a service called **GoToMyPC** (www.gotomypc.com). The service provides a Web-based interface so you can access and manipulate a distant PC from anywhere — even a cybercafe — provided your "target" PC is on and has an always-on connection to the Internet (such as RoadRunner cable access). The service offers top-quality security, but if you're worried about hackers, use your own laptop to access GoToMyPC system.

If you're bringing your own computer, check your ISP's Web site or call its toll-free number and ask how you can use your current account away from home via a local access number and how much it will cost.

If you're traveling outside your ISP's reach, the **iPass** network has dial-up numbers in most of the world's countries. You have to sign up with an iPass provider, who then tells you how to set up your computer for The Bahamas. For a list of iPass providers, go to www.ipass.com and click on "Individuals." One solid provider is **i2roam** (☎ 866-811-6209 or 920-235-0475; www.i2roam.com). Wherever you go, bring a **connection kit** with the right power and phone adapters, a spare phone cord, and a spare Ethernet network cable.

Most business-class hotels offer dataports for laptop modems, and some hotels in The Bahamas offer high-speed Internet access using an Ethernet network cable. You have to bring your own cables either way, so call your hotel in advance to find out what your options are.

Using a cellphone

The three letters that define much of the world's **wireless capabilities** are GSM (Global System for Mobiles), a big, seamless network that makes for easy cross-border cellphone use throughout Europe and dozens of other countries worldwide. In the U.S., T-Mobile, AT&T Wireless, and Cingular use this quasi-universal system; in Canada, Microcell and some Rogers customers use GSM; and all Europeans and most Australians use GSM.

If your cellphone is on a GSM system and you have a world-capable multiband phone, such as many Sony Ericsson, Motorola, or Samsung models, you can make and receive calls across much of the globe. Just call your wireless operator and ask to activate "international roaming" on your account. Unfortunately, per-minute charges are high — usually from $1 to $5.

That's why buying an "unlocked" world phone from the get-go is important. Many cellphone operators sell "locked" phones that restrict you from using any other removable computer-memory phone chip (called an **SIM card**) card other than the ones that they supply. If you have an unlocked phone, you can install a cheap, prepaid SIM card (found at a local retailer) in your destination country. (Show your phone to the salesperson; not all phones work on all networks.) You'll get a local phone number — and much, much lower calling rates. Getting an already-locked phone unlocked can be a complicated process, but you can have it done; just call your cellular operator and say that you're going abroad for several months and want to use the phone with a local provider.

Renting a phone is a good idea. Because of limited availability in The Bahamas, we suggest renting the phone before you leave home. This way you can give loved ones your new number, make sure the phone works, and take the phone wherever you go. Phone rental isn't cheap.

You usually pay $40 to $50 per week, plus airtime fees of at least a dollar a minute.

Two good wireless rental companies are **InTouch USA** (☎ 800-872-7626; www.intouchglobal.com) and **Roadpost** (☎ 888-290-1606 or 905-272-5665; www.roadpost.com). Give the company your itinerary, and a company representative can tell you which wireless products you need. InTouch also advises you for free on whether your existing phone will work in The Bahamas; simply call ☎ 703-222-7161 between 9 a.m. and 4 p.m. EST, or go to http://intouchglobal.com/travel.htm.

Keeping Up With Airline Security Measures

With the federalization of airport security, security procedures at U.S. airports are more stable and consistent than ever. Generally, you'll be fine if you arrive at the airport **two hours before a flight** to The Bahamas.

Bring a **current, government-issued photo ID,** such as a driver's license or passport. Keep your ID at the ready to show at check-in, the security checkpoint, and sometimes even the gate. (Children under 18 do not need photo IDs for domestic flights, but they do need them for international flights to most countries.)

The Transportation Security Administration (TSA) phased out **gate check-in** at all U.S. airports. And **E-tickets** have made paper tickets nearly obsolete. Passengers with E-tickets can beat the ticket-counter lines by using airport **electronic kiosks** or even **online check-in** from your home computer. Online check-in involves logging on to your airline's Web site, accessing your reservation, and printing out your boarding pass — and the airline may even offer you bonus miles to do so!

If you're using a kiosk at the airport to check-in, bring the credit card you used to book the ticket or your frequent-flier card. Print out your boarding pass from the kiosk and simply proceed to the security checkpoint with your pass and a photo ID. If you're checking bags or looking to snag an exit-row seat, you're able to do so using most airline kiosks. Even the smaller airlines employ the kiosk system, but always call your airline to make sure these alternatives are available. **Curbside check-in** is also a good way to avoid lines, although a few airlines still ban curbside check-in; call before you go.

Security lines are getting shorter, but long ones still remain. If you have trouble standing for long periods of time, tell an airline employee; the airline can provide a wheelchair. You can speed up security by **not wearing metal objects,** such as big belt buckles or clanky earrings. If you have metallic body parts, a note from your doctor can prevent a long chat with the security screeners. Keep in mind that only **ticketed passengers** are allowed past security, except for folks escorting passengers with disabilities or children.

Federalization has also stabilized **what you can carry on** and **what you can't**. The general rule is that sharp objects are out, nail clippers are okay, and your food and beverages must pass through the X-ray machine — but security screeners can't make you drink from your coffee cup. Bring food in your carry-on rather than checking it because explosive-detection machines used on checked luggage have mistaken food (especially chocolate, for some reason) for bombs. Travelers in the U.S. are allowed one carry-on bag, plus a "personal item," such as a purse, briefcase, or laptop bag. Carry-on hoarders can stuff all sorts of things into a laptop bag; as long as it has a laptop in it, it's still considered a personal item. The TSA issued a list of restricted items; check its Web site (www.tsa.gov/public/index.jsp) for details.

Part III
New Providence: Nassau, Cable Beach, and Paradise Island

In this part . . .

In this part, we guide you through the details of getting to (and around) New Providence, home of the Bahamas' historic capital. We also help you sift through the wide array of accommodations in Cable Beach, Nassau, and Paradise Island, and point you to the best sights to see after you settle in.

We offer you tips on finding the most authentic local cuisine and give you our top picks of everything from fast food to fine dining. Sure, you can hit the casinos and duty-free shops, but we also steer you to plenty of other diversions, both in the ocean and on dry land.

Chapter 10

Settling into New Providence

• •

In This Chapter

▶ Knowing what to expect when you get here
▶ Getting around New Providence
▶ Discovering all New Providence has to offer

• •

*A*fter surveying the choice of islands awaiting you in Chapter 3,
you're ready to embark on the actual exploration of Nassau/Cable
Beach or Paradise Island, the bustling hub of a nation and the country's
major tourist attraction.

Most of The Bahamas is about escapism. Not New Providence Island —
it's where the action is. Expect elegant bars, gargantuan gambling par-
lors, dance clubs, the best restaurants, sprawling resorts, and blocks
and blocks of shops with discounted merchandise. The island's a bit of
a circus, but that's what many vacationers are seeking.

Paradise Island is sleeker and more upscale than Cable Beach, even
though it's overbuilt and overly commercialized. Most visitors opt for
the beachfront properties and visit Nassau only for its shops and
attractions.

Arriving at the Airport

When Bahamians come to the end of a journey, they say, "Ya reach."
You receive a special New Providence welcome as "ya reach" **Nassau
International Airport** (☎ 242-377-1759). Spirited live calypso or
Bahamian Junkanoo music greets you in the arrivals' hall. The beat of
the music will have your shoulders bouncing and your feet tapping.

The airport is hassle-free. From collecting your bags and passing
through Customs to finding the taxi or van that will take you to your
hotel, everything runs quickly and smoothly. You can find the ATMs at
the airport in the arrivals' hall, and you also find a Tourist Information

Booth (☎ 242-377-6806), open daily from 8:30 a.m. to 11:30 p.m. The booth's staff dispenses vacation brochures and free maps.

Navigating your way through passport control and Customs

Start filling out your Immigration Arrival/Departure Card as soon as you join one of the lines marked "Visitors." This way, you're ready to roll when it's your turn to present the card along with your passport or birth certificate, photo ID, and your return- or onward-bound airline ticket. Remember where you stick your copy of the immigration card because you need to show it before you leave the country.

Getting through Customs usually takes about 15 minutes, depending on how many different pieces of luggage you have. Even if you declare that you're not bringing in anything illegal, Customs may single you out for a more thorough search.

Getting from the airport to your hotel

Cable Beach, the main resort area on New Providence, is about a 15-minute drive from the airport. **Paradise Island,** joined to New Providence by bridge, is 30 minutes away. If your hotel package includes transportation, you'll receive a coupon or voucher to use upon arrival. When you find the right bus going to your hotel, show the driver the voucher. Buses are labeled and easy to find. Otherwise, you have to take a taxi, which costs about $20 for two passengers to Cable Beach or about $28 to Paradise Island.

 To save money, you can share a cab with another couple heading to the same hotel and pay $3 for each additional person — but pretend that you've known each other since kindergarten. If you reveal that you just met at the airport, the driver may try to charge each couple the full rate. Drivers expect, and sometimes request, a 15 percent tip.

In most cases, you can get around New Providence without a car. If you decide that you need wheels, you can pick up your car at the airport if you rented through a major agency. Try to make your car-rental reservation before leaving home. For more information, see the section "Getting Around New Providence" later in this chapter.

Cruising into New Providence

Sometimes nearly a dozen cruise ships are in port at one time at **Prince George Dock,** also known as **Prince George Wharf.** If you're among the passengers, your ship is as much of an attraction as its destination, meaning that you don't have a whole lot of time for exploring dry land. However, because you disembark near Rawson Square in the heart of

Nassau, you're just a stroll away from the **Straw Market** and all the shops and restaurants of **Bay Street,** the main avenue. Read more about these attractions in Chapter 13.

A *jitney,* or public bus, takes you to the sandy shores of Cable Beach or to the foot of the Paradise Island bridge. You can walk across the bridge (and pay the 25¢ toll) to **Paradise Beach,** the most popular beach on Paradise Island. Of course, taxis can take you from downtown Nassau across the bridge (for a $2 toll), but the most convenient way for cruise-ship passengers to get to Paradise Island is to take one of the ferries from Prince George Dock for $2 each way.

Choosing Your Location

The capital city of **Nassau** dominates **New Providence Island.** Most of the beach resorts are at **Cable Beach,** a ten-minute drive west of Nassau. **Paradise Island,** which is connected by bridge to Nassau, is also packed with beachfront hotels.

Nassau, where Bahamians live and work, and the resort areas of Cable Beach and Paradise Island have distinct personalities. A hotel in downtown Nassau can put you on or across from a beach; it can also place you within walking distance of a slew of restaurants, the Straw Market, duty-free shops, horse-and-buggy rides, and historic sites. However, Nassau isn't a safe place to be at night. For many visitors, life on scenic Cable Beach revolves around the casinos, while the draw for others is the long stretch of golden sand. Paradise Island is short on historic attractions but long on water fun, designer shops, nightlife, and first-rate (but expensive) cuisine.

 If you want to stay on the beach but not cause serious damage to your wallet, look for choices on Cable Beach and Nassau. On Paradise Island, the best hotels — whether on or off the beach — are more expensive.

The casino in Cable Beach sits between the Nassau Marriott and the Radisson. On Paradise Island, the casino is located at the Atlantis Resort. Shuttle buses take you to these gambling meccas if you choose to stay at one of the other hotels.

You can easily reach other attractions, such as museums, old forts, and the **Ardastra Gardens and Zoo** (see Chapter 13) from Cable Beach, downtown Nassau, or Paradise Island. To get to these points of interest, you can take a taxi, guided tour, public bus, or go on foot. You can also make arrangements through your hotel to sail to one of the beach-rimmed offshore islets that offers aquatic activities, including dolphin and stingray encounters. Some of these side trips are popular among cruise-ship passengers, so depending on when you go, these uninhabited islands may host large crowds.

Getting Around New Providence

Two parallel bridges — with traffic flowing in opposite directions — link Nassau and Paradise Island. The older bridge — the *only* bridge for decades before the most spectacular section of the multimillion-dollar Atlantis resort sprouted on Paradise Island in the late 1990s — goes from Paradise Island to Nassau.

The bridge to Paradise Island is about a mile from the center of downtown Nassau. You can walk the whole distance, take a jitney to the foot of the bridge and walk across, or take a taxi from Nassau all the way across. Every time you cross the bridge from Nassau to Paradise Island, you must pay a toll: 25¢ on foot, $2 by taxi, and $1 by car.

Here are more tips about the various modes of transportation in New Providence.

Exploring on foot

Historic downtown Nassau is suitable for walking but is congested between 9 a.m. and 5 p.m. on weekdays. (For details on what sights you can expect to see, check out Chapter 13.)

The city's streets are desolate after dark, so lone strolls at night aren't safe. If you like wandering under the stars, Cable Beach and Paradise Island are your best bets.

Taking a bus

Some hotels along Cable Beach and on Paradise Island offer guests free bus service within the resort areas. To go elsewhere, you can take taxis or rent a car and brave Nassau traffic. Or, you can get almost anywhere you want to go on New Providence on a jitney. These small buses or large vans travel up and down West Bay Street (the road in front of Cable Beach hotels) to beaches, through downtown Nassau, and to other parts of the island. They run from approximately 6 a.m. to 7 p.m. At $1 a ride, they're a convenient, inexpensive way to get around. You need exact change or a $1 bill. When you see a jitney coming, flag it down. The buses wait to fill up at depots and are often tightly packed, but with reggae or calypso pumping on the radio, the mood is always festive.

To go east from downtown Nassau toward the Paradise Island bridges, catch a bus at Frederick and Bay streets, near the Straw Market. These buses don't go over the bridge, so you have to walk or take a cab across. To go west toward Cable Beach, catch a bus near the British Colonial Hilton at Bay Street. If you're traveling from Cable Beach to Paradise Island or vice versa, you must change buses in town.

Taking a taxi

Taxis wait outside Cable Beach and Paradise Island hotels, and they're also plentiful in downtown Nassau. Drivers take the same routes so often that many don't bother to use their meters. Therefore, before you hop into a cab, ask your hotel staff the approximate fare to wherever you're going. From Cable Beach to downtown Nassau, you pay about $10 for two passengers. Likewise, the trip from Cable Beach to Paradise Island costs about $15.

Driving around

If you want to rent a car, you must drive on the left side of the road, a holdover of British tradition. If you come from small-town America, drivers in Nassau may appear reckless to you. You can make car-rental arrangements at the airport or through your hotel (see Chapter 9 for more information).

Ferrying from island to island

Ferries run between Prince George Dock, in downtown Nassau, and Paradise Island about every ten minutes daily from 9 a.m. to 5:30 p.m. The round-trip cost is $6. A ferry is the most scenic way to get from Paradise Island to Nassau and vice versa. Go to the dock and climb aboard the next ferry that's leaving for a brief sail across the harbor.

Other fun ways to get around

Here are other options for getting around New Providence and Paradise Island.

- **Touring town in a horse-drawn carriage:** Riding around in a horse-drawn surrey with fringe on top is the most romantic way to see Nassau. Your horse may even have a droopy flower stuck in his straw hat. Carriages wait for passengers at **Rawson Square,** in the heart of Nassau, not far from where the cruise ships dock. For a 20-minute ride, expect to pay about $10 per person for up to three adults plus one or two children.

- **Riding bicycles:** Because traffic is often crazy in and around Nassau, two-wheelers aren't the best way to get from place to place. If you want to bike, you can do so in front of any large hotel complex. (Ask the hotel staff for information on bike rentals.) A guided tour is your best bet along scenic and shoreline trails. A half-day bicycle tour with **Bahamas Outdoors Ltd.** (☎ 242-362-2772) costs $59.

- **Buzzing by on a motor scooter:** Some vacationers love zipping around on mini-motorcycles or scooters, but the often speedy Nassau traffic makes them far from safe. If you're feeling brave, wear a helmet and set out on your adventure, staying on the left side of the road. Ask your hotel staff for the closest scooter-rental outfit. Rates run about $50 per day.

Fast Facts: New Providence

American Express

If you need help with traveler's checks or other American Express services, visit the office at Destinations on Shirley Street, between Parliament and Charlotte streets (☎ 242-322-2931). It's open Monday to Friday 9 a.m. to 5 p.m.

ATMs

Major banks throughout Nassau include the Royal Bank of Canada (☎ 242-322-2420), Bank of Nova Scotia (☎ 242-356-1517), and Barclays (☎ 242-356-8000), each has ATMs. However, some accept cards only in the Cirrus network (☎ 800-424-7787 or 800-4CIRRUS), while others take only Plus (☎ 800-843-7587). ATMs at both the Paradise Island and Cable Beach casinos also dispense quick cash. You can also find ATMs at the airports.

Baby-sitting

Hotel staff can help you make arrangements to hire an experienced sitter. Expect to pay around $10 to $15 an hour, plus $3 an hour for each additional child.

Emergencies

For any major emergency, call ☎ 919.

Hospitals

The government-run Princess Margaret Hospital (☎ 242-322-2861) is located on Shirley Street in downtown Nassau. Before your trip to The Bahamas, check out whether your health insurance covers you while you're abroad. If not, you may want to purchase a traveler's insurance plan with emergency medical expense coverage (see Chapter 9 for details).

Information

Contact the Ministry of Tourism at Rawson Square (☎ 242-328-7810) or ask your hotel staff for good local maps and other visitor information.

Internet Access

Check out Cybercafe at The Mall at Marathon (☎ 242-394-6254). Here you can get online from your own laptop or log on to one of the computers. The cost is 15¢ per minute. Some of the larger hotels also offer guests Internet access for a small fee.

Newspapers and Magazines

The Tribune Daily and *The Nassau Guardian,* both published in the morning, are the country's two competing daily newspapers. At your hotel and visitor information stations, you can find various helpful magazines, brochures, and booklets.

Pharmacies

The Prescription Parlourx Pharmacy (☎ 242-356-3973) on East Street South is open daily from 7 a.m. to 11 p.m. You can have whatever you need delivered to your hotel for about the cost of a round-trip taxi ride to the pharmacy. The delivery charge is $6 from about 7 a.m. to 9 p.m. and $25 until 11 p.m. Another reliable pharmacy that also delivers is Cole Thompson, open 8:30 a.m. to 6:00 p.m. at Bay and Charlotte streets (☎ 242-322-2062).

Police

In an emergency, call ☎ 919.

Post Office

The main post office is at the juncture of East Hill Street and East Street in Nassau (☎ 242-322-3344).

Restrooms

Downtown Nassau has free public toilets, which are adjacent to both the cruise ship docks and other docks near the Straw Market on Bay Street. But when nature calls, most locals opt to duck into one of the better-maintained restrooms of the many bars or casinos scattered throughout the city. The toilets in McDonald's on Bay Street are a good bet.

Safety

Just as you should anywhere in the world, exercise caution and common sense. For example, don't wear flashy jewelry to the beach or turn your back on your camera or handbag. Stay away from desolate or run-down areas — whether residential or commercial — at night. Cable Beach and Paradise Island are always packed with visitors and are safer places for walking and exploring after dark.

Taxis

Taxis wait outside Cable Beach and Paradise Island hotels, and they're also plentiful in Nassau. Before you hop into a cab, ask your hotel staff the approximate fare to wherever you're going. From Cable Beach to downtown Nassau, you pay about $9 for two passengers. Likewise, the trip from Cable Beach to Paradise Island costs about $15.

Chapter 11

Staying in Style in New Providence

● ●

In This Chapter
▶ Deciding among hotel locations
▶ Evaluating the top hotel choices

● ●

*N*ew Providence reigns supreme when it comes to the number of resorts and activities. You can also find a bed-and-breakfast or a small beach hotel away from the crowds.

Surveying the Scene

Most accommodations in New Providence are high-rises with hundreds of rooms. In fact, one — Atlantis Paradise Island — is actually more like an aquatic theme park than a hotel, weighing in with some 2,349 rooms.

In addition to large hotels and a few small ones, New Providence offers villas, townhouses, and condos. These options have fewer services, such as restaurants or staff to help make arrangements for tours and activities. Many villas, townhouses, and condos are a distance from sights and attractions, and you have to provide your own transportation. Keep in mind that while you have all the comforts of home, you also have all the work that goes along with it. However, these types of accommodations are good for families or groups of friends who prefer doing their own cooking and are looking for a private vacation. For long-term vacationers, these types of accommodations are a great money-saving tactic for an extended island stay.

The following rack rates are for two people spending one night in a double room in winter or early spring. These charges are published rates available to anybody who walks in off the street and requests a room. You can get discounted hotel rates in many ways (see Chapter 7 for more details). Rates at Breezes and Sandals Royal Bahamian may seem extraordinarily high when compared with our other recommendations, but these two hotels are all-inclusive, so their charges include meals, beverages, tips, taxes, transportation to and from the airport, entertainment, and most activities.

 If a view is important to you, make sure that you clarify this point when you reserve a room. The most expensive rooms invariably have ocean views; the less expensive accommodations with a view open onto a pool or a garden. Sometimes another building obscures views from a room. Ask so that you aren't unpleasantly surprised with a vista of a wall after checking in.

Most New Providence hotels don't quote prices for a meal plan, such as MAP (modified American plan or breakfast and dinner). When they do, the extra cost per person is indicated.

The Best Accommodations

Here are our top hotel picks in Nassau, Cable Beach, and Paradise Island, along with some handy maps.

 ## Atlantis Paradise Island Resort & Casino
$$$$$ **Paradise Island Beach**

The Atlantis is a $850-million, 2,349-room resort that sprawls from one shore of Paradise Island to the other, opening onto a long stretch of white sandy beach. Stay here if you'd like to lodge in a mega-resort and mini-city. Check into the nearby Ocean Club Golf & Tennis Resort (see the listing for this property later in the chapter) if you're seeking more tranquility and exclusivity.

Dozens of restaurants, bars, lounges, designer boutiques, and a mammoth casino that's open day and night keep many visitors glued to the premises. The resort's comfortable, sleekly decorated rooms vary in size, view, and location. Although all rooms have small balconies, many of these balconies in the plush Royal Towers (the priciest section) are wide enough for only two pairs of feet. The Beach Tower is the least expensive wing, with Coral Towers in the middle. Bathrooms are spacious and well maintained. Room service is available around the clock, and you can stay busy on the tennis, volleyball, and basketball courts, the putting green, in exercise classes, or at the spa. However, the centerpiece of the hotel is its dazzling water wonderworld of aquariums, freshwater pools, snorkeling lagoons, waterslides, and a white sand beach.

Take one of the waterslides down the life-size replica of a Mayan temple. An 18m (60-ft.), nearly vertical drop zips you along a clear tunnel that slices through a shark tank. The 15m (48-ft.) high corkscrew slide, however, lets you view the sharks at a more leisurely pace. Other aquatic playgrounds range from a shallow children's pool and beachlike zero-entry pool (instead of having steps, the shallow end gradually slopes from dry land, just like a beach) to a river pool that carries you along in an inner tube, as well as a series of pools linked by waterslides. In other words,

Nassau and Paradise Island Accommodations

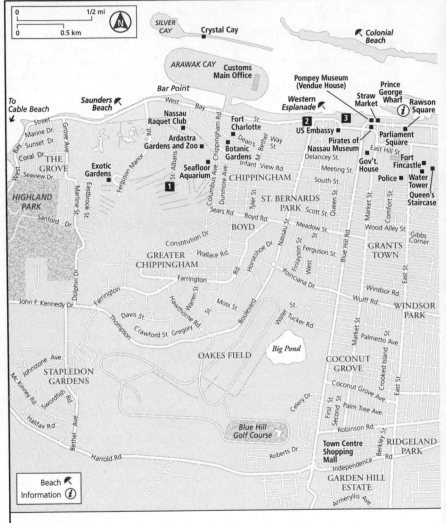

0 — 1/2 mi
0 — 0.5 km

SILVER CAY
Crystal Cay
Colonial Beach
ARAWAK CAY
Customs Main Office
Bar Point
Pompey Museum (Vendue House)
Prince George Wharf
Straw Market
Rawson Square
To Cable Beach
Saunders Beach
West Bay Street
Western Esplanade
Nassau Raquet Club
Fort Charlotte
2
3
US Embassy
Parliament Square
Marine Dr.
Grove Ave.
Bay
Sunset Dr.
Ardastra Gardens and Zoo
Dean's Way
Bethel St.
Pirates of Nassau Museum
East Hill St.
Coral Dr.
THE GROVE
Exotic Gardens
Botanic Gardens
Infant View Rd.
Delancey St.
Gov't. House
Fort Fincastle
Seaview Dr.
West
Seafloor Aquarium
Dunmore Ave.
CHIPPINGHAM
Meeting St.
Police
Water Tower
HIGHLAND PARK
Marine St.
Eastbrook St.
Ferguson Manor
St. Albans
Columbus Ave.
South St.
Queen's Staircase
Sanford Dr.
Sears Rd.
Tyler St.
ST. BERNARDS PARK
Scott St.
Queen St.
Market St.
Comfort St.
Gibbs Corner
Boyd Rd.
BOYD
Meadow St.
Wood Alley St.
GRANTS TOWN
Constitution Dr.
GREATER CHIPPINGHAM
Wallace Rd.
Horseshoe Dr.
Nassau St.
Ferguson St.
Finlayson St.
West
Blue Hill Rd.
John F. Kennedy Dr.
Dolphin Dr.
Farrington
Farrington
Hawthorne Rd.
Warren St.
Moss St.
Boulevard
Poinciana Dr.
Windsor Rd.
Wulff Rd.
East St.
WINDSOR PARK
Davis St.
Thompson
Crawford St.
Gregory St.
Water St.
Tucker Rd.
Market St.
Palmetto Ave.
Johnstone Ave.
STAPLEDON GARDENS
OAKES FIELD
Big Pond
COCONUT GROVE
Crooked Island
East St.
Mc Kinney Rd.
Swordfish Rd.
Coconut Grove Ave.
Celery Dr.
First St.
Second St.
Palm Tree Ave.
Halifax Rd.
Bethel Ave.
Blue Hill Golf Course
Robinson Rd.
Berkley St.
RIDGELAND PARK
Harrold Rd.
Town Centre Shopping Mall
Roberts Dr.
Independence Rd.
Beach
Information (i)
GARDEN HILL ESTATE
Armeryllis Ave.

BIMINI ISLANDS
GREAT HARBOUR CAY
Miami
BERRY ISLANDS
FLORIDA
PARADISE ISLAND
Nassau
NEW PROVIDENCE ISLAND
Straits of Florida
Tongue of the Ocean
ANDROS ISLAND
0 — 50 mi
0 — 50 km

Atlantis Paradise Island Resort & Casino **4**

British Colonial Hilton **3**

Comfort Suites Paradise Island **5**

Dillet's Guest House **1**

Holiday Inn Junkanoo Beach Nassau **2**

Ocean Club Golf & Tennis Resort **7**

Sunrise Beach Club and Villas **6**

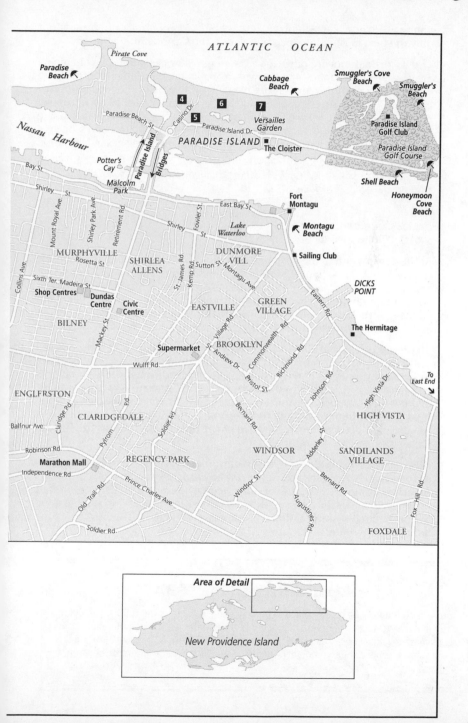

ATLANTIC OCEAN

Pirate Cove

Paradise
Beach

Cabbage
Beach

Smuggler's Cove
Beach

Smuggler's
Beach

4

Paradise Beach St.

Casino Dr.

6

5

Paradise Island Dr.

Versailles
Garden

Nassau Harbour

PARADISE ISLAND

The Cloister

Paradise Island
Golf Club

Paradise Island
Golf Course

Potter's
Cay

Paradise Island
Bridges

Bay St.

Shell Beach

Shirley   St.

Malcolm
Park

Honeymoon
Cove
Beach

Mount Royal Ave.

Shirley Park Ave.

Retirement Rd.

East Bay St.

Fowler St.

Shirley   St.

Fort
Montagu

Lake
Waterloo

Montagu
Beach

MURPHYVILLE

Rosetta St.

SHIRLEA
ALLENS

St. James Rd.

Kemp Rd.

Sutton St.

DUNMORE
VILL

Montagu Ave.

Sailing Club

DICKS
POINT

Collins Ave.

Sixth Ter. Madeira St.

Shop Centres

Dundas
Centre

Civic
Centre

EASTVILLE

GREEN
VILLAGE

Eastern Rd.

The Hermitage

BILNEY

Mackey St.

Supermarket

Village Rd.

St. Andrew Dr.

BROOKLYN

Commonwealth Rd.

Richmond Rd.

Wulff Rd.

Bristol St.

Johnson Rd.

To
East End

ENGLERSTON

Claridge Rd.

Rd.

Bernard Rd.

High Vista Dr.

HIGH VISTA

Balfour Ave.

CLARIDGEDALE

Pyfrom

Soldier Rd.

WINDSOR

Adderley St.

SANDILANDS
VILLAGE

Robinson Rd.

Marathon Mall

REGENCY PARK

Bernard Rd.

Fox Hill Rd.

Independence Rd.

Old Trail Rd.

Prince Charles Ave.

Windsor St.

Augustines Rd.

FOXDALE

Soldier Rd.

Area of Detail

New Providence Island

you're at Disney. The Atlantis's activity-packed children's program is not only the best in The Bahamas but also in the Caribbean.

Twenty restaurants are on-site, so the range of prices and types of cuisine are greater than in many small towns. You can take the kids to chow down on burgers, or you can dine more elegantly on some of the most superior cuisine in The Bahamas, prepared by top Bahamian, American, or European chefs. For example, Villa d'Este offers a refined Northern Italian cuisine that's almost as grand as you'd get in Italy, whereas Mama Loo's or Five Twins features Asian food that equals some of the finest places in New York.

See map p. 138. Casino Dr. ☎ *800-ATLANTIS or 242-363-3000. Fax: 242-363-3524.* www.atlantisresort.com. *Parking: $5 valet, free self-parking. Rack rates: $346–$490 double, $810 suite. AE, MC, V.*

Breezes Bahamas
$$$$$ Cable Beach

At the eastern end of the strip of Cable Beach hotels, all-inclusive Breezes, run by SuperClubs, is designed mainly for adult couples and singles, but children are welcome, too, as long as they're 16 or older. The other major all-inclusive, Sandals (reviewed later in this chapter), is more stylish and upscale with better amenities, but that Jamaican chain only accepts male/female couples whereas Breezes is more democratically open to all.

The hotel opens onto one of the best beaches along the entire coastal strip. You entertain yourself with everything from toga and pajama parties to talent shows and comedy cabarets. Island traditions, such as dancers and musicians dressed in whimsical costumes, make lively appearances in Junkanoo Jamborees and steel-band performances. A large, heated freshwater swimming pool is on-site. You can also snorkel or take scuba lessons. A short walk along the road or the beach takes you to the Crystal Palace Casino (see Chapter 13).

Breezes' refurbished hotel rooms with wooden furniture and Formica tops are comfortable, but frankly never rise beyond the standard of a first-class American hotel. Although Breezes' price tag sounds expensive at first, it includes all meals, beverages, and most activities. Diners can sample good but unremarkable international cuisine at a food court. The best bet is the Italian dining room.

Ice skating in Nassau

Breezes Bahamas guests can play ice hockey and ice skate at the resort. The country's first ice-skating rink is synthetic, of course, but nothing's artificial about the daily puck fests. Hockey sticks and skates are available, if you forget your own. Feeling the urge to do a triple axel at midnight? This 488m (1,600-ft.) rink is open for skating 24 hours a day.

Cable Beach Accommodations

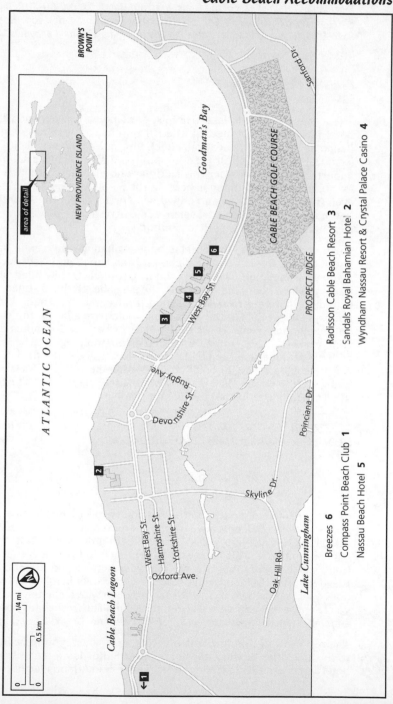

ATLANTIC OCEAN

BROWN'S POINT

Goodman's Bay

Sanford Dr.

CABLE BEACH GOLF COURSE

PROSPECT RIDGE

NEW PROVIDENCE ISLAND

area of detail

West Bay St.

Rugby Ave.

Devonshire St.

Poinciana Dr.

Skyline Dr.

West Bay St.
Hampshire St.
Yorkshire St.
Oxford Ave.

Oak Hill Rd.

Lake Cunningham

Cable Beach Lagoon

1/4 mi
0.5 km

Breezes **6**
Compass Point Beach Club **1**
Nassau Beach Hotel **5**

Radisson Cable Beach Resort **3**
Sandals Royal Bahamian Hotel **2**
Wyndham Nassau Resort & Crystal Palace Casino **4**

See map p. 141. Just east of the Nassau Beach Hotel. ☎ *800-GO-SUPER* (800-467-8737) or 242-327-5356. Fax: 242-327-1209. www.superclubs.com. *Rack rates: $592–$745 double, $748 suite. Rates include all meals and most activities. AE, DISC, MC, V.*

British Colonial Hilton
$$$ Nassau

The grande dame of all Nassau hotels, this landmark seven-floor, 291-room hotel has been fine tuned by the Hilton chain. If you're going to The Bahamas for a beach vacation, check into one of the hotels at Paradise Island or Cable Beach. If the shopping and sights of Nassau are more important to you, consider this landmark hotel. A beach that's adequate for sunning and swimming is here, but it's a bit small. The hotel doesn't even try to attract the casino crowd, who prefer either the Atlantis or the Nassau Marriott. Business travelers come here, and so do visitors who are more interested in buying than gambling.

Plush and glamorous, the hotel is once again a worthy venue for James Bond. Scenes from such 007 flicks as *Thunderball* and *Never Say Never Again* were shot here. The hotel even has a Double O suite filled with Bond memorabilia. The rooms open onto the small beach that's situated on the channel separating New Providence from Paradise Beach. A dignified atmosphere prevails in the bedrooms, which are a bit on the small side but many offer scenic views of the Nassau harbor. Bedrooms are quite comfortable and are capped with rich crown moldings and accessorized with tile or stone-sheathed bathrooms. The cuisine at the British Colonial is good standard fare, although it can't compete with top Nassau restaurants, such as Buena Vista or Sun And . . . (see Chapter 12). The hotel features a medium, unheated freshwater pool.

See map p. 138. 1 Bay St. ☎ *800-HILTONS* (800-445-8667) in the U.S. and Canada, or 242-322-3301. Fax: 242-302-9009. www.hilton.com. *Parking: $8. Rack rates: $239–$299 double, suite from $350. AE, DC, DISC, MC, V.*

Comfort Suites Paradise Island
$$$–$$$$ Paradise Island

Here you're offered modern suites, but don't expect yours to have separate rooms or even a balcony. Instead, you get one comfortable motel-like room with sitting and sleeping areas. For families or groups of friends, the rooms offer pull-out sofas. This hotel isn't on the beach and you can't see the ocean from your bedroom, but across from your hotel is the Atlantis Paradise Island Resort & Casino (see this resort's entry earlier in this chapter), which does open onto a beautiful white sandy beach with a sheltered marina. So you're only a five-minute walk from the sands. The freshwater pool is small and unheated. An open-air restaurant serves only breakfast and lunch.

The real draw of Comfort Suites is that, as a guest, you have full access to the amenities at the Atlantis. Comfort Suites is a quieter three-story hotel and is a good choice if you want access to Atlantis facilities without staying at the overwhelming mega-resort. For the most privacy at Comfort Suites, ask for a room that's not along a walkway. Children under age 16 stay free with one or two adults.

See map p. 138. Paradise Island Drive. ☎ *800-517-4000 or 242-363-3680. Fax: 242-363-2588.* www.choicecaribbean.com. *Rack rates: $258–$308 double. Rates include continental breakfast. AE, MC, V.*

Compass Point Beach Club
$$$–$$$$$ **Gambier**

This colorful beach resort is the most fun place to stay in New Providence. Eighteen octagonal cottages with louvered windows are painted in vivid hues of lemon, orange, teal, mauve, and blue. These wooden buildings — some on stilts, and some with one or two bedrooms — stud the waterfront and gently sloping hillside. Junkanoo festival motifs, such as fish, roosters, and sunbursts, decorate all buildings, and rocking chairs sit on the decks. Inside, the decor is elegantly rustic, with West African batik fabrics and natural wood furniture. Most units don't have air-conditioning, but ceiling fans and cross ventilation keep you cool. The bathrooms are spacious and feature the best recorded bathroom music in Nassau. The owner is music-industry mogul Chris Blackwell, who launched the career of reggae star Bob Marley. All units contain refrigerators, and some units come with open-air kitchenettes and dining patios.

The beach in front of the cottages may be small, but the larger Love Beach, which is popular for snorkeling, is just next door. A small, unheated freshwater pool is on-site. The cottages's oceanfront restaurant prepares some of the island's most imaginative cooking.

See map p. 141. Adjacent to Love Beach, about a ten-minute drive west of Cable Beach. ☎ *800-688-7678 or 242-327-4500. Fax: 242-327-3299.* www.compasspoint resortandvillas.com. *Rack rates: $245 cabana, $305–$390 one-bedroom cottage, $390–$470 two-bedroom cottage. AE, DC, MC, V.*

Dillet's Guest House
$$ **Nassau**

In a residential neighborhood, this bed-and-breakfast is within strolling distance of Saunders Beach, downtown Nassau, and bus stops. Iris Knowles, who runs Dillet's with her daughter, Danielle, was reared in this handsome home, which was built in 1928 by her father. The inn has only seven rooms, which are decorated with white wicker and pastels. All the guest quarters offer sitting areas, air-conditioning, and ceiling fans. The bathrooms are also attractive but small, each with a shower. Taking up an entire block, the grounds — which include a small, unheated freshwater pool — are planted with tropical greenery. You're treated to a Bahamian breakfast featuring sweet johnnycake and banana bread or potato bread flavored with coconut.

See map p. 138. Dunmore Avenue and Strachan streets. ☎ *242-325-1133. Fax: 242-325-7183.* www.islandeaze.com/dillets. *Rack rates: $125 double. Rate includes breakfast. No credit cards.*

Holiday Inn Junkanoo Beach Nassau
$$–$$$ Nassau

If you like spending your cash on purchases other than your hotel room, this place may be for you. Just west of downtown Nassau, this hotel is within easy reach of shops, restaurants, and historic sites of Bay Street, the main drag. The hotel's right across the street from the small but adequate Junkanoo Beach. If you're ready to hit a casino, Paradise Island's casino is 3km (2 miles) northeast and Cable Beach's casino is 5km (3 miles) west.

The medium-size bedrooms have a view of either the beach or Nassau Harbour, and they come with extras that you don't always find in a moderately priced choice, including alarm clocks, phones with two lines, and a desk. Bathrooms are a bit small. With diversions such as Nintendo on hand, the kid suites on the ground floor around the swimming pool are good for families; these rooms have a king-size bed, plus a second room (it's small and windowless, however) with bunk beds. The hotel boasts two unheated freshwater pools, one small and one large. The on-site Bay Street Grille is not reason alone to stay here, although you dine outside in a tropical courtyard overlooking the pool.

See map p. 138. Across West Bay Street from the beach, on the edge of downtown Nassau. ☎ *800-465-4329 or 242-356-0000. Fax: 242-323-1408.* www.holiday-inn.com. *Rack rates: $154 double, $179 suite. AE, DISC, MC, V.*

Nassau Beach Hotel
$$–$$$ Cable Beach

Next door to its sibling, the flashier Wyndham Nassau Resort & Crystal Palace Casino (reviewed later in this chapter), and across the road from the Cable Beach Golf Course, the Nassau Beach Hotel has been going strong since the 1940s. Spruced up during the 1990s, it has weathered competition from the newer, glitzier resorts nearby. Claiming a prime slice of the white sand beachfront, this hotel is one of the more dignified in the area. But don't let the Georgian-style architecture, gleaming marble and tile lobby, and hushed hues fool you. The Nassau Beach Hotel knows how to party. Check out the nightly Bahamian revue at the popular King & Knights club, the loud Friday evening Junkanoo parade at Café Johnny Canoe out front, or at one of the hotel's various bars. When hunger hits, you can choose from seven on-site restaurants serving standard international cuisine — except for the Beef Cellar, which grills the juiciest, most tender, and succulent steaks on Cable Beach.

The midsize accommodations contain summery rattan pieces, comfortable beds, and a marble bathroom. All rooms come with a balcony or patio, but make sure you ask about the view when you make your reservation. Although you can see the ocean from most rooms, some rooms overlook buildings instead. Watersports are extensive, and the hotel also has six tennis courts (four are floodlit for night play) and a fitness center. Two unheated freshwater pools are also on-site.

See map p. 141. Near the Crystal Palace Casino. ☎ *888-NASSAU-B (888-627-7282) or 242-327-7711. Fax: 242-327-8829.* www.nassaubeachhotel.com. *Rack rates: $145–$250 double, $300–$350 suite. AE, DISC, MC, V.*

Ocean Club Golf & Tennis Resort
$$$$$ Paradise Island

Tucked away on the quiet eastern side of Paradise Island, this elegant colonial style resort is as understated as the Atlantis is extravagant. For class and style, nothing matches it on the island. In a past life, Ocean Club was the private estate of A&P grocery-chain heir Huntington Hartford. The resort stretches from a white sandy beach to the harbor side of the island. At the core of the resort are formal terraced gardens, inspired by Versailles, where stone steps, hand-laid rock ridges, and European bronze and marble statues set off bougainvillea and hibiscus plants. Striking stone arches of a 12th-century Augustinian cloister, which Hartford had shipped from France and reassembled, overlook the gardens and the harbor.

Guest rooms are spacious, with views of the gardens or the beach and ocean. All rooms come with patios or balconies, and some have king-size mahogany four-poster beds, cane chairs, tall potted palms, hardwood floors, and sisal rugs, plus luxurious private bathrooms. Every afternoon, champagne and strawberries mysteriously appear in your room. The on-site restaurants offer the finest hotel dining on Paradise Island — better than the hotel dining rooms in Nassau or Cable Beach. Tennis courts, a large, heated freshwater pool, and a spa are also on the premises. Take the shuttle bus or a short walk to the 18-hole championship golf course. Because Atlantis and Ocean Club share the same owners (Sun International), Ocean Club guests have full access to all the facilities at theme-park Atlantis (see its review earlier in this chapter). A courtesy bus links Ocean Club to Atlantis.

See map p. 138. Ocean Club Drive. ☎ *800-321-3000 or 242-363-2501. Fax: 242-363-2424.* www.oceanclub.com. *Rack rates: $795–$995 double, from $1,250 suite, from $1,350 villa. AE, DC, MC, V.*

Radisson Cable Beach Resort
$$$–$$$$ Cable Beach

With a broad, white sandy beach and an extensive children's program, the Radisson resort is a good choice for families. Offering beach olympics, arts and crafts, treasure hunts, storytelling, and other well-supervised activities, the complimentary half- or full-day programs at Camp Junkanoo are open to children between the ages of 4 and 11. Children under age 12 stay free, with one or two adults. Featuring five freshwater swimming pools, the Radisson's tropical waterscape also includes rock formations, waterfalls, and whirlpools.

Some 700 guest rooms in two nine-story wings form a U that cups the pools and beautiful sandy shore. Views from lower floors showcase the gardens while higher rooms overlook the ocean. Bedrooms are modern and comfortable, with large windows, balconies, and a midsize bathroom. The hotel features a fitness center on the premises and a golf course is across the road. When you're not working out or teeing off, go snorkeling, scuba diving, sailing, or play some tennis. You can dine at several good restaurants and, at night, listen to live music at the hotel. If you prefer, however, you can head to the adjoining casino complex for other eats, shops, and entertainment.

See map p. 141. Adjacent to the Crystal Palace Casino. ☎ 800-333-3333 or 242-327-6000. Fax: 242-327-6987. www.radisson.com. *Rack rates: $450 double, from $700 suite. Three meals $99 per person extra or $65 ages 13 to 16, $45 ages 4 to 12. AE, DC, DISC, MC, V.*

Sandals Royal Bahamian Hotel
$$$$$ Cable Beach

Opening onto a white sand beach, this Jamaican chain member is a more upscale, all-inclusive hotel than Breezes Bahamas. With its Romanesque statues, European spa, first-class restaurants, and two large, unheated freshwater pools surrounded by columns, Sandals Royal Bahamian is an elegant but more expensive alternative. A shuttle ride or a leisurely stroll west of the Crystal Palace Casino, the hotel is removed from the busiest section of Cable Beach. Sandals appeals to newlyweds, and many couples get married on the hotel's grounds. With romantic touches such as four-poster beds and luxurious bathrooms, the individual rooms, suites, and villas at Sandals are exclusively for couples (heterosexual ones, that is).

As soon as you enter the lobby that's decked out in marble with chandeliers hanging from fresco-painted ceilings, you feel regal. You can spend a week here and splash in a different pool every single day. You can sail off to the hotel's private island, complete with its own pool and restaurant, or go snorkeling, scuba diving, or water-skiing. The cuisine at more than half a dozen restaurants ranges from home-style Bahamian and Japanese Teppanyaki to classic French and Northern Italian. Although the food is plentiful, entirely presentable, and prepared with first-rate ingredients, the Sandals kitchen never rises to the sublime. After dark, head to the theater for live performances by local bands, dancers, and other entertainers, or spend a quiet evening at the piano bar.

See map p. 141. A short drive or comfortable walk from the Crystal Palace Casino. ☎ 800-SANDALS or 242-327-6400. Fax: 242-327-6961. www.sandals.com. *Rack rates: $3,832–$7,665 per couple for seven days in double room, including all meals, beverages, and activities. Minimum two-night stay. AE, DISC, MC, V.*

Sunrise Beach Club and Villas
$$$$–$$$$$ Paradise Island

This sprawling low-rise resort, drawing mostly European vacationers, is the kind of place you picture when you think of a tropical getaway. Narrow paths snake through the colorful grounds that are thick with palm trees, hibiscus, crotons, and bougainvillea. This property offers only 35 units for rent, so the atmosphere is far quieter than it is at Paradise Island resorts, such as Atlantis.

With varying architectural styles and décor, the one-, two-, and three-bedroom villas and townhouses are set in different areas. Some units are tucked into the flourishing gardens, while the preferred ones overlook the two pools (one with a cave, waterfall, and children's wading section) or the sand beach. Cabbage Beach, one of the best beaches in The Bahamas, is only a short stroll to the east. A winding staircase may lead to the bedroom in your unit, or your master bathroom may sport a whirlpool tub. Glass and rattan, chrome, and stained glass highlight some accommodations, while others feature more hardwood. All come with kitchens — some larger, some smaller. Because all the accommodations here have more or less the same comfort level, your selection will depend on your needs. A one-bedroom townhouse is fine for a couple, whereas families or groups may prefer the two-bedroom apartments or even the three-bedroom villas, if the brood is large enough.

Living up to its name, the resort's Jungle Bar makes a scenic spot for a drink, a conch burger (a fried conch sandwich), or other light fare.

See map p. 138. Casino Drive. ☎ 800-451-6078 or 242-363-2250. Fax: 242-363-2308. Rack rates: $315 one-bedroom apt, $551 two-bedroom apt., $998 three-bedroom apt. AE, MC, V.

Wyndham Nassau Resort & Crystal Palace Casino
$$$$ **Nassau**

Adjacent to the casino that also adjoins the Radisson (which has a better beach), this large, sprawling hotel is an epic extravaganza. Without going outside, you can walk directly from the hotel towers to an array of restaurants, shops, and a fitness center. Most people hang out around the large, heated freshwater pool with its swirling aqua-slide. If you're traveling with kids, consider the modest children's program and playground.

The Wyndham doesn't have all the glitz of mega-resort Atlantis, but it is the island's second-largest hotel. With its rainbow-hued towers and wings, it's far flashier than the Radisson and is good for party-loving types. The hotel sells entertainment aggressively but houses you well in its accommodation towers, most of which are far enough away from the noisy public areas for light sleepers. We prefer the Casino Tower and Tower F because they have the grandest seafront vistas. You'll find some of the country's most lavish suites here, and you can live out your fantasies — for example, you can become Valentino in the Sheik-in-the-desert suite decorated for a sultan.

See map p. #141. Neighboring the Radisson. ☎ 800-222-7466 or 242-327-6200. Fax: 242-327-4346. www.wyndhamnassauresort.com. Parking: $6 valet, free self-parking. Rack rates: $179–$250 double, $250–$500 suite. MAP $47 per person or $24 children under 12. AE, DC, DISC, MC, V.

Chapter 12

Dining Out in New Providence

· ·

In This Chapter

▶ Finding the best food beyond your hotel dining room
▶ Locating restaurants with island ambience

· ·

From familiar fast-food chains to first-class international dining rooms, New Providence offers vacationers dozens of dining choices. The less-expensive places are in and around downtown Nassau, while the widest selection of expensive restaurants is on Paradise Island. What you won't find are restaurants devoted to a healthy cuisine, although almost every dining room offers dishes that would win the approval of your doctor.

Getting a Taste for New Providence

You have a choice of three areas for dining: Nassau, Paradise Island, and Cable Beach. Most visitors patronize the Nassau restaurants during the day while on shopping and sightseeing jaunts, preferring to dine at Cable Beach and Paradise Island in the evening.

Nassau can be dangerous after dark because of muggings. However, a few restaurants in Nassau, such as **Chez Willie,** are so special that you may want to dine there. In that case, take a taxi to the restaurant. When you finish dinner, have the staff summon a cab to return you safely to your hotel.

First-class restaurants always require reservations, especially during the winter months.

Most restaurants host happy hour (actually two or three hours starting around 5 p.m.), which is a good time to sample whatever tropical rum-based concoction the establishment features. Dining rooms often close between meals, but fast-food joints can satisfy your hunger. A few restaurants in the casino complexes don't allow young children.

See Chapter 2 for details about local specialties and the Introduction for an explanation of the price categories we use.

Dining at Nassau's Best Restaurants

Bahamian Kitchen
$ Nassau   BAHAMIAN

For real local flavor and a down-home taste, head to this little eatery next to Trinity Church. This restaurant is one of our favorites of the local dives, enjoying a popularity that exceeds Café Skan's (see the review later in this chapter). The Bahamian Kitchen is one of the best places to try that Bahamian delicacy, freshly made conch salad. Some of the other delights include *stew fish* (fish marinated in spices and vegetables), a creamy curried chicken, okra soup, or pea soup and dumplings. Most dishes come with peas and rice. If you want to eat like your Bahama mama might have cooked for you, try such fare as corned beef and grits, all served with johnnycake. Baked pork chops and grouper also appear on the menu. If the weather is nice, you can order takeout and have a Bahamian picnic on the beach.

See map p. 150. Trinity Place, off Market Street. ☎ *242-325-0702. Lunch main courses: $6–$13; dinner main courses: $11–$32. AE, MC, V. Open: Mon–Sat 11 a.m.–10 p.m.*

Buena Vista
$$$$$ Nassau   CONTINENTAL

Only Graycliff and Sun And . . . (see reviews later in this chapter) do Continental cuisine better. For more than half a century, this two-story, 19th-century mansion has been a citadel of fine food enjoyed by candlelight in mellow areas decorated with antique paintings. A pianist entertains softly in winter, recapturing the flavor of the early '40s when the Duke and Duchess of Windsor ran The Bahamas. In fair weather, request a table on the garden terrace and order the bartender's special: a rum punch with coconut milk. Meals are served on the kind of delicate china that your grandmother keeps locked behind glass in a cabinet. The cookery is natural, straightforward, and classic, making the best use of quality ingredients, such as tender rack of lamb, roast duckling in a zesty orange sauce, stone crab with mustard sauce (our favorite), and an especially delectable filet mignon in a peppercorn sauce. Chefs prepare these dishes to perfection (if you like heavy sauces), although they hardly tax the imagination of the kitchen staff, who has been making them for years. Since 1946, the house's special dessert has been Mrs. Hauck's orange pancakes with a Grand Marnier sauce.

See map p. 150. Delancy and Meeting streets, behind the Roman Catholic cathedral, a block west of Government House. ☎ *242-322-2811. Reservations recommended. Jackets requested for men. Main courses: $32–$72; fixed-price dinner: $42. AE, MC, V. Open: Mon–Sat dinner only.*

Nassau and Paradise Island Dining

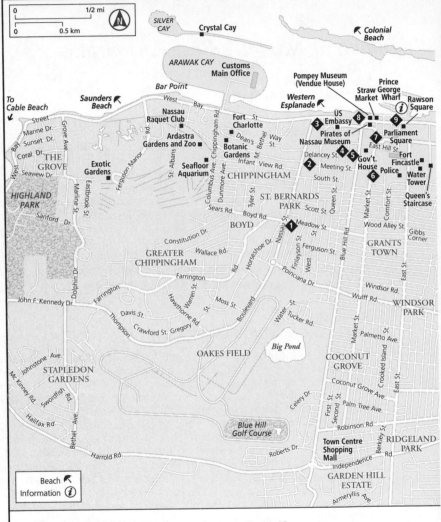

Anthony's Caribbean Grill **15**	Dune **16**
Bahamian Club **13**	Five Twins **14**
Bahamian Kitchen **7**	Gaylord's **10**
Buena Vista **2**	Graycliff **5**
Café at the Great Hall of Waters **13**	Marketplace **12**
Café Matisse **9**	Palm Tree **6**
Café Skan's **8**	The Poop Deck **17**
Chez Willie **3**	Shoal Restaurant and Lounge **1**
Conch Fritters Bar & Grill **4**	Sun And ... **11**
Courtyard Terrace **16**	

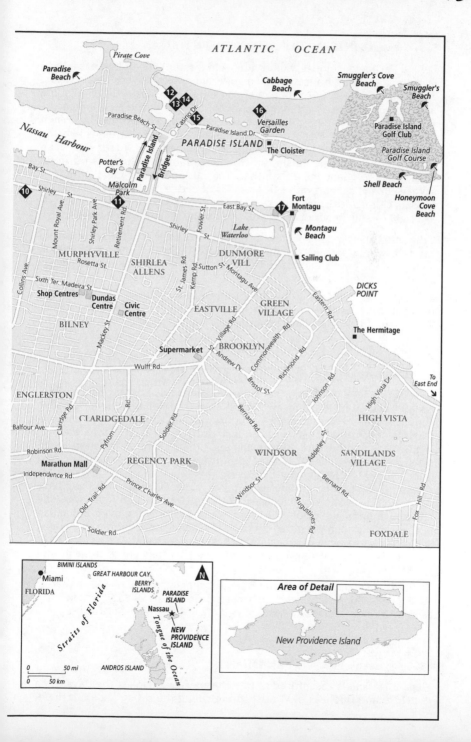

ATLANTIC OCEAN

Pirate Cove

Paradise Beach

Cabbage Beach

Smuggler's Cove Beach

Smuggler's Beach

Paradise Beach St.

Casino Dr.

Paradise Island Dr.

Versailles Garden

Paradise Island Golf Club

Paradise Island Golf Course

Nassau Harbour

Paradise Island Bridges

PARADISE ISLAND

The Cloister

Potter's Cay

Shell Beach

Honeymoon Cove Beach

Bay St.

Shirley St.

Malcolm Park

Mount Royal Ave.

Shirley Park Ave.

Retirement Rd.

East Bay St.

Fowler St.

Fort Montagu

Shirley St.

Lake Waterloo

Montagu Beach

MURPHYVILLE

Rosetta St.

SHIRLEA ALLENS

St. James Rd.

Kemp Rd.

Sutton St.

Montagu Ave.

DUNMORE VILL

Sailing Club

DICKS POINT

Collins Ave.

Sixth Ter. Madeira St.

Shop Centres

Dundas Centre

Civic Centre

EASTVILLE

GREEN VILLAGE

Eastern Rd.

BILNEY

Mackey St.

Village Rd.

Commonwealth Rd.

Richmond Rd.

The Hermitage

Supermarket

St. Andrew Dr.

BROOKLYN

Wulff Rd.

Bristol St.

Johnson Rd.

High Vista Dr.

To East End

ENGLERSTON

Clarridge Rd.

CLARIDGEDALE

Soldier Rd.

Bernard Rd.

HIGH VISTA

Balfour Ave.

Pyfrom Rd.

Robinson Rd.

Marathon Mall

REGENCY PARK

WINDSOR

Adderley St.

SANDILANDS VILLAGE

Independence Rd.

Old Trail Rd.

Prince Charles Ave

Windsor St.

Augustines Rd.

Bernard Rd.

Fox Hill Rd.

Soldier Rd.

FOXDALE

BIMINI ISLANDS

GREAT HARBOUR CAY

Miami

BERRY ISLANDS

FLORIDA

Straits of Florida

Nassau

PARADISE ISLAND

NEW PROVIDENCE ISLAND

Tongue of the Ocean

0   50 mi
0   50 km

ANDROS ISLAND

Area of Detail

New Providence Island

Café Matisse
$$$ Nassau INTERNATIONAL/NORTHERN ITALIAN

Behind Parliament House, this century-old former private home is a local favorite, attracting both Bahamian government employees and visitors. The joint effort of a Bahamian chef and his Italian-born wife results in a harmonious cuisine that reaches from the islands to the Mediterranean. The Matisse in the name comes from reproductions of paintings by French impressionist Henry Matisse. The restaurant serves pizzas, especially the best *frutti di mare* pie in town; this dish is topped, of course, with fresh local seafood. But the cuisine of Greg and Gabrielle Curry is far more advanced and challenging than that. You can open your meal with their savory curried shrimp with a fragrant jasmine rice or the best calamari in Nassau. Our favorite main courses are the grilled seafood, which emerges just right — still juicy, not dried out, and the cannelloni with lobster sauce.

If the smell of cigar smoke doesn't thrill you, steer clear of the second-floor veranda, where patrons sipping pre- and post-dinner drinks fill the small tables. Happy hour runs from 5 to 7 p.m., and the restaurant has live jazz a couple of nights a week.

See map p. 150. Bank Lane at Bay Street, near Parliament Square. ☎ *242-356-7012. Reservations recommended. Lunch main courses: $13–$24; dinner main courses: $26–$30. AE, MC, V. Open: Tues–Sat noon–3 p.m. and 6–10 p.m.*

Café Skan's
$ Downtown Nassau BAHAMIAN/AMERICAN

Good, filling food that's easy on the wallet keeps this bustling cafe packed. Located across from the Straw Market, this establishment is more coffee shop than cafe. The food is just as substantial as what you'd get at a regular restaurant, although you can also drop in for lighter fare, such as sandwiches and burgers. Bahamians pile in here early in the morning to devour dishes like their mamas made for them, including corned beef and grits, *chicken souse* (chicken parts and vegetables in a seasoned broth), stew fish, and broiled grouper with johnnycake. Of course, you can have "the usual" — a stack of pancakes, fluffy omelets, and French toast. The chefs turn out savory conch fritters or conch chowder, even Bahamian bean soup with dumplings, along with rib-sticking pork chops. Everything is accompanied by generous side dishes, like peas and rice or macaroni and cheese. The cuisine has no pretense: It's just good, honest, and straightforward food.

See map p. 150. Bay Street at Market Plaza, across the street from the Straw Market. ☎ *242-322-2486. Reservations not accepted. Breakfast: $3–$9.50; sandwiches: $5.95–$9.95; main-course platters: $5.95–$18. MC, V. Open: Mon–Sat 8 a.m.–5 p.m.*

Chez Willie
$$$$ Nassau FRENCH/BAHAMIAN

Elegant Nassau is recaptured at this charmer that evokes the days when the Duke and Duchess of Windsor were ruling the roost. On a fair night, opt for an alfresco dining as you listen to piano music, perhaps a Cole Porter tune. The host is Willie Armstrong, and his romantic spot is worth a journey by taxi into Nassau at night. Regal statuary rings a courtyard with a fountain. Chefs imaginatively prepare tip-top foodstuffs or else follow classic recipes — perhaps delicate stone-crab claws in a Dijon mustard sauce or a fresh Bahamian tuna and crab mousse. Main courses are well-executed, including lobster Thermidor and a sautéed Dover sole in a tarragon-laced tomato sauce. The typical Bahamian grouper gets a fancy touch, encased in puff pastry with crabmeat and served with a creamy coconut sauce. Other classics are beef Wellington, a delicate chateaubriand, or a roast rack of lamb — indeed, the Duke's favorite dishes from the '40s.

See map p. 150. West Bay Street. ☎ *242-322-5364. Reservations required. Jacket preferred for men. Main courses: $30–$48; fixed-price menu for two: $60–$100 per person. AE, MC, V. Open: Daily 6:30–10 p.m.*

Conch Fritters Bar & Grill
$–$$ Downtown Nassau   BAHAMIAN/AMERICAN

This casual bar and grill is the best place in the center of Nassau for you to sample conch in many variations, including not only the best conch fritters in town but also cracked conch, which is the mollusk's version of breaded veal cutlet. The first local restaurant you notice when coming in from Cable Beach to Nassau, the eatery enjoys a mixed following of locals and visitors. Even if you don't like conch, the chefs turn out many other good-tasting dishes, including some excellent crispy fried chicken or that Florida favorite from the '50s — surf and turf. This is one of the places that offers the famous Bahamian specialty, guava duff, for dessert. The bright décor is enlivened by plants and wood parrots, and live music is presented on most nights.

See map p. 150. Marlborough Street, opposite the British Colonial Hilton. ☎ *242-323-8801. Burgers, sandwiches and platters: $9.95–$36. AE, MC, V. Open: 7 a.m.–midnight.*

Gaylord's
$$ Nassau   INDIAN

For a change of pace, you can try some northern Indian cuisine, the best in Nassau. This restaurant is in a distinctive 19th-century building, and inside, silk drapes across the ceilings, decorative brass plates and sculpture are on display, and Indian music plays. With plenty of vegetarian choices, the menu ranges from mild, creamy *kormas* (balls of ground meat or vegetables in a thick, seasoned sauce) to bold *curries* (stew-like meat, fish, or vegetable dishes flavored with curry), and *tandoori* (marinated meat or fish cooked in a clay oven) main courses. Along with lamb, beef, chicken, and fish, you're likely to find the inevitable conch worked into the selections. Tandoori conch was a first for us, and it's a tasty way to prepare this mollusk. *Vegetable samosas* (pastries filled with curried vegetables or meat) make good starters. We can make a meal just out of the freshly baked breads alone, especially when they're filled with flavored onions or cheese. For dessert, try the carrot pudding.

See map p. 150. Dowdeswell Street, in front of Princess Margaret Hospital. ☎ 242-356-3004. Reservations recommended. Main courses: $14–$30; fixed-price lunch: $12–$25; fixed-price dinner: $25–$50; vegetarian dinner: $25. AE, MC, V. Open: Mon–Fri noon–3 p.m. and daily 6:30–11p.m.

Graycliff
$$$$$ Nassau   CONTINENTAL

Opposite Government House, Graycliff is in the most atmospheric mansion in Nassau and is far more elegant than Buena Vista. Once there, you enter a world of antiques, elegant china, and old English silverware. This restaurant — where you should dress in your most formal resort wear — is no longer "the tops" in The Bahamas, a position it held for years. Sun And . . . , for example, offers even better food. But for the allure of yesterday, Graycliff still ranks high. You can order a drink on the balcony bar or ask for a table on the cool terrace, while listening to the soft piano tunes of Coward, Gershwin, and Cole Porter. The cuisine is basically the type that pleased gourmets in decades past before the "revolution" came: perfectly grilled and choice steaks, lobster Graycliff in a white-wine medora sauce, plump juicy pheasant in a pineapple sauce, and grouper in a Dijon mustard sauce. Graycliffe continues to attract diners whose big night out involves the consumption of Iranian caviar, fine brandy, a Grand Marnier soufflé, Cuban cigars, as well as a selection from a *carte* of some 175,000 wine bottles.

See map p. 150. West Hill Street and Blue Hill Road, across from Government House. ☎ 242-322-2796. Reservations required. Jackets advised for men for dinner. Lunch main courses: $9–$29; dinner main courses: $38–$48. AE, MC, V. Open: Mon–Fri noon–2:45 p.m. and daily 7–9:30 p.m.

Palm Tree
$ Nassau   BAHAMIAN/AMERICAN

An island matriarch, Lydia Russell, lived here until she died in the 1980s. Her heirs took over the site and opened this local restaurant, serving a classic native cuisine. The restaurant adjoins their other place, **Mama Lyddy's** (☎ 242-322-4201), where you can get takeout for the makings of a great island picnic. At Palm Tree, the chefs prepare all the classic dishes that are familiar to generations of islanders. The joke among locals is that the food has changed a bit, at least since the landing of Columbus. Expect time-tested fare, including some of the town's best *cracked conch,* which is like breaded veal cutlet — crisp on the outside and tender inside, though a bit rubbery. Try their perenially popular baked pork chops or go for the fried or steamed grouper. Classically, this restaurant broils lobster, but you can also order it minced. The side dishes make meals unto themselves: fresh beets, macaroni and cheese, fried plantains, potato salad, or creamy corn.

See map p. 150. Corner of Market Street at Cockburn Street. ☎ 242-328-6849. Main courses: $6–$10. No credit cards. Open: Tues–Sat 7:30 a.m.–11 p.m.

The Poop Deck
$$–$$$ Nassau   BAHAMIAN/SEAFOOD

Even if this place didn't serve good food (which it does!), we'd still hang out here at night. We're drawn to its open-air, waterside location with a panoramic view of the marina — which lights up at night near the bridge to Paradise Island. In such a setting, only a nautical atmosphere with seafaring artifacts will do. A lot of the food attracts beer-drinking, cigarette-smoking, sports-loving devotees, but it's straightforward and prepared with fresh ingredients. A tasty appetizer is the crab-stuffed mushrooms. A local dish that we recommend is the Bahamian steamed chicken, flavored with tomatoes, onions, and sweet peppers in the Creole style, and accompanied with mango salsa and sweet-potato fish cakes. The cracked lobster, which is batter coated and sautéed, lures in many a diner. If you're dropping by for lunch, the burgers and sandwiches are tempting. The chef's version of the celebrated guava duff was the best we've sampled in New Providence.

To sit at one of the best tables (at the edge of the balcony), get here just before noon for lunch or 5 p.m. for dinner. Don't come alone, though, because single diners aren't seated at these front tables.

See map p. 150. East Bay Street, next to Nassau Yacht Haven. ☎ *242-393-8175. Reservations recommended. Lunch main courses: $10–$30; dinner main courses: $15–$42. AE, MC, V. Open: Daily noon–4:15 p.m. and 5–10:15 p.m.*

Shoal Restaurant and Lounge
$–$$ Nassau   BAHAMIAN

This restaurant is one we return to again and again, although its food is only slightly better than the grub served at other local favorites, such as Conch Fritters or Café Skan's. At times, the chefs at all these local dives seem to use the same recipes handed down from generations. We like to go truly Bahamian here and drop in for breakfast with friends to sample *boil fish,* cooked with salt pork, onions, and green peppers. This dish is always served with johnnycake. Chicken souse is a real morning eye-opener, but it might be strictly for devotees, not for the faint of heart. We asked our waiter what it's made with. He advised, "You wouldn't want to know. Just eat and enjoy." When we go to this no-frills restaurant at night, we order the crawfish salad or the steamed conch. Of course, the menu always features steak and lobster, too. Dishes come with fried plantain and mounds of peas and rice. Once very scarce on menus, guava duff is now almost a mandatory offering at every restaurant, and a sublime version is offered here as well. The restaurant will provide transportation to and from your hotel. You'll need all the help you can get returning to your hotel if you down several of the bartender's lethal Bahama Mamas.

See map p. 150. Nassau Street, near the College of the Bahamas. ☎ *242-323-4400. Main courses: $9–$30. AE, MC, V. Open: Daily 7:30 a.m.–11 p.m.*

Sun And . . .

$$$–$$$$ Nassau CONTINENTAL

Nassau's finest fare, even better than that of Graycliff or Buena Vista, is served by candlelight on a patio by a rock pool. Near Fort Montagu, Sun And . . . is a classic citadel of refined cuisine and service offered with an overlay of English colonial charm. A fountain-studded Iberian-style courtyard, complete with fountains and a drawbridge, sets the romantic aura. Sun And . . . is truly a world-class restaurant. Chefs prepare the exceptional ingredients with a finely honed technique. We can't predict what will be on the menu when you visit, but if we awarded stars for grand cuisine, we'd give them to the chef's smoked moulard duck breasts or the duck-stuffed ravioli with porcini mushrooms. Focus on the absolutely sensational boiled lobster or the classic roast spring lamb, which is almost melt-in-your-mouth tender. The soufflés are incomparable — better than Graycliff's. Most diners opt for the Grand Marnier soufflé, but our favorite is the soufflé with rum raisins and Black Label Bicardi.

See map p. 150. Lakeview Road off Shirley Street. ☎ 242-393-1205. Reservations recommended. Jackets requested for men. Main courses: $32–$40. AE, DISC, MC, V. Open: Tues–Sun 6:30– 9 p.m. Closed Aug–Sept.

Checking Out Paradise Island's Best Restaurants

Anthony's Caribbean Grill

$$ Paradise Island AMERICAN/CARIBBEAN

Near the Atlantis Resort and Comfort Suites, this laid-back tropical spot offers a pleasant alternative to hotel dining rooms. Brightly decorated with Bahamian artwork, Anthony's features an extensive menu that includes familiar but well-prepared dishes that never achieve greatness but are full of flavor, seasoning, and spice. For a taste of the islands, we go for the peppery jerk chicken on a bed of multicolored pasta, known as "Rasta pasta." Named after the music of The Bahamas, the 20-ounce Junkanoo steak with well-seasoned vegetables is only for the trencherman. The ribs sizzle in their salsa laced with coconut and mango. But in general, this restaurant is an upscale version of TGI Fridays, serving the usual array of pizzas (some of the pies studded with lobster), burgers, and fried chicken. The bartender is known for his 48-ounce sparklers, with rum, vodka, amaretto, and fruit punch. "With two of these," the bartender assured us, "we'll carry you out on a stretcher."

See map p. 150. Casino Drive, across from Comfort Suites. ☎ 242-363-3152. Lunch platters and main courses: $10.95–$39. AE, MC, V. Open: Daily 7:30 a.m.–11 p.m.

Bahamian Club

$$$$ **Paradise Island** **FRENCH/INTERNATIONAL**

Within the sprawling mega-resort of the Atlantis, this restaurant is a rather chic dining room imbued with the aura of the days of British colonialism. No place in either New Providence or Paradise Island serves such good cuts of meat, especially T-bone steaks and perfectly roasted prime rib. Diners come here in search of robust flavors. The menu still features classics, such as broiled lobster, Dover sole, and salmon steak. You might begin your meal with a fresh jumbo shrimp cocktail or a fresh salad of baby spinach leaves. Even though the restaurant imports its main ingredients, they don't taste that way after the skilled chefs work their magic in the kitchen.

See map p. 150. In the Coral Towers of the Atlantis Resort. ☎ *242-363-3000. Reservations required. Main courses: $41–$45. AE, DC, DISC, MC, V. Wed–Mon 6–11 p.m.*

 ## Café at the Great Hall Of Waters

$$$$$ **Paradise Island** **INTERNATIONAL**

This restaurant gives you a splashy look at the water wonderland of the Atlantis Resort, even if you're not a guest of the hotel. Paradise Island has better restaurants, notably Five Twins (reviewed later in this chapter), but none are this dramatic. You feel like a scuba diver as you look through gigantic picture windows that display the illuminated "ruins" of the lost city of Atlantis. Everywhere you look, rainbow-hued fish swim past stone "archaeological" remains, and rows of lobsters parade through the sand. With a ceiling that seems miles away, the cafe's multilevel dining areas are located on the lower floor of the Royal Towers. The restaurant offers a kids' menu, and little ones love taking walks along the aquarium walls between courses. In such a setting, the food becomes almost secondary, although it's quite good. Lobster is a specialty, but you can also order well-prepared versions of crab legs or grilled salmon. The chefs import top-quality ingredients, such as lamb, and work their magic with it. Desserts are uniformly luscious.

See map p. 150. In the Royal Towers of the Atlantis Resort. ☎ *242-363-3000. Reservations required. Main courses: $25–$45. AE, MC, V. Open: Thurs–Mon 7 a.m.– 11 a.m.; 11:30 a.m.–2:30 p.m.; and 6–10 p.m.*

Courtyard Terrace

$$$$$ **Paradise Island** **CONTINENTAL**

Within Paradise Island's most exclusive hotel, the Ocean Club, you dine in a romantic setting. Picture it: Your table is near a pool with a splashing fountain, candle flames dance in the trade winds, and a four-piece ensemble plays music on the balcony. You dine amid palms and flowering shrubs, surrounded by colonial-style verandas. The menu is strong on the classics, and the chef excels in making dishes that have pleased discerning palates for decades. Here you're served freshly grilled grouper or snapper, each perfectly seasoned, prepared, and never allowed to dry out. The lobster quiche is light and lively, and the calves' lyonnaise is as good as that served in a typical Left Bank Parisian bistro. The service is smooth, and the wine list is carefully chosen, although you don't have a massive selection like you do at Graycliff. Evenings can get a bit chilly, so you may want to bring along an evening wrap.

See map p. 150. In the Ocean Club Resort, Ocean Club Drive. ☎ 242-363-3000. Reservations required. Jacket and tie required for men during the winter season. Main courses: $40–$52. AE, DC, DISC, MC, V. Open: Daily 6:30–9 p.m.

Dune
$$$$ Paradise Island   INTERNATIONAL

The brilliantly talented Jean-Georges Vongerichten, a reigning chef in New York, is the guiding force behind Dune, the most cutting-edge restaurant on Paradise Island or even New Providence. Although he'd be competing in a sea of similarity of fine restaurants in New York, in The Bahamas, the French-born chef reigns supreme. He's not on Paradise Island all the time, but the dishes bear his imprint. The restaurant ships in marvelous luxury products and treats them with care and sensitivity in the kitchen. Such delights as fresh shrimp dusted with orange powder, served with artichokes and arugula, may rest on your platter. Begin, perhaps, with the delectable and freshly made spring rolls with soybean salsa. The shiitake cakes or the chicken and coconut milk soup are impressive appetizers, and an unexpected delight is a goat-cheese-and-watermelon salad.

See map p. 150. In the Ocean Club Resort, Ocean Club Drive. ☎ 242-363-2000, ext. 64739. Reservations required. Lunch main courses: $12–$25; dinner main courses: $22–$50. AE, DC, DISC, MC, V. Open: Daily 7–11 a.m., noon–3 p.m., and 6–10:30 p.m.

Five Twins
$$$$$ Paradise Island   ASIAN/SEAFOOD

Save this dining mecca for a special evening. While a singer croons smooth melodies, you can eat by candlelight on fine china, either inside or outside on a terrace that overlooks the marina. Attracting high rollers from the nearby casino, this restaurant is the best in the Atlantis's massive gambling-and-entertainment complex. Revolving around seafood, the Thai-Japanese-Indonesian cuisine is contemporary Pacific Rim with a European flair. Color, texture, artistic presentation and, of course, flavor play major roles in each dish, whether you choose freshly caught grouper, snapper, shrimp, or lobster. You can start with nuanced chilled oysters with apple slaw or a pepper-cured salmon with vegetable tempura. The restaurant also features a sushi bar as well as a separate upscale rum-and-cigar lounge. After dinner, a DJ spins party tunes from a booth suspended above the dance floor. Children under age 12 aren't allowed in the restaurant.

See map p. 150. In the Casino complex of the Atlantis Resort. ☎ 242-363-3000. Reservations required. Main courses: $40–$60. AE, DC, MC, V. Open: Daily 6–10 p.m., with a sushi and satay bar open daily 6:30–11 p.m.

Marketplace
$$$$ Paradise Island INTERNATIONAL

Decorated with old vases and terra-cotta tiles, this large buffet-style restaurant is reminiscent of a sprawling market. It serves the finest buffet on Paradise Island and is located in the Royal Towers of the Atlantis Resort. The food is fresh, but it's a mass feeding station. You go here to fill up, not to find food as good as that at Conch Fritters Bar & Grill. Before you start loading your plate, browse the various cooking stations and do some strategic planning. From fresh fruit to omelets, you can make breakfast as light or as heavy as you want. At lunch and dinner, you can find everything from fresh seafood and made-to-order pastas to freshly carved roast beef and lamb. No intimate affair, this place seats some 400 diners. Sit inside or on the patio overlooking a lagoon.

See map p. 150. In the Royal Towers of the Atlantis Resort. ☎ *242-363-3000. Full buffets: $47–$60. AE, DC, MC, V. Open: Daily 7–11 a.m., 11:30 a.m.–2:30 p.m., and 5:30–10 p.m.*

Dining at Cable Beach's Best Restaurants

The Black Angus Grill
$$$$ Cable Beach STEAK

The casino crowd flocks to this popular restaurant where beef is the star of the show, but poultry and seafood play supporting roles. Because Bahamian cattle farms don't exist, the restaurant imports frozen meat. The meat is always juicy, however, and the chef knows how particular some carnivores are. So, rare means rare, medium-rare means medium-rare, and you won't see any pink if you ask for your meat well-done, whether you order prime rib, filet mignon, or a T-bone steak. If you want both seafood and meat, you can order the surf and turf — the lobster tail is sweet and plump. Another good choice is the chicken carbonara (made with Parmesan cheese, bacon, garlic, and white wine).

See map p. 160. On the second level of the casino complex of the Wyndham Nassau Resort & Crystal Palace Casino. ☎ *242-327-6200. Main courses: $28–$40. AE, DC, DISC, MC, V. Open: Mon–Sat 6–11 p.m. (hours may vary; call in advance).*

Café Johnny Canoe
$–$$ Cable Beach BAHAMIAN/INTERNATIONAL

This brightly decorated eatery is so wild and festive that at first, you may think it's truly a tourist trap. It's obviously geared toward visitors, but the island cuisine is very authentic and full of regional flavor. At breakfast, the pancakes are light, and the omelets are fluffy. If you're adventurous and are here on a Saturday and Sunday, try old-fashioned Bahamian recipes, including tuna and grits, boil fish, or stewed conch, each dish comes with johnnycakes. For substantial Bahamian fare, you can devour the classic cracked conch with peas and rice or enjoy the grilled mahimahi with

Cable Beach Dining

The Black Angus Grill **2**
Café Johnny Canoe **3**
The Restaurant at Compass Point **1**
Sole Mare **2**

macaroni and cheese. The icing on the cake, so to speak, is the guava duff for dessert. On Friday at 8 p.m., a Junkanoo band performs, turning the place into a carnival.

See map p. 160. West Bay Street, in front of the Nassau Beach Hotel. ☎ 242-327-3373. Breakfast: $2.75–$10; salads, sandwiches, and lunch and dinner platters $9.95–$24. AE, DISC, MC, V. Open: Daily 7:30 a.m.–midnight.

The Restaurant at Compass Point
$$–$$$ Gambier   CALIFORNIAN/INTERNATIONAL

Music mogul Chris Blackwell attracts most visiting celebrities to New Providence to his chic little enclave set along the oceanfront. Informal, low-key, and casually hip, it dazzles diners with its Junkanoo decorations of everything from inlaid conch shells to flamboyant island colors. The cuisine has more modern flair and imagination than any other on New Providence. The chef pairs seemingly odd combinations of flavors, such as conch sushi with mango. However, most of these marriages of flavors come off beautifully. We're especially fond of the blackened grouper with a tropical sweet and sour salsa. Treat yourself to the spicy-jerk chicken salad or the crab cakes with a papaya relish.

See map p. 160. On the water in Gambier Village, about ten minutes west of Cable Beach. ☎ 242-327-4500. Reservations required. Lunch main courses: $10–$22, dinner main courses: $19–$35. AE, MC, V. Open: Daily 7:30 a.m. –10 p.m.

Sole Mare
$$$$ Cable Beach   NORTHERN ITALIAN

Overlooking the ocean from the second level of the casino complex in the Wyndham Nassau Resort & Crystal Palace Casino, this restaurant serves an admirable Northern Italian cuisine and even pleases some diners who claim "you can't eat good Italian in The Bahamas." With candlelit tables and a guitarist playing soft tunes, Sole Mare is one of the most elegant choices in Cable Beach. One standout dish is the pasta with lobster and shrimp sautéed in garlic olive oil and white wine. The veal sautéed with endive, capers, and white wine makes another enticing choice, along with the al dente cappellini with a zesty tomato sauce.

See map p. 160. In the Wyndham Nassau Resort & Crystal Palace Casino. ☎ 242-327-6200. Reservations required. Jackets preferred for men. Main courses: $17–$39. AE, DC, DISC, MC, V. Open: Tues–Sat 6–11 p.m. (hours may vary; call ahead).

Chapter 13

Having Fun On and Off the Beach in New Providence

● ●

In This Chapter

▶ Catching some rays on New Providence's best beaches
▶ Enjoying the island's watersports
▶ Exploring land attractions, shopping, and nightlife
▶ Taking two great day trips

● ●

As the home of **Nassau** (The Bahamas' history-packed capital), **Cable Beach** (the hotel-lined resort), and **Paradise Island** (the flashy vacation mecca just offshore), New Providence offers more action, both wet and dry, than anywhere else in The Bahamas. Watersports — from scuba diving and snorkeling to Jet-Skiing and parasailing — keep vacationers entertained when they aren't playing golf or tennis, horseback riding, mountain biking, or just strolling the streets of downtown Nassau. In this chapter, we present the hottest nightlife, the widest selection of duty-free shops and designer boutiques, and the best human-made attractions — from botanical gardens to intriguing museums.

Combing the Beaches

Although mega-resorts discourage non-guests from relaxing on their beaches, you can find plenty of unmarked, unnamed public beaches on New Providence and Paradise Island.

Beaches that are absolutely accessible to the public are

▸ **Cabbage Beach:** On Paradise Island, this beach is the real show-case. Its broad, white sands stretch for at least 3km (2 miles). Casuarines, palms, and sea grapes border it. This beach draws crowds in winter, but you can find a little more elbow room by walking to the northwestern stretch of the beach. You can reach Paradise Island from downtown Nassau by walking over the bridge, taking a taxi, or boarding a ferry at Prince George Dock. Cabbage Beach doesn't have public bathroom facilities, but you can patronize one of the handful of bars and restaurants nearby and use its facilities. Technically, you should be a customer even if you buy only one soft drink.

✔ **Cable Beach:** The name "Cable Beach" refers to a string of resorts and beaches that lie in the center of New Providence's northern coast. This beachfront is the most popular area in The Bahamas. It offers 7km (4 miles) of soft, white sand, and the hotels that line the waterfront offer diverse restaurants, snack bars, and watersports. Calypso music floats to the sand from hotel pool patios, where vacationers play musical chairs and see how low they can limbo. Vendors wind their way between sunblock-slathered bodies. Some sell armloads of shell jewelry, T-shirts, beach cover-ups, and fresh coconuts for sipping the sweet "water" straight from the shell. Others offer their hair-braiding services or sign up visitors for water-skiing, Jet-Skiing, and banana-boat rides. Kiosks advertise parasailing, scuba diving, and snorkeling trips, as well as party cruises to offshore islands.

Waters can be rough and reefy, but a little farther along the shore, they can be calm and clear. Because guests of the resorts use their hotel facilities, no public restrooms are available here. (If you're not a guest of the hotel, you're not supposed to use the facilities.) The Cable Beach resorts begin 5km (3 miles) west of downtown Nassau. Even though resorts line much of this long swath of beach, the public can access various sections of the beach without crossing through private hotel grounds.

✔ **Caves Beach:** On the north shore, past the Cable Beach properties, Caves Beach lies some 11km (7 miles) west of Nassau. It stands near Rock Point, right before the turnoff along Blake Road that leads to the airport. Because visitors often don't know of this place, it's another good spot where you can escape the hordes. This beach has soft sands. No toilets or changing facilities are available here.

✔ **Delaporte Beach:** Just west of the busiest section of Cable Beach, Delaporte Beach is another public-access beach where you can escape the crowds. It opens onto clear waters and boasts white sands, although it has no facilities, including toilets. Nonetheless, it's an option.

✔ **Goodman's Bay:** This public beach is east of Cable Beach on the way toward the center of Nassau. Goodman's Bay and Saunders Beach (see reviews later in this section) often host local fund-raising cook-outs where vendors sell fish, chicken, conch, peas and rice, or macaroni and cheese. People swim and socialize to blaring reggae and calypso music. To find out when one of these beach parties is happening, ask the staff at your hotel or pick up a local newspaper. This beach has a playground, plus toilets.

Fun in New Providence

ATTRACTIONS
Ardastra Gardens & Zoo **2**
Atlantis Aquarium **30**
Atlantis Paradise Island Resort
 & Casino **30**
Fort Charlotte **3**
Fort Fincastle and the
 Water Tower **19**
Government House **6**
Hairbraider's Centre **28**
Junkanoo Expo **28**
Nassau General Post Office **18**
Nassau Public Library and Museum **21**
National Art Gallery of The Bahamas **5**
Parliament Square **23**
Pirates of Nassau Museum **7**
Potter's Cay **32**
Prince George Wharf **28**
Queen's Staircase **20**
Rawson Square **27**
The Retreat **35**
Straw Market **10**
Versailles Garden and Cloister **31**

SHOPPING
Bahamas Post Office
 Philatelic Bureau **18**
Balmain Antiques **14**
Barry's Limited **9**
The Beauty Spot **11**
Bonneville Bones **8**
Brass & Leather Shop **17**
Coin of the Realm **15**
Cole's of Nassau **25**
Fendi **16**
Gucci **26**
John Bull **13**

Kennedy Gallery **24**
Leather Masters **22**
The Linen Shop **14**
Mademoiselle, Ltd **12**
Marlborough Antiques **4**
Nassau International Bazaar **29**
The Perfume Bar **28**
The Perfume Shop **11**
Prince George Plaza **28**
Pyfroms **13**
Sea Grapes Boutique **1**
Tropique International
 Smoke Shop **1**

ATLANTIC OCEAN

Pirate Cove

Paradise Beach

Cabbage Beach

Smuggler's Cove Beach

Smuggler's Beach

30

Paradise Beach St.

Casino Dr.

Paradise Island Dr.

31

Nassau Harbour

32

PARADISE ISLAND

Paradise Island Bridges

Potter's Cay

Bay St.

Shirley St.

Malcolm Park

East Bay St.

33

Shirley St.

Fowler St.

Lake Waterloo

Fort Montagu

Montagu Beach

Shell Beach

Honeymoon Cove Beach

Paradise Island Golf Club

Paradise Island Golf Course

Mount Royal Ave.

Shirley Park Ave.

Retirement Rd.

MURPHYVILLE

Rosetta St.

Sixth Ter. Madeira St.

Shop Centres

Collins Ave.

Dundas Centre

34

Civic Centre

BILNEY

Mackey St.

SHIRLEA ALLENS

St. James Rd.

Kemp Rd.

Sutton St.

Montagu Ave.

DUNMORE VILL

EASTVILLE

Village Rd.

BROOKLYN

Supermarket

St. Andrew D.

Wulff Rd.

Commonwealth Rd.

Richmond Rd.

Bristol St.

GREEN VILLAGE

Eastern Rd.

Sailing Club

DICKS POINT

The Hermitage

Johnson Rd.

To East End

ENGLERSTON

Clarirge Rd.

Balfour Ave.

Robinson Rd.

Marathon Mall

Independence Rd.

CLARIDGEDALE

Pyfrom Rd.

Soldier Rd.

REGENCY PARK

Prince Charles Ave.

Old Trail Rd.

Soldier Rd.

Bernard Rd.

WINDSOR

Windsor St.

Adderley St.

SANDILANDS VILLAGE

Bernard Rd.

HIGH VISTA

High Vista Dr.

35

Fox Hill Rd.

NIGHTLIFE

Atlantis Paradise Island
Resort **30**

Club Waterloo **33**

The Crystal Palace
Casino **1**

Dragons **30**

Dundas Center for the
Performing Arts **34**

King & Knights
Night Club **1**

Zoo Nightclub **1**

Nassau Harbour

Pompey Museum

Woodes Rogers Walk

Prince George Wharf

0   1/8 mile
0   100 meters

Marlborough St.

West St.

Queen St.

George St.

9   10   11   12   13   14

7   8

28

27   Rawson Square

24

Frederick St.

Charlotte St.

Parliament St.

East St.

16   17

15

25   23

22   21

20

26   Parliament Square

29

Bay St.

4

West Hill St.

Duke St.

5   6

East Hill St.

18

Market St.

Cumberland St.

Sands Rd.

19   20

Elizabeth Ave.

Shirley St.

   ✔ **Paradise Beach:** This gem is one of Paradise Island's best beaches. *Chikees* (thatched huts) — which are great when you've had too much sun — dot this white sandy beach. Guests of the Atlantis mainly use this beach becase it lies at the far western tip of the island. If you're not a resident of the Atlantis, getting access to the beach is difficult. If you're staying at a hotel in Nassau and want to come to Paradise Island for a day at the beach, you're better off going to Cabbage Beach (see earlier review in this section).

   ✔ **Saunders Beach:** This beach, located east of Cable Beach, is where many islanders go on the weekends. To reach it, take West Bay Street from Nassau in the direction of Coral Island. This beach lies across from Ft. Charlotte, just west of Arawak Cay. Like Goodman's Bay (see review earlier in this section), it often hosts fun local fund-raising cookouts that are open to the public. This beach doesn't have any public facilities.

   ✔ **Western Esplanade (also called Junkanoo Beach):** If you're staying at a hotel in downtown Nassau, such as the British Colonial, this is a good nearby beach to visit. It's a narrow strip of sand and has a snack bar, changing facilities, and toilets.

Playing in the Surf

Most water action jumps off from **Cable Beach, Paradise Beach,** and **Prince George Dock** in downtown Nassau. For a change of scenery, many folks board tour boats to **Blue Lagoon Island** and **Rose Island,** two popular cays just offshore.

Jet-Skiing, parasailing, banana-boat rides, water-skiing, and windsurfing are available on the beaches in front of Cable Beach and Paradise Island hotels. In many cases, however, independent vendors who aren't affiliated with the hotels run these sports, which means that the resorts aren't responsible for any problems that may arise.

Snorkeling and parasailing

If you want shallow diving and snorkeling without having to go out on a boat, New Providence Island offers dozens of possibilities. Our favorite spot is **Love Beach,** near the Compass Point hotel. Also attracting snorkelers are such scenic areas as **Rose Island Reefs, Booby Rock Channel,** and **Gambier Deep Reef,** plus some underwater wrecks lying in shallow water.

In the western part of the island, the nature reserve at offshore **Gouldings Reef Cay** offers some of the best snorkeling on the island, and it's never crowded. You can see some of the most majestic elkhorn coral in all of The Bahamas. Scenes from *Splash!* and *Cocoon* were shot here.

Excursions by boat take you to the best and most dramatic snorkeling sites — sites that are more impressive than what you can do yourself off the coast. **Barefoot Sailing Cruises** (☎ 242-393-0820) is based at **Bayshore Marina,** on East Bay Street near the Paradise Island bridge. Their 12m (41-ft.) sailboat takes no more than 16 passengers; their 17m (56-ft.) sailboat holds a maximum of 30, and their 20m (65-ft.) catamaran accommodates 65. The size and type of boat that you sail on depends on the number of people booked on any given day. A half-day snorkel sail to **Atholl Island** or **Spruce Cay** runs $49 per person, including beverages and snacks, while the full-day trip costs $69 with lunch.

Another good choice is **Flying Cloud** (☎ 242-393-4430), which is based at the ferry terminal on Paradise Island. This 17m (57-ft.) catamaran takes a maximum of 50 passengers. Snorkeling cruises go to **Rose Island** for a half-day of fun that costs $45 per person; a two-and-half-hour sunset cruise costs $45 per person. Snorkel gear and lessons, if necessary, are included in the price, along with transportation to and from your accommodation.

Parasailing is another exhilarating sport. You're strapped to a parachute that's tied with a long leash to a boat. As the boat takes off, you float gently into the air as if you're flying. Independent operators along Cable Beach and Paradise Island Beach charge about $40 for eight to ten minutes in the sky.

Scuba diving

If you visit any of the Out Islands, you may want to save your under-water scuba time for those less-visited reefs. The waters around New Providence offer excellent dive sites, but too many scuba divers may be admiring all the tropical fish, huge sponges, and varied coral reefs around the dramatic caves, cliffs, ocean holes, ledges, and wrecks.

On New Providence Island, **Southwest Reef** lures scuba divers with its giant coral heads that stand in anywhere from 4 to 8m (12–25 ft.) of water, with staghorn corals and elkhorn along with rainbow-hued fish.

Another great dive site is **Shark Wall,** lying 16km (10 miles) off the coast, along with such sites as **Razorback, Booby Rock Reef,** and **Rose Island Reef.** Dive outfitters can also lead you to the many old **shipwrecks** off the coast, along with caves and cliffs. Wrecks include *Mahoney* and *Alcora*, and the wreck used in the James Bond film, *Never Say Never Again.* Divers also explore the airplane propeller used in another Bond film, *Thunderball.*

Neophytes can take a quickie "resort course," also known as a beginner's class (about $70). Full-certification courses run anywhere from $495 to $695. Plan to pay about $70 for a two-tank dive, $55 to $65 for a night dive, and $100 to $125 for a shark dive. Most operators sell you a videotape of your aqua-action for about $50, and they transport you to and from your hotel.

With more than three decades of experience, **Bahama Divers** (☎ 242-393-5644), at the Nassau Yacht Haven by the bottom of the Paradise Island bridge, is Nassau's oldest and most reliable company.

Even if you're not a scuba diver, you and your kids can still breathe underwater. Try helmet diving with **Hartley's Undersea Walk** (☎ 242-393-8234; www.underseawalk.com) at the **Nassau Yacht Haven** on East Bay Street. During this three-and-a-half-hour excursion (about $75), you take a 30-minute boat ride out to a reef. After donning a lead and glass helmet, you descend a ladder into 4 to 5m (12–15 ft.) of water. Air is pumped into the helmet through a long tube. You can keep your glasses on or your contact lenses in, because your face and hair stay completely dry. Folks have even taken their helmet-clad dogs under. Following the instructions of your guide, you spend about 20 minutes wandering in slow motion around the ocean floor, past crayon-colored sea plants, corals, and fish. To secure your reservation, arrive 30 minutes before your scheduled departure time.

Climbing Aboard

You can experience Bahamian waters and marine life firsthand without getting wet. But remember that these are Atlantic waters, not the tranquil Caribbean Sea, and the waves can be rough at times, causing seasickness for those who aren't used to it. If you're prone to motion sickness, check the sea conditions before you set out.

Sailing

For the best sailing charter to some of the Out Islands, try **Amarok Sailing Charters** (☎ 719-379-4605 or 242-477-4471). The crewed 12m (41-ft.) Amarok ketch carries up to six passengers and specializes in six-day trips to the Exumas, which are about five hours from Nassau. The trip costs around $1,740 per couple. You can read more about the Exumas in Chapter 24.

For a shorter sailing adventure, **Barefoot Sailing Cruises** (☎ 242-393-0820) offers a two-hour champagne sunset cruise ($39, including cold hors d'oeuvres). You sail through Nassau Harbour, under the bridges, into Montagu Bay, by the cruise ships, and maybe along the northern coast of Paradise Island. You can munch cheese and crackers as you sip your bubbly, and you don't need to dress up — many passengers wear shorts. The price includes ground transportation. Depending on the number of vacationers booked, you may cruise on a 12m (41-ft.) sailboat carrying no more than 16 passengers or a 16m (54-ft.) sailboat taking a maximum of 30.

Flying Cloud (☎ 242-393-4430) carries up to 50 passengers on its 17m (57-ft.) catamaran. Depending on the time of year that you go, the two-and-a-half-hour evening cruise takes in the setting sun ($45, including hot and cold hors d'oeuvres). During the three-hour dinner cruise ($45), you can chow down on soup, salad, fish, beef, rice, vegetables, and dessert, served with wine. All rates cover transportation to and from your hotel.

Between Barefoot Sailing Cruises and Flying Cloud, we find cruises aboard Barefoot more adventurous and fun, especially when the passengers are few. For a real sailing experience, book on a sailboat instead of the larger catamaran. If the catamarans are crowded, you may feel like you're riding on a cattle boat, especially with all the eating and drinking. On a sailboat, the atmosphere is more romantic, and the night is yours.

Another option is **Majestic Tours Ltd.** (☎ 242-322-2606), which books three-hour cruises on two of the biggest catamarans in the Atlantic. These tours offer views of the water, sun, sand, and outlying reefs. These cruise boats are affordable and the most professionally run, but we find that too many other passengers are aboard. If you don't mind sailing with a crowd, the *Yellow Bird* is suitable for up to 250 passengers. It departs from Prince George's Dock; ask for the exact departure point when you make your reservation. The cost is $18 per adult, $9 for children under 10, and snorkeling equipment is $10 extra. The outfitter also has another boat, the *Robinson Crusoe,* which holds 350 passengers. On Wednesday, Friday, and Sunday, cruises run from 10 a.m. to 4:30 p.m.; adults cost $45 per person and children 11 and under are half-price. Sunset dinner cruises are on Tuesday and Friday from 7 to 10 p.m.; adults cost $50 per person and children are half-price.

Dolphin diversions and other ocean adventures

Are dolphins really smiling? Why is their skin so warm and smooth? Can they understand each other's chatter? Find out the answers to these questions and many more during a **Dolphin Encounter** on **Blue Lagoon Island** (☎ 242-363-1003 or 242-363-6790). This popular activity is often booked well in advance.

The Close Encounter program ($85) enables you to stand in shallow water and pet the dolphins, and the Swim with the Dolphins program ($165) lets you delve deeper. Both sessions last about three hours, including the boat ride to and from Blue Lagoon, a part of Salt Cay, which is about 5km (3 miles) northeast of Paradise Island.

Several tour operators take visitors to and from Blue Lagoon Island, but you can't book a Dolphin Encounter through all of them.

 Some marine studies show that contrary to popular belief, dolphins don't like being touched by humans. So you can decide whether you want to interact with an animal that may not be enjoying your company all that much.

Enjoying semi-submarine rides

To see coral reefs, you can take a ride in a semi-submarine. Contact **Seaworld Explorer** (☎ 242-356-2548) to board its 45-passenger semi-submersible observatory. The trip begins with a 15-minute catamaran ride and narrated tour along Nassau's coastline. Then you spend about an hour in the "sub." The vessel doesn't actually dive, but it does have windows that are about 3m (10 ft.) below the surface of the ocean, so you get close-up views of fish, coral, and a shipwreck. This 90-minute excursion takes you to **Sea Gardens Marine Park** and costs $37 for adults and $19 for children ages 3 to 12. You can arrange transportation between your hotel and the trip's starting point — Bay Street and Elizabeth Avenue in downtown Nassau — for an additional $3 each way.

Fishing for fun

Bahamian waters are thick with game fish, and some travelers spend every day of their vacations casting lines. The best time to fish for wahoo is from November to February; for blue marlin, June and July; and for bonito and blackfin tuna, May to August. For a half-day charter for two to six anglers, you can spend anywhere from $400 to $600 or, for a full day, $800 and up. If you want to join a group for a half day (usually in the morning), you spend about $70 per person. Two of New Providence's best companies are **Born Free Charters** (☎ 242-363-4144; www.born freefishing.com) and **Nassau Yacht Haven** (☎ 242-393-8173; www.nassauyachthaven.com).

Exploring on Dry Land

Wandering the historic streets of Nassau is an adventure in itself. Seeing the sights from a horse-drawn carriage makes you feel as if you've been transported into the past. From impressive old forts, small museums, and attractive pink and white government buildings to manicured gardens, aquariums, and a zoo, New Providence and Paradise Island can keep you busy.

To get around New Providence, you can rent a car, take taxis, or hop aboard the far cheaper *jitneys* (public buses or vans that run in front of Cable Beach hotels and throughout Nassau). These vans may take a while, but they eventually get you within shouting distance of the attractions in this area. Jitney routes are often roundabout, but you're treated to impromptu tours of neighborhoods that you may otherwise miss.

To get to Paradise Island, you can take a taxi across the bridge from Nassau or you can walk. After you're there, you can take shuttle buses around the island or hoof it.

The following attractions are the best that New Providence offers.

Ardastra Gardens & Zoo
Nassau

The gardens here are a treat for the eyes, but the animals are the real draw. You see creatures great and small, from iguanas, *hutias* (indigenous rodents), and peacocks, to monkeys, lemurs, and various felines. You can even stroke a tame boa constrictor or get your photo snapped with a colorful macaw on your shoulder.

The zoo is known for its marching flamingos' performances, which hit the stage three times a day. The fun begins when the leggy pink birds trot en masse into the arena. Like a drill sergeant, their trainer shouts commands, and the flamingos all stop, abruptly change direction, or stretch out their wings. The trainers summon audience members to join the flock in hilarious poses. After the performance, you can ask the flamingos for their autographs as they gather by the lake with the wild ducks and Australian black swans. Allow about 90 minutes for the show.

See map p. 164. West Bay Street and Chippingham Road, near Ft. Charlotte. www.ardastra.com. *From Cable Beach, take bus #10 that travels along West Bay Street or you can take a brief taxi ride. Admission: $12 for adults, $6 for children. Open: Daily 9 a.m.–4:30 p.m.*

Atlantis Aquarium
Paradise Island

The world's largest tropical aquarium exhibits some 50,000 sharks, stingrays, turtles, and other fish and sea creatures collected from around the planet. Plan to spend about 90 minutes here.

If you want to slide down the waterfall on the "Mayan temple" through a clear tube that cuts through a shark tank, you have to book a room at the Atlantis Resort or one of its sibling properties (the Ocean Club or neighboring Comfort Suites). Only guests of these hotels can ride down the waterslides, swim in the elaborate pools, and enjoy the many other outdoor aquatic attractions.

Both guests and non-guests, however, can walk through the acrylic underwater tube, looking up to see hammerheads that seem to swim past palm trees through the sky above you. In the dim passageways of "The Dig," colorful fish swarm around streets and statues evocative of Atlantis.

Feedings of the giant green moray eels occur twice a day; before you visit, check the times. At the touch tank, children get a kick out of handling the spiky sea urchins, large conch shells, soft starfish, and surprisingly heavy sea cucumbers.

See map p. 164. Royal Towers, Atlantis Resort. ☎ 800-ATLANTIS or 242-363-3000. Admission: $25 for adults, $12.50 for children 12 and under. Tours last one hour and occur daily from 10 a.m. to 6 p.m.

Atlantis Paradise Island Resort & Casino
Paradise Island

Although gambling is the main event here, there's so much to see at the entertainment complex of this mega-resort. Although most casinos keep the outdoors outdoors, the unusual design of this huge casino allows sunshine to stream in through skylights. Designer boutiques, watering holes, restaurants — all on the expensive side — and plenty of gaping vacationers surround the casino.

See map p. 164. Casino Dr., Paradise Island, just across the bridge. ☎ 800-ATLANTIS or 242-363-3000. Admission: Free. Open daily 24 hrs.

Ft. Charlotte
Nassau

If you have the time or desire to see only one fort in New Providence, make it Ft. Charlotte. With a commanding view of the harbor, it was built in 1788 by Lord Dunmore, the royal governor, and named for Queen Charlotte, the wife of King George III. Tour guides tell visitors all about the moat, draw-bridge, cannons, underground passages, and dungeons, but relate no stories of battles because the fort never saw one. You aren't charged for admission, but your guide expects a tip. You can combine a visit here with a trip to nearby **Ardastra Gardens & Zoo** and **Arawak Cay** (where local chefs whip up Bahamian favorites in small, no-frills restaurants).

See map p. 164. West Bay Street and Chippingham Road, about a mile west of downtown Nassau. ☎ 242-325-9186. Admission: Free. Open: Mon–Sat 8 a.m.–4 p.m.

Ft. Fincastle and the Water Tower
Nassau

Like Ft. Charlotte, Nassau's other major fort, Fincastle, never saw a battle, either. It was a lighthouse until 1816 when it was turned into a signal tower, 61m (200 ft.) above the sea. Its 38m (126-ft.) tall Water Tower, which you can reach by taking an elevator to the observation platform, gives you the most panoramic view of New Providence. The fort is named in honor of Lord Dunmore, the royal governor who ordered its construction in 1793. His second title was Viscount Fincastle.

Young men hang out here, insisting that you go on a guided tour, but you can easily see the remains and enjoy the view on your own. These would-be tour guides are hard to shake off, however.

See map p. 164. Bennett's Hill, Elizabeth Avenue, just south of Shirley Street. Admission for Water Tower: $1. Open: Mon–Sat 9 a.m.–4 p.m.

Hairbraider's Centre
Nassau

Whether you want a single beaded plait, cornrows in an intricate design, or many itty-bitty loose braids with colorful rubber bands, this open-air pavilion is the place to go. Depending on what style you want, the cost ranges from $2 to more than $100, and styling can take anywhere from minutes to hours to complete. At one time, hairbraiders roamed the shores of Cable Beach and Paradise Island in search of customers. Although you still may find some of these nimble-fingered women hawking their services on the sand, the government set up the Hairbraider's Centre to cut down on beach vendors. Normally, you can find braiders here Monday through Saturday between 9 a.m. and 3:30 or 4 p.m. A few braiders might show up on a Sunday if they need money and some cruise ships are in port.

Agree on a price and style before your Bahamian beautician touches your tresses. Put plenty of sunblock on your newly exposed scalp to avoid a wicked sunburn.

See map p. 164. Prince George Dock, near Rawson Square, downtown Nassau.

Historic Nassau

Set aside a couple of hours for some good old-fashioned Nassau street-walking. You won't even get arrested. As you wander through the capital, you'll see that the past is well preserved. The best time for an amble is after 10 a.m. and before 4 p.m., Monday through Saturday. Many stores and museums close on Sunday, and on Saturday, the streets are congested because that's when the Changing of the Guard takes place at Government House. Try to find out from the staff at your hotel when the fewest cruise ships are in port, because those passengers really clog the center of town.

A good place to begin your tour is **Rawson Square**, which links **Bay Street**, the main thoroughfare, with **Prince George Wharf**, also known as **Prince George Dock**, where the cruise ships dock. Horse-drawn carriages — each carrying up to three passengers — wait here to give leisurely tours. You can also see a statue of former shopkeeper Sir Milo Butler, the country's first native Bahamian — and first post-independence — governor. On the northern side of the square, the **Ministry of Tourism Information Booth** doles out helpful maps and brochures. Across the way is **Parliament Square**, with its statue of a young Queen Victoria and its pink, white-trimmed Georgian-style government buildings that date back to the late 1700s and early 1800s.

Nassau Public Library and Museum, on Bank Lane, is an octagonal building, which has been here since around 1797, and was once the Nassau Gaol (in other words, the local slammer). Shelves of books line the small prison cells. History buffs can check out the time-worn prints and colonial documents in the little museum. Stamp collectors head for the **Nassau General Post Office** at the end of Parliament Street. You can then walk northeast to the foot of **Queen's Staircase.** These 65 steps lead to **Ft. Fincastle** and the **Water Tower,** both of which offer views of Nassau and the harbor.

To the west, at Duke and George streets, stands the pink-and-white **Government House.** Since 1801, this house has been the official residence of the governor-general, the Queen's representative. A statue of Christopher Columbus stands midway up the front steps. The stately white columns and wide circular driveway make this mansion the perfect setting for the dignified **Changing of the Guard Ceremony** that takes place outside every other Saturday at 10 a.m. The real crowd-pleaser of this event is the **Royal**

Bahamas Police Force Band. The music is at least as colorful as the uniforms: stark-white tunics, navy trousers with bright red stripes, and white pitch helmets with crimson bands.

If you're into antiques, walk north (back toward Bay Street) to the restored **Balcony House,** located at Market Street and Trinity Place. This 18th-century, two-story house with a balcony is Nassau's oldest wooden residential building. Furniture from the early 1800s through the 1940s decorates the rooms, and most visitors rave about the handsome mahogany staircase that was salvaged from a wrecked ship during the 1800s. You can spend a half-hour here. A donation is expected.

Finally, stroll over to the open-air **Straw Market** at Market Street, where vendors sell items such as shell jewelry, clothing made from African and Indonesian fabrics, woodcarvings, sun hats, baskets, place mats, and bags woven from straw. East of the Straw Market is the waterfront **Woodes Rodgers Walk,** which is lined by mail boats, sponge boats, and vendors hawking fruit, vegetables, fish, and conch. Continue your stroll until you reach the imposing cruise ships docked back at Prince George Wharf.

Junkanoo Expo
Nassau

Unless you're vacationing during Christmas or New Year's, you'll miss the beloved **Junkanoo Festival.** This country's answer to Carnival and Mardi Gras begins with a parade in the wee hours of Boxing Day (December 26) and New Year's Day. However, at the Junkanoo Expo, which is housed in an old customs shed, you feel as if you're witnessing the real deal. With a little imagination, you can picture the colorful costumes and whimsical masks on dancers and musicians as they parade down Bay Street. You can also watch the video of last year's bash. Some of the handcrafted costumes on display take months to create.

See map p. 164. At the entrance to Prince George Dock. ☎ *242-356-2731. Admission: $2 for adults, 50¢ for children. Open: Daily 9 a.m.–5:30 p.m.*

National Art Gallery of The Bahamas
Nassau

At long last, this nation has a national gallery to showcase its talented artists. In a restored historic building in the center of Nassau, the gallery displays Bahamian art, past and present. Bahamian art, as an entity, has existed for only 50 years. Museum curators claim that the current collection is only the nucleus of a long-range strategy to beef up the number of works. Most paintings in the exhibit are divided into a historical and a contemporary collection. The collection honors pioneering Bahamian artists, as well as younger and more modern painters. Even though some paintings fall into the realm of primitive or even native art, many of the paintings are quite sophisticated — especially Amos Ferguson's *Snowbirds.* In this painting, Ferguson used house paint on cardboard to create a remarkable portrait.

See map p. 164. Villa Doyle, West Hill Street. ☎ *242-328-5800. Admission: $3 for adults, $2 for seniors and students, $1 for children 14 and under. Tues–Sat 11 a.m.–4 p.m.*

Amos Ferguson: The painting painter

The Bahamas' best known artist, Amos Ferguson, used to be a house painter. Born on Exuma in 1920, he once ran a small farm and helped with his father's carpentry business. When he later moved to Nassau, he took up house painting. Using house paint instead of oil or acrylic, he started creating striking color-rich "naïve" pictures. Many vacationers got to know his early work through a Nassau Straw Market vendor named Bea, who eventually became his wife.

During the 1980s, Ferguson tumbled onto the international art scene. His often whimsical works — still created with house paint — are now owned by collectors around the world. His thought-provoking themes revolve around Biblical and historical images, nature and folklore, and the masks, costumes, and music of the Bahamian Junkanoo festival. You can see his paintings at the permanent exhibition at the **Pompey Museum** on Bay Street in downtown Nassau.

Pirates of Nassau Museum
Nassau

You need half an hour for the self-guided tour through this museum that brings Nassau's buccaneering days to life. During the 18th century, pirates ruled the waves around New Providence as they grew rich from the goods they pillaged from merchant ships. You can go below deck on a replica of a pirate ship, *Revenge*, where you can view the kitchen area, hammocks, cannons, and animals, such as goats, chickens in crates, and, of course, rats. Battles rage through the special effects of sounds and lights, and the dungeon feels damp and creepy. You can hear pirates planning their next attack and smell the sea air. Kids of all ages enjoy the wax figures and the recreated ship and buildings, including the favorite pirate hangout: the tavern. Exhibits tell the story of Woodes Rodgers, who the English crown shipped here to clean up the pirate pandemonium.

See map p. 164. Corner of King and George streets, a block south of the Straw Market. ☎ *242-356-3759. Admission: $12 for adults, $6 for children 3–18, free 2 and under. Open: Mon–Sat 9 a.m.–6 p.m.*

Pompey Museum
Nassau

Plan to spend at least an hour in this intriguing museum in **Vendue House,** named for the man who led a 19th-century revolt against slavery in the Exumas. This limestone building has stood here since around 1769. It was the site of New Providence's slave market until 1834, when the practice of selling people was outlawed throughout the British Empire. While viewing the exhibits on human bondage, the abolition movement, and emancipation, you get a clearer picture of the racial, economic, and political forces that have shaped the present day Bahamas. A 30-minute video presentation focuses on Bahamian history, heritage, and culture. An upstairs exhibition shows the powerful work of Amos Ferguson, the Bahamian "naïve" (meaning simple and one-dimensional; almost childlike) painter that some call "the father of Bahamian art." (See the sidebar "Amos Ferguson: The painting painter" in this chapter.)

Vendue House, Bay Street between George and Market streets. ☎ *242-326-2566. Open: Mon–Wed and Fri–Sat 9:30 a.m.–4:30 p.m; Thurs 9:30 a.m.–1 p.m., Sun 12:30 p.m.–3:30 p.m. Admission: $5 adults, $3 seniors, $2 children ages 13–18, $1 12 and under.*

Potter's Cay
Nassau

In the islands, the local market is an integral part of daily life. Already visited the Straw Market? Fine, but that overcrowded bazaar is for tourists. On the other hand, Potter's Cay, located beneath the original Paradise Island bridge, is for Bahamians. This place is an ideal spot for watching sloops from the Out Islands bring in huge mounds of glistening fish and conch. Seeing restaurant chefs buying fresh seafood straight off the boats isn't unusual.

You can even take notes for your own kitchen while a fisherman prepares conch salad that couldn't be any fresher: He bores a hole into the shell, extracts the unfortunate conch, skins it, dices it, marinates it in lime juice, and seasons it with onions and peppers. In the stalls that line the water's edge, vendors sell this zesty salad along with conch fritters, conch chowder, fresh herbs, and pineapples (many from Eleuthera), bananas, papayas, limes, and other just-plucked fruit.

Vendors here don't appreciate having their photographs taken, especially if you're not purchasing anything. Point a camera in their direction, and they make their objections abundantly clear. As colorful as this site can be, abstain from capturing it on film, unless you have a very long lens or a wide angle lens — or a 007-style camera hidden in your sunglasses.

See map p. #164. Located directly under the bridge that links Nassau and Paradise Island.

Queen's Staircase
Nassau

During the 1790s, enslaved men cut 65 steps out of solid limestone to form a staircase leading from old Nassau to the top of Ft. Fincastle. Later, this 31m (102-ft.) staircase was named in honor of the 65-year reign of Queen Victoria.

At the bottom of the stairs, guides wait to present the history of the staircase. Their recitations are so well memorized that some of them sound like robotic recordings. At the top, you can easily walk to Ft. Fincastle and the Water Tower.

See map p. 164. Across Shirley Street, toward the rise away from the harbor, and near Princess Margaret Hospital in downtown Nassau.

The Retreat
Nassau

You can visit the Botanical Gardens, but the 4 hectares (11 acres) of this National Trust property are better maintained. Two-hundred species of rare and exotic palms from around the world, other unusual trees, and delicate native orchids fill these flourishing grounds.

 The Retreat is the place for birders to see and hear all kinds of feathered friends, such as banana quits, northern mocking birds, black and white warblers, and red-legged tanagers.

You can take a half-hour tour on Tuesday, Wednesday, or Thursday at noon, or visit on your own. The Retreat is about a 20- to 30-minute taxi ride from Cable Beach, depending on traffic. If you don't mind a longer trip, you can also take a public bus from the hotel areas.

See map p. 164. Village Road, across from Queens College, just east of downtown Nassau. ☎ *242-393-1317. Admission: $2 for adults, $1 for children. Open: Mon–Fri 9 a.m.–5 p.m. Tours given Tues–Thurs at noon (price of admission includes the tour).*

Versailles Gardens and Cloister
Paradise Island

Europe is literally transported to The Bahamas in these gardens. This 12th-century cloister was originally built by Augustinian monks in southwestern France and was reassembled here, stone by stone. Huntington Hartford, the A&P grocery heir, purchased the cloister from the estate of William Randolph Hearst at San Simeon in California. Unfortunately, after Hearst bought the cloister, it was hastily dismantled in France for shipment to America, but the parts weren't numbered — and they all arrived unlabeled on Paradise Island. But the reassembly of the complicated monument didn't follow most conventional construction methods. The monument puzzle remained unsolved until artist and sculptor Jean Castre-Manne set about to reassemble it, piece by piece. It took him two years, and what you see today presumably bears some similarity to the original. Tropical flowers and classic statues fill the gardens, which extend over the rise to Nassau Harbour. Although the monument remains a timeless beauty, recent buildings have encroached on either side, marring Huntington Hartford's original vision.

See map p. 164. Adjacent to the Ocean Club Resort, Paradise Island. Admission: Free.

Walking tours
Nassau

Goombay Guided Walking Tours, arranged by the Ministry of Tourism, leave from the Tourist Information Booth on Rawson Square daily from 9 a.m. to 3 p.m. Tours last for one hour and include descriptions of some of the city's most venerable buildings, with commentaries on Nassau's history, customs, and traditions. The tours require advance reservations because schedules may vary. The cost is $10 for adults and $5 for children under 12. Call ☎ 242-323-3102 to confirm that tours are on schedule.

Tourist Information Booth on Rawson Square in Nassau. ☎ *242-323-3102. Admission: $10 for adults, $5 for children under 12. Tours: Open: Daily 9 a.m.–3 p.m. Tour schedule varies; advance reservations required.*

Keeping Active

Most of the sports action in and around New Providence is linked to the Atlantic. But when you're ready to dry off, you have plenty of choices.

Biking

A half-day bicycle tour with **Bahamas Outdoors Ltd.** (☎ 242-362-1574; about $59) can take you on a 5km (3-mile) bike ride along some scenic forest and shoreline trails in the Coral Harbour area on the southwestern coast of New Providence. You pass along a trail that has mangrove creeks and pine forests as a scenic backdrop and can take time off for a kayak trip to a shallow for snorkeling.

Some of the major hotels on Paradise Beach and Cable Beach rent bikes to their guests. You can bike along Cable Beach or the beachfront at Paradise Island, but Nassau traffic is too congested.

Golfing

New Providence courses frequently host international tournaments. At the 18-hole **Radisson Cable Beach Golf Course** (☎ 242-327-6000), The Bahamas' oldest course, greens fees run $140 with carts included. This course is the most convenient for many vacationers because it's just across the road from the main Cable Beach hotels. Although the **South Ocean Golf Club** (☎ 242-362-4391) is a half-hour drive from Nassau, this 18-hole course is the best course on New Providence and one of the best in the country. The rolling terrain of this challenging course overlooks the ocean. Here, greens fees run $100, including the cart. **Ocean Club Golf Club** on Paradise Island Drive (☎ 242-363-6682) at the east end of the island is an 18-hole championship golf course designed by Tom Weiskopf. This course overlooks both the Atlantic Ocean and Nassau Harbour. Attracting every caliber of golfer, the par-72 course is famous for its Hole 17, which plays entirely along the scenic Snorkelers Cove. Greens fees, including cart, are $245 per player, and rental clubs and shoes are available.

Gyms and spas

Many of the large hotels have exercise rooms for guests to use. Some also offer spa facilities, including **Sandals Royal Bahamian** and the **Crystal Palace Casino** complex, both on Cable Beach, and **Atlantis Paradise Island Resort & Casino** and **Ocean Club Golf & Tennis Resort,** both on Paradise Island. If your hotel doesn't have a gym or spa, or if you need more extensive equipment or pampering to keep up your routine, check out **Gold's Gym** (☎ 242-393-4653; daily equipment rates begin at $8), located at the foot of the Paradise Island bridge in Nassau. Or try **Windermere Spa & Salon** (☎ 242-393-0033) at the Harbour Bay Shopping Centre on East Bay Street in Nassau.

Horseback rides

Small groups of riders spend 90 minutes riding along wooded and beach-side trails through **Happy Trails Stables** (☎ 242-362-1820). The $95 price tag includes transportation between your hotel and the stables. The stables are in the Coral Harbour area in southwestern New Providence, about 20 minutes from Cable Beach and 45 minutes from Paradise Island. You have to make reservations to go on one of these guided rides, which go out twice a day.

Tennis

Among the hotels with tennis courts — some lit for night play — are the **Radisson, Sandals,** and **Nassau Beach Hotel** on Cable Beach, and the **Atlantis** and **Ocean Club** on Paradise Island. Some hotels allow in-house guests to play for free, but other hotels charge a small hourly fee. If your hotel doesn't have courts, you can arrange to play elsewhere, usually for $10 to $15 an hour, plus about $6 for racquet rental.

Shopping the Local Stores

You can find a variety of bargains in Nassau, including Swiss watches, Japanese cameras, French perfumes, Irish crystal and linens, and British china.

You don't have to pay import duties on 11 categories of luxury goods, including china, crystal, fine linens, jewelry, leather goods, photography equipment, watches, fragrances, and other merchandise. Antiques, of course, are exempt from import duty worldwide. But even though prices are duty-free, you can still end up spending more on an item in The Bahamas than you would back in your hometown. It's a tricky situation.

 If you're contemplating a major purchase, such as a good Swiss watch or some expensive perfume, do some research in your hometown discount outlets before making a serious purchase in The Bahamas. Although the alleged 30 to 50 percent discount off stateside prices may apply on some purchases, that's not true in most cases. We discovered that certain cameras and electronic equipment are listed in The Bahamas at, say, 20 percent or more below the manufacturer's "suggested retail price." That sounds good, except the manufacturer's "suggested retail price" may be a lot higher than what you'd pay in your hometown. You aren't getting the discount you think you are. Some shoppers even take along department-store catalogs from the States to determine whether the items they're considering are indeed a bargain.

Mostly European, American, and Asian imports fill vacationers' shopping bags. Bahamian-made goods are much scarcer. Even at Nassau's **Straw Market,** between Bay Street and Woodes Rodgers Walk, you may be surprised at the number of items made in China, Indonesia, and Kenya. But at this open-air market, you also find plenty of locally produced straw goods, along with Bahamian sauces and seasonings, perfumes, woodcarvings, shell jewelry, dolls, and art.

Be prepared for persistent vendors. Someone may slip a necklace around your neck in an attempt to convince you that you can't live without it. In addition to the large Bay Street Straw Market, you find similar setups across from the Radisson and Wyndham hotels on Cable Beach.

 Pay the first price you're quoted, and the vendor will look at you as if you have three eyes. Bargaining is a way of life here. Don't be afraid to turn your back on something you really want. Chances are, the previously stubborn vendor will call after you with a suddenly reduced price that's "only for you."

Although bargaining is *expected* at straw and produce markets, it isn't welcome at all in most stores. At glitzy boutiques, such as the ones at Atlantis Paradise Island Resort & Casino, salespeople give you a price and stand firm.

Antiques

Marlborough Antiques (corner of Queen and Marlborough streets; ☎ 242-328-0502) carries the type of antiques you'd expect to find in a shop in London: antique books, antique maps and engravings, English silver (both sterling and plate), and unusual table settings (fish knives and so on). Among the store's most appealing objects is its collection of antique photographs of the islands. Works by Bahamian artists Brent Malone and Maxwell Taylor are also on display.

Art

Although many locals come to **Kennedy Gallery** (on Parliament Street; ☎ 242-325-7662) for custom framing, the gallery also sells original artwork by well-known Bahamian artists, including limited-edition prints, handicrafts, pottery, and sculpture.

Brass and copper

With two branches on Charlotte Street, the **Brass and Leather Shop** located at 12 Charlotte St., between Bay and Shirley streets, ☎ 242-322-3806) offers English brass, handbags, luggage, briefcases, attachés, and personal accessories. Shop number two, located at Marathon Mall on Marathon Road, sells handbags, belts, scarves, ties, and small leather goods from such famous designers as Furla, Bottega Veneta, Pierre Balmain, and others. If you look and select carefully, you can find some good buys here.

Cigars

Many cigar aficionados come to the **Tropique International Smoke Shop** (in Wyndham Nassau Resort & Crystal Palace Casino, West Bay Street; ☎ 242-327-7292) to indulge their passion for Cubans, which are hand-picked and imported by Bahamian merchants. The staff at this outlet trained in Havana, so they know their cigars.

 Remember, the United States prohibits the importation of Cuban cigars because of the trade embargo. If you buy them, you're supposed to enjoy them in The Bahamas.

Coins and stamps

At the **Bahamas Post Office Philatelic Bureau** (in the General Post Office at the top of Parliament Street on East Hill Street; ☎ 242-322-1112), you'll find beautiful Bahamian stamps slated to become collector's items. One of the most sought-after stamps has a seashell motif.

Coin of the Realm (Charlotte Street, just off Bay Street; ☎ 242-322-4497) is a family-run shop located in a lovely building hewn out of solid lime-stone over 200 years ago. The shop offers not only fine jewelry, but also mint and used Bahamian and British postage stamps and rare (and not-so-rare) Bahamian silver and gold coins. It also sells old and modern Bahamian paper currency.

Fashion

One of Nassau's more formal and elegant clothing stores, **Barry's Limited** (Bay and George streets; ☎ 242-322-3118) sells garments made from lamb's wool and English cashmere. Elegant sportswear (including Korean-made guayabera shirts) and suits are sold here. Most of the clothes are for men, but women often stop in for a look at the fancy handmade Irish linen handkerchiefs and the stylish cuff links, studs, and other accessories. The name **Bonneville Bones** (Bay Street; ☎ 242-328-0804) hardly describes what's inside this store. This men's store is the best we've found in Nassau. You can find everything from standard T-shirts and designer jeans to suits here. **Cole's of Nassau** (Parliament Street; ☎ 242-322-8393) offers the most extensive selection of designer fashions in Nassau. Women can buy everything from swimwear and formal gowns to sportswear and hosiery. Cole's also sells gift items, sterling-silver designer and costume jewelry, hats, shoes, bags, scarves, and belts.

Fendi (Charlotte Street at Bay Street; ☎ 242-322-6300) is Nassau's only outlet for the well-crafted, Italian-inspired accessories endorsed by this famous leather-goods company. With handbags, luggage, shoes, watches, cologne, wallets, and portfolios to choose from, the selection may well solve some of your gift-giving quandaries.

Mademoiselle, Ltd (Bay Street at Frederick Street; ☎ 242-322-5130) specializes in the kinds of resort wear that look appropriate at either a tennis club or a cocktail party. It features locally made batik garments by Androsia. Swimwear, sarongs, jeans, and halter tops are the rage here, as are the wonderfully scented soaps and lotions. The store's on-site Body Shop boutique supplies all the paraphernalia you need for herbal massages and beauty treatments.

Handicrafts

Sea Grape Boutique (West Bay Road, next to Travelers Rest; ☎ 242-327-1308) is the finest gift shop on New Providence, with a fascinating inventory of exotic decorative items. It includes jewelry crafted from fossilized coral, sometimes with sharks' teeth embedded inside, beadwork from Guatemala, Haitian paintings, silver from India, hairbrushes shaped like parrots, and clothing that's well-suited to the sometimes steamy climate of The Bahamas. A second branch of this outfit, **Sea Grape, Too,** is located in the Radisson Hotel's Mall, on Cable Beach (☎ 242-327-5113).

Jewelry

The jewelry department at **John Bull** (corner of Bay and Charlotte streets; ☎ 242-322-4253) offers classic selections from Tiffany & Co.; cultured pearls from Mikimoto; the creations of David Yurman, Stephen Lagos, Carrera y Carrera, and Sea Life by Kanbana; Greek and Roman coin jewelry; and Spanish gold and silver pieces. John Bull is the best name in the business. The store also features a wide selection of watches, cameras, perfumes (including Estée Lauder, Chanel, and Calvin Klein at discount prices — though you should check carefully to make sure that you're getting a bargain), cosmetics, leather goods, and accessories. This store is one of the best places in The Bahamas to buy a Gucci or Cartier watch. The outlet has been the authorized agent for Rolex in The Bahamas for 30 years, and the store itself has been doing business since 1929.

Leather

In addition to the stores mentioned in this section, another good store for leather goods is the **Brass and Leather Shop,** which we describe in the "Brass & Copper" section.

Gucci (Saffrey Square on Bay Street; ☎ 242-325-0561), is the best place to buy leather goods in Nassau. The wide selection includes handbags, wallets, luggage, briefcases, gift items, scarves, ties, casual clothes, evening wear for men and women, umbrellas, shoes, sandals, watches, and perfume, all by Gucci of Italy.

The well-known retail outlet **Leather Masters** (Parliament Street; ☎ 242-322-7597) carries an internationally known collection of leather bags, luggage, and accessories by Ted Lapidus, Lanvin, and Lancel of Paris; Etienne Aigner of Germany; and i Santi of Italy. Leather Masters also carries luggage by Piel and Marroquinera of Colombia; leather wallets by Bosca; and pens, cigarette lighters, and watches by Colibri. The store also sells silk scarves, neckties, and cigar accessories.

Linens

The Linen Shop (Ironmongery Building on Bay Street, near Charlotte Street; ☎ 242-322-4266) is the best outlet for linens in Nassau. It sells beautifully embroidered bed linens, Irish handkerchiefs, hand-embroidered women's blouses, and tablecloths. Look also for the most exquisite children's clothing and christening gowns in town.

Maps

Balmain Antiques (second floor of Mason's Building on Bay Street, near Charlotte Street; ☎ 242-323-7421) offers a wide and varied assortment of 19th-century etchings, engravings, and maps, many of them antique and all reasonably priced. Other outlets have minor displays of these collectibles, but this outlet has the finest. Some items are 400 years old. Discussing your interests with Mr. Ramsey, the owner, is usually best so that he can direct you to the proper drawers. His specialties include The Bahamas, America during the Civil War, and black history. He also has a collection of historical military items.

Markets

The **Nassau International Bazaar** (from Bay Street down to the water-front, near Prince George Wharf) consists of some 30 shops selling international goods in a new arcade. A pleasant place for browsing, the $1.8 million complex sells goods from around the globe. With cobbled alleyways and garretted storefronts, the area looks like a European village.

Prince George Plaza (Bay Street) is popular with cruise-ship passengers. Many fine shops, such as Gucci, are located here. When you get tired of shopping, you can eat at the one of the several nearby restaurants and cafes.

The **Straw Market** (Straw Market Plaza on Market Street) seems to be on every shopper's itinerary. Even those who don't buy anything come here to look around. Bahamian craftspeople weave and pleat straw hats, handbags, dolls, placemats, and other items, including straw shopping bags to hold your purchases. You can buy items ready-made (often from Taiwan) or order special articles, sometimes bearing your initials. You can also have fun bargaining for the lowest price. The Straw Market is open daily from 7 a.m. to 7 p.m.

Music

One of the finest record stores in the Bahamas, **Jam Productions** (Shirley Street in the Island Plaza; ☎ 242-364-0604) specializes in rare and hard-to-find music from the Caribbean and abroad.

Perfumes and cosmetics

Nassau has several good perfume outlets that also stock a lot of nonperfume merchandise.

- **The Beauty Spot:** The largest cosmetic shop in The Bahamas, this outlet sells duty-free cosmetics by Lancôme, Chanel, Yves Saint Laurent, Elizabeth Arden, Estée Lauder, Clinique, Prescriptives, and Biotherm, among others. It also operates facial salons. Bay and Frederick streets; ☎ 242-322-5930.

- **Bonneville Bones:** This store carries a wide selection of duty-free fragrances and cosmetics. It's known for the quality of its goods and service. Bay and George streets; ☎ 242-322-2095.

- **The Perfume Bar:** This little gem has exclusive rights to market Boucheron and Sublime in The Bahamas. It also stocks the Clarins line (but not exclusively). Bay Street; ☎ 242-322-3785.

- **The Perfume Shop:** In the heart of Nassau, within walking distance of the cruise ships, the Perfume Shop offers duty-free savings on world-famous perfumes. Treat yourself to a flacon of Eternity, Giorgio, Poison, Lalique, Shalimar, or Chanel. Those are just a few of the scents for women. For men, the selection includes Drakkar Noir, Polo, and Obsession. Corner of Bay and Frederick streets; ☎ 242-322-2375.

Steel drums

If you fall under the Junkanoo spell and want to take home some steel drums, visit **Pyfroms** (Bay Street; ☎ 242-322-2603). The drums will always be useful if island fever overtakes you after you return home.

Living It Up After Dark

Nassau, Cable Beach, and Paradise Island were designed for party time. After dark, the bars at the larger hotels and at plenty of restaurants are packed. Vacationers and residents bump hips on the crowded dance floors of local nightclubs. For many visitors, the casinos are the focal point of nightlife — and for some, day life as well.

The newer of New Providence's dynamic duo, the casino complex at **Atlantis Paradise Island Resort** (☎ 242-363-3000) is the largest in The Bahamas and the Caribbean. Craps tables, baccarat, blackjack, roulette, Caribbean stud poker, and more than 1,000 slot machines give you plenty of excuses to try your luck. Tables are open only from 10 a.m. to 4 a.m. daily, but the one-arm bandits are ready around the clock. Also on-site and drawing a party crowd is **Dragons Night Club,** open from 9 p.m. to 1 a.m.

The **Crystal Palace Casino** (☎ 242-327-6200) lies between the Wyndham Nassau and Radisson resorts on Cable Beach. Tables are open from 10 a.m.

to 4 a.m. during the week, and 24 hours a day on weekends. Slot machines, of course, are willing to eat your coins anytime, day or night.

If you want to see a performance that evokes the spirit of the islands, make a reservation for the **King & Knights Night Club** (☎ 242-327-5321) at the Nassau Beach Hotel showroom on Cable Beach. Performances here revolve around limbo, steel drums, fire dancing, and Bahamian Goombay and Junkanoo music and costumes. Of course, expect this place to be filled with visitors, not locals. The damage is about $25 (including one drink). If you like, you can arrive early to have dinner as well; main courses range from $10 to $30.

If you're craving a real slice of local life, find out what's happening at the **Dundas Center for the Performing Arts** (on Mackey Street in Nassau; ☎ 242-393-3728). These plays and musicals, put on by local or foreign performers, give you a taste of Nassau's artsy scene.

Conveniently located on West Bay Street, across from Saunders Beach and between Cable Beach and downtown Nassau, the **Zoo Nightclub** (☎ 242-322-7195) is the hottest dance club in town. The $10 to $25 cover charge gets you access to five different bars, including a sports bar, a cafe, and three levels of dance floors. The doors open around 8:30 to 9 p.m., but most patrons — an equal mix of locals and visitors — don't start showing up until between 10:30 and 11:30 p.m. The house rocks until 3 a.m.

Often featuring live bands, **Club Waterloo** (☎ 242-393-7324) on East Bay Street, just east of the Paradise Island exit bridge, is another popular dance spot with a choice of bars. The owner doesn't like reggae, so instead you hear rock 'n' roll, calypso, R&B, and club music. This place draws an eclectic blend of locals, Europeans, and American vacationers, both singles and couples. The place is open from 8 p.m. to 4 a.m., but the crowd is sparse before 10 or 11 p.m. If all that dancing makes you hungry, don't despair: Club Waterloo serves snack-type food.

The official cover charge can climb as high as a whopping $30 at Waterloo, but many people know better: Buy a $5 pass from your cab driver, and then pay an additional $5 at the door.

Going Beyond Nassau

Tour operators take vacationers to the two most popular offshore cays, activity-packed **Blue Lagoon Island** and the more tranquil **Rose Island.** You decide whether you want to be in a small, personalized group or part of a huge crowd that descends on one of these peaceful islands.

Trip #1: Rose Island respite

One of the most serene sails to the tranquil Rose Island beach, located 13km (8 miles) east of downtown Nassau, is with **Barefoot Sailing Cruises** (☎ 242-393-0820). Based at Bayshore Marina, on East Bay Street near the Paradise Island Bridge, this company uses three different boats: two sailboats and a catamaran that carries between 16 and 65 passengers. The vessel you end up on depends on the number of people booked. For the full-day trip, the $69 charge covers lunch, snacks, drinks, snorkeling gear, and transportation to and from your hotel.

As you sail past small, scenic cays off the coast of New Providence, you realize that half the fun is getting to Rose Island. The sail is a six-hour event, so you have time for sunning, swimming, and snorkeling in water no deeper than 3.6m (12 ft.). The day begins with coffee and doughnuts and ends with fruit and cookies, with a barbecue lunch sandwiched in between. Rum punch and soft drinks flow freely.

Trip #2: Blue Lagoon action

About 5km (3 miles) northeast of Paradise Island, **Blue Lagoon Island,** also known as **Salt Cay,** snags vacationers with its seven beaches, seaside hammocks, live bands, army of water toys (from snorkeling gear to aqua-bikes and kayaks), children's play area, and dolphin and stingray encounter programs.

Taking a trip here is enjoyable, but parts of the island get crowded at times because cruise ships and several tour operators ferry passengers over for day trips. Most visitors plop right down at the first beach they see. To find the quietest corners, walk as far as you can after disembarking.

Nassau Cruises Ltd. (☎ 242-363-1000), based between the bridges on Paradise Island, offers a variety of ways to sample Blue Lagoon Island. Packages begin at $25 per adult and $15 per child, covering only transportation to and from the island. For $65 per adult and $35 per child, you also get lunch, two drinks (fruit or rum punch), and use of all non-motorized watersports equipment. Add a snorkeling excursion to **Stingray City Marine Park,** and you pay $85 per adult and $50 per child. Because the cruise line offers several departure and return times, you can come and go to Blue Lagoon Island when you want. For details about the Dolphin Encounter Program (run by another outfit), see "Dolphin diversions and other ocean adventures" earlier in this chapter.

Part IV
Grand Bahama

In this part . . .

*I*f Grand Bahama — a low-key yet high-impact island — appeals to you, this part introduces you to the best ways you can make the most of your stay. You can use the advice about arriving and exploring the island to help familiarize yourself with the lay of the land.

We help you find accommodations that fit your style and your budget. Whether you want a meal at the water's edge or in a British-style pub, we give you Grand Bahama's best bets. We also offer plenty of suggestions on how to spend your days and nights, from savoring a beachside nature preserve to rolling the dice.

Chapter 14

Settling into Grand Bahama

●●

In This Chapter

▶ Knowing what to expect when you get to Grand Bahama
▶ Getting around Grand Bahama
▶ Discovering Grand Bahama from A to Z

●●

*G*rand Bahama was the dream of Virginian financier Wallace Groves, who envisioned it as a miniature Miami Beach. Today, with its high-rise hotels, golf courses, marinas, international bazaars for shopping, a bevy of Continental restaurants, and golden sand beaches, that dream has been realized. Grand Bahama is the second-most popular tourist destination in The Bahamas, rivaled only by Nassau and Paradise Island. It's the northernmost and the fourth-largest landmass in The Bahamas, stretching for 188km (73 miles).

Both **Freeport** and **Lucaya** lack the upscale chicness of Paradise Island or even Nassau, but they do have fabulous beaches. The afford-able hotels and restaurants make Freeport and Lucaya the preferred destinations for middle-class families (as opposed to the high rollers who are attracted to Cable Beach and Paradise Island). Lucaya was developed about a decade later than Freeport, but today the tourist facilities of the two major resort areas have more or less merged into an indistinguishable whole.

But Grand Bahama is so big that many areas remain unspoiled. You can find these natural gems in either the **West End** or the **East End,** which host very few resorts or restaurants. You can also get close to nature at the Rand Memorial Nature Centre and the Garden of the Groves. And the Lucayan National Park, with its underwater caves, forest trails, and a secluded beach, is another major attraction for adventurous travelers.

Arriving at the Airport

Although some people arrive in cruise ships, most visitors swoop down on Grand Bahama in planes. Getting through **Freeport International Airport** (☎ 242-352-2052) is generally quite easy. Upon your arrival, you're launched into your vacation with the sound of live calypso or reggae music.

Navigating your way through passport control and Customs

With your passport (or birth certificate and photo ID), return airline ticket, and a completed Immigration Arrival/Departure Card, get in the shortest visitors' line. Hold on to your copy of the immigration card because you need to present it before leaving The Bahamas.

The well-marked airport is easy to navigate. You collect your baggage and declare that you haven't brought in any contraband. Customs officials may or may not open your luggage to confirm your claim. You can then pick up maps and helpful brochures at the tourist information desk, get some extra cash in U.S. dollars from an ATM, and head for the exit.

Getting from the airport to your hotel

Metered taxis greet each flight, ready to whisk vacationers off to hotels. (The cab-driver lobby is powerful enough to ban buses at the airport, so you'll have to rely on a taxi.) The cost is about $10 to Freeport and $15 to Lucaya, plus a 15 percent tip. Downtown Freeport is only a five-minute ride from the airport; Lucaya, the beach resort area, is a ten-minute ride.

If your vacation package includes hotel transfers, present your voucher to the driver of a van that's clearly marked to go to your hotel. If you want to explore Grand Bahama at your own pace, you can pick up a rental car at the airport (see "Getting Around Grand Bahama" later in this chapter).

Cruising into Grand Bahama

Freeport is a popular port of call for major cruise ships. If you opt for one of these floating resorts, expect limited time ashore.

On Grand Bahama Island, your cruise ship will dock at a dull industrial-looking wasteland on the western part of the island, far removed from the center of all the action at Freeport or Lucaya. For shopping, sightseeing, the best beaches, or gambling, you must take a $10 taxi ride over to the resort areas. Taxis await all arriving cruise ships.

Island hopping

If you want to visit some other islands while on Grand Bahama, you can do so aboard a small commuter-type airline, **Major's Airlines,** which flies out of Freeport International Airport (☎ 242-352-5778). This airline offers regular flights to Bimini for $130 round-trip; to Abaco for $150 round-trip; to Andros for $180 round-trip; and to Eleuthera for $200 round-trip. Most of its carriers transport 9 to 15 passengers. Flights aren't available every day, so call for schedules, reservations, and other information.

Choosing Your Location

Until 2003, guests to Grand Bahama Island had to make a decision: Is gambling more important than beaching it? However, with the opening of the casino at **The Westin and Sheraton at Our Lucaya,** you can now stay in Lucaya and beach it during the day, and then gamble the night away at an on-site casino without having to journey to Freeport.

Therefore, Lucaya has become more popular than Freeport, because Freeport is a 15-minute bus ride from the beach. Lucaya has hardly put Freeport out of business, though, because thousands of visitors still prefer staying in Freeport to take advantage of the incredible facilities at the **Crowne Plaza Golf Resort & Casino** and to shop at the nearby **International Bazaar.** Also, Freeport's hotels usually are less expensive than the ones at Lucaya.

But the International Bazaar is looking a little tired these days, and the **Port Lucaya Marketplace** is giving it a run for its money. Many of the major stores at the International Bazaar also opened branches at the Port Lucaya Marketplace, charging the same prices for the same kinds of merchandise.

Although both Freeport and Lucaya have plenty of good places to leave your money, we prefer leaving our money at Port Lucaya because of its gingerbread-trimmed, wooden buildings and the live music heard most evenings in **Count Basie Square.**

Even if you stay in Freeport, you can still sample Lucaya's attractions — buses, minivans, and taxis connect these resort areas. Neither area is far from Grand Bahama's golf courses, horse stables, and natural attractions, such as **Garden of the Groves, Rand Memorial Nature Center,** and **Lucayan National Park.** Check out Chapter 3 for more background info on — and a map of — this location.

Getting Around Grand Bahama

Whether you board a bus, catch a taxi, mount a motor scooter, pedal a bike, or walk, getting to the most interesting parts of this island is relatively easy. For the most flexibility, you can rent a car, although you don't need one to get around.

Exploring by foot

Nearly devoid of hills, Grand Bahama Island is good for long strolls because outside Freeport and Lucaya, it's largely undeveloped. Flourishing botanical gardens and nature reserves, such as **Lucayan National Park** and **Bahamas National Trust Rand Nature Centre,** are prime locales for hoofing it. For guided nature hikes, contact **Kayak Nature Tours (☎ 242-373-2485).** If human-made wonders are more to your liking, the International Bazaar and its surroundings in Freeport and the Port Lucaya Marketplace and its Lucaya seaside neighborhood are best for a shopper's stroll.

Taking a bus

Grand Bahama's public bus service, run by privately licensed minivans, makes getting around Freeport and Lucaya almost hassle-free. You typically wait five to seven minutes at any given stop. Sometimes vans sit longer because drivers often don't leave until they have a minimum number of passengers. The fare is $1 for adults and 50¢ for children, and drivers request exact change, either in U.S. or Bahamian money. When you board, tell the driver your destination.

Taking a taxi

The majority of taxis are limousines. The government sets fares and requires cabs to have working meters, but many drivers don't turn them on for routine trips; instead, they quote you a flat fare. If you're not sure what the approximate cost of a taxi ride should be, ask someone at your hotel desk before you leave. One or two passengers pay $3 for the first kilometer (⅗ mile) and 40¢ for each additional half-kilometer (¼ mile). Each additional passenger over the age of 3 costs a flat fee of $2, and for each piece of luggage beyond two, the driver collects 50¢. Taxis wait outside hotels, restaurants, and attractions and cruise the streets where you can flag them down. Two reliable companies to call are **Freeport Taxi (☎ 242-352-6666)** and **G.B. Taxi Union (☎ 242-352-7101).**

Driving around

Unlike Nassau, driving on Grand Bahama, with its long, broad roads, is easy. A car comes in handy if you'd rather not rely on taxis and minivans. Much of the island is undeveloped, so heavy traffic isn't a problem, and you can easily find places to park. Like the British, islanders drive on the left.

You can find car-rental companies around Freeport International Airport. Cars begin at $50 a day, jeeps at $70, and vans at $120. Availability varies, so if you haven't made a reservation before you arrive, you may have to call around until you find the size or type of car that you want. The major companies are **Avis** (☎ 242-352-7666), **Dollar** (☎ 242-352-9325), and **Hertz** (☎ 242-352-9250).

Other fun ways to get around

Mopeds and **minibikes** may seem like an ideal way to get around Grand Bahama. But if you're used to driving on the right side of the road, a miscalculation while riding a moped on the left here can end up being painful. If you're willing to risk it, plan on spending about $15 for the first hour, plus $5 for each additional hour, or $40 to $55 a day. You need to have a valid driver's license and leave your credit card or $100 cash as a deposit. Wearing helmets — provided with each rental — is mandatory. You can make arrangements to rent through your hotel or at one of the scooter rental shops you see near gas stations and other spots along the road. If you arrive on Grand Bahama by cruise ship, you can rent motor scooters at Freeport Harbour.

Another option you have is **bicycling.** Pancake-flat Grand Bahama seems designed for bicycling. As you're whizzing by (riding on the left side of the road), the breeze can mask the sun's power, so be sure to slather on plenty of sunblock. Wearing a brimmed hat is also a good idea. Some hotels offer complimentary bikes, while other accommodations, along with roadside bike-rental outfits, let you rent one for $15 to $20 a day. See Chapter 17 for more on biking and other activities in Grand Bahama.

Fast Facts

American Express

The Scotiabank ATM accepts American Express cards. For any other services, however, contact the office on New Providence, because no Amex representative is on Grand Bahama.

ATMs

The international ATMs at Bank of Nova Scotia branches dispense both Bahamian and U.S. currency. This bank also operates two ATMs that dispense only U.S. dollars at Crowne Plaza Resort & Casino in Freeport. For 24-hour access to your funds, head to the ATMs at the Royal Bank of Canada, located at East Mall

Drive and Explorers Way or Boulevard Service Station on Sunrise Highway; these machines offer only Bahamian currency. Bank of Nova Scotia and Royal Bank of Canada ATMs accept MasterCard, Visa, and any credit or bank card linked to the Plus or Cirrus network. The Scotiabank ATM also accepts cards on the Novus network, along with American Express.

Baby-sitting

Hotel staff can help you make arrangements to hire an experienced sitter.

Doctors

See "Hospitals."

Emergencies

Ambulance: ☎ 242-352-2689.

Bahamas Air Sea Rescue Association (BASRA): ☎ 242-352-9246.

Fire Brigade: ☎ 242-352-8888.

National Park Service: ☎ 242-352-5438.

Police: ☎ 919.

Hospitals

Government-run Rand Memorial Hospital (☎ 242-352-6735) is on East Atlantic Drive. For information about a clinic close to your hotel, call the hospital or ask the staff at your accommodation. Before you leave home, check your health insurance to see whether you're covered while traveling abroad. If you're not, you may want to purchase a traveler's insurance plan with emergency medical expense coverage (see Chapter 9 for details).

Information

Contact the Grand Bahama Island Tourism Board (☎ 242-352-8044 or 242-352-6909). You can find tourist information desks at the airport, the International Bazaar, Port Lucaya Marketplace, and the larger hotels.

Internet Access

Visit the Cyberclub at Seventeen Center, (☎ 242-351-4560; cyberclub@grand bahama.net). It's open Monday through Saturday from 9 a.m. to 8 p.m.

Newspapers and Magazines

To keep abreast of island happenings, including fund-raising beach cookouts, plays, and other events, check out *Freeport News,* the local daily. You can also get *The Tribune* and *The Nassau Guardian,* both published in Nassau, here. *What-to-Do* and *Island Scene* are free magazines geared toward vacationers; they're full of dining and shopping tips, as well as information about Grand Bahama

attractions. You can find them at hotels, shops, and tourist offices.

Pharmacies

Try the Sunrise Medical Center (☎ 242-373-3333) on Sunrise Highway in Freeport or Lucayan Medical East (☎ 242-373-7400) on East Sunrise Highway in Lucaya.

Police

In an emergency, call ☎ 919.

Post Office

Located in downtown Freeport on Explorer's Way (☎ 242-352-9371), the post office is open Monday through Friday from 9 a.m. to 5:30 p.m.

Restrooms

Public toilets are available at the airport, the International Bazaar, as well as the Port Lucaya Marketplace. Except for Xanadu Beach at Lucaya, don't expect any of the other more remote beaches on island to have public toilets.

Safety

Freeport and Lucaya are usually safe, as long as you take the same precautions you would anywhere else in the world: Don't venture into deserted areas alone, especially at night, and be discreet with your money, jewelry, and other valuables. Traveling by the island's privately run minivans is safe.

Taxis

Although all taxis have meters, many drivers don't use them. Rates for two passengers are $3 for the first kilometer (¾ mile), plus 40¢ for each additional half-kilometer (¼ mile); additional passengers over age 3 cost a flat fee of $2. If you have more than two pieces of luggage, each additional piece costs 50¢. Taxis are easy to come by, but if you'd like to call one, try Freeport Taxi (☎ 242-352-6666) or G.B. Taxi Union (☎ 242-352-7101).

Chapter 15

Staying in Style in Grand Bahama

• •

In This Chapter

▶ Deciding where to stay
▶ Evaluating the top choices

• •

*I*n this chapter, we describe the accommodations that appeal to most first-time visitors. We considered locations, amenities, quality of service, architecture, and proximity to Grand Bahama's best attractions.

Surveying the Scene

Here you have a choice of more than 4,000 bedrooms or suites, ranging from simple double bedrooms common to most American roadside motels to one- or two-bedroom condo units of time-shares, some of which may be someone else's vacation home when she is off island.

Of course, you have your choice of sprawling resorts, just as you do on Paradise Island (prices, however, are cheaper on Grand Bahama). Many of these resorts offer various meal plans. The cost is usually less expensive if you book in on half-board terms (that is, breakfast and dinner), leaving you free to have lunch somewhere else during your exploration of the island.

If you want a beachfront location, opt for Lucaya. If gambling and shopping are more important to you, a hotel in Freeport may be just fine. For escapists, you can find some resorts in the distant East End, away from everything but those white sandy beaches.

Rack rates are for two people spending one night during the high season of winter and spring, unless we indicate otherwise. *Rack rates* simply mean published rates, but you can often do better (see Chapter 7 for details). Room rates at all-inclusive resorts include not only all meals and beverages, but also tips, taxes, transportation to and from the airport, and most activities and entertainment.

Grand Bahama Island abounds in package deals, appealing to honeymooners, golfers, gamblers, scuba divers, and others. The best deals are offered from mid-April to mid-December.

The Best Accommodations

Here are our top hotel picks on Grand Bahama Island.

Best Western Castaways Resort & Suites
$$ Freeport

The 118-room Castaways is a modest and unassuming hotel despite its excellent position adjacent to the International Bazaar and the casino. Guests stay here because of its location and low price. The hotel isn't on the beach, but a free shuttle can take you to nearby Williams Town Beach or Xanadu Beach. Gardens surround the four-story hotel, and the hotel has a pagoda roof and an indoor/outdoor garden lobby with shops, a game room, and tour desks. Rooms are a basic motel style, and the best units are on the ground. The hotel has a large, unheated freshwater pool with a wide terrace and a pool bar that offers sandwiches and cool drinks. The Flamingo Restaurant features unremarkable Bahamian and American dishes. The Yellow Bird Show Club stays open until 3 a.m. and features limbo dancers and fire-eaters Monday through Saturday. A children's playground adjoins the pool.

See map p. 198. East Mall Drive. ☎ *800/780-7234 or 242-352-6682. Fax: 242-352-5087.* www.bestwestern.com. *Rack rates: $120 double, $150 suite. Children under 12 stay free in parent's room. AE, MC, V.*

Crowne Plaza Golf Resort & Casino
$$–$$$ Freeport

This mammoth complex (also known as the Royal Oasis) actually consists of two differently styled resorts combined under one umbrella: the ten-story Crowne Plaza tower and the less glamorous, three-story Crowne Plaza Country Club. Reinventing the resort to stay competitive, the owners spent some $42 million on the once-tired, 1960s-era properties, hoping to revive some of their old glitz and glamour.

Flanked by a pair of fine golf courses, the Ruby and the Emerald, and catering to the convention crowd, the resorts sit on 1,000 hectares (2,500 acres) of tropical grounds. Because the resort lies inland from the sea, the complex doesn't have its own natural beach. One of the grandest additions is a marine park and a man-made, landlocked beach; otherwise, you can take frequent shuttle buses to good natural beaches nearby. The two sections also share one of the largest casinos in the entire country; the casino is a serviceable site, but it's nowhere near as flashy as the Atlantis Casino on Paradise Island.

The Crowne Plaza Country Club attracts families, honeymooners, frugal couples, golfers, and others who don't need or want luxury. The hotel's design is like an enormous wagon wheel; at the core of this "wheel" is a Disney-inspired mini-mountain surrounded by a swimming pool. Nine wings of the hotel stretch from the pool, making up the "spokes" of the wheel. The hotel is so spread out that guests often complain that they need ground transport just to reach their bedrooms. Some of the rooms have kitchenettes and are sold as timeshare units. Even standard rooms are well equipped, with two comfortable double beds, dressing areas, and full-size bathrooms. Rooms in the 900 wing are the largest and best furnished — and they're usually the ones that sell out first. The resort also rents out a number of suites, which are furnished in summery fabrics plus beachy but durable furniture.

Crowne Plaza Tower lies across East Mall Drive from its larger sibling. The tower is smaller, more tranquil, and a bit more posh, containing 20 suites and 362 luxuriously furnished large units. The tower adjoins the casino and the International Bazaar. A light, California-style décor prevails, and rooms most often contain cherry hardwood furnishings. Lots of conventioneers, folks on quick getaways from Florida, and high rollers tend to stay here.

See map p. 198. East Mall Drive and Sunrise Highway. ☎ *800-545-1300 or 242-350-7000. Fax: 242-350-7002.* www.theroyaloasis.com. *Rack rates: Crowne Plaza Country Club $145–$155 double, $240 suite; Crowne Plaza Tower $175–$205 double, $350 suite. Up to two children under 12 stay free in parent's room. AE, MC, V.*

Paradise Cove
$$ Paradise Cove

This seven-room property is a secluded hideaway on a beach, with an informal series of one-bedroom apartments and two-bedroom cottages rented to those who like to escape the glitz and glam of Freeport or Lucaya. Away from the crowds, Paradise Cove is like Grand Bahama used to be before the tourist hordes invaded, and it teems with rainbow-hued tropical marine life and a vast array of coral that will delight snorkelers. Yet you're only a 20-minute drive east of **West End.** Snorkeling, swimming, kayaking, and sunbathing fill the day here. All units are good sized and have full kitchens for guests who want to cook their own grub.

See map p. 198. Paradise Cove. ☎ *242-349-2677. Fax: 242-352-2003.* www.deadmans reef.com. *Rack rates: $100 apartment, $125 cottage, $195 two-bedroom villa. AE, MC, V.*

Pelican Bay at Lucaya
$$–$$$ Lucaya

On a peninsula jutting into a series of inland waterways, this hotel has more architectural charm than any other on the island, evoking a Danish seaside village. Located next door to the Underwater Explorers Society (UNEXSO), the 69-unit Pelican Bay attracts scuba divers. Lucaya's finest beach is across the road. Townhouse-style buildings, trimmed with white latticework and gingerbread, are painted in earth tones. Each large unit has a wet bar and bathrobes. Balconies offer vistas of the marina, waterway, whirlpool, or two large, unheated freshwater pools. For the breeziest stay,

Grand Bahama Accommodations

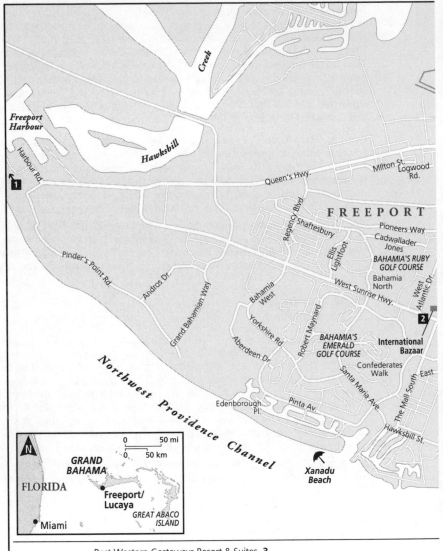

Best Western Castaways Resort & Suites **3**

Crowne Plaza Golf Resort & Casino **2**

Paradise Cove **1**

Pelican Bay at Lucaya **5**

Port Lucaya Resort and Yacht Club **4**

Ritz Beach Resort **7**

Taino Beach Vacation Club **8**

Viva Wyndham Fortuna Beach **9**

The Westin & Sheraton at Our Lucaya **6**

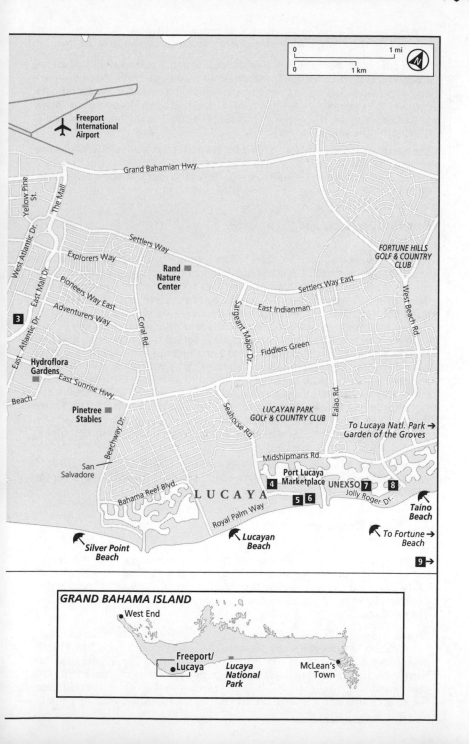

Freeport International Airport

Grand Bahamian Hwy.

Yellow Pine St.

The Mall

West Atlantic Dr.

East Mall Dr.

East Atlantic Dr.

Settlers Way

Explorers Way

Pioneers Way East

Adventurers Way

Rand Nature Center

Settlers Way East

FORTUNE HILLS GOLF & COUNTRY CLUB

East Indianman

West Beach Rd.

Coral Rd.

Sargeant Major Dr.

Fiddlers Green

3

Hydroflora Gardens

East Sunrise Hwy.

Beach

Pinetree Stables

Beachway Dr.

Seahorse Rd.

LUCAYAN PARK GOLF & COUNTRY CLUB

Ealao Rd.

To Lucaya Natl. Park →
Garden of the Groves

San Salvadore

Bahama Reef Blvd.

Midshipmans Rd.

L U C A Y A

Port Lucaya Marketplace **4**

UNEXSO **7**

8

5 **6**

Jolly Roger Dr.

Taíno Beach

Royal Palm Way

Lucayan Beach

To Fortune →
Beach

Silver Point Beach

9 →

GRAND BAHAMA ISLAND

West End

Freeport/ Lucaya

Lucaya National Park

McLean's Town

0   1 mi
0   1 km

request one of the end rooms that offer cross-ventilation. The older rooms look out on the marina, while the newer deluxe units overlook the bay.

If you dine at the **Ferry House Restaurant,** which is just a brief stroll away, you can charge the excellent meals to your room. Along the marina, a passageway leads directly to Port Lucaya Marketplace and the watersports vendors. You shouldn't take this route if you had a few Goombay Smashes or Bahama Mamas; the walkway has no outer wall or railing, so you could fall right in the water.

See map p. 198. Royal Palm Way, by Port Lucaya Marketplace and UNEXSO, the dive operator. ☎ *800-600-9192 or 242-373-9550. Fax: 242-373-9551.* www.pelicanbay hotel.com. *Rack rates: $155–$195 double, $250 suite. Rates include breakfast. AE, MC, V.*

Port Lucaya Resort and Yacht Club
$$ **Lucaya**

With its own 50-slip marina, this 163-room hotel and yacht club attracts boaters and shoppers. Despite being adjacent to Port Lucaya Marketplace, the resort is surprisingly tranquil and has a secluded feel. Buildings one through six are the quietest because they're removed from the music and bustle of the marketplace. Deluxe rooms overlook the marina, and bathrooms are tidy, well maintained, and have adequate shelf space. An Olympic-size, unheated freshwater pool is set off by a whirlpool, and you can sip a drink from the poolside Tiki Bar. Plenty of watersports are at or near the hotel, and you can reach the beach by walking across the road and through the huge Lucayan resort. If you're traveling with children, consider dropping them off at Our Lucaya's Camp Lucaya (see the review of The Westin and Sheraton at Our Lucaya later in this section). The **Trade Winds Café,** Port Lucaya Resort's main restaurant, serves standard fare at breakfast and dinner, but you can find far better and more varied dining options at the nearby marketplace.

See map p. 198. Next to Port Lucaya Marketplace. ☎ *800-582-2921 or 242-373-6618. Fax: 242-373-6652.* www.portlucayaresort.com. *Rack rates: $100–$145 double, $175–$250 suite. AE, MC, V.*

Ritz Beach Resort
$$ **Lucaya**

This newly built hotel is adjacent to the **Taino Beach Vacation Club** (see the listing later in the chapter), sharing all the fun and amenities of its elaborate water park. Enveloped by semitropical gardens, the Ritz (not related to other fabled hotel chain) also is adjacent to the **Pirates of The Bahamas Theme Park.**

The origins of this resort date back to 1995. Over the years, it was constructed in three different phases. The resort is made up of two buildings, and it also embraces a 50-room complex called Coral Suites. All the bedrooms are in concrete coral buildings, and your options range from efficiency and studio units to one-bedroom suites to elaborate villa and penthouse accommodations. The bedrooms are spacious and well furnished.

Your amenities depend on how much you want to pay. Penthouses are located on the third and fourth levels and include such accommodations as a studio penthouse, which is multilevel with its own sun deck and private pool. The hotel's eating facilities are actually at the Taino Beach Vacation Club where guests can patronize two international restaurants and five bars. The Ritz also has a pool bar.

See map p. 198. Jolly Roger Drive, Taino Beach. ☎ *242-373-9354. Fax: 242-373-4421.* www.ritzbeach.com. *Rack rates: $125 efficiency, $175 studio, $300 penthouse. Children 12 and under stay free in parent's room. AE, MC, V.*

Taino Beach Vacation Club
$$ Lucaya

This 37-unit resort on the southern shore offers breezy one-, two-, and three-bedroom condos furnished in a semitropical motif. These highly desirable oceanfront accommodations are set in tropical gardens; the hotel has a strong emphasis on sports, such as volleyball. The resort is near an excellent 457m (1,500-ft.) strip of white sands, only a six-minute ride from Port Lucaya. Although no beach in The Bahamas is private, this one comes the closest to being so because of its seclusion and the lack of harassment from beach vendors. It's adjacent to a water park and the Pirates of The Bahamas Theme Park.

See map p. 198. Jolly Roger Drive, Taino Beach. ☎ *242-373-4682. Fax 242-373-4421.* www.tainobeach.com. *Rack rates: $125 one-bedroom condo, $175 two-bedroom condo, $225 three-bedroom condo. AE, DISC, MC, V.*

Viva Wyndham Fortuna Beach
$$$$ Lucaya

Evoking an Italian version of a Club Med, this property sits on 11 secluded hectares (26 acres) in front of one of the island's best white sand beaches. Although the Viva Wyndham welcomes families and hosts a children's program, most vacationers here are young couples. This European-owned resort has a definite Italian accent. You hear more *ciaos* than hellos. Guests play bocce ball on the beach and dine on Italian and some Bahamian cuisine. Because of its strong Continental overlay, the cuisine is better here than at your typical Grand Bahama hotel.

Not far from the **Bahamas National Trust Rand Memorial Nature Centre** and **Lucayan National Park,** this beach resort has a one-size-fits-all price tag. You don't need to dig into your pocket for food, drinks, nightly entertainment, or most activities, although you have to pay extra for scuba diving, fishing, water-skiing, and horseback riding. Six kilometers (4 miles) from Lucaya and 10km (6 miles) from Freeport, this resort is an attractive getaway. More than half the comfortable rooms have views of the water while the others overlook the gardens. If you want accommodations in an isolated setting, you won't mind staying here and having to rent a car to explore the rest of the island.

See map p. 198. Doubloon Road and Churchill Drive, 6km (4 miles) east of Lucaya. ☎ *242-373-4000. Fax: 242-373-5555.* www.vivaresorts.com. *Rack rates:*

$240–$344 double, $312–$442 triple, $384–$550 quad. Rates include all meals and most activities. Children under 11 stay free in parent's room. AE, MC, V.

The Westin and Sheraton at Our Lucaya
$$$–$$$$ Lucaya

This massive $400 million resort, one of the largest in The Bahamas, is firmly anchored at the center of two of the best white sandy beaches in The Bahamas — **Lucayan Beach** and **Taino Beach.** Expect nearly 3 hectares (8 acres) of soft, white sand. Freeport/Lucaya, which was losing tourists to Paradise Island, got a big boost in 1999 when this sprawling metropolis opened its doors.

The first three sections of this resort were completed late in 1998 under the name **Sheraton at Our Lucaya.** It's the only one of the three branches of Our Lucaya that focuses exclusively on all-inclusive holidays. Here, the one set price includes all your meals, drinks, and most activities. With a vague South Beach Art Deco design, the resort is a massive, open-sided hexagon, with rooms facing the beach and the swimming pool. The 528-room resort is contemporary but relaxed; the developers created a young vibe that draws a lot of families. The bedrooms are whimsical and fun, thanks to fabrics you'd expect on a loud Hawaiian shirt and maple-veneered furniture, all put together with the kind of artful simplicity of a California beach house.

In 2000, two newer subdivisions of Our Lucaya opened, neither of which is an all-inclusive property. The smaller and somewhat more private of the two is **Westin Lighthouse Pointe,** a 322-unit, low-rise complex that focuses specifically on an adult clientele. Its larger counterpart is the 528-unit **Westin–Breakers Cay,** a grand, ten-story, white-sided tower. The three sections stretch in a glittering profile along a narrow strip of beachfront, allowing residents to drop into any of the bars, restaurants, and gardens. A complex this big contains a staggering variety of restaurants, each designed with a different theme and ambience.

Each of the three properties has a dramatic or unconventional swimming pool that's consistent with its theme. For example, the Sheraton at Our Lucaya's pool was designed around a replica of a 19th-century sugar mill, complete with an aqueduct that might be worthy of the ancient Romans. And in recent years, a spa and fitness center, a quartet of tennis courts, a convention center, a state-of-the-art casino, and a shopping mall have all been added to the resort. Plus, increasing emphasis is being put on golf, thanks to the opening of the spectacular Reef Course. And Camp Lucaya will amuse and entertain children ages 2 to 12 throughout daylight hours every day.

See map p. 198. Royal Palm Way, across from Port Lucaya Marketplace. ☎ *800-LUCAYA-1 or 242-373-1333. Sheraton fax: 242-373-8804. Westin fax: 242-350-5060. www.ourlucaya.com. Rack rates: Sheraton $189–$249 double, including all meals and activities; Westin Lighthouse Point or Breakers Cay $189–$229 double; Sheraton or Westin $449 suite. AE, DC, DISC, MC, V.*

Chapter 16

Dining Out in Grand Bahama

• •

In This Chapter

▶ Finding the best food beyond your hotel dining room
▶ Discovering restaurants with island ambience

• •

*M*ost restaurants in Freeport and Lucaya don't give your wallet as much of a workout as those in Nassau and Paradise Island. You don't have as many dining options either, but from fast food to fine food, the choices of locales and cuisine are plentiful enough. Menus spotlight locally caught seafood and typical Bahamian dishes, but you also find the usual array of international fare. Restaurants import nearly all foodstuffs, especially meats, fruits, and vegetables.

Have a casual lunch at a waterside cafe, followed by an elegant candlelit dinner at a hotel. Or try an unassuming, family-run spot that specializes in Bahamian favorites. Islanders head to the rustic restaurants and bars in the **West End** for the freshest — and cheapest — snapper, jack fish, grouper, conch, and other local seafood. Sunday night is party night in the West End. The trip is a 40km (25-mile) drive from Freeport by taxi or rental car.

The **East End** begins east of the Lucayan National Park, 45km (28 miles) east of Freeport/Lucaya at the settlement of High Rock. Only the adventurous escape the resort-studded Freeport/Lucaya area and venture into this sparsely inhabited section for lunch while they're driving around the island. Don't expect any fancy dining — just some local eateries serving Bahamian favorites with homemade goodness. And, yes, a view of the sea.

Getting a Taste for Grand Bahama

Grand Bahama chefs aim for international appeal, turning out the usual array of food to please everybody: pasta, barbecued ribs, burgers, even quesadillas, souvlaki, sushi, or Wiener schnitzels. Early-bird specials and festive happy hours with discounted drinks lure patrons to various spots. Some Freeport and Lucaya restaurants open only for dinner, and some close between meals; so even when reservations aren't necessary, you may want to call before going out of your way.

See the Introduction at the beginning of the book for an explanation of the price categories used in this chapter. For details about Bahamian specialties, turn to Chapter 2.

Dining at Grand Bahama's Best Restaurants

Barracuda's
$$ Lucaya INTERNATIONAL

With high ceilings and big windows, this space is the size of an airplane hangar, and it's done up with playful art and a whimsical, hip décor that would be at home in Miami's South Beach. The kitchen turns out light international dishes that are loaded with flavor. Examples include grilled grouper tuna and white-bean salad; stone crab claws; leek tart with mozzarella and apples; and chicken breast with fresh ginger. If you want to drink your dessert, consider a China Beach, a chocolate-laced affair that's made with crème de cacao, Kahlúa, and Carolans Irish cream.

See map p. 206. In the Reef Village Hotel at the Lucayan Beach & Golf Resort, Royal Palm Way. ☎ *242-373-1333. Breakfast: $13.50; buffet: $16. AE, DC, MC, V. Open: Daily for breakfast 7–10:30 a.m. and Sat–Sun 6:30 p.m.–midnight.*

Beckey's Restaurant & Lounge
$-$$ Freeport BAHAMIAN

Beckey's culinary creations make you think that you've stumbled into a Bahamian home. No matter what time of day you get to this friendly dining spot, you can order fluffy pancakes, scrambled eggs, or local breakfast favorites, such as stew fish or *boil fish* (fish cooked with salt pork, onions, and green peppers) with grits. For lunch or dinner, the steamed snapper, pan-fried grouper, or cracked conch are island favorites that are prepared with zest. We prefer the local specialties instead of the regular American-style food. The bartender makes a Beckey's Special, a lips-to-hips concoction of coconut rum and vanilla ice cream with a splash of brandy. During happy hour, complimentary conch fritters come with the two-for-one mixed drinks. About a five-minute drive from the International Bazaar, Beckey's is just across from Hydroflora Garden.

See map p. 206. East Sunrise Highway at East Beach Drive. ☎ *242-352-5247. Breakfast: $5–$10; lunch: $7–$17; dinner main courses: $8–$24. AE, MC, V. Open: Daily 7 a.m.–11 p.m.*

Bishop's Restaurant

$ East End   BAHAMIAN

For down-home dishes, known mainly by locals, this establishment is an East End favorite. The restaurant opens onto views of the sea. Far from the high-rise hotels, this little restaurant and lounge is reminiscent of The Bahamas of the 1920s and '30s. It serves some of the best cracked conch we've sampled on Grand Bahama Island; the cooks roll the conch in a light batter and fry it in piping hot oil so that its crust is slightly crunchy. Another favorite that's always on the menu is fried grouper with classic peas and rice. Or, for a savory dish, order the chicken barbecued in zesty sauce.

See map p. 206. High Rock. ☎ *242-353-4515. Main courses: $9–$12. No credit cards. Open: Daily 9 a.m.–9 p.m.*

Captain's Charthouse

$$ Lucaya   INTERNATIONAL

Come to Captain's Charthouse for old-fashioned favorites. Seafood, especially lobster, is the star of this restaurant, which serves only dinner. The chef also does a good job with prime rib, pork chops, chicken, and other comfort food that seems plucked from the 1950s. Filling up on the delicious, freshly baked bread or the salad bar before your main course arrives is easy to do. Captain's Charthouse is located away from the tourist fray, but you can arrange complimentary transportation to and from your hotel.

See map p. 206. East Sunrise Highway and East Beach Drive. ☎ *242-373-3900. Reservations recommended. Main courses: $16–$24; early bird dinner: $8–$16 (5–5:30 p.m.). AE, DISC, MC, V. Open: 5–11 p.m. (last seating).*

China Temple

$ International Bazaar   CHINESE

This restaurant is a Chinese joint that also offers takeout. Over the years, this food has proved to be the dining bargain of the bazaar. The menu is familiar and standard: chop suey, chow mein, and sweet-and-sour dishes. The food's certainly not gourmet Asian fare, but it's cheap and it might hit the spot when you're craving something different.

See map p. 206. International Bazaar. ☎ *242-352-5610. Lunch main courses: $7–$8.75; dinner main courses: $10–$15.50. AE, DISC, MC, V. Open: Mon–Sat 11 a.m.–10 p.m.*

Club Caribe

$ Lucaya   AMERICAN/BAHAMIAN

This casual, laid-back eatery lies 11km (7 miles) east of the International Bazaar beside a beach swept by the trade winds. A funky, offbeat charmer, it's a good place to escape from the tourist hordes, especially on cruise-ship

Grand Bahama Dining

The Pub on the Mall **7**
  Islander's Roost
  Prince of Wales Lounge
  Red Dog Sports Bar
The Rib Room **4**
Shenanigan's Irish Pub **13**
Silvano's **3**
The Star Club **1**
The Stoned Crab **16**
Willy Broadleaf **14**
Zorba's Greek Cuisine **12**

Barracuda's **15**
Beckey's Restaurant & Lounge **8**
Bishop's Restaurant **17**
Captain's Charthouse **9**
China Temple **5**
Club Caribe **18**
Fatman's Nephew **12**
Ferry House Restaurant **14**

Geneva's Place **6**
Giovanni's Café **11**
Luciano's **12**
Palm Grill & Coconut Bar **4**
The Pepper Pot **10**
Pier 1 **2**
Pisces **13**
The Pub at Port Lucaya **12**

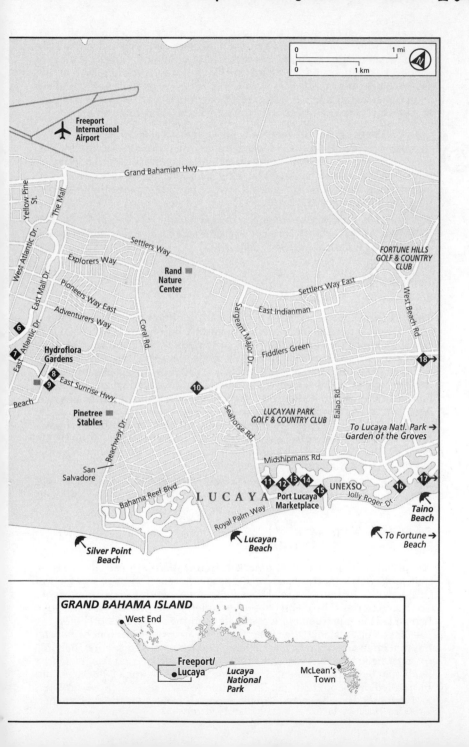

arrival days. You can spend the day on the beach or check out its offshore reef. Just bring some snorkel gear to get up close and personal with all the rainbow-hued fish swarming the reef. In between dips, sample the sandwiches, barbecued ribs, or salads for lunch or the cracked conch or the savory blackened mahimahi for dinner. Rent a lounge chair, relax, and sip a tall rum cocktail, such as a raspberry-coconut Ocean Breeze or a Mango Mama. The Friday-night fish fry from 6 to 9 p.m. is big fun, too.

Club Caribe is off the beaten path, but you don't need to bother with a rental car or taxi. Make your reservation in the morning — or better yet, the day before — and you can arrange complimentary round-trip transportation from your hotel. The ride is about 15 minutes from the International Bazaar area and about seven minutes from accommodations near the Port Lucaya Marketplace.

See map p. 206. Churchill Beach, Mather Town, just east of Taino Beach. ☎ 242-373-6866. Reservations required. Main courses: $7.50–$35, lunch main courses: $5–$14. AE, DISC, MC, V. Open: Tues–Sun 11 a.m.– 6 p.m.

Fatman's Nephew
$–$$ Lucaya BAHAMIAN

The next generation carries on the culinary tradition of the late Fatman, a chef whose Grand Bahama restaurant once had countless loyalists. At this newer location overlooking the Port Lucaya Marketplace Marina, the focus is on seafood. You can sample various grilled or spicy Cajun-style fish or try local favorites, such as cracked conch. On most days, you encounter at least eight kinds of game fish, including wahoo and kingfish. The menu features other island dishes, too, like curried chicken, daily specials, burgers, and steaks. Sometimes an especially authentic dish appears on the menu, such as Bahamian-style shark soup made from the flesh of hammerheads. Not every dish wins an award, but the place is an enduring favorite. The casual atmosphere is idyllic for having drinks and appetizers on the breezy terrace above the water.

See map p. 206. Port Lucaya Marketplace. ☎ 242-373-8520. Main courses: $5–$35. DISC, MC, V. Open: Mon, Wed–Sat 10 a.m.–midnight, Tues and Sun 5 p.m.–midnight.

Ferry House Restaurant
$–$$ Lucaya INTERNATIONAL

A short stroll from Port Lucaya Marketplace, the Ferry House sits in a tranquil spot away from the crush of shops and hotels. The huge windows of this dockside restaurant are always flung open, offering views of pleasure boats and ferries. The menu changes frequently, depending on what fresh fish and other ingredients are available. And the staff bakes bread on the premises. For breakfast, the Danish pastries are a treat. For lunch, you can have an open-faced Danish sandwich, piled with smoked salmon, herring, or roast beef. You may also find filling salads and quesadillas. Icelandic lamb may be on the menu at dinnertime, along with duck à l'orange, and butterflied or coconut shrimp. In addition to local fish (snapper, grouper, and dolphin), the chef may prepare imported trout, tuna, or even sushi.

See map p. 206. Bell Channel, near the Pelican Bay Hotel and the Port Lucaya Marketplace. ☎ *242-373-1595. Reservations recommended for dinner. Lunch platters: $9–$18; dinner main courses: $19–$30. AE, DISC, MC, V. Open: Mon–Fri noon–2:30 p.m. and Tues–Sun 6–9 p.m.*

Geneva's Place
$ Freeport   BAHAMIAN

Ask a native Bahamian where to go for the best local food, and chances are you'll end up at this unassuming dining spot in downtown Freeport. Run by an amiable family, Geneva's serves up hefty portions of the kind of home-cooking you'd get from your own mother — if she were Bahamian. Tender conch comes cracked, stewed, or in a savory chowder. Order your grouper steamed, broiled, or pan-fried and your thick pork chops steamed or fried. Peas and rice is the best side dish.

See map p. 206. Kipling Lane, The Mall at West Sunrise Highway. ☎ *242-352-5085. Main courses: $10–$25; lunch sandwiches and platters: $8–$11. No credit cards. Open: Daily 7 a.m.–11 p.m.*

Giovanni's Café
$ Lucaya   ITALIAN/SEAFOOD

Tucked away in one of the pedestrian thoroughfares of the Port Lucaya Marketplace, you find a yellow-sided clapboard house that opens into a charming 38-seat Italian trattoria. The chefs (including head chef Giovanni Colo) serve Italian-influenced dishes of local seafood, specializing in seafood pasta (usually prepared only for two diners) and lobster. Giovanni stamps each dish with his Italian verve and flavor, whether it's Bahamian conch, local seafood, or scampi. Dishes show off his precision and rock-solid technique, exemplified by sirloin steak with fresh mushrooms, delectable shrimp scampi, and an extremely good spaghetti carbonara.

See map p. 206. Port Lucaya Marketplace. ☎ *242-373-9107. Lunch main courses: $5–$9; dinner main courses: $11–$20. AE, MC, V. Open: Mon– Sat 8 a.m.–10 p.m.*

Luciano's
$$$–$$$$ Lucaya   CONTINENTAL

This elegant restaurant overlooks the Port Lucaya Marketplace Marina and has a certain Continental charm. Whet your appetite with a seafood crêpe, garlic-infused escargot, or chilled melon with port. Inspired by classical European recipes with some local flair thrown in, the seafood and meat courses are uniformly excellent. You can try the Bahamian grouper filet with toasted almonds and lemon butter. Flambéed with cognac, the scampi is another palate pleaser. The duckling breast comes in a green peppercorn sauce, and the rack of lamb (served for two) is carved tableside. Dessert brings a velvet-smooth crème brûlée, pears over vanilla ice cream topped with raspberry sauce, and more crêpes, among other treats.

See map p. 206. Port Lucaya Marketplace. ☎ *242-373-9100. Reservations required. Main courses: $21–$59. AE, DISC, MC, V. Open: Mon–Sat 5:30–10 p.m. (last seating).*

Palm Grill & Coconut Bar
$ Freeport BAHAMIAN/SEAFOOD/INTERNATIONAL

Part of the Royal Oasis resort, this eatery offers two distinct dining experiences. The Palm Grill is a fashionable bistro with tables inside or out. The staff serves a beautifully roasted prime rib, however you want it prepared; fettuccine Alfredo with the tantalizing addition of fresh shrimp; and Bahamian snapper cooked just right — still moist — and served with grilled vegetables. At the more convivial Coconut Bar, you can order well-stuffed sandwiches, juicy burgers and fries, freshly made salads and, of course, conch and other main courses. All dishes come from the same kitchen.

See map p. 206. Crowne Plaza Golf Resort & Casino, The Mall at West Sunrise Highway. ☎ *242-350-7000. Palm Grill lunch main courses: $6.25–$12; dinner main courses: $12–$22. Coconut Bar main courses: $7.50–$18. AE, DC, DISC, MC. Open: Palm Grill daily 6:30–11:30 a.m., noon–3 p.m., and 5:30–11 p.m.; Coconut Bar daily 10 a.m.–1 a.m.*

The Pepper Pot
$ Freeport BAHAMIAN

This restaurant may be the only place on Grand Bahama that specializes in Bahamian takeout food. You'll find this establishment in a tiny shopping mall after about a five-minute drive east of the International Bazaar. You can order the best guava duff on the island, a savory conch chowder, the standard fish and pork chops, chicken souse (an acquired taste), cracked conch, sandwiches and hamburgers, and an array of daily specials.

See map p. 206. East Sunrise Highway. (at Coral Road). ☎ *242-373-7655. Breakfast: $3–$5.50; main courses: $7–$8.25; vegetarian plates: $2.50–$5.50. No credit cards. Open: Daily 24 hours.*

Pier 1
$$$ Freeport BAHAMIAN/SEAFOOD

For some dramatic sunset watching, reserve a table at this seafood restaurant perched on stilts above Freeport Harbour. Kids love "walking the plank" to get inside Pier 1. Fish-filled aquariums and other nautical touches decorate the comfortable dining areas. The evening feedings at the shark pool are a special attraction. In fact, baby shark, prepared in a variety of ways, is a house specialty. You can try it blackened, curried and served with bananas, pan-fried, or in spicy fritters. Spicy food is also a specialty at Pier 1: The house salad dressing can clear your sinuses, and the Bahamian conch salad is fiery, too. If you have a tender palate, go for the fried calamari, Bahamian cracked conch, stone crab claws, or coconut shrimp. Pasta is also on the menu, as are dishes of 12-ounce sirloin and chicken.

Because Pier 1 isn't far from the cruise-ship dock, it's often packed with passengers from the ships.

See map p. 206. Near the cruise-ship dock, Freeport Harbour. ☎ *242-352-6674. Reservations required for dinner. Main courses: $17.95–$46.50. AE, DISC, MC, V. Open: Mon–Fri 10 a.m.–10 p.m., Sat–Sun 3–10 p.m.*

Pisces
$-$$ Lucaya   BAHAMIAN/INTERNATIONAL

This restaurant is our favorite among the many in the Port Lucaya Market-place, and we're seconded by a healthy mix of locals and yacht owners who pack the place every weekend. Decorated with Tiffany-style lamps and captain's chairs, it boasts the most charming wait staff on Grand Bahama Island. Lunches are relatively simple affairs, with fish and chips, sandwiches, and salads. You can order pizzas anytime, and they're available in 21 varieties, including one with conch, lobster, shrimp, and chicken. Dinners are more elaborate and better tasting, and you have a choice of curries (including a version with conch); lobster in cream, wine, and herb sauce; all kinds of fish and shellfish; and several kinds of delicious pasta dishes.

See map p. 206. Port Lucaya Marketplace. ☎ 242-373-5192. Reservations recommended. Lunch main courses: $8.95–$11.95; pizzas: $12–$27; dinner main courses: $14.95–$30. AE, MC, V. Open: Mon–Sat 5 p.m.–1:30 a.m.

The Pub at Port Lucaya
$-$$ Lucaya   ENGLISH/BAHAMIAN

By day, you can dine on typical English pub grub. Along with fish and chips, you can find dependable chicken and asparagus pie, shepherd's pie, and steak-and-ale pie. Fat burgers add an American twist to the menu. At dinner, Bahamian dishes rule, including grilled fish or cracked conch served with a heaping mound of peas and rice. Dine inside or alfresco, overlooking the water. Although you shouldn't feel any discomfort here, opt for a Painkiller, a rum-filled cocktail that can leave you smashed.

See map p. 206. Port Lucaya Marketplace. ☎ 242-373-8450. Main courses: $10–$35; sandwiches and burgers: $6.90–$13.80. AE, MC, V. Open: Daily 11 a.m.–11 p.m. (bar until 1 a.m.).

The Rib Room
$$$-$$$$ Freeport   STEAKS/SEAFOOD

Serious meat-eaters gravitate to this restaurant, which resembles a British hunting lodge, decked out in dark leather, wood, and brick. Plates come loaded with juicy slabs of steak and prime rib and sides of potatoes and Yorkshire pudding. If you don't want beef, you can choose among fruits of the sea, such as shrimp, Bahamian lobster, and grouper, or opt for chicken. However, the folks in the kitchen clearly cater to carnivores.

See map p. 206. Crowne Plaza Golf Resort & Casino at the Royal Oasis, at West Sunrise Highway. ☎ 242-352-6721. Reservations recommended. Jackets required for men. Main courses: $20–$34. AE, DC, MC, V. Open: Fri–Wed 5:30–10:30 p.m.

Shenanigan's Irish Pub
$-$$$ Lucaya   CONTINENTAL

Dark and beer-stained from the thousands of pints of Guinness, Harp, and Killian's that have been served and spilled here, this pub is the premier

---

The Pub on the Mall

No matter what type of food you're in the mood for, chances are you can find it at one of the four watering holes under one roof at the **Pub on the Mall** (located at The Mall and Ranfurly Circus, opposite the International Bazaar). A meal usually costs $21, including soup or access to the salad bar, but not dessert; or you can order bar food for $5 per platter.

Inexpensive pub fare, from fish and chips to T-bone steak and lamb, draws diners to **Prince of Wales Lounge** (☎ 242-352-2700; open Mon–Sat noon–1 a.m., Sun 5 p.m.–midnight). Arrive between 5 and 7 p.m., and you can feast on salad, one of two main courses, dessert, and coffee, all for only about $8. Thirsty? Try a potent Pub Special: coconut rum, tequila, cherry brandy, pineapple juice, orange juice, grenadine, and bitters served in a pint mug.

Sit on the balcony at **Islander's Roost** (☎ 242-352-5110; reservations recommended; open Mon–Sat 5:30 p.m.–midnight). The steak, prime rib, and fish here are nothing special, but the frozen daiquiris are sumptuous, and the tropical décor puts you in a vacation mood.

A 243cm (96-in.) satellite TV broadcasting American and European sports dominates the **Red Dog Sports Bar** (☎ 242-352-2700; open daily noon–midnight). If you need energy for all that rootin', hootin', and hollerin', order chicken and fries, fish 'n' chips, or other pub grub, washed down with a brew or two.

Boston Irish hangout on Grand Bahama Island. Many visitors come just to soak up the suds — sometimes for hours at a time — and perhaps eventually order some food. If you get hungry, you can order surf and turf, French-style rack of lamb for two, seafood Newburg, and several preparations of chicken. Don't expect more than comfort food — it's satisfying and affordable unless you order the expensive steak and lobster combo.

See map p. 206. Port Lucaya Marketplace. ☎ 242-373-4734. Main courses: $8.95–$42. AE, DC, DISC, MC, V. Open: Mon–Thurs 5 p.m.–midnight, Fri–Sat 5 p.m.–2 a.m.

Silvano's
$–$$ Freeport   ITALIAN

The only authentic Italian dining spot in Freeport, this 80-seat restaurant serves a fine, but not exceptional, cuisine. The standard repertoire from mama's kitchen is presented here with quality ingredients, most often shipped in from the United States. The grilled veal steak is our favorite, although the homemade pastas are equally alluring. The pastas are served with a wide variety of freshly made sauces. The chef also works his magic with fresh shrimp. Service is polite and helpful.

See map p. 206. Ranfurly Circus. ☎ 242-352-5111. Reservations recommended. Lunch main courses: $5.50–$11; dinner main courses: $13–$36. AE, MC, V. Open: Daily noon–3 p.m. and 5:30–11 p.m.

The Star Club
$ West End BAHAMIAN

Among the unassuming places to chew and sip in the West End — about a 45-minute drive from downtown Freeport — The Star Club is the one with the most character. Opened in 1946 as Grand Bahama's first hotel, this colonial wooden and concrete two-story building sits on the waterfront. In its heyday, it welcomed such guests as Ernest Hemingway, Sidney Poitier, and Martin Luther King, Jr. Bahamians know that when other nightspots close, The Star Club is still a happening place because it's open nearly 24 hours a day. After partying elsewhere on the island, many locals head here to listen to music (recorded or the occasional live band), play pool, and watch the sunrise.

Conch in all its incarnations, fried chicken, burgers, and fish and chips are on the menu, along with peas and rice. The cook will fill you up with a satisfying meal or snack, but you won't be on the phone to the editors of *Gourmet* magazine. When the weather cooperates, you can watch men prepare fresh conch salad out front at a waterside stand. The owner here claims that it's common knowledge that The Star Club's conch salad is the best on the island. We agree. The bartender won't divulge the secret recipe for his club's legendary Bahama Mamas, but these drinks keep folks coming back for more.

See map p. 206. Bayshore Road. ☎ *242-346-6207. Main courses: $10–$16. No credit cards. Open almost around the clock (hours vary, so call ahead).*

The Stoned Crab
$$$ Lucaya SEAFOOD

The most romantic restaurant on island, The Stoned Crab sits beneath a soaring pyramid-shaped roof at the edge of the beach. You can eat inside, but the best seats in the house are on the alfresco patio. The stone crab claws here are some of the sweetest you'll ever taste, and the fish — try the wahoo, yellowfin tuna, or swordfish — are also beautifully prepared. Other good selections are the crab and avocado cocktail and the broiled seafood platter that's aromatically seasoned with oregano, garlic, and white wine. For guests not wanting to eat fish, the restaurant offers a number of Continental dishes nightly, including chicken parmigiana. If you're not the designated driver, be sure to order a Stoned Crab, which is a potent rum and fruit juice cocktail, or an Irish coffee. Because the seafood is freshly caught, not everything on the menu is always available.

See map p. 206. Taino Beach. ☎ *242-373-1442. Reservations strongly recommended. Main courses: $19–$39. AE, MC, V. Open: Daily 5–10:30 p.m.*

Willy Broadleaf
$$ Lucaya INTERNATIONAL/BUFFET

At the first-class Westin and Sheraton at Our Lucaya, you're treated to one of the most lavish buffet dinners in the entire Bahamian chain. The chefs conceive of their lavish offering as a giant spread of exotic dishes based on recipes from around the globe. The décor fits the cuisine, evoking a court-yard patio in Mexico, a marketplace in old Cairo, the dining hall of an Indian maharajah, even an African village; from India comes tandoori chicken, from Greece moussaka. Another tasty treat is a sausage made from wild boar. Expect freshly made salads, hot and cold dishes, and luscious desserts.

See map p. 206. The Westin and Sheraton at Our Lucaya, Royal Palm Way. ☎ *242-373-1333. Buffet: Sun–Thurs $30, Fri–Sat $38. AE, DC, MC, V. Open: Daily 6:30–10 p.m.*

Zorba's Greek Cuisine
$–$$ Lucaya GREEK/BAHAMIAN

First thing in the morning, locals are standing in line for the Bahamian breakfasts served at Zorba's. From chicken souse to corned beef and grits, all the island eye-openers are on the menu. Eggs and fluffy Greek pastries snag less daring early risers. Lunch may be a fat gyro or a souvlaki kebab. Dinner can begin with a Greek salad and then move on to moussaka, with baklava for a sweet finish. We can't pretend the food here is like a trip to the Greek isles, but it's satisfying in every way. At this casual dining spot, you can eat inside or enjoy your meal alfresco.

See map p. 206. Port Lucaya Marketplace. ☎ *242-373-6137. Lunch main courses $7–$13; dinner main courses: $10–$23. AE, DISC, MC, V. Open: Daily 7 a.m–11 p.m.*

Chapter 17

Having Fun On and Off the Beach in Grand Bahama

● ●

In This Chapter

▶ Catching some rays on Grand Bahama's best beaches

▶ Enjoying the island's watersports

▶ Exploring Grand Bahama's land attractions, shopping, and nightlife

▶ Taking two great day trips

● ●

*F*rom booze cruises and snorkeling excursions to fishing trips and kayak paddles, Grand Bahama keeps water lovers busy. The variety of beaches rimming the island allows devotees to spend their entire vacations sun-worshipping. Landlubbers can enjoy excellent golf, tennis, horseback riding, hiking, biking, shopping, and sightseeing. Compared with Nassau and Paradise Island, Grand Bahama may not be party central after dark, but you can find more than enough nightspots for drinking, dancing, and romancing.

Combing the Beaches

White sandy beaches hug Grand Bahama's southern shores, some 97km (60 miles) of strands. Footprints are few and far between on most of these shores. The busiest and best beaches are in **Lucaya,** the island's watersports mecca, where you find the cluster of resort hotels. Built inland, Freeport hotels shuttle their guests to nearby sandy shores. **Xanadu Beach,** located at a resort near Freeport, is a favorite for guests with beachless accommodations and cruise-ship passengers. This beach can be crowded at times in winter, but that's because of its gorgeous, soft, white powdery sands that open onto tranquil waters. The beach, which stretches for a kilometer and a half (1 mile), has a backdrop of coconut palms and Australian pines. Here you find some of the best watersports on the island, including snorkeling, boating, Jet-Skiing, and parasailing. On weekends, residents head to the sands at **William's Town,** east of Xanadu Beach and south of Freeport. Many visitors get their first glimpses of golden **Taino Beach,** just east of Lucaya, when they stop by The Stoned Crab

Fun in Grand Bahama

SHOPPING

Bahamian Things **6**

International Bazaar **2**

   Bahamas Coin and Stamp Ltd.

   Caribbean Cargo

   Cleo's Boutique

   Columbian Emeralds International

   Far East Traders

   Flovin Gallery

   Island Galleria

   Les Parisiennes

   Paris in The Bahamas

The Perfume Factory Fragrance of The Bahamas **3**

Port Lucaya Marketplace **8**

   Androsia

   Bandolera

   Columbian Emeralds International

   Flovin Gallery II

   Harley-Davidson of Freeport

   Jeweler's Warehouse

   UNEXSO Dive Shop

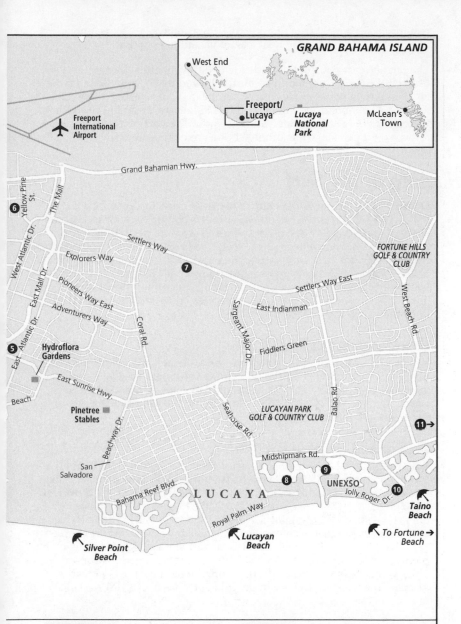

ATTRACTIONS

Lucayan National Park **11**

Parrot Jungle's Garden of the Groves **11**

Perfume Factory **3**

Pirates of The Bahamas Theme Park **10**

Rand Nature Centre **7**

NIGHTLIFE

Casino at Westin & Sheraton at Our Lucaya **9**

Count Basie Square **8**

Royal Oasis Casino **4**

Star Club **1**

Superior Watersports **8**

Yellowbird Showroom **5**

restaurant for a meal (see Chapter 16). Parasailing, Jet-Skiing, and banana-boat rides at Taino Beach keep vacationers active.

The farther east you go, the less crowded the beaches become. You hit **Churchill Beach**, then **Smith's Point**, followed by **Fortune Beach** (where an all-inclusive resort draws many Europeans), and **Barbary Beach**. About a 20-minute drive from the hotels in Lucaya, stunning **Gold Rock Beach** slumbers at **Lucayan National Park**. One part of it lures residents for weekend picnics, while other sections remain secluded.

Playing in the Surf

Ocean Motion Water Sports Ltd., Sea Horse Lane, Lucayan Beach (☎ 242-374-2425) is the largest watersports company on Grand Bahama. It offers a wide variety of daily activities — weather permitting — from 9 a.m. to 5 p.m. Parasailing, for example, costs $50 per person; snorkeling trips cost $35 for 1½ hours; water-skiing costs $25 per 3km (2-mile) pull; Hobie Cats cost $20 per person; windsurfing costs $30 per hour; and banana-boating costs $10 per person for a 3km (2-mile) ride. Call for information on or to arrange other activities, including deep-sea fishing, bottom-fishing, and kayaking.

Banana-boating

You can join a row of other riders on one of these long, yellow inflated boats for a bouncy trip. As the boat snakes through the waves, you get splashed, so hold on tight to the handles! Try **Sea Affairs Ltd.** at Xanadu Beach, Lucaya (☎ 242-352-2887). In general, the $10 price applies to both kids and adults.

Diving and dolphin encounters

Both the National Association of Underwater Instructors (NAUI) and the Professional Association of Diving Instructors (PADI) hold diving certification classes at the **Underwater Explorer's Society (UNEXSO)** (☎ 888-365-3483 or 242-373-1244; www.unexso.com), Port Lucaya Marketplace, which offer three full days of training for $400. UNEXSO is one of Grand Bahama's oldest and most reliable companies. The half-day quickie resort course ($75) includes a shallow reef dive. Dives start at about $25 for a one-tank plunge and $50 for a two-tank dive, with all necessary gear. The more dives you have in your package, the more the per-dive cost decreases. At night, the colors of the ocean are brilliantly intense. A UNEXSO night dive costs $35.

A goal of most scuba divers is to visit *Theo's Wreck* — one of the most famous wrecks — lying off the coast of Freeport. In 1982, The Bahamian government sunk this 70m (230-ft.) freighter knowing that it would become a haven for marine life. You can see some of the most varied marine life off island, ranging from moray eels to sea turtles. Other popular dive sites include **Golden Rock, Pygmy Caves,** and **Silver Point Reef.**

Bahamian-owned **Caribbean Divers,** at the Bell Channel Inn, opposite Port Lucaya (☎ 242-373-9111), is another good outfitter. Its certification courses begin at $350, and its resort course runs $89. Prices begin at $35 for a one-tank dive and $65 for a two-tank dive, including equipment. Caribbean Divers also offers night dives for $70 and shark dives starting around $100. You can rent underwater cameras for $40. For the optimal experience underwater, the company limits groups to a maximum of 18 divers.

Another outfitter is **Xanadu Undersea Adventures** at Xanadu Beach Resort (☎ 800-327-8150 or 242-352-3811). Certification courses begin at $425, and resort courses run $89. You can have your dive videotaped for $35 or rent your own underwater camera for $25 to $30, plus film. Dives begin at $37 for one tank and $66 for two tanks. Ask about shark dives for $72 and night dives for $52.

If you want to dive with dolphins, you can do so through UNEXSO's **The Dolphin Experience.** For the **Close Encounter** ($69 for adults, free for children age 5 and younger), a ferry takes you from Port Lucaya Marketplace to Sanctuary Bay, 3km (2 miles) away. Atlantic bottlenose dolphins nuzzle your dangling legs as you sit on a partially submerged dock. Participants stand waist-deep in the water and pet some of these powerful creatures. The butter-smooth skin of these amiable mammals feels amazingly soft and warm. While small groups take turns going into the water, an expert tells you all about the origins, behaviors, likes, and dislikes of the dolphins. You spend only about 15 minutes body-to-body with Flipper's cousins.

If you want more time up close and personal, opt for the **Swim with the Dolphins** program ($159). When you're underwater, you can hear their clicks and clucks as they converse with each other. Contact UNEXSO for more information.

No matter which dolphin program you choose, reserve as far in advance as possible.

UNEXSO pioneered shark diving ($100) in The Bahamas, and UNEXSO schools you on proper human-shark interaction and takes all kinds of precautions to ensure your safety.

You can have your shark dive videotaped for $20 and up. If you'd rather snap shots yourself, you can rent underwater cameras from UNEXSO for $10 and up.

Jet-Skiing and water-skiing

Like aquatic motorcycles, Jet Skis let you zoom across the waves. Some people object to this form of fun, saying that it's at odds with Grand Bahama's tranquility and calm waters. However, if you're interested in this adventure, **Sea Affairs Ltd.,** at Xanadu Beach (☎ 242-352-2887) can arrange it for you. The rental costs $30 for 15 minutes or $50 for 30 minutes.

If water-skiing is more to your liking, you can also book with **Sea Affairs Ltd.,** at a price of $20 per person for a 2.4km (1½-mile) ride.

Kayaking

To explore Grand Bahama's more pristine corners, you can rent Funyaks through **Paradise Watersports** at Xanadu Beach (☎ 242-352-2887). Rentals cost $8 for 30 minutes or $12 for an hour, plus a $10 deposit.

Or, combine a kayak trip with a guided nature walk: Make a reservation with **Kayak Nature Tours** (☎ 242-373-2485), run by Bahamian-German husband-wife team Ed and Erika Gates. You spend 90 minutes of this six-hour adventure paddling double kayaks along a tidal creek and through a mangrove forest with branches that create a shady canopy. As fish dart by, you can spot egrets, greenback herons, and other sea birds. A trek through **Lucayan National Park** introduces you to ancient Lucayan Indian caves, and you're treated to a picnic lunch on **Gold Rock Beach,** where you can swim. The excursion costs $69 for adults, $30 for children ages 11 to 16, and is free for kids age 10 and under. Kayak Nature Tours provides air-conditioned transportation to and from your hotel, complete with drivers who provide a running narration about Bahamian history, lore, and sights. The ride is about 40 minutes from the International Bazaar and 30 minutes from Port Lucaya Marketplace. Kayak Nature Tours also hosts trips to nearby islands (see "Going Beyond Grand Bahama" later in this chapter).

Parasailing and snorkeling

For parasailing, you're strapped into a harness that's attached to a parachute on one end and a boat on the other. When the boat takes off, away you go, up toward the clouds. The people, ocean, and beach below shrink to toy-size. Although you're airborne for only about five minutes, the thrill lasts much longer in your memory. Contact **Reef Tours** at the Port Lucaya Dock (☎ 242-373-5880; http://reef.ilucaya.com). It costs $50 per person.

The waters around Grand Bahama are clear and ideal for snorkelers, who can spot such varied marine life as sea turtles, moray eels, and horse-eyed jacks. **Ben's Cave** is a favorite. This panoramic cavern is part of the Lucayan Cave system. The coral beds at **Silver Point Reef** and **Gold Rock** also draw snorkelers. Most hotels either host their own snorkeling excursions or can help you make arrangements for trips elsewhere. Reef Tours runs one-hour-and-45-minute excursions that cost $35 for adults and $16 for children.

Climbing Aboard

You can find plenty of opportunities to explore sea life without getting wet.

Sailing local waters

Superior Watersports, Port Lucaya Marketplace (☎ 242-373-7863) offers trips on its *Bahama Mama,* a two-deck 22m (72-ft.) catamaran. Its Robinson Crusoe Beach Party, offered daily from 11 a.m. to 4 p.m., costs $59 per person. The company also has a shorter sunset booze cruise that goes for $29. (In summer, these cruises are on Tues, Thurs, and Sat 6–8 p.m.) Call for information about how to hook up with this outfitter.

For an underwater cruise, try the company's quasi-submarine, the *Seaworld Explorer.* The sub itself doesn't descend; instead, you walk down into the hull of the boat and watch the sea life glide by. The "sub" departs daily at 9:30 a.m., 11:30 a.m., and 1:30 p.m. The cost is $39 for adults and $25 for children 12 and under.

 To see Grand Bahama's underwater beauty, climb aboard a glass-bottom boat and watch the fish swarm around a diver with dinner. Try **Paradise Watersports** on Xanadu Beach (☎ 242-352-2887). The ride costs $25 for adults and $15 for children.

Ocean Wonder, run by **Reef Tours, Ltd.** (☎ 242-373-5880; http:// reef.ilucaya.com), is supposedly the world's largest twin-diesel-engine glass-bottom boat. Cruises depart from Port Lucaya behind the Straw Market on the bay side at 9:30 a.m., 11:15 a.m., 1:15 p.m., and 3:15 p.m., except Friday, when only two tours leave at 9:30 and 11:15 a.m. The tour lasts 1½ hours and costs $25 for adults, $15 for children ages 6 to 12, and is free for children 5 and under. When calling for a reservation, confirm the departure times because they may vary by season.

Going fishing

The clear waters off Grand Bahama Island are great for snapper, yellow-tail, grouper, wahoo, barracuda, and kingfish. Off the coast, fishermen catch some of the largest game fish in the world, and many fishermen pursue dolphinfish. In the eastern part of the island, the great fishing grounds are in **Deep Water Cay.** The best outfitter is **Reef Tours, Ltd.,** Port Lucaya Dock (☎ 242-373-5880; http://reef.ilucaya.com), which offers one of the least expensive ways to go deep-sea fishing around Grand Bahama Island. Adults pay $85 to fish and $45 if they go along only to watch. Four to six people can charter the entire 13m (42-ft.) craft for $520 per half-day or $950 per whole day. The 10m (32-ft.) craft can be chartered for $350 per half-day and $675 for a whole day. Departures for the half-day excursion are daily at 8:30 a.m. and 1 p.m. Bait, tackle, and ice are included in the cost.

Through **Xanadu Undersea Adventures** on Xanadu Beach (☎ 800-327-8150 or 242-352-3811), you can arrange a 3½-hour fishing trip for $45 per adult and $30 per child. Trips depart at 9 a.m. and 1 p.m.

 By law, each person can catch only six wahoo, dolphinfish, or kingfish per day.

Another good sport-fishing operation you can try is **Running Mon Marina,** Kelly Court, Freeport (☎ 242-352-6834). For renting boats, the most convenient marinas are Running Mon, **Port Lucaya Marina** (☎ 242-373-9090), and **Xanadu Marina and Beach Resort** (☎ 242-352-6783), Dundee Bay Drive, Lucaya.

Exploring on Dry Land

Youthful Freeport and Lucaya keep visitors amused with **golf, tennis, horseback riding, gardens,** and **nature reserves.** Even if you're not interested in shopping, the **International Bazaar** in Freeport and the **Port Lucaya Marketplace** in Lucaya are scenic places to wander.

You can visit attractions by taxi, bus, foot, rental car, or on a guided tour. You have the most flexibility if you strike out on your own, of course. But if you'd rather let a Bahamian take you, perhaps to several far-flung attractions, consider taking a guided tour.

The top attractions

Lucayan National Park
Lucaya

Lucayan National Park is a tropical wilderness preserve on 16 hectares (40 acres), where you may want to spend at least a couple of hours exploring as you follow trails and elevated walkways through the thick forest. You'll come to **Gold Rock Creek,** which is fed by a spring from what may be the world's largest underground freshwater cave system. Visitors can walk into two caves. One cave, however, is closed during bat-nursing season — late spring to midsummer. Spiral wooden steps take you down to the freshwater pools, where you can see fish darting back and forth. Through UNEXSO (☎ 888-365-3483 or 242-373-1244; www.unexso.com), adventurous folks can arrange to go on a cave dive. In the caves, people have found bones and pottery shards of the Lucayan Indians, who once collected fresh water here.

Across the road from the park entrance, you find a boardwalk trail that leads through a mangrove forest down to one of the island's best beaches, Gold Rock Beach. Pack a lunch and eat it at a seaside picnic table or on the dunes, and then cool off in the aquamarine waves.

Before heading out to this remote national park, purchase a ticket ($3 per adult; free for children age 12 and under) at **The Bahamas National Trust headquarters,** located at East Settler's Way, a half-kilometer east of Coral Road (☎ 242-352-5438). Lucayan National Park is a 30-minute drive east of Freeport and 25 minutes east of Port Lucaya Marketplace. You can take a taxi or join a bus tour.

See map p. 216. Forty-two kilometers (26 miles) from Freeport, and 32km (20 miles) east of Lucaya. ☎ 242-352-5438. Admission: $3 adults, free for children age 12 and under. Open: Daily 9 a.m.–4 p.m.

Parrot Jungle's Garden of the Groves
Lucaya

This attractive 5 hectare (12-acre) oasis has a pond full of alligators and a petting zoo with Vietnamese potbellied pigs, Pygmy goats, and a cockatoo. Macaws on perches welcome visitors, and you can spot an iguana, a peacock, ducks, and raccoons. Allow at least 45 minutes to see the animals and to wander across footbridges and along paths past waterfalls, fruit trees, flowers, and lacy ferns. You can spend a few quiet moments in the historic chapel that sits on a rise overlooking the garden. Built with native stone, the chapel is topped by a Spanish tile roof. The garden — 25 minutes from the International Bazaar and 15 minutes from the Port Lucaya Marketplace — honors American financier and developer Wallace Groves, who founded Freeport with his wife, Georgette.

See map p. 216. On Magellan Drive, off Midshipman Road, Lucaya. ☎ *242-373-5668 or 242-373-1456. Admission: $9.95 adults, $6.95 ages 3–10, free for children under 3. Open: Daily 9:30 a.m.–4 p.m.*

Perfume Factory
Freeport

Touring the fragrance laboratory housed in a replica of a 19th-century Bahamian mansion takes a mere five minutes. You can discover how the company produces perfumes, colognes, and lotions from tropical ingredients. You're then invited to purchase some. But most people find the mix-your-own sessions here the best reason to visit. Be prepared for an olfactory workout. For $30, you can sniff honeysuckle, lavender, gardenia, jasmine, cinnamon, ginger, and an array of other aromas to decide which two or three essential oils to combine into your own signature creation. You can name your concotion and have it bottled and labeled. Choosing your special scent can take anywhere from 15 minutes to a half hour.

See map p. 216. Behind International Bazaar. ☎ *242-352-9391. Admission: Free. Open: Mon–Fri 9:30 a.m.–5:30 p.m., Sat noon–4 p.m.*

Pirates of The Bahamas Beach Theme Park
Taino Beach

Islanders think of this amusement park as their Disney World. This theme park is one of the largest watersports centers in The Bahamas, featuring pools for diving and swimming, along with an array of activities, such as parasailing, banana-boating, snorkeling, kayaking, paddle-boating, and Jet-Skiing. Children have their own Captain Kidd's Camp with a supervised playground. Something's always happening here, including beach or bonfire parties. The park doesn't charge a general admission fee, but you're charged for some of the attractions, such as the 18-hole mini-golf course ($6 per person). The Bonfire Party Night on Tuesday, Thursday, and Sunday lasts from 6 p.m. to midnight and costs adults $50, children $20, and includes free transportation from your hotel, live entertainment, and an all-you-can-eat buffet dinner. A restaurant and bar are housed in a wooden structure that evokes a Spanish galleon.

See map p. 216. Jolly Roger Drive. ☎ 242-373-8456. Admission: Free. Open: Mon–Fri 8 a.m.–4 p.m., Thurs–Sun 2–10:30 p.m.

Rand Nature Centre
Freeport

Nature buffs, especially bird lovers, need at least two hours to appreciate this 40 hectare (100-acre) reserve run by the Bahamas National Trust, a nonprofit conservation association. Named in honor of philanthropist James H. Rand, this slice of wild Grand Bahama is 3km (2 miles) from the International Bazaar and less than 6km (3½ miles) from Port Lucaya Marketplace. One of the highlights is a pond studded with a flock of pink flamingos, The Bahamas' national bird. You can get a close-up look at this endangered species, so bring your camera. Other feathered friends you may spot are a red-legged thrush, a banana quit, or a Cuban emerald hummingbird. A pair of binoculars comes in handy, especially for the two-hour guided bird walk that's held the first Saturday of each month, starting at 8 a.m. A variety of orchids is among more than 100 different types of plants here. Several species of Bahamian boa constrictors reside in the exhibit room, along with other indigenous and imported creatures. Taxis and buses take you to the exhibit room.

See map p. 216. East Settler's Way, less than a half-kilometer east of Coral Road. ☎ 242-352-5438. Admission: $5 adults, $3 children 5–12, free for ages 5 and younger. Open: Mon–Fri 9 a.m.–4 p.m.

Guided tours

Several tour companies offer informative tours of Grand Bahama Island. One reliable company is **H. Forbes Charter Services Ltd.,** The Mall at West Sunrise Highway, Freeport (☎ 242-352-9311; www.forbescharter. com). From its headquarters at the International Bazaar, this company offers half- and full-day bus tours. The most popular option is the half-day Super Combination Tour, priced at $35 per adult and $25 per child under 12. The tour includes guided visits to the botanical gardens, drive-through tours of residential areas and the island's commercial center, and stops at the island's deep-water harbor. The tour also includes shopping and a visit to a wholesale liquor store. Tours depart Monday through Saturday at 9 a.m. and 1 p.m.; the tour lasts 3½ hours.

If you're a nature lover, escape from the casinos and take a bush-and-sea safari with **East End Adventures** (☎ 242-373-6662). The safari takes you through dense pine forests and along deserted beaches, and you go inland on hikes to such sites as *blue holes* (natural pools where freshwater floats on top of saltwater), mangrove swamps, and underground caverns. You may even learn how to crack conch. You eat a native lunch on a serene beach in Lightbourne's Cay, a remote islet in the East End. Most of the tour is laid-back; you can snorkel in blue holes or shell hunt. The company conducts safaris daily between 8 a.m. and 5:30 p.m. The cost is $110 for adults and $55 for kids ages 2 to 12.

Trekking to the "Wild" West End

Rent a car or hire a taxi and head to **West End,** which is about 45 minutes from downtown Freeport. Fishing boats recline along the one narrow road that parallels the coastline. This tranquil fishing community is the place to go when you're in the mood to have a few drinks or swap a tale or two with locals or when you have a taste for fresh home-style seafood. Small roadside kitchens move snapper, jack fish, and grouper from the ocean to the frying pan in record time.

Once the capital of Grand Bahama, West End is inhabited by descendants of the first settlers of the island. Freeport and Lucaya may be new compared to Nassau, but other parts of Grand Bahama were developed long before its modern resort areas. West End is the site of the island's annual Junkanoo parades on Independence Day (July 10) and Boxing Day (December 26). On your way to West End, you pass other old seaside settlements — some dilapidated, and some in colorful ruins. Many of the tiny houses are painted bright blues, yellows, and greens. You may also come upon a *blue hole* (a natural pool where fresh water floats on top of saltwater). When the tide is right, many locals swim in these pools.

Keeping Active

Beaches are paramount, but you can find much more to island life than making waves. Grand Bahama gives visitors many options for staying active on solid ground.

Biking

A guided bike trip is an ideal way to see parts of Grand Bahama that most visitors miss. Starting at **Barbary Beach,** you can pedal a mountain bike along the southern coast parallel to the beach. Stop for a snack, lunch, and a dip. Finally, you reach **Lucayan National Park,** some 19km (12 miles) away. Explore the cave where the Indians buried their dead in the days when Grand Bahama was theirs. Crabs here have been known to come up though holes in the ground carrying bits of bowls once used by the Lucayans. **Kayak Nature Tours** (☎ 242-373-2485), the company that sponsors these trips, transports you home to your hotel by van, so you don't have to exhaust yourself in the heat cycling back. The cost is $79 for adults, half-price for children ages 10 to 16. All equipment, sustenance, and round-trip transportation from your hotel is included.

Golfing

Grand Bahama is home to more golf courses than any other Bahamian island. Open to the public throughout the year, the golf courses host a variety of international tournaments. No need to worry if you don't feel like lugging your own clubs — you can rent clubs from any Freeport or Lucaya pro shop.

Emerald Golf Course, The Mall South, at the Crowne Plaza Golf Resort & Casino (☎ 242-350-7000), is the site of the annual Grand Bahama Pro-Am Tournament. The course has plenty of trees along the fairways, as well as an abundance of water hazards and bunkers. The toughest hole is the ninth, a 498m (545-yd.) par 5 from the blue tees. In winter, greens fees are $95 per day, and in summer, they're reduced to $85.

The championship **Ruby Golf Course,** also at Crowne Plaza Golf Resort & Casino (☎ 242-350-7000), received a major upgrade in 2001 by Jim Fazio Golf Design, Inc. The new design lengthened Ruby course to increase the rating and to enhance play. It also added a fully automated irrigation system. Greens fees are the same as the ones at the Emerald Golf Course. The Ruby course has a total of 6,172m (6,750 yd.), if you play from the championship blue tees.

Fortune Hills Golf & Country Club, Richmond Park, Lucaya (☎ 242-373-4500), was originally intended to be an 18-hole course, but the back 9 holes were never completed. You can replay the front 9 for 18 holes and a total of 6,323m (6,916 yd.) from the blue tees. Par is 72. Greens fees are $31 for nine holes and $43 for 18 holes.

The best-kept and most manicured course on Grand Bahama is the par-72 **Lucayan Park Golf & Country Club,** Lucayan Beach (☎ 242-373-1066). Recently made over, it's quite beautiful and is known for a hanging boulder sculpture at its entrance. Greens are fast, and the course has a couple of par 5s more than 457m (500 yd.) long, totaling 6,239m (6,824 yd.) from the blue tees and 5,932m (6,488 yd.) from the white tees. Greens fees are $100 for 18 holes, including a mandatory shared golf cart. Even if you're not a golfer, sample the food at the club restaurant, which offers everything from lavish champagne brunches to first-rate seafood dishes.

The first golf course to open in The Bahamas since 1969 made its premiere in 2000. **The Reef Course** at Royal Palm Way, Lucaya (☎ 242-373-2002), was designed by Robert Trent Jones, Jr., who called it "a bit like a Scottish course but a lot warmer." The course requires precise shot-making to avoid its numerous lakes: Water is on 13 of its 18 holes, with various types of long grasses swaying in the trade winds. The course boasts 6,327m (6,920 yd.) of links-style playing grounds. Residents of Our Lucaya, the resort which the course is associated with, pay $100 for 18 holes or $50 for 9 holes. Nonresidents pay $110 for 18 holes and $65 for 9 holes.

Hiking and birding

Early freed slaves carved out the **Heritage Trail** as they made their way from one part of the roadless island to the other. This 13km (8-mile) trek, which runs parallel to the beach, takes you to the flourishing Lucayan National Park. At the park, you can spot birds and explore old caves that the island's Native Americans once used for fishing, collecting fresh water, and burying their dead. But the best part of this all-day excursion is the picnic lunch on a dune, shaded by casuarinas overlooking the beach, and,

of course, the swim afterward. You won't have to hike back to your starting point because **Kayak Nature Tours** (☎ 242-373-2485) provides transportation. The cost of the tour is $69 per person. This company also takes
vacationers on early morning bird-watching tours that include snacks and
transportation to and from hotels.

Horseback riding

Take a ride with **Pinetree Stables** (☎ 242-373-3600), Beachway Drive,
along a wooded trail through a mangrove swamp to a golden sand
beach. These stables are conveniently located halfway between the
International Bazaar and the Port Lucaya Marketplace. The two-hour
ride costs $75 per person. Groups of up to ten people go out with two
guides per trip two times a day, Tuesday through Sunday. Make reservations as far in advance as you can, especially in the summer.

Tennis

In Freeport, most visitors play tennis at the nine hard-surface courts at
the **Crowne Plaza Golf Resort & Casino** (☎ 242-352-9661). The cost is
$10 an hour for guests and $12 for non-guests. Six courts have lights for
night play (for an extra $12). In Lucaya, **The Westin and Sheraton at Our
Lucaya** (☎ 242-373-1333) has four courts, each available for $10 to $18
an hour for guests and non-guests alike. You can rent racquets (for $5)
and balls ($3) and take lessons ($55 per hour) at either of these hotels.

Shopping the Local Stores

 If you're in the market for watches, leather, crystal, china, perfume, or
gemstone and 14-carat gold jewelry, European and American imports
can be considerably less expensive here than at home. Of course, list
prices prevail, and knowing what these prices are back home is always
good so that you can determine whether you're indeed getting a bargain.

Not a whole lot in the stores is actually produced in The Bahamas —
that is, beyond some clothing, lotions, fragrances, crafts, and straw
goods. Many of the items at the island's straw markets come from elsewhere, including all those colorful, flowing Indonesian fabrics that are so
popular for women's wear.

Port Lucaya Marketplace is an open-air shopping and dining complex
that sprawls along the waterfront in Lucaya. Fire-engine red British telephone booths stand near pastel shingle-roofed buildings festooned with
bougainvillea. Many restaurants are on second-story balconies overlooking the channel. Nearly 100 pubs, restaurants, and boutiques draw both
visitors and residents. Some afternoons and most evenings, live music
spills from the bandstand in the lacy harborside gazebo at **Count Basie
Square.**

At the older **International Bazaar,** near Crowne Plaza Golf Resort & Casino in Freeport, the shops, eateries, and architecture take visitors around the world. You enter through a towering *torii* archway, a symbol of welcome in Japan. Designed in the 1960s, the place has a somewhat seedy feel. In many cases, merchandise and food are only loosely related to the countries represented by the architecture of the section where they're sold. Yet, strolling along the maze of slender, meandering walkways is still amusing. Turn a corner and your surroundings suddenly change from Tokyo to the Left Bank of Paris, from Latin America to Africa, from East India to Hong Kong. You may have a hard time comparison-shopping because figuring out how to get back to a place you came from can be tricky. For the most part, prices here are good — in many cases 20 to 40 percent lower than in the United States.

Behind the entrance to the International Bazaar, the **Straw Market** is packed with stalls where vendors call out to passers-by, "It doesn't cost anything to look!" Baskets, wide-brimmed hats, bags, place mats, and dolls are among the most popular straw goods. Tables are also piled high with T-shirts, beach towels, shell jewelry, magnets, mugs, and mahogany African-style Bahamian woodcarvings. The **International Arcade,** which links the bazaar with the Casino at Bahamia, houses branches of glitzy stores, such as Parfum de Paris, Columbian Emeralds, and the Leather Shop. Here, you can also find artisans in booths, including glass blowers and jewelry designers.

International Bazaar

Here are some worthwhile shops you'll find at the bazaar.

Art

Flovin Gallery (☎ 242-352-7564) sells original Bahamian and international art, frames, lithographs, posters, and Bahamian-made Christmas ornaments and decorated coral. It also offers handmade Bahamian dolls, coral jewelry, and other gift items. Another branch is at the **Port Lucaya Marketplace.**

Crystal and china

Island Galleria (☎ 242-352-8194) boasts an awesome collection of crystal. The store includes works of utilitarian art in china and crystal by Waterford, Aynsley, Lenox, Dansk, Belleek, and Swarovski. The store can pack and ship anything you buy. Another branch is located in the Port Lucaya Marketplace (☎ 242-373-4512).

Fashion

Cleo's Boutique (☎ 242-351-3340) offers everything from evening wear to lingerie, as well as everything in between. A warm and inviting destination, Cleo's prides itself on capturing the Caribbean woman in all her moods. You can also find a wide array of costume jewelry beginning at $20 a piece.

Far East Traders (☎ 242-352-9280) sells Asian linens, hand-embroidered dresses and blouses, silk robes, lace parasols, smoking jackets, and kimonos. A branch is located inside the Island Galleria at the Port Lucaya Marketplace.

Paris in The Bahamas (☎ 242-352-5380) contains the biggest selection of luxury goods under one roof in the International Bazaar. The staff wears couture black dresses, and everywhere there's a sense of French glamour and conspicuous consumption. The store offers both Gucci and Versace leather goods for men and women; crystal from Lalique, Baccarat, Daum, Kosta Boda, and Orrefors; and a huge collection of cosmetics and perfumes.

Gifts

Caribbean Cargo (☎ 242-352-2929) is one of the island's best gift shops, specializing in such items as picture frames, candles, clocks, and clothes.

Unusual Centre (☎ 242-373-7333) is exactly what its name suggests. Where else can you find a wide array of items made of eel skin or goods made from exotic feathers, such as peacock? Another branch is located at the Port Lucaya Marketplace (☎ 242-352-5994).

 In addition to these gift shops in the bazaar, **Bahamian Things,** 15B Poplar Crescent (☎ 242-352-9550), sells an array of locally handcrafted items, including books on The Bahamas, Abaco ceramics, woodwork, and even handmade Christmas decorations.

Jewelry

Colombian Emeralds International (☎ 242-352-5464) is a branch of the world's foremost emerald jeweler, offering a wide array of precious gemstone jewelry and one of the island's best watch collections. Careful shoppers will find significant savings over U.S. prices. The outlet offers certified appraisals and free 90-day insurance. Two branches are also located in the Port Lucaya Marketplace (☎ 242-373-8400).

Leather

The Leather Shop (☎ 242-352-5491) is another good outlet, carrying a much more limited Fendi line but also many other designers, including Land and HCL. Additional leather goods include shoes and gift items. Other locations include the Port Lucaya Marketplace (☎ 242-373-2323) and **Regent's Centre** (☎ 242-352-2895).

Perfume

Les Parisiennes (☎ 242-352-5380) offers a wide range of perfumes, including the latest from Paris. It also sells Lancôme cosmetics and skincare products. A branch is at the Port Lucaya Marketplace (☎ 242-373-2974).

The Perfume Factory Fragrance of The Bahamas (☎ 242-352-9391) is the top fragrance producer in the country. The shop is housed in a model of an 1800s mansion, and visitors can go inside to hear a five-minute commentary and to see the mixing of fragrant oils. A "mixology" department lets you create your own fragrance from a selection of oils. The shop's well-known products include Island Promises, Goombay, Paradise, and Pink Pearl (which has conch pearls in the bottle). The shop also sells Guanahani, a fragrance created to commemorate the 500th anniversary of Columbus's first landfall in the New World. ("Guanahani" was the Indian name for the southern Bahamian island of San Salvador, traditionally believed to be the site of Columbus's landing.) Other perfumes and colognes include Sand, the number-one Bahamian-made men's fragrance in the country.

Stamps and coins

Bahamas Coin and Stamp Ltd. (☎ 242-352-898) is the major coin dealer on the island. It specializes in Bahamian coin jewelry, ancient Roman coins, and relics from sunken Spanish galleons. It also carries a vast selection of antique U.S. and English coins and paper money.

Port Lucaya Marketplace

The following are some of the highlights of the marketplace.

Androsia (☎ 242-373-8387) is the Port Lucaya outlet of the famous batik house of Andros Island. Its designs and colors capture the spirit of The Bahamas. Fabrics are handmade on the island of Andros. The store sells quality cotton resort wear, including simple skirts, tops, jackets, and shorts for women, and it also offers a colorful line of children's clothes.

Bandolera (☎ 242-373-7691) carries a collection of chic women's clothing that's many, many cuts above the usual run of T-shirts and tank tops. The staff can be rather haughty here, however.

Flovin Gallery II (☎ 242-373-8388) is a branch of the art gallery that's located in the International Bazaar. It sells a collection of oil paintings (both Bahamian and international), along with lithographs and posters. In its limited field, it's the best in the business. It also features a number of gift items, such as handmade Bahamian dolls and decorated corals.

Harley-Davidson of Freeport (☎ 242-373-8269) is one of only two registered and licensed Harley outlets in The Bahamas. You can special-order a motorcycle if you feel flush with funds from a casino, or you can content yourself with T-shirts, leather vests, belts, caps, sunglasses, and gift items.

Jeweler's Warehouse (☎ 242-373-8401) is a place for bargain hunters looking for good buys on discounted, closeout 14-karat gold and gemstone jewelry. Discounts can be up to 50 percent, but the quality of many of these items remains high. You can get guarantees and certified appraisals.

UNEXSO Dive Shop (☎ 242-373-1250) is the premier dive shop of The Bahamas. It sells everything related to the water: swimsuits, wet suits, underwater cameras and video equipment, shades, hats, souvenirs, and state-of-the-art diving equipment.

Living It Up After Dark

In Freeport, most of the nightlife spins around the **Royal Oasis Casino,** located at the Crowne Plaza Golf Resort & Casino, The Mall at West Sunrise Highway (☎ 242-350-7000). This casino is a mammoth, glittering, Moroccan-style palace, and is one of the largest casinos in either The Bahamas or the Caribbean. Visitors play games of chance and attend Las Vegas-inspired floor shows. Giving Freeport major competition is the **Isle of Capri Casino** at The Westin and Sheraton at Our Lucaya Beach & Golf Resort, Royal Palm Way (☎ 242-373-1333), which at long last has brought gambling to the Lucaya area. This casino offers guests their choice of games, ranging from baccarat to Caribbean stud poker, as well as 400 slot machines. Both casinos are open daily from 10 a.m. to 2 a.m.

For an evening with more island appeal, try the **Yellowbird Showroom** at **Best Western Castaways Resort,** East Mall Drive, Freeport (☎ 242-352-6682). Fire eaters, calypso singers, and limbo dancers put on a festive show Monday through Saturday from 9 to 11 p.m. ($20 per person, including one drink, or $32 per person for the show, dinner, and drinks). About a 45-minute drive from Freeport, **West End** is a local after-hours target, particularly **The Star Club** (☎ 242-346-6207), which usually stays open until dawn. Where Grand Bahama's local nightclubs leave off, hotel and restaurant bars and lounges pick up the slack, with crowded dance floors.

In the Port Lucaya Marketplace's waterfront **Count Basie Square,** live music pumps from the gazebo almost every night, starting around 7:30 p.m. You can hear calypso played on steel drums, a reggae band, a Junkanoo troupe, or a gospel group. Some say that the idea for the marketplace itself originated with the Count, the legendary American jazz pianist and bandleader who spent his last years on Grand Bahama. Most of Port Lucaya's stores close after dark, but the marketplace still throbs with activity under the stars. The bars and restaurants surrounding the square are serious hangout spots for both residents and visitors.

After many vacationers see the waters surrounding Grand Bahama, they can't get enough, even after dark. To be wined, dined, and entertained at sea, make a reservation for a moonlight dinner cruise with **Superior Watersports** (☎ 242-373-7863). You can feast on steak and lobster on a fun-filled 22m (72-ft.) catamaran. Cruises run Monday, Wednesday, and Friday from 6 to 9 p.m. and depart from Port Lucaya Marketplace; the cost is $59 for adults and $39 for children.

Going Beyond Grand Bahama

Whether you're a novice or an experienced kayaker, one of the following excursions can introduce you to another side of The Bahamas.

Trip # 1: Kayak and snorkel adventure to Peterson Cay

You can go from Grand Bahama, one of the country's largest islands, to one of its smallest by kayak. Nearby uninhabited **Peterson Cay** is an itty-bitty national park on a reef. After you reach this pristine slip of land edged by a luscious beach, Freeport and Lucaya seem like Las Vegas. You can go on this excursion with **Kayak Nature Tours** (☎ 242-373-2485). When you arrive at the tour's starting point — about a 25-minute drive from Freeport — you paddle for about 30 minutes to the cay. For about 90 minutes, you can snorkel around the island with the colorful fish and marine life. A trip with Kayak Nature Tours costs $69 per person. The company keeps snorkel groups to a maximum of ten people, even when more participants are in the total group of kayakers. The company provides all the necessary gear, and your driver entertains you with a running narration about Grand Bahama as you're transported to and from your hotel.

Trip # 2: Kayak trip to Indian Cay

Another kayak adventure offered by **Kayak Nature Tours** (☎ 242-373-2485) costs $89 per person and takes seven hours. This trip combines a kayak adventure with a snorkeling tour and is excellent for first-time snorkelers *and* adventures. The tour's launched by sightseeing in the old hamlet of West End, site of the first settlement on Grand Bahama Island. Then guests go by kayak to **Indian Cay,** one of the most remote of all the islands in the North Bahamas. According to legend, Ponce de Léon discovered this cay and named it *La Vieja* (the old one) after an old Lucayan woman he found there. Upon seeing her, he knew at once that he hadn't found the Fountain of Youth he so eagerly sought. Adventurers take a short nature walk across this tiny cay that time forgot. Later, back on "mainland" Grand Bahama, tour guides direct participants along the underwater trails at Old Bahama Bay Resort. At the resort, visitors have lunch served on a private beach.

Part V
The Abacos: Prime Out Islands

The 5th Wave   By Rich Tennant

AFTER SAILING AROUND ELBOW CAY, DERK AND HEATHER HEAD FOR THE INTERESTING GROTTOS OF NOSE CAY.

In this part . . .

We explore The Abacos, which lie north of New Providence. You discover what makes the most popular of these serene landfalls special, whether you're considering an inn at a marina in Marsh Harbour, a small beach hotel on Elbow Cay, an upscale yacht club on Green Turtle Cay, or a modern resort on Treasure Cay. In this part, we give you plenty of suggestions for having fun in the sun and sampling everything from conch fritters to lobster. Most importantly, you find out the best ways to travel among these small, scenic cays by air, land, and sea.

Chapter 18

Marsh Harbour and Great Abaco Island

After New Providence Island (where you find Nassau and Paradise Island) and Grand Bahama Island (home to Freeport and Lucaya), the "prime" grouping of islands is the Abaco archipelago. The island chain is the most visited of the Out Islands, and it's a prime destination for boaters and fishermen.

When people speak of **"the Abacos,"** they're referring not just to one island but to a boomerang-shaped archipelago of mostly minor cays, lying in the northeastern part of the island nation. The Abacos begin at tiny Walker's Cay in the north and stretch for 209km (130 miles) in a southwesterly direction. Most of these cays are uninhabited.

As the center of Abaconian commerce, **Marsh Harbour** is the best refueling stop in all the Out Islands, with the largest range of facilities, including marinas, shopping centers, banks, and pharmacies. Even though Marsh Harbour is large enough to boast a Pizza Hut, it's still small enough to walk around; it has only one traffic light. However, the town lacks the quaint New England charm of either New Plymouth (see Chapter 20) or the allure of Hope Town (see Chapter 19).

Marsh Harbour is also the major transportation hub of the Abacos, with its airport functioning as the main arrival point for most visitors — at least those who didn't sail in on a boat.

Arriving at the Airport

Regardless of where you're going in the Abacos, Marsh Harbour is the easiest town to reach. Minor airstrips are in the Abacos, including

Marsh Harbour

Treasure Cay (see Chapter 21), but Marsh Harbour offers the most convenient flights servicing the Abaco chain.

The airport is a ten-minute drive south of Marsh Harbour. Upon arrival, you'll find taxis waiting to take you where you want to go, along with restrooms, phones, and a little snack bar. No car-rental agencies are at the airport; you have to make arrangements after you reach Marsh Harbour.

Choosing Your Location

Marsh Harbour is at the crook of the bend in the archipelago (just opposite of Elbow Cay). **Treasure Cay** lies to the north, a distance of 45km (28 miles) from Marsh Harbour, and you reach it by taking a badly paved road.

If you're an adventurer, you'll want to drive 40km (25 miles) farther north to **Little Abaco Island.** Birders come here to look for the West

Indian red-bellied woodpecker, and sometimes you can still see wild horses. On the way to Little Abaco, you pass the Treasure Cay airport and the dock where visitors take a ferry to **Green Turtle Cay.** The last town on **Great Abaco Island** is a hamlet called **Cooper's Town.** After that, you can take a causeway that links Great and Little Abaco islands.

Little Abaco's small settlements are hardly worth a stopover, taking in Cedar Harbor (with a few good beaches) and Mount Hope, which you reach after another 8km (5 miles) and mainly known for its drugstore and grocery. A drive 8km to the northwest delivers you to the hamlet of **Fox Town,** which may be the end of your tour, with its post office and police station. The actual end of the line is another 3km (2 miles) ahead when you come to **Crown Haven.** After this point, you have to turn around and go back south to Marsh Harbour.

Although there are tiny harbors of no importance in Great Abaco, when locals refer to "the harbor," they mean the yacht-filled Marsh Harbour in the center of the Abacos. Marsh Harbour opens onto the Sea of Abaco. To better understand the geography of the Abacos, refer to the map "The Abaco Islands" in Chapter 3.

Where you stay in the Abacos — Marsh Harbour, Elbow Cay, Green Turtle Cay, or Treasure Cay — depends on your tastes and interest. Before you make a decision, go through all four of these island chapters to see which one appeals to you, because each island of the Abacos has its devotees as well as its detractors. For example, Green Turtle Cay may draw a snobby yachting crowd who may not be charmed at all by the more middlebrow allures of Marsh Harbour.

Getting Around Marsh Harbour and Great Abaco

In many of the smaller islands of the Abacos, including Treasure Cay and Green Turtle Cay (see Chapters 21 and 20, respectively), you can manage without a car. If you plan to stay in Marsh Harbour and visit one of the off-shore islands, such as Elbow Cay (reached by ferryboat; see Chapter 19), you still don't need a car. But if you want to explore "mainland" Great Abaco Island, including points south such as **Bahamas National Trust Sanctuary,** you need a car.

- ✔ **Hoofing it:** Marsh Harbour is a small town, and you can get around on foot, but you won't really find that much to see. We suggest saving your legs for a day-trip to Elbow Cay (see Chapter 19), where you can walk endlessly along its beaches of golden sand.

- ✔ **Driving around:** You don't need a car to get around the town itself, but if you want to explore the rest of the island on your own, you can rent a car, usually for $70 to $80 a day or $350 to $400 per week (be prepared for bad roads, though). In Marsh Harbour, call **A&P**

Rentals (☎ 242-367-2655), Don MacKay Boulevard, to see whether any vehicles are available.

✔ **Peddling around: Rental Wheels of Abaco** (☎ 242-367-4643), Queen Elizabeth Drive, rents bikes for $8 a day or $35 a week and mopeds for $35 a day or $185 a week. The best place to go biking is to take the long road heading south from Marsh Harbour, perhaps finding a secluded beach to beat the heat of the day.

✔ **Taking a taxi:** Unmetered taxis, which you often have to share with other passengers, meet all arriving flights. They can take you to your hotel if it's on the Abaco "mainland"; otherwise, they can drop you at a dock where you can hop aboard a water taxi to one of the neighboring offshore islands, such as Green Turtle Cay or Elbow Cay. Most visitors use a combination taxi and water-taxi ride to reach the most popular hotels. From Marsh Harbour Airport to Hope Town on Elbow Cay, the cost is about $12 for the transfer. You can also make arrangements for a taxi tour of Great or Little Abaco. These tours, however, are expensive, and you don't really see that much. Sightseeing on foot in one of the Loyalist settlements, such as New Plymouth, is better. Taxis are independently owned and operated, so there's no central number to call. But you can easily find a taxi at the airport. If you need one otherwise, you can ask the staff at your hotel to summon one for you.

✔ **Boarding a boat:** Because Marsh Harbour is the boating capital of The Bahamas, some Bahamians use boats more frequently than a car for getting around. **Albury's Ferry Service** (☎ 242-367-3147) can take you to the most interesting offshore islands, including Elbow Cay and Great Guana Cay.

Staying in Style

Abaco Beach Resort & Boat Harbour
$$$–$$$$ **Marsh Harbour**

This 82-room beachfront resort — the biggest and best in Marsh Harbour — is a good choice, especially if you're serious about diving or fishing. This property extends over a sprawling acreage at the edge of town and meets up with a small beach. The business has several different faces: the hotel, with its handsomely furnished rooms that overlook the Sea of Abaco; the well-managed restaurant and bar; the Boat Harbour Marina, which has slips for 180 boats and full docking facilities; and a full-fledged dive shop. The beach here is small and gravel studded and isn't reason enough to check in. The beach is also private, reserved only for residents of the hotel. The bedrooms are better equipped than the ones at its rival, Conch Inn Hotel (see next review). At the Abaco Beach Resort, the rooms are air-conditioned and include a TV and extras, such as a minibar, hair dryer, and safe. **Angler's**

Restaurant is one of Marsh Harbour's best (see the review in the "Dining Out" section later in the chapter). A swim-up bar and beachfront bar serve light snacks and grog. Two tennis courts, a fitness center, sauna, and massage services are on-site. Staff can also arrange boat rentals for you at the marina.

See map p. 236. The Sea of Abaco. ☎ *800-468-4799 or 242-367-2158. Fax: 242-367-4154.* www.abacoresort.com. *Rack rates: $199–$285 double, $390 one-bedroom suite, $550 cottage for up to 4. AE, DISC, MC, V.*

Conch Inn Hotel & Marina
$$ **Marsh Harbour**

Slightly downscale from the Abaco Beach Resort & Boat Harbour (see previous review), this little nine-room inn lies at the southeastern edge of the harbor. One of the world's largest yacht-chartering companies, The Moorings, leases this casual, one-story hotel on a long-term basis. A number of sandy beaches are within driving distance. Its small motel-style bedrooms have two double beds, and you can get roll-aways if you have extra occupants. All units overlook the yachts bobbing in the nearby marina. A freshwater pool, fringed with palm trees, and a nearby branch of the Dive Abaco scuba facility are on the premises. The on-site restaurant and bar, the **Conch Crawl Restaurant** (see the review later in this chapter).

See map p. 236. East Bay Street. ☎ *242-367-4000. Fax: 242-367-4004.* www.conchinn. com. *Rack rates: $120 double. Extra person $20. MC, V.*

Dolphin Beach Resort
$$$ **Great Guana Cay**

Even better than any of the accommodations of Marsh Harbour is an escape to the offshore **Great Guana Cay** and this ten-room charmer (for more details on this cay, refer to "Going Beyond Marsh Harbour" later in this chapter). Set directly astride one of the best beaches in The Bahamas, a 15-minute walk north of Guana Cay's largest settlement (Guana Village), with miles of powder-soft sand in front of you, this resort offers informal but very comfortable lodgings. Four of the units are in the main house and have queen-size beds, ceiling fans, small refrigerators, and microwaves; three of them contain private screened-in decks with teakwood furniture. The oceanfront cottages, which accommodate between two and four guests, have queen-size beds, ceiling fans, air-conditioning, and kitchenettes. The showers are outside but are secluded and screened by island flora. The place is private, intimate, and laid-back. The on-site restaurant, **The Landing,** offers a "conch crawl," which is a Bahamian take on a lobster tank. **Nippers,** a beachfront bar and grill, is a five-minute walk away. A saltwater pool is on-site, and guests can also get bikes, kayaks, and snorkeling gear from the hotel.

Outside Guana Village. ☎ *800-222-2646 or 242-365-5137.* www.dolphinbeach resort.com. *Rack rates: $180–$195 double, $240–$350 cottage. MC, V.*

Lofty Fig Villas
$$ **Marsh Harbour**

This family-owned, six-unit bungalow colony overlooks the harbor. It doesn't have the services of a resort like Abaco Beach, but it's good for families and self-sufficient types. Built in 1970, the villas stand in a tropical landscape with a freshwater pool and a gazebo where you can barbecue. Rooms have one queen-size bed and a queen-size sofabed, a dining area, a kitchen, and a private screened-in porch. The hotel provides maid service Monday through Saturday. The hotel is about a ten-minute walk from a supermarket and shops, and you can find restaurants and bars just across the street. You can also find marinas, a dive shop, and boat rentals close by. From the Lofty Fig, you have to walk, bike, or drive a half-kilometer (1 mile) east to a point near the Marsh Harbour ferryboat docks for access to a sandy beach and a snorkeling site. (Many visitors opt to go to Great Guana Cay for their day at the beach.)

See map p. 236. East Bay Street. ☎ *and fax 242-367-2681. Rack rates: $120 daily or $780 weekly for two. Extra person $20. MC, V.*

Nettie's Different of Abaco
$$$ **Casuarina Point**

Set within the hamlet of **Casuarina Point,** 29km (18 miles) south of Marsh Harbour, a wide deck and a garden surround this 20-room, family-managed bonefishing club. This ecologically conscious place was built at the edge of a saltwater marsh favored by a variety of birds, wild hogs, and iguana; it's a good choice for bird-watchers and superb for bonefishing enthusiasts. It's not luxurious, but it's a peaceful place near good snorkeling and virgin beaches. The hotel is closely associated with several bonefishing guides in the neighborhood, any of whom can arrange full-day fishing excursions for around $375 per couple. (This cost doesn't include all equipment. Be sure that you understand the arrangements thoroughly before you commit yourself.) Each of the small to midsize bedrooms has a screened-in porch, a ceiling fan, a small bathroom, and simple furnishings; eight rooms have air-conditioning. During your stay, you're in the midst of a close-knit, isolated community that's firmly committed to preserving the local environment and heritage. You can even visit a living museum that takes you back through 100 years of the island's history. The hotel also has a bar and restaurant where the staff can recite a selection of simple Bahamian fare to you before you sit down for your meal. The food is quite good. Non-guests can drop in for meals.

Casuarina Point. ☎ *877-505-1850 or 242-366-2150. Fax: 242-327-8152.* www. differentofabaco.com. *Rack rates: $200 double; from $1,300 per week. AE, MC, V.*

Dining Out

Angler's Restaurant
$$ **Marsh Harbour** BAHAMIAN/SEAFOOD

At Boat Harbour, overlooking the Sea of Abaco, Angler's is the main restaurant of the town's major resort (Abaco Beach Resort & Boat Harbour; see our review earlier in this chapter). Within a few steps of your seat, dock pilings rise from the water, yachts and fishing boats come and go, and the place is open and airy. The menu changes daily, but it always features fresh seafood — which the chef prepares with finesse — along with a well-chosen selection of meat and poultry dishes. Begin with spicy lobster bisque, a timbale of grilled vegetables, or perhaps crab Rangoon, served on bean-sprout slaw with a pineapple-coconut sauce. Main dishes dance with flavor, notably the lobster stir in a mango chili sauce and the guava-glazed charred lamb chops. The chef also prepares the freshly caught red snapper with just the right infusion of fresh basil.

See map p. 236. In the Abaco Beach Resort & Boat Harbour. ☎ *242-367-2158. Reservations recommended for dinner. Main courses: $6–$29. AE, MC, V. Open: Daily 7:30 a.m.–2:30 p.m. and 6–9:30 p.m.*

The Conch Crawl Restaurant
$–$$ **Marsh Harbour** BAHAMIAN

Only the Angler's Restaurant (see our earlier review in this chapter) is more sophisticated than this winning choice. Located at the Conch Inn Hotel & Marina, Conch Crawl attracts a lot of yachties and visiting professional athletes. The cooks use local ingredients, such as freshly caught grouper and snapper, whenever they can. They also know every conceivable way to prepare conch. The regulars don't even consult the menu; they just ask, "What's good?" Diners also look for daily specials, such as curried chicken or steamed chicken. Fish and seafood are always on the menu. If you're frittering away a few hours, drop in for a Conch Crawl, a rum-based drink with secret ingredients. The bar, set beneath an octagonal gazebo near the piers, is a fine place to meet people.

A taste of the Abacos

In Marsh Harbour, conch salad is sold right on the docks. "It'll make a man out of you," one local vendor tells everybody, even if the person is a woman. If you stick around long enough, you'll see Billy Thompson coming by in his little truck. He's said to make the world's best homemade soursop-and-mango ice cream. If you want to go really casual, try **Island Bakery,** Don MacKay Boulevard (☎ 242-367-2129), which has the best Bahamian bread and cinnamon rolls on the island, often emerging fresh from the oven. You may even pick up the makings for a picnic.

See map p. 236. At the Conch Inn (The Moorings), East Bay Street. ☎ 242-367-4444. Lunch salads, sandwiches, and platters: $6–$14; dinner main courses $16–$28. MC, V. Open: Daily 7 a.m.–11 p.m.

The Jib Room
$–$$ Marsh Harbour   BAHAMIAN/AMERICAN

This funky restaurant/bar is a hangout for local residents and boat owners who savor its welcoming spirit. If you want the house-special cocktail, a Bilge Burner, get ready for a head-spinning combination of apricot brandy, rum, coconut juice, and vodka. Saturday night brings Jib's steak barbecue, when the staff serves up as many as 300 steaks. The only other dinner nights are Wednesday and Thursday, when grilled baby back ribs may be the featured dish of the day. Other choices include a seafood platter, New York strip steak, and broiled lobster — and yes, you've had it all before in better versions, but dishes are well prepared. Go for the convivial atmosphere rather than the food.

See map p. 236. Marsh Harbour Marina, Pelican Shores. ☎ 242-367-2700. Lunch platters: $7.50–$10; fixed-price dinner: $20. MC, V. Open: Wed–Sat 11:30 a.m.–2:30 p.m. and Wed–Thurs and Sat 7–11 p.m.

Mangoes Restaurant
$–$$ Marsh Harbour   BAHAMIAN/AMERICAN

Set near the harborfront in one of the town's most distinctive buildings, Mangoes is the best — and certainly the most popular — restaurant on the island, drawing both yachties and locals. It boasts a cedar-topped bar and a cathedral ceiling that soars above a deck jutting out over the water. Somehow the chefs seem to try a little harder here, offering a typical menu but adding a hint of island spirit. They dress up grilled grouper with a bit of mango and tomatoes, and cracked conch makes an appearance as well. Your best bet, as is the case in nearly all Bahamian restaurants, is the fresh catch of the day, and Mangoes is no exception. At lunch, you can sample their locally famous "conch burger."

See map p. 236. Front Street. ☎ 242-367-2366. Reservations recommended. Lunch: $5–$15; dinner main courses: $14–$30. AE, MC, V. Open: Daily 7 a.m.–3 p.m. and 6:30–9 p.m. (bar daily 11:30 a.m.–midnight).

The premier yachting event

In July, Marsh Harbour hosts **Regatta Time in Abaco**, attracting sailboats and their crews from around the world. Every year, the event is held sometime between Independence Day in the United States and Independence Day in The Bahamas (in other words, between July 4 and July 10). Many of the yachties participating in this event stay at the Green Turtle Club. For event registration forms and more information, visit www.go-abacos.com/regatta/rtia-regatta.html.

Mother Merle's Fishnet
$ Dundas Town BAHAMIAN

Mother Merle's Fishnet prepares many of the meals eaten aboard the yachts and sailing crafts in the nearby harbor. The restaurant doesn't have a dining room on the premises, so don't expect a place to sit and linger, although the well-prepared food — if you don't mind hauling it off to another venue — makes the limitations most palatable. The setting is a cement house on the town's main street. Inside, you find the gentle but aging matriarch Merle Williams, who's assisted by her able-bodied daughters, Angela and Shirley. As Mother Merle tells it, all Bahamian women are good cooks, and you might believe her words when you taste her family's three different preparations of chicken, all prepared according to secret family recipes. Locals swear that Mother Merle makes the best cracked conch in the Abacos, and she's also known for her different preparations of grouper.

Dundas Town, the hamlet that adjoins Marsh Harbour, lying directly north of the center. ☎ *242-367-2770. Main courses: $8–$17. No credit cards. Open: Tues–Sat 6:30–10:30 p.m.*

Sapodilly's Bar & Grill
$ Marsh Harbour BAHAMIAN

One of Marsh Harbour's better restaurants occupies an open-air pavilion across the road from the harborfront in an area of town known as "the tourist strip." Even if you eventually head into the high-raftered interior dining room, take time out for a drink or two on the covered open-air deck, surrounded by vibrant Junkanoo colors and a crowd of local hipsters, yacht owners, marina workers, and businessmen visiting from other parts of The Bahamas. Lunch may consist of grilled fish sandwiches, burgers, salads, and quiche. Dinners are more elaborate, with 12-ounce New York strip steak, flavor-filled shrimp kebabs in teriyaki sauce, and zesty curried filets of grouper. Live music plays every Friday and Saturday from 8 to 11 p.m.

See map p. 236. East Bay Street. ☎ *242-367-3498. Reservations recommended. Lunch platters and sandwiches: $8–$15; dinner main courses: $19–$28. MC, V. Open: Mon–Sat 11:30 a.m.–3 p.m. and 6–9 p.m. (bar daily 11:30–closing).*

Wally's
$$ Marsh Harbour BAHAMIAN/INTERNATIONAL

This eatery sits across the street from the water and occupies a tidy pink colonial villa on a lawn dotted with hibiscus. It has an outdoor terrace, a boutique, and an indoor bar and dining area filled with Haitian paintings. The special house drink is a Wally's Special, which contains four kinds of rum and a medley of fruit juices. The chef prepares the best Bahamian cracked conch at Marsh Harbour, as well as tender filet mignon, lamb chops, tarragon chicken, and an excellent version of smothered grouper. Main dishes come with a generous house salad and vegetables. The place really hops at lunchtime, when things can get very busy as hungry diners devour dolphinfish burgers, several kinds of chicken platters, and some well-stuffed sandwiches.

See map p. 236. East Bay Street. ☎ *242-367-2074. Reservations recommended for dinner. Lunch sandwiches and platters: $10–$13; dinner main courses: $25–$30. AE, DISC, MC, V. Open: Mon–Sat 11:30 a.m.–3 p.m., Fri–Sat 6–9 p.m. Closed six weeks during Sept–Oct.*

Enjoying the Sand and Surf

Exploring almost-deserted beaches and sailing to nearby islands, such as Elbow Cay, are part of the fun of any visit to Great Abaco Island.

Combing the beaches

Of the major towns of the Out Islands, Marsh Harbour has one of the least appealing sets of beaches. You can opt for any of a trio of private beaches, but none is very enticing, and all carry the stigma of not really wanting outsiders. The easiest of these three beaches to circumvent is the one at the Abaco Beach Resort, but it's small, not really fabulous and, again, private. Buy a drink for a local at the hotel bar, and you're in, but that, at best, is a somewhat uncomfortable arrangement.

To compensate, beachgoers get into their cars and head south of Marsh Harbour. After 15 to 20 minutes of southbound driving, and at points south of Little Harbour, lots of good beaches begin to appear. The beaches in the vicinity of the hamlet of **Casuarina Point** benefit from some battered, all-Bahamian restaurants in the vicinity.

Some swimmers heading south from Marsh Harbour make it a point to go eastward from the main highway whenever an offshoot road appears, usually at points near Little Harbour or at points south of Little Harbour. Other times, they simply stop their cars wherever they feel like it.

 None of the beaches of Great Abaco Island has facilities or lifeguards. Guard your valuables and be safe.

Playing in the surf

Divers swim to the **Abacos Train Wreck,** which you can explore in 4.5 to 6m (15–20 ft.) of water; the wreck consists of two almost-intact locomotives lying on their sides. Yet another wreck nearby, the *Adirondack,* lies in shallow water some 3 to 7.5m (10–25 ft.) deep. Many divers also come here to explore the government-protected **Sea Preserve and Fowl Cay Land,** which teems with multi-colored sea life in shallow reefs.

One of the best places to snorkel, with a colorful offshore reef, moray eels, and a plethora of beautiful rainbow-hued fish, is **Mermaid Reef.** It lies on a narrow, scrub-covered peninsula known as **Pelican Shore,** which forms the northernmost edge of Marsh Harbour's harborfront. You can drive to a point near the origin of Pelican Shore, trek across a stretch of scrub and sand, and then swim out to Mermaid Reef. Alternatively, some hardy locals sometimes swim from central Marsh Harbour across the harbor, walk across the very narrow sands of Pelican Shore, and then swim once again the short distance to Mermaid Reef.

Dive Abaco, at the Conch Inn Hotel & Marina (☎ 800-247-5338 in the U.S. or 242-367-2787; www.diveabaco.com), provides services as simple as renting snorkeling gear or as in-depth as offering full dive trips to tunnels and caverns in the world's third-longest barrier reef. Uncertified novice divers can take all-inclusive resort courses for $152. Two-tank dives, including tanks and weights for certified divers, are $82. Snorkeling is $52. Trips depart daily at 9:30 a.m., and demand dictates afternoon trips. **Sea Horse Boat Rentals,** at the Abaco Beach Resort & Boat Harbour (☎ 242-367-2513), also rents snorkeling gear.

Climbing aboard

Because the Abacos are the boating capital of The Bahamas, many visitors arrive for only one purpose: to charter a boat and go sailing.

Ask about the depth of the harbor before you rent and, even more importantly, before you attempt to navigate your way in or out of Marsh Harbour, because Hurricane Floyd changed the configuration of the channel. People with yachts that have deep drafts have reported trouble getting in and out of the port.

If you want to try *bareboating* in The Bahamas — seagoing without a captain or crew — **Abaco Bahamas Charters** (☎ 800-626-5690, or 242-366-0151; www.abacocharters.com), can set you up. Weekly charters with a choice of boats begin at $1,625, with a $1,500 deposit required. Only experienced sailors can rent.

The Moorings (☎ 800-535-7289 or 242-367-4000) is one of the leading charter sailboat outfitters in the world. It operates from an eagle's nest perch behind the Conch Inn Hotel & Marina, overlooking a labyrinth of piers and wharves — at least 80 berths, with more on the way — where hundreds of upscale watercrafts are tied up (many of them for rent). With one of its vessels, you can enjoy short sails between the islands, stopping at white sandy beaches and snug anchorages. Yacht rentals generally range from $455 to $1,280 a day, with a skipper costing another $144 per day, and an onboard cook (if you want one) priced at an additional $124 per day.

For the more casual boater, **Sea Horse Boat Rentals,** at the Abaco Beach Resort (☎ 242-367-2513), offers some of the best rentals. A 5.5m (18-ft.) Boston Whaler rents for $140 per day, and you can also book a 6.5m (22-ft.) Privateer for $155 per day. You can also rent other vessels, and all boats are equipped with a Bimini top, coolers, a compass, and a swimming platform, along with life jackets, a paddle, docking lines, and other equipment.

Exploring on Dry Land

In monuments or sightseeing attractions, Nassau doesn't fear competition from little Marsh Harbour, which some regard as a mere refueling stopover. However, Marsh Harbour is the best center for exploring the nature-created sights of Great Abaco Island, which consists of both Great Abaco and Little Abaco.

A fully graded and tarred main highway links all the settlements on the "mainland," with such colorfully named hamlets as Fire Road, Mango Hill, Coopers Town, Joe Creek, Red Bays, Snake Cay, Little Harbour, Sandy Point, Cherokee Sound and, our favorite, Hole in the Wall, which lies at the "bottom" of Great Abaco. (See "The Abaco Islands" map in Chapter 3 to help you visualize the area.)

Driving south for 40km (25 miles) from Marsh Harbour along the **Great Abaco Highway,** you come first to **Cherokee Sound,** with a population of 150. Cherokee Sound is located at the end of a peninsula that juts out into Cherokee Sound. Residents are descendents of Loyalists who fled the mainland U.S. in 1783 and remained faithful to the British Crown.

These people faced an inhospitable land, and for two centuries have tried making a living as best they can. The men dive for lobsters or go out at night "sharking." They sell the jaws of the sharks in Marsh Harbour. They also hunt down tiniki crabs as well as pigeon and wild boar in the remote pinelands of the Abacos.

From Cherokee, you can head north to **Little Harbour,** a settlement about 12km (8 miles) south. While in Little Harbour, visit **Pete Johnston's Foundry** (☎ 242-367-3067). In the Abaco gift and souvenir shops, you'll see a remarkable book, *Artist on His Island,* detailing the true-life adventures of Randolph and Margot Johnston, who lived a Swiss Family Robinson-type adventure with their three sons. Arriving on this southerly point of the Abacos aboard their old Bahamian schooner, the *Langosta,* they lived in one of the natural caves on the island until they eventually erected a thatched dwelling for themselves in 1951. The Johnstons, including son Pete, have achieved international fame as artists and sculptors — though they still live at Little Harbour, a cay shaped like a circle, with a white sand beach running along most of it.

Pete Johnston, using an old "lost-wax" method, casts his bronze sculptures, many of which are in prestigious galleries today. Margot Johnson creates porcelain figurines of island life — birds, fish, boats, and fishers. She also works in glazed metals. They welcome visitors at their studio daily from 10 to 11 a.m. and from 2 to 3 p.m. You can also purchase their art, which comes in a wide price range.

Before leaving the foundry, you can stop in for a drink at the laid-back **Pete's Pub.** This rustic pub is beloved by yachties throughout the Abacos. The artwork is intriguing, and the beer is cold. The pub was constructed in part by the timbers of the *Langosta*. In the evening, Pete Johnson may sing a medley of sea chanties, accompanying himself on his guitar.

After leaving Cherokee and Little Harbour, you can return to the Great Abaco Highway, heading south once again to reach the little fishing village of **Casuarina Point,** west of Cherokee Sound. Here you find a lovely stretch of golden sands and some jade-colored boneflats.

If you keep going south, you come to **Crossing Rocks,** a little fishing village 64km (40 miles) south of Marsh Harbour, noted for its kilometer-long beach of golden sand. The hamlet where locals barely eke out a living takes its name from the isthmus where Great Abaco Island narrows to its thinnest point.

If you continue traveling south, you come to a fork in the road: the southern road going to the **Abaco National Park** (also called Bahamas National Trust Sanctuary) and the aptly named **Hole in the Wall,** which is the end of the line for Great Abaco.

Protected by the government, the 8,296 hectare (20,500-acre) Abaco National Park, established in 1994, sprawls across the southeastern portion of Grand Abaco Island. Some 2,023 hectare (5,000 acres) of it is pine forest, with a lot of wetlands that are home to native bird life, including the endangered Bahama parrot. Hardwood forests, sand dunes, and mangrove flats fill the area. Rangers under the sponsorship of the **Bahamas National Trust** (☎ 242-393-1317), which operates occasional tours of the sanctuary, protect this area.

Touring on your own can be extremely difficult, and any private outfitters in the area aren't very well organized. An exception is **Ron and Erin Lowe-Pagliaro** (www.abacooutback.com), who offer sea-kayaking, snorkeling, and land tours and birding excursions. A half-day kayak trip costs $55 per adult or $35 for children 11 and under; a full day costs $85 for adults and $45 for children. They also offer a tour that goes 2½ hours south of Marsh Harbour through the Abaco National Park to Hole in the Wall; these trips cost $95 per adult or $55 per child. Contact them via their Web site.

Living It Up After Dark

The most popular gathering spot in Marsh Harbour is the **Sand Bar** at the Abaco Beach Resort & Boat Harbour (☎ 242-367-2158), opening onto the Sea of Abaco. The yachting crowd, often from Miami, hangs out here, swapping tall tales of the sea while downing lethal rum punches. Another good hangout is at **Wally's,** East Bay Street (☎ 242-367-2074), the second-most frequented place to hang out. You can enjoy Wally's special punch on an outdoor terrace or inside a cozy bar. On Wednesday and Saturday, live entertainment often performs. **Sapodilly's Bar & Grill**

(☎ 242-367-3498), East Bay Street, attracts an interesting blend of locals and visitors, some of whom play at its pool table, others preferring to mix and mingle at the bar.

Going Beyond Marsh Harbour and Great Abaco

The greatest day-trip is to Hope Town on **Elbow Cay** (see Chapter 19). **Great Guana Cay** is lesser known but is also an intriguing jaunt by ferry from Marsh Harbour.

Longest of the Abaco cays, Great Guana, on the east side of the island chain, stretches 4km (7 miles) from tip to tip and lies between Green Turtle Cay and Man-O-War Cay. The beachfront runs the length of the cay and is spectacular — one of the loveliest in The Bahamas. The reef fishing is superb, and bonefish are plentiful in the shallow bays.

The settlement stretches along the beach at the head of the palm-fringed **Kidd's Cove,** named after the pirate, and the ruins of an old sisal mill near the western end of the island make for an interesting detour. The island has about 150 residents, most of them descendants of Loyalists who left Virginia and the Carolinas to settle in this remote place.

As in similar settlements in New Plymouth and Man-O-War Cay, houses here resemble those of old New England. Over the years, the traditional pursuits of the islanders have been boatbuilding, carpentry, farming, and fishing. It doesn't take long to explore the village because it has only two small stores, a one-room schoolhouse, and an Anglican church.

Albury's Ferry Service, Marsh Harbour (☎ 242-365-6010), runs three ferries per day to Great Guana Cay. A round-trip ticket costs $15; one-way is $10.

Instead of driving around the island, most people get around in small boats. On the cay, you can charter a boat for a half-day or a full day (or a month, for that matter). One company to try is **Seagull Fishing Charters** (☎ 242-366-0266) in Hope Town. Carrying up to six passengers in a 9.4 m (31-ft.) Stapleton, Seagull offers sails from Elbow Cay to Lubbers Quarters for $390 for 4 hours; from Marsh Harbour to Man-O-War for $440 for four hours, and from Marsh Harbour or Elbow Cay to Guana Cay, $490 for four hours.

If you want to stay at this remote location, **Dolphin Beach Resort** is a good hotel. (See the listing in the "Staying in Style" section earlier in this chapter.) Most visitors come just for the day, returning to Marsh Harbour for the night.

For fun on the beach, head for **Nipper's Beach Bar & Grill** (☎ 242-365-5143), a dive where visitors hang out with the locals. Right on the sands, you sit in split-level gazebos and take in the most stunning seascape in the Abacos, with a snorkeling reef just 11m (12 yd.) offshore. Burgers and well-stuffed sandwiches satisfy your hunger at lunch. But the best time to go is on a Sunday afternoon for a pig roast. One guest supposedly consumed five "Nipper Trippers" — the bartender's specialty, a mix of five different rums along with tropical juices — and lived to tell about it.

Fast Facts: Marsh Harbour and Great Abaco

ATMs

You find few ATMs in the Out Islands. If you must have cash on your Out Island trip, make arrangements before you leave Nassau or Freeport; we counted just seven ATMs in the entire chain of Out Islands, including the one at the post office in Marsh Harbour.

Emergencies

Call **919** for medical, dental, or hospital emergency. To report a fire call **411**.

Hospitals

The best medical clinic in the Abacos is at the Government Clinic, Queen Elizabeth Drive (☎ 242-367-2510). Hours are Monday through Friday from 9 a.m. to 5 p.m.

Information

Contact the Abaco Tourist Office at Queen Elizabeth Drive in the commercial heart of town (☎ 242-367-3067). The office is open Monday through Friday from 9 a.m. to 5:30 p.m.

Internet Access

Check with your hotel to see whether it provides Internet access.

Pharmacies

Go to the Chemist Shop Pharmacy, Don MacKay Boulevard (☎ 242-367-3106). It's

open Monday through Saturday from 8:30 a.m. to 5:30 p.m.

Police

Call the police at ☎ **242-367-2560**. The station is located in the center of town near Marsh Harbour's sole traffic light.

Post Office

The Marsh Harbour Post Office is on Don MacKay Boulevard (☎ 242-367-2571).

Safety

More crime occurs in Marsh Harbour than anywhere else in the Abacos, but that doesn't mean it's the venue for gangland slayings evocative of Chicago in the 1920s. Remember to take the same precautions that you would take at home. Keep valuables in a safe place and don't go into deserted, unfamiliar areas alone at night.

Taxis

Taxis meet incoming flights at the Marsh Harbour airport. During your stay, the staff at your hotel can call one for you whenever you need one.

Chapter 19

Elbow Cay

· ·

In This Chapter

▶ Navigating Elbow Cay

▶ Finding Elbow Cay's best accommodations and restaurants

▶ Enjoying the beaches, watersports, and attractions

· ·

*V*isit Elbow Cay and you risk coming back year after year, as so many Canadians, Americans, and Europeans who now own vacation homes do. The main settlement is Hope Town, a charming Cape Cod-like village with narrow paved streets, saltbox cottages, little clapboard houses with white picket fences around flowering gardens, and a red-and-white striped lighthouse.

Autumn is quiet in these parts, so some hotels and restaurants close in September and October. Elbow Cay isn't a bustling island with big resorts, so you find few places that have TVs or even phones in the rooms.

Arriving in Elbow Cay

Anyone can board a plane and get off in a vacation spot, but you have to be a traveler who's determined not to have an ordinary beach vacation to choose an island like Elbow Cay. Not only do you have to board a plane — or two — but you also have to take a taxi, a ferry, and a shuttle van to get to your hotel. That is, unless you sail in on a boat.

The best way to get to Elbow Cay is to fly into **Marsh Harbour** (see Chapter 18), home of the Abacos' main (but small and easy-to-navigate) airport. From here, you take a taxi to the dock to catch the ferry across Whale Cay Channel to **Hope Town,** about 20 minutes away ($10 one way, same-day round-trip $15). Service is three times a day.

 You need to coordinate your flight arrival and departure with the ferry schedule. Ask the staff at your hotel for details or call **Albury's Ferry Service** (☎ 242-365-6010). If you contact your hotel, your hotel staff can meet you at the ferry dock.

Elbow Cay

HOTELS ■
Abaco Inn **6**
Club Soleil Resort **2**
Hope Town Harbor Lodge **1**
Hope Town Hideaways **10**
Sea Spray Resort Villas & Marina **7**

RESTAURANTS ◆
Abaco Inn **6**
Boat House Restaurant **8**
Cap'n Jacks **3**
Club Soleil **2**
Harbour's Edge **4**
Hope Town Harbour Lodge **1**
Munchie's **5**
Rudy's Place **9**

Choosing Your Location

Elbow Cay's long and secluded white sand shores, some backed by sandy dunes, are serious contenders for The Bahamas' most stunning locales. Elbow Cay is practically divided by White Sound, a small, tranquil body of water. Accommodations are on or near sandy shores in Hope Town and White Sound, but because the hotels are small and few in number, beaches remain virtually vacant.

Getting Around Elbow Cay

Many visitors rent boats to get around the island, explore nearby cays, and go on fishing and snorkeling trips. Even if you're not interested in playing sea captain, you can still move easily around Elbow Cay by.

- ✔ **Hoofing it:** The quiet, narrow streets of Hope Town are reserved for pedestrians, and you can walk to many other parts of tiny Elbow Cay.

- ✔ **Wheeling around:** You can't rent a car on Elbow Cay, but that isn't a problem. Hope Town, the scenic seaside village, bans all motor vehicles. If you want a golf cart delivered to your hotel, call **Island Cart Rental** (☎ **242-366-0448**; www.islandcarrentals.com); these gas or electric carts go for $40 to $45 a day or $240 to $270 week. Hotels provide shuttle vans to and from town. Some dining rooms offer pick-up and drop-off service at dinnertime, if you call ahead. Bicycles — often free for hotel guests — are available at or near most accommodations.

Staying in Style

Abaco Inn
$$ White Sound

This sophisticated, 22-unit adult retreat — popular with honeymooners — faces a white sandy beach on White Sound. The inn stands at the narrowest point in Elbow Cay. On the east side, the more turbulent surf of the ocean washes in. Up the shore is a secluded beach where some buffs sun in the nude, which is technically illegal in The Bahamas. More of a resort than its chief rivals, Hope Town Harbour Lodge and Club Soleil Resort, Abaco Inn offers you a choice of eight luxury villa suites with sunrise and sunset sea views or a series of simply but comfortably furnished guest cottages fronting either the Atlantic or White Sound. Shaded by sea grape and palm trees, hammocks wide enough for two hang outside cottages. A stone fireplace is in the cozy lounge in the main house. Yachties favor the bar or the on-site restaurant, one of the island's finest (see the review later in the chapter). Vans periodically take guests to and from Hope Town. Bicycles are complimentary, and many people rent boats.

See map p. 251. Three kilometers (2 miles) south of Hope Town. ☎ *800-468-8799 or 242-366-0133. Fax: 242-366-0113.* www.abacoinn.com. *Rack rates: $140–$165 double. AE, DISC, MC, V.*

Club Soleil Resort
$$ Hope Town

This colorfully landscaped seven-room hotel, with the popular seafood restaurant **Club Soleil** (reviewed later in this chapter), is across Hope Town Harbour. The accommodations aren't as fine as those at Abaco Inn (see previous review), but they're comfortable and far more tranquil because of the secluded property near the lighthouse on the western edge of Hope Town. You reach the resort by boat — either one you rent and moor at the hotel's marina or else a hotel boat that's sent to bring you over. At the resort, you find several lovely golden sand beaches and an on-site saltwater pool. The midsize accommodations feature a clean-cut, tasteful décor. Bedrooms have amenities such as private balconies that open onto the water and cedar-lined closets for storing your belongings. You don't have a phone, but you get a TV with VCR. In addition, the staff can arrange all sorts of watersports.

See map p. 251. Near the lighthouse at Hope Town Harbour. ☎ *800-688-4752 or 242-366-0003. Fax: 242-366-0254.* www.clubsoleil.com. *Rack rates: $130 double, $1,000 weekly two-bedroom apt. AE, MC, V. Closed Sept.*

Hope Town Harbour Lodge
$$–$$$ Hope Town

This Hope Town landmark sits on a narrow bluff between the harbor, with its red-and-white striped lighthouse, and the ocean, with its white sand beach. Snorkeling is idyllic at the reef just offshore, where spotting turtles and dolphins along with all kinds of crayon-colored fish is the norm.

 Some of the 19 cheerfully decorated guest rooms have decks overlooking the pool and the ocean. Book one of these units, located across the road from the main building, if you want a mini-fridge and, more importantly, if you don't want to climb many stairs. Other rooms in the main building are smaller and have views of the town and harbor. A few paces down the road from the main building is the historic **Butterfly House** — one of the oldest surviving homes in Hope Town. The hotel owners transformed it into a two-bedroom, two-bathroom, two-deck vacation cottage with a full kitchen. As many as six people can stay here comfortably. You can dine by the saltwater pool, on the terrace high above Hope Town Harbor, or in the more formal wood-paneled restaurant (see the listing later in the chapter). The staff can arrange boat rentals and watersports for you.

See map p. 251. Between Hope Town Harbour and the beach in Hope Town. ☎ *800-316-7844 or 242-366-0095. Fax: 242-366-0286.* www.hopetownlodge.com. *Rack rates: $135–$180 double, $325–$425 Butterfly House for 4–6 people. MC, V.*

Hope Town Hideaways
$$$ Hope Town

Staying in Hope Town Hideaways is like living in your own second home in The Bahamas. These five gingerbread-trimmed villas lie across the harbor from where the ferryboats from Marsh Harbour arrive. On 4.5 hectares (11 acres) of grounds, which you reach by boat, this hideaway lives up to its name. The accommodations are part of a larger complex of privately owned homes, surrounded by grounds handsomely landscaped with orange trees, mangoes, and flamboyant bougainvillea. One or two couples — the maximum is six guests — can sleep comfortably in the units, each with a large kitchen, dining room, a living area with two single daybeds, and two bedrooms with queen beds. Furnishings are custom built. You're not on the beach, but you can enjoy the freshwater pool instead.

See map p. 251. Near the lighthouse, on a 12-slip marina. ☎ *242-366-0224. Fax: 242-366-0434.* www.hopetown.com. *Rack rates: $250 cottage for two people, $370 cottage for three or four people, $420 cottage for five or six people. MC, V.*

Sea Spray Resort Villas & Marina
$$–$$$ White Sound

These villas are on 2.5 hectares (6 acres) of landscaped grounds 6km (3½ miles) south of Hope Town near the southernmost tip of Elbow Cay. With its jagged limestone coast, the beach at this hotel may not be good for swimming, but surfers have a ball in the rolling waves. Fortunately, a good sandy beach is just a five-minute walk away, and either an energizing hike or an invigorating bike ride can take you to beautiful, secluded Tahiti Beach. Sea Spray's five oceanside and harborside cottages range from one-bedroom, one-bathroom to two-bedroom, two-bathroom. All have decks, barbecue pits, air-conditioned bedrooms, and ceiling fans. Kitchens are fully equipped, but you don't need to cook because you can find a good restaurant, the **Boat House** (reviewed below in "Dining Out"), right on the premises. Unlike some home-like accommodations that have limited housekeeping service, these villas come with daily maid service. Grounds are handsomely landscaped, and the waterfront swimming pool is a relaxing spot. Most guests rent boats here at the 60-slip marina.

See map p. 251. About 5km (3 miles) south of Hope Town. ☎ *242-366-0065. Fax: 242-366-0383.* www.seasprayresort.com. *Rack rates: $1,325–$1,950 per week. AE, MC, V.*

Dining Out

You can find a decent variety of culinary offerings on Elbow Cay, from Bahamian favorites to gourmet international dishes. Most restaurants serve variations of rum punch, and every menu has both Key lime pie and coconut pie.

You don't need to dress up at most restaurants here — shorts and a T-shirt are fine. However, **Abaco Inn, Club Soleil,** and **Hope Town Harbour Lodge** have the most upscale dining, so casual resort clothes are more appropriate. Several restaurants provide complimentary transportation to and from your hotel.

Abaco Inn
$$$–$$$$ White Sound   BAHAMIAN/INTERNATIONAL

This beachside inn offers Elbow Cay's best food, served in a semi-elegant alfresco setting. The finest tables are outside on the bluff overlooking the water. The breakfast menu may include a colorful frittata. Lobster salad and pasta dishes are the best choices at lunchtime. Before dinner, guests gather on the deck for drinks. Try a Bahama Breeze (Bacardi Gold, coconut rum, banana rum, apricot brandy, and fruit punch). The evening meal, always changing, may be coconut-crusted grouper or tender New Zealand lamb chops, followed by a smooth crème brûlée.

See map p. 251. Three kilometers (2 miles) south of Hope Town. ☎ *242-366-0133. Reservations recommended at night. Lunch sandwiches, salads, and platters: $7–$14;*

main courses: $18–$32. DISC, MC, V. Open: Daily 8–10:30 a.m., noon–3 p.m., and 6–8 p.m. Call to arrange complimentary transportation to and from the inn.

Boat House Restaurant
$$–$$$ White Sound BAHAMIAN/INTERNATIONAL

You can dine inside, but why would you want to when you can also sit out-side on the deck overlooking the marina? For dinner, the chef's signature calypso grouper gets top billing: A filet, sautéed in lemon and lime juices with a medley of herbs, then broiled with Nassau Royale (a Bahamian liqueur) and served with freshly toasted almonds and mixed vegetables. Lobster here comes any way you like it. For more variety, try the seafood platter, which includes lobster tail, grouper, and savory conch. On Monday nights, catch the Bahamian barbecue buffet, complete with local special-ties, such as cracked conch, grouper fingers, savory barbecued chicken or ribs, johnnycake, peas and rice, and coconut pie. After your plate is full, you can feast to the live sounds of Bahamian music.

See map p. 251. 6km (3½ miles) south of Hope Town, at the Sea Spray Resort. ☎ *242-366-0065. Reservations recommended at night. Main courses: $15–$28. MC, V. Open: Mon–Sat 8–11 a.m., 11 a.m.–3 p.m., and 6:30–9 p.m.; Sun 8 a.m.–3 p.m. Call to arrange complimentary transportation to and from Sea Spray Resort.*

Cap'n Jacks
$ Hope Town BAHAMIAN

Depending on when you come, you may find turtle burgers or crawfish on the menu at this casual alfresco dining spot at the edge of the harbor. Any time of year, the grouper and conch are well prepared and are the freshest food on the menu. Landlubbers gravitate toward the more routine fried chicken and burgers. The Key lime pie and the chocolate silk pie are justi-fiably popular dessert choices. Try Cap'n Jacks' version of the omnipresent Goombay Smash. Come on Wednesday or Friday between 8 and 11 p.m. for the live local music.

See map p. 251. On Hope Town Harbour. ☎ *242-366-0247. Main courses: $7.25–$15. MC, V. Open: Mon–Sat 8 a.m.–9 p.m.*

Club Soleil
$$$ Hope Town SEAFOOD

Windows around this breezy wood-paneled dining room at the edge of the harbor make you feel as if you're on a boat. You look out to Hope Town, just across the water. Vernon Malone (brother of Rudy Malone, owner of this hotel and restaurant) depicted a miniature version of town in the restaurant's driftwood wall sculpture. Sunday brunch is the big deal here, with the eggs Benedict getting rave reviews from us. Dinner may be poached salmon or a seafood platter, with Key lime pie for dessert. The chefs competently prepare all dishes with imported ingredients and turn out a very tempting menu, although one that doesn't reach the level of the

Abaco Inn. For a cocktail, try a Tropical Shock, made from dark, light, and coconut rum with fruit juices.

 Make reservations through your hotel or Vernon's Store in Hope Town. If you don't have your own boat, arrange to be picked up at the post office dock in town and ferried across.

See map p. 251. Near the lighthouse at Hope Town Harbour. ☎ *242-366-0003. Reservations recommended for dinner and Sunday brunch. Main courses: $16–$26. MC, V. Open: Tues–Sat 7–10 a.m. and 5:30–10 p.m.; Sun 11:30 a.m.–1:30p.m.*

Harbour's Edge
$$–$$$$ Hope Town BAHAMIAN

Harbour's Edge is almost always busy, if "busy" is an adjective you can use to describe sleepy Elbow Cay. The deck is topped with wooden picnic tables that give you a front-row seat for viewing the candy-cane lighthouse and the boat-packed harbor. At lunch, patrons eagerly gobble up the *gullywings* (chicken wings), conch chowder, crawfish salad, and fish sandwiches. Chefs competently prepare dinners of grilled, blackened, or fried grouper, as well as steamed or grilled Bahamian crawfish. With afternoon happy hours, a Saturday-night DJ, and the island's only pool table, this place is a lively hangout for a loud, young crowd. Try an Over the Edge, the restaurant's signature drink, made with banana rum and fruit juices.

See map p. 251. Just north of the public dock in Hope Town. ☎ *242-366-0292. Lunch main courses $7–$13; dinner main courses: $12–$30. MC, V. Open: Wed–Mon 11:30 a.m.–3 p.m. and 6–9 p.m. (bar Wed–Mon 10 a.m.–midnight). Closed mid-Sept–mid-Oct.*

Hope Town Harbour Lodge
$$$–$$$$ Hope Town BAHAMIAN/INTERNATIONAL

Lunch by the pool that overlooks a sandy beach is a special affair at the Hope Town Harbour Lodge. Popular midday treats are the curried tuna, the curried lobster, and the grouper Rueben. You eat dinner either in the dining room, with its pickled wood-paneled walls, or on the terrace above the harbor. Consider tasting the Chinese-style grouper spring rolls with a mustard-laced chutney or the peppered filet mignon. The menu is hardly inventive, but the staff properly seasons and prepares dishes well.

See map p. 251. Between the beach and Hope Town Harbour in Hope Town. ☎ *242-366-0095. Reservations recommended for dinner. Lunch main courses: 6–9 p.m.; dinner main courses: $17–$30. MC, V. Open: Daily 11:30 a.m.–2:30 p.m.; Tues–Sun 6:30–8 p.m.*

Munchie's
$ Hope Town BAHAMIAN

Bahamian-born, European-trained Norris Smith spent years as the acclaimed chef at Hope Town Harbour Lodge before opening this snack stand in 1993. He now whips up the island's best burgers and sandwiches made from turkey, beef, conch, or grouper, along with peas and rice, macaroni and cheese, and other local favorites that have brought him a loyal following among both residents and repeat visitors. Take your food with you to the beach or relax at one of the umbrella-shaded tables.

See map p. 251. On Back Street, across from Vernon's Store. ☎ 242-366-0423. Main courses: $5–$10. Open: Mon–Sat 10 a.m.–10 p.m. Closed mid-Sept–mid-Oct.

Rudy's Place
$$ Just outside Hope Town   BAHAMIAN

At Rudy's, you feel as if you've been invited to dine with friends, because this rustic restaurant is in a former private residence. The hearty meals include the island's best conch fritters, soup (maybe potato, lima bean, or broccoli), a fresh salad, freshly baked warm bread, and dessert (try the "chocolate suicide" cake). Your main course could be New York strip steak or lamb chops with mint jelly. The most justifiably popular choice is the crawfish; the chef removes the meat from the shell, lightly batters and fries it, places it back in the shell, and then bakes it with Parmesan cheese. The wine list offers a good selection of French, German, Portuguese, and American vintages.

Don't be surprised if your waiter is a child — the son or daughter of one of the other workers. When you call to make a reservation, you can arrange complimentary transportation to and from your hotel.

See map p. 251. Center Line Road. ☎ 242-366-0062. Reservations recommended. Fixed-price dinner: $20–$30. MC, V. Open: Mon–Sat 6:30–8:30 p.m. Closed Sept–Oct.

Exploring the Sand and Surf

Exploring empty beaches and sailing to nearby cays are activities central to any Elbow Cay vacation. On dry land, the small harborside village known as **Hope Town** is the place to wander.

Combing the beaches

In Hope Town, you'll find sandy beaches right at your doorstep, and beaches in the south are only about a 15-minute ride away. Near Sea Spray Resort in White Sound, **Garbanzo Beach** lures many surfers. Isolated **Tahiti Beach,** at the southern end of the island (a little more than a half-kilometer, or 1 mile, from Sea Spray), got its name from its thick wall of palms. At low tide, the shelling can be excellent along this gorgeous curve of sand, and these shallow waters make for good bonefishing, too. Across the water, you can see uninhabited **Tilloo Cay** and the thrashing waves of the Atlantic in the distance.

Tahiti Beach is about a ten-minute bike ride from Sea Spray and about 20 minutes from Abaco Inn, both in the White Sound area. To get here, you may have to walk your bike up and down a few of the small but rocky rises.

Along the way, you pass sea grape trees, fluffy long-needled pines, and other varied roadside vegetation. Turn left when you come to the first major left (by the house on the bluff). Turn right when you see two stone pillars. Go downhill and turn left at the end of the road at the wire fences. Take this path to the end. Walk along the dense palm grove to the beach. Because you're heading for the shore, which is public, ignore the PRIVATE — NO TRESPASSING signs.

With their irresistible deserted beaches, pencil-thin Tilloo Cay and the tiny **Pelican Cays** lie to the south of Elbow Cay. They make excellent targets for a day's sail. The waters around Tilloo Cay, packed with grouper and conch, are particularly good for both fishing and swimming. In the **Pelican Cays Land and Sea Park, Sandy Cay Reef** is one of the most colorful dive sites around. The area is protected, so line fishing, spear fishing, craw fishing, and shelling are all taboo.

Playing in the surf

In the Abacos, Elbow Cay is one of the best places for snorkeling. A favorite strip of beach for snorkelers is **Mermaid Beach,** with its colorful reef that teems with moray eels and various tropical fish. The beach is at **Mermaid Reef,** 3km (2 miles) north of Hope Town on the eastern side of the island. If you need snorkeling equipment, check with the folks at **Sea Horse Boat Rentals** (☎ 242-367-2513).

Through scuba-outfitter **Froggies Out Island Adventures** (☎ 242-366-0431), two-tank dives start at $100, plus equipment. Resort courses run $140, and certification courses are $500. Half-day snorkel boat trips start at $40, and you can spend plenty of time – as much as two whole hours — in the water. If you prefer sticking closer to shore, most hotels have snorkel gear on hand to rent or lend to guests who don't bring their own.

The waves and breezes at **Garbanzo Beach,** in the White Sound area, make it prime hang-ten territory. If you don't bring your own surfboard, the staff at nearby **Sea Spray Resort** (☎ 242-366-0065) can help you get one.

Climbing aboard

The waters off the coast of Elbow Cay are a popular spot for boating and fishing. Head down to the marina if you want to join in the fun.

For boat rentals, starting at about $90 a day for a 5m (17-ft.) Boston Whaler, call **Island Marine** (☎ 242-366-0282; www.islandmarine.com), near Hope Town, or **Sea Horse Boat Rentals** (☎ 242-367-2513; www.seahorseboatrentals.com) in Marsh Harbour. Ask about recommendations for local fishing guides.

If you want to forego the 20-minute ferry ride to Elbow Cay after you arrive at the airport in Marsh Harbour, you can rent a boat to get here on your own and then use the boat for your entire vacation. At **The**

Moorings (☎ 800-535-7289 or 242-367-4000; www.moorings.com), rates start at around $455 a day for an 11m (36-ft.) monohull boat that can carry a maximum of six people.

Exploring on Dry Land

No cars are allowed in the heart of Hope Town. Bikers and pedestrians have these narrow paved streets, with names like Loves' Lane, to them-selves. What you do find are some harborside restaurants and pastel-painted saltbox cottages with purple and orange bougainvillea tumbling over stone and picket fences. Amid the usual island fare at the handful of souvenir shops, you see resort wear made out of *Androsia,* the fabric produced on the Bahamian island of Andros.

Stores in Hope Town are shut tight on Sunday, and the various churches — surprising in number for such a tiny village — are in full swing. You may happen upon the outdoor Catholic service held in waterfront **Jarret Park Playground,** next to the main dock.

To find out why "Malone" is such a common surname, stop by the **Wyannie Malone Museum** (officially open most days from 10 a.m. to noon but unofficially open "whenever"). This small collection of island lore pays tribute to the South Carolinian widow and mother of four who founded Hope Town around 1783. Like other parts of the Abacos, including Green Turtle Cay and Man-O-War Cay, Elbow Cay was settled by European Americans loyal to the British Crown. Unwilling to face the out-come of the American Revolution, they began new lives in The Bahamas.

The most photographed site in the Out Islands is Hope Town's red-and-white striped **lighthouse** at the edge of the Hope Town Harbour. Before the lighthouse was erected in 1838, many of Hope Town's residents made a good living luring ships toward shore to be wrecked on the treacherous reefs and rocks, turning the salvaged cargoes into cash. To protect their livelihood, some people tried in vain to destroy this beacon while it was being built. Today, you can climb to the top of the 40m (130-ft.) tower for panoramic views of Hope Town Harbour and town. Most weekdays between 10 a.m. and 4 p.m., the lighthouse keeper is happy to give you a peek. The lighthouse is within walking distance of Club Soleil and Hope Town Hideaways. If you're staying elsewhere, you can make arrange-ments through your hotel for a visit.

Living It Up After Dark

On Saturday nights, a young party crowd gathers at **Harbour's Edge** (☎ 242-366-0087), a Hope Town bar and restaurant that has the island's only pool table. On Monday nights, Bahamian barbecues draw many people to **Sea Spray Resort** (☎ 242-366-0065), about 5km (3 miles) from Hope Town. The food is as good as the low prices, and you can hear live music. Other evenings, people hang out at the bars of hotels and restaurants — or they turn in early to rest up for yet another day of exploring.

Going Beyond Elbow Cay

Spend a day not only scuba diving or snorkeling but also island hopping with **Froggies Out Island Adventures** (☎ 242-366-0431). You have easy access in and out of the water from this company's double-deck 10.6 and 16.7m (35- or 55-ft.) yachts, which come complete with bathrooms. While you sit on the top deck or in the shade down below, your boat may pass a pod of dolphins. You stop at **Fowl Cay Land,** filled with caves and 17m (55-ft.) pillars of coral. If you're snorkeling, you may not be able to swim in and out of the grottoes, but you can see plenty of fish, including frown-faced groupers and other colorful marine life. You may even spot sharks.

You also stop at **Great Guana Cay,** a pretty island that's even quieter than Elbow Cay, for lunch at a restaurant, and then you head to **Man-O-War Cay** to roam around the handsome old shipbuilding village. (For more details about Man-O-War Cay, see Chapter 21.) Nature walks and beachcombing are part of this excursion. Adult snorkelers are $50 and children are $35.

Fast Facts: Elbow Cay

American Express and ATMs

No Amex services or ATMs are available on Elbow Cay. You can access your cash at an ATM in Marsh Harbour.

Emergencies

Call the police at ☎ 242-367-2560.

Hospitals

You need to head to the medical center in Marsh Harbour, a 20-minute boat ride away. In an emergency, contact the staff of your hotel.

Information

Contact the Abaco Tourist Office in Marsh Harbour at ☎ 242-367-3067.

Internet Access

Check with your hotel for Internet access. No cybercafes are located on Elbow Cay.

Pharmacies

Some hotels and shops in Hope Town carry over-the-counter medications and toilet articles but, for prescriptions, you need to go to Marsh Harbour on the mainland, 20 minutes away by ferry.

Police

See "Emergencies."

Post Office

At the end of the "post office dock" (the main public dock in Hope Town), the post office (☎ 242-366-0098) is open weekdays from 9 a.m to 5 p.m. but is closed for lunch, usually between 1:30 and 2:30 p.m.

Safety

Elbow Cay is a very safe island. Remember to take the same precautions that you would whether you're at home or on vacation: Keep valuables in a safe place and don't go into deserted, unfamiliar areas alone at night.

Taxis

Taxis meet incoming flights at the Marsh Harbour airport, and they greet arriving ferries as well. During your stay, the staff at your hotel can call one for you whenever you need one.

Chapter 20

Green Turtle Cay

Green Turtle Cay is about 5km (3 miles) west of Great Abaco Island, the "mainland." The beach-rimmed coastline of this 5.6km (3½-mile) long, 0.8km (½-mile) wide island dips in and out of bays and sounds. Most vacationers get around by boat — usually on a rented craft. If you don't charter your own boat, you can easily join fishing, snorkeling, or diving excursions.

One of the best ways to spend a day is exploring deserted beaches on nearby uninhabited islets. On some trips, your captain may spear a few lobsters, catch some fish, and grill it for you right on shore.

Coral colonies starting in relatively shallow water make for exceptional snorkeling, and diving is good here as well. Anglers and boaters flock to Green Turtle Cay, especially during the spring and summer. The fewest visitors check in to hotels in the fall.

Arriving in Green Turtle Cay

Fly to **Treasure Cay Airport** (see Chapter 21), where a taxi can take you to the ferry dock for departures to Green Turtle Cay. At the dock,

A tip on tipping

As your taxi pulls up to the ferry dock on the Treasure Cay side, chances are young boys will be waiting to load your bags onto the boat, whether you need help or not. Because dozens of stores aren't around this area, these children can't make pocket change bagging groceries — and shoveling snow is out of the question. Be as gracious and as generous as you can.

Green Turtle Cay

HOTELS ■
Bluff House Beach Hotel **3**
Coco Bay Cottages **1**
Green Turtle Club & Marina **2**
New Plymouth Club & Inn **4**

RESTAURANTS ◆
Bluff House **3**
Green Turtle Club & Marina **2**
Laura's Kitchen **5**
New Plymouth Club & Inn **4**
Plymouth Rock Liquors
  and Café **6**
Rooster's Rest Pub
  and Restaurant **7**
The Wrecking Tree **5**

you may have to wait a while for the ferry. Green Turtle Cay is about a 15- to 20-minute ride from the dock. The ferry takes you directly to the **Green Turtle Club,** if you're staying there, or to **New Plymouth.** This land-and-sea transfer costs $16 per person round-trip.

 Treasure Cay Airport is one of three airports in the Abacos, so be sure that you book the right destination. If you fly into Marsh Harbour, you have to take a 45-minute taxi ride for $80 to the Green Turtle Cay ferry dock. Before making your airline reservations, check the ferry schedule with your hotel to be certain that your flight doesn't arrive too late or too early.

Choosing Your Location

The island's two main resorts are on the water in the north. **Bluff House** borders both a quiet sandy bay and a marina, and the **Green Turtle**

Club, a short walk from a good beach, sprawls along a marina. If you're vacationing with friends or family, consider renting a beachside cottage. If you seek historic charm, head for the **New Plymouth Inn,** located in New Plymouth, the New England-style, 18th-century village at the southern end of the island.

Getting Around Green Turtle Cay

Although you can walk to many parts of Green Turtle Cay, water is the most common mode of transportation. Some hotels provide water transport to town or to weekly hotel parties. Many vacationers rent boats (see "Exploring the Sand and Surf" later in this chapter), but if you prefer not to, you still have other options for getting around.

   ✔ **Hoofing it:** Most of the island is accessible on foot. The virtually car-free streets of New Plymouth, a quiet 18th-century seaside village, are prime walking territory.

   ✔ **Going by golf cart:** On Green Turtle Cay, golf carts stand in for rental cars. **D & P Rentals** (☎ 242-365-4655), at the Green Turtle Club Marina, lets you use one of theirs at $45 for eight hours or $60 per day.

   ✔ **Pedaling around:** You can bike all over the island, and pedaling is especially scenic in historic New Plymouth. For $12 a day, **Brendal's Dive Center** (☎ 242-365-4411), at the Green Turtle Club Marina, rents cruisers and ten-speeds.

Staying in Style

Green Turtle Cay has only two large places to stay. "Large" here means fewer than 35 rooms. Although some units are plush, don't count on finding a TV or phone in yours. Like the other Abaco Islands, Green Turtle Cay is for vacationers who want a retreat. If you're expecting a large, amenity-studded resort, you'll be disappointed.

Bluff House Beach Hotel
$$–$$$ **Between White Sound Harbour and Sea of Abaco**

With a popular, elegant restaurant, Bluff House sits on the highest spot on the island, which is only 24m (80 ft.). The marina hugs one side of the property while a cozy beach borders another. The view of the water from the main house and the pool deck is panoramic. Originally built as a private house during the 1950s, Bluff House grew over the years as the owners added rooms for visiting friends. Today guests — often honeymooners — stay in 30 units, ranging from ordinary hotel rooms to plush three-bedroom villas. The décor is as varied as the accommodations, with hardwood, tiled, or carpeted floors, Oriental rugs, and antique floral patterns in some rooms, and airy wicker furniture in others. Spacious, split-level suites with balconies overlook the ocean. Guests receive complimentary use of snorkel gear, and the staff can make arrangements for other watersports. (If you swim out to the rocky ledge around the corner, you can find some good snorkeling.) A shuttle bus transports guests to New Plymouth, in the southern part of the island, three times a week.

Wooden boardwalks and stairs lead up and down the hilly grounds. Don't think about taking high heels to this terrain; if you have any trouble walking, don't even consider Bluff House.

See map p. 263. Northern end of the island between White Sound Harbour and Sea of Abaco. ☎ *800-745-4911 or 242-365-4247. Fax: 242-365-4248.* www.bluffhouse. com. *Rack rates: $150–$180 double, $225–$340 one-bedroom villa. AE, DISC, MC, V.*

Coco Bay Cottages
$$$ At the Sea of Abaco

On the north end of Green Turtle Cay, at a point where 152m (500 ft.) of land separates the Atlantic Ocean from the Sea of Abaco, this four-unit cottage complex opens onto a beach on the Atlantic side of the island and another sandy beach on the more tranquil bay. This accommodation is ideal for guests who want to anchor in for a while (literally — lots of folks arrive by private boat, which you can moor here for free; otherwise you can come directly by water taxi from the airport dock). Furnished in a refreshing style of Caribbean furnishings and pastel colors, the oceanfront property occupies 2 hectares (5 acres), dotted with some 50 tropical fruit trees. Each cottage has two bedrooms, a living room, a dining room, and a fully equipped kitchen with a microwave. Rebuilt in 1988 and renovated in 1996, the spacious cottages have improved over the years. Linens and kitchen utensils are provided (you can also stock up on groceries at three shops in New Plymouth), and ceiling fans and trade winds cool the rooms.

See map p. 263. In the north near the Sea of Abaco. ☎ *800-752-0166 or 242-365-5464. Fax: 242-365-5465. Rack rates: $200–$250 daily or $1,300–$1,600 weekly. MC, V.*

Green Turtle Club & Marina
$$$ White Sound Harbour

Although the fanciest hotel in the Abacos, the Green Turtle Club is far from stuffy. Witness the lively crowd that gathers in the clubhouse lounge for conversation, backgammon, and predinner cocktails. Yachting flags hang from the ceiling beams, and business cards and dollar bills scrawled with names paper the walls. During the coolest time of year, a fire often roars in the hearth in this cozy lounge. With plenty of fishermen and boaters arriving, spring and summer are the most popular — and most expensive — seasons here. The 34 rooms and villas vary in size, view, and décor and are spread out along the marina and near a pool. In your room, you're likely to find a Queen-Anne dresser and four-poster mahogany bed, an Oriental throw rug and vase, an oak floor and wood-trimmed door, a snazzy bathroom with a dressing area, and a patio. Some of the deluxe rooms even have TVs. Calm **Coco Bay Beach** is about a five-minute walk from here, and the rougher ocean beach is just ten minutes away. Talk to the staff to arrange a variety of watersports. Once a day, a shuttle bus takes guests into town. *See map p. 263. Northern end of the island in White Sound Harbour.* ☎ *800-963-5450 or 242-365-4271. Fax: 242-365-4272.* www.greenturtleclub.com. *Rack rates: $190–$210 double, $225 suite, $325–$455 villa. MAP $41 adults, $26 children. AE, DISC, MC, V.*

New Plymouth Club & Inn
$$ New Plymouth

A true charmer, this nine-room inn is one of the best values in the Abacos. Not only is it a bed-and-breakfast, but it's also a bed-and-dinner. New Plymouth Club & Inn isn't on the beach; however, it does have a freshwater swimming pool, and the sandy shores aren't far. You can easily schedule fishing, snorkeling, and scuba-diving trips. Apart from its location right in the center of the pretty town, the best thing about the New Plymouth Club & Inn is the building it occupies: a handsome, two-story home, evocative of New England. Islanders say the ghost of Captain Billy Roberts, once a resident, haunts the place from time to time. Perhaps he can't get enough of the broad verandas, flower beds, and old English-style rooms decorated with antiques and handmade quilts. Try to book the room with the canopy bed — if some of the inn's many repeat guests haven't snagged it first. The bar, lounge, and popular dining room overlook the gardens and pool patio, where visitors sip daiquiris (among other drinks) in the afternoons.

See map p. 263. Across the road from the Memorial Sculpture Garden. ☎ *242-365-4161. Fax: 242-365-4138. Rack rates: $150 double. MAP $25. MC, V. Closed Sept–Oct.*

Dining Out

The hotel restaurants are the fanciest — and, of course, the most expensive — places to dine. They all have just one seating for dinner, so be sure to make reservations. Folks tend to dress up for dinner at **Bluff House** and **Green Turtle Club & Marina.** Although this practice may mean shirts with collars for men, neither restaurant requires jackets or ties. In New Plymouth, you can find several casual, local restaurants to try. Lobster season is during August and September.

Bluff House
$$ Between White Sound Harbour and Sea of Abaco BAHAMIAN/CONTINENTAL

At this hilltop hotel restaurant, dinner is served on a deck overlooking the harbor. Thursday — with a barbecue buffet and a live band — is a big night, and a one-man band usually performs on Tuesday nights. Other evenings are more subdued, with guests sharing boating, fishing, and diving stories over first-rate food at candlelit tables. The house drink is a rum and fruit juice concoction called the Tranquil Turtle. One night you may order the prime rib or lobster, while another evening you can sample the roast lamb wrapped in bacon with honey-rosemary glaze or try the crispy duck breast with a grapefruit and Grand Marnier sauce. Many of the homemade desserts come from local recipes. The chef can handle special requests, such as dishes for vegetarians or diabetics.

See map p. 263. In the north between White Sound Harbour and Sea of Abaco. ☎ *242-365-4247. Reservations required (call by 5 p.m.). Complete dinner: $32 for adults, $22 for children. AE, MC, V. Open: Daily 7:30 p.m. until closing (bar 6:30–11 p.m.).*

Green Turtle Club & Marina
$$$–$$$$ White Sound Harbour   AMERICAN/BAHAMIAN

Breakfast and lunch are casual here, served on a screened-in patio shadowed by a buttonwood tree. Dinner is in the elegant dining room, and women dress up and men wear shirts with collars. Guests often gather for drinks and to swap tales in the bar, and then a staff member escorts them to candlelit tables with high-backed Queen-Anne chairs in the dining room. The menu changes daily, but whether you're having New York strip steak, ginger lobster medallions, or broiled grouper in guava sauce, your meal is served on fine china. A well-prepared vegetarian dish is always available. The cuisine is invariably excellent. The Green Turtle Club offers musical entertainment three times a week, with Wednesday being the most popular night.

See map p. 263. In the north, in White Sound Harbour. ☎ *242-365-4271. Reservations required. Main courses: $21–$35. AE, MC, V. Open: Daily 8 a.m.–6 p.m.*

Laura's Kitchen
$$ New Plymouth   BAHAMIAN

Cozy, family-run Laura's Kitchen may not win awards for its simple décor, but this handsome old cottage is a good place to find Bahamian favorites. The menu includes good-tasting dishes, such as cracked conch, tasty grouper, fried shrimp, lobster, fried chicken, and steak. Although vacationers often visit, Laura's has a loyal local following as well.

See map p. 263. King Street, near the ferry dock. ☎ *242-365-4287. Reservations recommended for dinner. Lunch main courses: $4–$12; dinner main courses: $14–$20. MC, V. Open: Daily 11 a.m.–3 p.m. and 6–9 p.m. Closed Sept and Dec 25.*

New Plymouth Club & Inn
$$ New Plymouth   BAHAMIAN/CONTINENTAL

Sunday brunch at New Plymouth Club & Inn draws plenty of hungry people. You have serious competition if you want to sit on the screened-in sun porch overlooking the swimming pool and the fragrant oleander, bushy almond leaves, and hibiscus. Before you make your dinner reservation, check the menu to see what the chef is whipping up that day. Surrounded by colonial furnishings, your elegant candlelit evening meal may be grilled lamb chops, veal, grouper almondine, or chicken with an orange glaze. You can fill up on the homemade Bahamian bread, which is slightly sweet and pillow soft.

See map p. 263. Parliament Street, across from the Memorial Sculpture Garden.
☎ *242-365-4161. Reservations required for dinner (call by 5 p.m.). Breakfast: $12; lunch: $15; dinner $35. MC, V. Open: Daily 6 a.m. to 9 p.m.*

Plymouth Rock Liquors and Café
$ New Plymouth   BAHAMIAN

Plymouth Rock may be a liquor store, but with counter and takeout service for breakfast and lunch, this establishment is more than that. For breakfast, you can order eggs or *chicken souse* (a hot and spicy soup-like Bahamian specialty). For lunch, try a conch burger, cracked conch platter, or a more prosaic hamburger. For dessert, many patrons choose the apple turnovers or the hummingbird cake (sweetened with banana and pineapple). Shelves aren't only packed with alcohol (the store has 60 types of rum for sale), but you can also browse through a mega-selection of hot sauces from The Bahamas and elsewhere. When you're through feeding your body, you can tend to your spirit at the art gallery next door.

See map p. 263. Parliament Street, next to Barclay's Bank. ☎ *242-365-4234. Menu items: $4–$8.50. DISC, MC, V. Cafe open: Mon–Sat 9 a.m.–3:30 p.m.*

Rooster's Rest Pub and Restaurant
$ Just outside New Plymouth   BAHAMIAN

Rooster's Rest is best known for the live reggae and calypso music that turns it into party central on Friday and Saturday nights. But it's also a good place to sample generous portions of the usual local suspects: fried grouper, cracked conch, peas and rice, and, of course, a Goombay Smash or two.

See map p. 263. Gilliam's Bay Road, across from The Bahamas Telephone Company and the school. ☎ *242-365-4066. Reservations recommended for dinner. Lunch burgers and snacks: $8–$12; dinner main courses: $10–$20. MC, V. Open: Mon–Sat 11:30 a.m.–9:30 p.m.*

The Wrecking Tree
$ New Plymouth   BAHAMIAN

A large, shady cedar tree grows up through the front porch of this popular eatery. Some people say that the Wrecking Tree got its name because 19th-century wrecking vessels brought their salvage to this spot, but many residents can tell you the true origin: People used to sit under the tree and drink until they got "wrecked." Stop here for pastries, cool drinks, or a Bahamian meal. Start off with zesty conch fritters, and then try the fish, conch, pork chops, ribs, turtle steak, or crawfish.

See map p. 263. Bay Street. No phone. Complete dinner: $13–$15. No credit cards accepted. Open Mon–Sat 11 a.m.–9 p.m.

Exploring the Sand and Surf

Along with sampling Green Turtle Cay's aquatic activities, you can visit a museum and wander the streets of New Plymouth, the historic waterfront village.

Combing the beaches

About a ten-minute walk from Bluff House and five minutes from the Green Turtle Club, **Coco Bay** is one of the most beautiful crescents in The Bahamas. Shaded by casuarina pine trees and lapped by lazy waves, this long beach is often empty. The rougher **Ocean Beach,** about a ten-minute stroll from either Bluff House or the Green Turtle Club, is another stunner. Frothy waves thrash the stark white sand, which is set off by the intense blue of the Atlantic.

 You can take a boat trip to one of the nearby uninhabited islands that are ringed with even more pristine beaches. On **Manjack Cay,** for example, the expanse of sugar-white sand seems to go on forever, and the shallow, clear water is a brilliant shade of turquoise. There's no regular service from the ferry dock; negotiate with one of the local boatmen or hook up with one of the trips offered by **Captain Ray** (☎ 916-933-3766; www.abaco.tv/manjack-cay-bahamas.asp).

Playing in the surf

With one of the world's largest barrier reefs, the Abacos offer some of The Bahamas' best and least crowded snorkeling and diving sites, with plenty of variety. You can get an eyeful of reefs starting at depths of just 1.5m (5 ft.) and ranging to 18m (60 ft.) and more. Like sheets on a clothesline, sprawling schools of fish billow by coral caverns, huge tube and barrel sponges, and fields of elk and staghorn coral. Sea turtles and large groupers are common sights. In fact, the waters are so clear that you can often see farther than 30m (100 ft.).

Scuba divers can poke around the wreck of the *San Jacinto,* an American steamship that was built in 1847 and sank two decades ago. At this site, you can feed the resident bright green moray eel. Plan to spend about $135 for a scuba resort course, $500 for full certification, $55 for a one-tank dive, and $75 for a two-tank dive.

If you like small groups and big fun, try **Brendal's Dive Center** (☎ 242-365-4411; www.brendal.com) at the Green Turtle Club Marina. Whether you're an experienced diver or snorkeler or you're just getting your feet wet, the personal attention you get makes the difference here. Originally from Acklins, a small Bahamian island to the south, the dive company has more than two decades of underwater experience. A special treat for snorkelers is the wild dolphin encounter trip ($75 per person), which includes stops at undisturbed islands. This company also rents kayaks

($10 per hour for singles, $12 per hour for doubles, or $190 a week for the single and $250 a week for the double). You can also hook up with **Green Turtle Divers** (☎ 242-365-4271).

Climbing aboard

If you've had enough of sitting on the beach and relaxing, you can explore the ocean. From boat rentals to fishing expeditions, Green Turtle Cay offers an array of offshore activities.

Based at the Green Turtle Club Marina, **Brendal's Dive Center** (☎ 242-365-4411) can take you on a group sunset cruise (complete with rum punch) on a 8.8m (29-ft.) sailboat for $60 per person (up to eight passengers). To see the coral without getting wet, Brendal's hosts glass-bottom boat trips for $50 per person.

Contact **Donny's Boat Rentals,** in Black Sound, (☎ 242-365-4119) for speedboats. This company rents Whalers and Makos (types of motorboats) starting at $65 a day. Or you can try **Reef Rentals,** directly across from the ferry dock in New Plymouth (☎ 242-365-4145). This fleet includes a sleek motorboat made on Man-O-War Cay, the nearby island long known for its excellent boatbuilding. Rentals start at $265 for three days for a 5.7m (19-ft.) Wellcraft boat.

Reserving a boat when you make your hotel and airline reservations is a good idea, particularly during the busy spring and summer.

Some of America's most devoted anglers arrive here just to fish the coast off this cay. You find giant game fish as well as tropical fish in these waters, including a few dolphinfish, yellowfin tuna, and even the big game wahoo.

Fishing charters run from $140 to $250 for a half-day and $240 to $350 for a full day. You can make arrangements through your hotel. The annual **Green Turtle Club Fishing Tournament** (☎ 800-688-4752 or 242-365-4271) was on hold at press time, but call for information to see whether it's on when you're visiting in May.

Exploring on Dry Land

Walking in New Plymouth is to journey back in time. To get a taste of how Green Turtle Cay and the rest of the Abacos came to be, poke around the **Albert Lowe Museum** (☎ 242-365-4094), on Parliament Street in New Plymouth. Housed in a charming old cottage, the museum was founded in 1976 by acclaimed local artist Alton Lowe, who named the place after his father, Albert, a direct descendant of one of the European-American families who settled the island and an avid model shipbuilder. You can see some of his mini-schooners on display, along with paintings by Alton (whose prints are for sale), timeworn photographs, and other historical artifacts, some dating back to the 18th century. Admission is $5 for adults and $2.50 for students; children 5 and under are free. The museum is usually open Monday through Saturday from 9 a.m. to 4 p.m. and closed for lunch between 11:45 a.m. and 1 p.m.

Across from New Plymouth Inn on Parliament Street, the **Memorial Sculpture Garden** honors residents of the Abacos, both living and dead. What blooms in this garden are busts of island notables on stone pedestals. Read about some of the American Loyalists who came to The Bahamas from New England and the Carolinas. Statues are also dedicated to their descendants and to those people who were enslaved in these islands. You can see everyone from Albert Lowe to African-Bahamian Jeanne I. Thompson, the second woman to practice law in The Bahamas. This garden is laid out in the pattern of the British flag.

Living It Up After Dark

On Friday and Saturday nights, a mostly young, local crowd parties to reggae and calypso music at **Rooster's Rest Pub and Restaurant** (☎ 242-365-4066) on Gilliam's Bay Road, just outside New Plymouth. During the week, the island's calypso-reggae band, the Gully Roosters, plays at the **Green Turtle Club** (☎ 800-963-5450 or 242-365-4271) one night and at **Bluff House** (☎ 800-745-4911 or 242-365-4247) another night. Both "venues" are on the northern end of the island.

Those fruity, rum-based cocktails known as Goombay Smashes are all over Green Turtle Cay. But **Miss Emily's Blue Bee Bar** (☎ 242-365-4181), located on Victoria Street in New Plymouth is supposedly the birthplace of this beloved, much-imitated drink. Of course, the original recipe, created by the late Miss Emily, is a well-kept secret. Everyone from Bahamian prime ministers to international TV stars has entered this tiny, unassuming hangout. Miss Emily's is open Monday through Friday from 11 a.m. until "whenever."

Going Beyond Green Turtle Cay

One of the island's best aquatic adventures is a day sail with **Brendal's Dive Center** (☎ 242-365-4411), located at the Green Turtle Club Marina. Whether you're a snorkeler or a scuba diver, the highlight comes when you get to hand-feed some graceful stingrays. Because you're giving them snacks, they aren't interested in nibbling on you. If you don't know how to snorkel or scuba dive, Brendal's is a good place to learn.

On the trip, you stop at a secluded beach on an island so small that you can circle it on foot in 20 minutes. After catching your fish or lobster, your captain grills it right on the beach and serves it along with conch salad, homemade bread, and a green salad. The weather, sea conditions, and your preferences determine exactly where else you go. Brendal manages to strike that rare balance between pure professionalism and laid-back flexibility, so you can design almost any trip you want.

For the most relaxing, intimate scuba or snorkeling excursion, make a special request for the sailboat that carries a minimum of four and a maximum of eight passengers. Otherwise, you'll probably travel in a motorboat that holds up to 24 divers (although that many divers are rarely on board).

Fast Facts: Green Turtle Cay

American Express and ATMs

No Amex services or ATMs are available on Green Turtle Cay. You can access your cash at an ATM in Marsh Harbour.

Emergencies

Call **919** for fire emergencies.

Hospitals

Contact the government clinic (☎ 242-365-4028), an eye-catching pink and white building in New Plymouth.

Information

For visitor-related information, contact the Abaco Tourist Office (☎ 242-367-3067).

Internet Access

Resorts generally offer Internet access. But Green Turtle Cay doesn't have any cybercafes.

Pharmacies

The only pharmacy in the Out Islands is the Chemist Shop Pharmacy (☎ 242-367-3106), located on Don MacKay Boulevard

in Marsh Harbour. It's open Monday through Saturday from 8:30 a.m. to 5:30 p.m.

Police

Call ☎ 242-365-4450.

Post Office

Open Monday through Friday 9 a.m to 5 p.m., the post office (☎ 242-365-4242) is on Parliament Street in New Plymouth.

Safety

Green Turtle Cay is a very safe island. However, you still need to take the same precautions that you should take anywhere you go: Keep valuables in a safe place and don't go into deserted, unfamiliar areas alone at night.

Taxis

Taxis meet incoming flights at the Treasure Cay Airport, and they greet arriving ferries as well. During your stay, the staff at your hotel can call one for you whenever you want.

Chapter 21

Treasure Cay

● ●

In This Chapter

▶ Traveling on Treasure Cay
▶ Reviewing Treasure Cay's accommodations and restaurants
▶ Enjoying watersports and land-based attractions

● ●

*A*ttractive condos and villas, a championship golf course, a marina, and a golden sand beach draw visitors to **Treasure Cay,** especially in winter.

Treasure Cay is a resort area, not an island — at least not anymore (see the sidebar "When an island isn't an island" later in this chapter). This resort area looks and feels like the planned vacation community that it is — a bit sterile for our tastes. Don't be surprised if your stay makes you forget that you're in The Bahamas.

Not much existed here before Treasure Cay was born in the 1960s, so don't expect to find any historic sites or long-standing communities full of local color. The good news is that you can sail to nearby islands — Green Turtle Cay, Man-O-War Cay, and Elbow Cay — to visit three of The Bahamas' oldest and most charming villages.

Arriving at the Airport

Treasure Cay International Airport (☎ 242-365-0605) is one of the three airports in the Abacos, the group of islands just west of Grand Bahama in the northern Bahamas. Taxis meet arriving flights, and they charge about $15 for one or two people for the 10- to 15-minute ride to the Treasure Cay resorts.

Choosing Your Location

You have a choice of two settings: either at a 150-slip marina, one of the best boat hangouts in the islands, or on a 5.6km (3½-mile) beach of stark white sand and calm, clear water.

Most vacationers rent golf carts or bikes to get to local restaurants and to explore their surroundings. The marina and golf course are

Treasure Cay

HOTELS ■
Banyan Beach Club **2**
Treasure Cay Hotel Resort
& Marina **3**

RESTAURANTS ◆
The Spinnaker Restaurant **4**
Touch of Class **1**

close to both hotels. At the shopping center near the marina, you find
the bank, post office, grocery store, and car rental and sports shops,
along with two souvenir stores.

Getting Around Treasure Cay

Renting a car isn't necessary. To get where you're going, you can walk,
bike, rent a golf cart, or take a taxi. Some restaurants outside the resort
even send a shuttle to pick you up from your hotel.

✔ **Taking a taxi:** Except for moving between the airport or ferry dock
  and your hotel, you won't need a cab. For details about taxi fares,
  call the **Treasure Cay Airport Taxi Stand** (☎ 242-365-8661). For
  that special occasion when you need airport pickups or a trip to
  dinner in style, call **Elegante Limo Service** (☎ 242-365-8248 or
  242-365-8053; $115 an hour for up to ten passengers); this company
  also rents golf carts.

✓ **Driving around:** The only real reason to rent a car is for the 35-minute drive to Marsh Harbour to catch the ferries to Elbow Cay and Man-O-War Cay, two offshore islands (see the "Going Beyond Treasure Cay" section later in this chapter). If you decide you want to do so, you can rent a car for $75 a day at the **Cornish Car Rental,** Treasure Cay Airport, (☎ 242-365-8623). A more scenic way to get to these islands is to rent or charter a boat from Treasure Cay (see recommendations later in this chapter).

✓ **Wheeling around on a bicycle or golf cart:** Through **Wendell's Bicycle Rentals** (☎ 242-365-8687), across from the bank in the Treasure Cay shopping center, you can rent *beach cruisers* (single-gear bikes with wide wheels) or *mountain bikes* (wide-wheeled bikes with multiple gears) for $7 a day or $42 a week. Four-seater electric golf carts go for $40 a day or $245 a week through Wendell's or **Claridge Golf Carts** (☎ 242-365-8248 or 242-365-8053), just outside town.

Staying in Style

The two hotels here offer a variety of accommodations, from standard rooms and suites to apartments and villas.

Rooms can be scarce in May when the place is packed with anglers angling for fame in one of the country's most popular fishing tournaments: the **Treasure Cay Billfish Championship.**

In addition to the cay's two main hotels, you can also arrange condo rentals. The best agency for this service is **Bahama Beach Club** (☎ 800-563-0014 in the U.S. or Canada). A three-night minimum stay is required, and prices are $300 per night for a two-bedroom unit, $350 a night for a three-bedroom unit, and $400 a night for a four-bedroom unit.

Banyan Beach Club

$$$ Treasure Cay Beach

Right on the beach that's widely known as one of the best in The Bahamas because of its gentle curve, white sand, and turquoise water, Banyan Beach Club offers 21 spacious condos that are ideal for families. Some of these one- and two-bedroom units have an additional sleeping area: a loft with two twin beds, which you reach by a spiral or ladder-style staircase. Queen-size beds are in downstairs rooms. Patios or balconies have expansive views. The one-bedroom units face the swimming pool, while the larger apartments, with two or three bathrooms, overlook the beach. All units come with kitchens complete with a dishwasher, microwave, blender, and coffeemaker. The upstairs apartments in both shingle-roof buildings have high-angled ceilings. Guests get acquainted at the Monday night cocktail parties or over hamburgers and hot dogs at the beach bar and grill. Treasure Cay's golf course is within strolling distance, but most people get

When an island isn't an island

Cay is pronounced "key" in The Bahamas, and it means "a little island." So how come Treasure Cay, on the east coast of Great Abaco, is part of the "mainland"? Well, Treasure Cay used to be a separate chunk of land, known as Lovel's Island, at least as far back as the 1780s. Eventually, landfill erased the sliver of Carleton Creek that ran between Treasure Cay and Great Abaco.

there on the golf carts they rent to cruise the resort. You can easily arrange watersports at the Treasure Cay Marina.

See map p. 274. Less than a kilometer (about a half-mile) north of Treasure Cay Hotel Resort & Marina. ☎ 888-625-3060 or 242-365-8111. Fax: 242-365-8112. www.banyan beach.com. *Rack rates: $130–$250 double. AE, DISC, MC, V.*

Treasure Cay Hotel Resort & Marina
$$$–$$$$ Treasure Cay Marina

One of the biggest of the Out Island resorts, this property attracts boaters, golfers, fishermen, and divers, as well as escapists seeking a remote retreat. Guests appreciate the House-and-Garden-style architecture, the spectacular beachfront, and the marina facilities. Simply furnished in tropical motifs, most accommodations overlook the dozens of sailing crafts moored in Treasure Cay Marina. The deluxe suites are very attractive, with fully equipped kitchens and two bathrooms. Renowned architect Dick Wilson designed the 18-hole golf course. Tennis courts are lit for night play, and you can rent watersports equipment. Guests sometimes rent electric golf carts (around $35 a day) or bikes to explore the far-flung palm and casuarina groves of the sprawling property. For a full review of the resort's restaurant, **The Spinnaker,** see the "Dining Out" section later in this chapter.

See map p. 274. Treasure Cay Marina. ☎ 800-327-1584 or 954-525-7711 for reservations, or 242-365-8801. www.treasurecay.com. *Rack rates: $170–$195 double, $315 suite. Full board $60 extra per person. AE, DISC, MC, V.*

Dining Out

Many vacationers to Treasure Cay stay in accommodations with kitchens or kitchenettes. However, if you know you're never going to feel like putting fire to a pan, consider purchasing your hotel's meal plan or dine at nearby local restaurants, some of which provide transportation.

You can find rather standard food at the **Beach Bar & Grill** at the Banyan Beach Club (☎ 242-365-8111), which opens daily from 11:30 a.m. to 6 p.m. Platters of food cost from $4 to $7. Another eatery worth considering is the roadside **Coconut's** on Queen's Highway (☎ 242-365-8885), which serves typically Bahamian fare, such as grouper and conch along with a few Italian specialties. Main courses range from $15 to $26, and it's open daily from 6 to 9:30 p.m.

The Spinnaker Restaurant
$$$ Treasure Cay Marina   AMERICAN/BAHAMIAN

Serving reliable seafood, steak, pasta, and Bahamian specialties, this resort restaurant at the Treasure Cay Marina has a prime waterside spot. For lunch, the cracked conch makes a good choice. At night, the portions of meat and potatoes or fresh fish (prepared in a variety of ways, from steamed to blackened) are generous. Guests of the Banyan Beach Club, less than a kilometer (about a half-mile) away, usually arrive by golf cart.

See map p. 274. On the water in Treasure Cay Marina. ☎ 242-365-8469. Reservations suggested for dinner. Main courses: $17–$30. AE, DC, MC, V. Open: Daily 7 a.m.– 9:30 p.m. Limited hours in autumn and early winter.

Touch of Class
$$-$$$ North of Treasure Cay resort   BAHAMIAN

Call ahead and this popular local eatery can send a courtesy van to pick you up at your hotel. Touch of Class is the spot when you're ready to try some real Bahamian food, such as fried freshly caught grouper filet with a sauce of tomatoes, sweet peppers, and onions; or tender cracked conch served with a mound of peas and rice. If you can't decide, try the seafood plate, which offers a sampling of grouper, lobster, and conch. Both the Key lime pie and the banana cream pie are luscious desserts.

See map p. 274. On Queen's Highway, a ten-minute drive from Treasure Cay resort. ☎ 242-365-8195. Main courses: $16–$28. MC, V. Open: Nightly 6–9 p.m.

Exploring the Sand and Surf

Highlighted by the Treasure Cay Billfish Championship each spring, watersports in Treasure Cay mean big fun. Golfers don't have to head to Nassau or Freeport for a great game. Treasure Cay may be far less developed than the more popular islands, but its golf course is a big draw.

Combing the beaches

If you desire a beach with some of the softest, whitest sand you can imagine and water in some of the most amazing shades of blue and green, then **Treasure Cay Beach** is for you. What's especially alluring about this beach is that — unlike eye-catching strands on busier, more built-up islands — this shore is never crowded because it extends for 5.5km (2½ miles).

Playing in the surf

Treasure Cay's excellent boating, fishing, scuba diving, and snorkeling make it tempting to spend most of your time in the water.

Certified divers can hook up with **Treasure Divers** (☎ 242-365-8465; www.treasure-divers.com). A shorter one-tank dive goes for $55 and a longer two-tank dive for $80. **Rich's Boat Rentals** (☎ 242-365-8582; www.richsrentals.com) can book you on a snorkel sail ($35 per person with a six-person minimum) or on a beach snorkel trip ($65 per person) after which the freshly caught grouper and lobster are grilled right on the beach.

Climbing aboard

Treasure Cay makes a good starting point for exploring the Abacos by sea. At **Rich's Boat Rentals** (☎ 242-365-8582; www.richsrentals.com), boats ranging from 6 to 8 meters (21–27 ft.) start around $130 a day. A guided charter starts at about $250 for a half-day or $400 for a full day. With 7 to 8m (24–26 ft.) fully equipped boats, **J.I.C. Boat Rentals** (☎ 242-365-8465) is another good outfit.

Treasure Cay's surrounding waters offer some of the country's best fishing, including **deep-sea, sea-bottom,** and **drift fishing.** Off the coast, fishermen pursue barracuda, grouper, yellowtail, snapper, tuna, marlin, dolphinfish, and wahoo. The cay's own bonefish flats are just a short boat ride from the Treasure Cay Marina. Charters start at $425 for a half-day and $550 for a full day. Make arrangements through your hotel, **Treasure Cay Marina** (☎ 242-365-8250), Rich's Boat Rentals, or J.I.C. Boat Rentals.

Exploring on Dry Land

If you prefer to stick to dry land, check out the following options.

The **Treasure Cay Golf Club** (☎ 242-365-8045) at the Treasure Cay Resort & Marina offers one of the best courses in The Bahamas. The course is a 72-par 18-holer. Greens fees run $85 for 18 holes or $60 for 9. Reserving tee times is necessary from October to June.

Treasure Cay Hotel Resort & Marina (☎ 242-365-8801) offers six tennis courts — three clay surfaces ($16 an hour) and three hard surfaces ($14 an hour) — all lit for night play. Check with the hotel to make arrangements to play.

Living It Up After Dark

Fishermen, yachties, and hotel guests head for the **Tipsy Seagull Bar** at the Treasure Cay Hotel Resort & Marina (☎ 242-365-8535), which presents live music in winter (only on Friday and Saturday nights off-season). When a fishing tournament is on island, this bar is jam-packed. The setting is an A-frame, and the décor is nautical memorabilia. Bar patrons who want to hang out can order such treats as pizza and lobster from the resort's adjoining The Spinnaker restaurant. Happy hour is nightly from 5 to 7 p.m. The bar closes in autumn, the early winter months, and during other slow periods.

Going Beyond Treasure Cay

You can get some local flavor and a blast from the past if you sail off to one, two, or three of the Abacos' nearby historic villages.

Trip #1: Green Turtle Cay

A brief ferry ride takes you across the water to Green Turtle Cay, one of the prettiest islands in The Bahamas. The hamlet of **New Plymouth** may make you think that you landed in Cape Cod because it shares a similar architectural heritage with that New England summer haunt. White picket fences enclose the front yards of the small clapboard houses. In this subtropical village, these buildings are trimmed in pastel pinks, blues, and greens and are shaded by bushy palm trees. Once the most prosperous settlement in the Abacos, New Plymouth was founded by British Loyalists who fled the U.S. after the American Revolution. Stroll around the quiet streets, sip a Goombay Smash, stop for a meal, and visit the art and maritime museum.

The ferry from Treasure Cay to Green Turtle Cay runs several times a day. To get to the ferry dock from the Treasure Cay Hotel, you have to take a 15-minute taxi ride to the departure dock. This ride costs $15 for one or two passengers. Before long, the ferry pulls up to New Plymouth (about $11 round-trip for adults and $7 for children). For more details about hotels, restaurants, sights, and activities on Green Turtle Cay, check out Chapter 20.

Trip #2: Elbow Cay and Man-O-War Cay

Elbow Cay and Man-O-War Cay, two nearby islands, make wonderful boating targets. The red-and-white striped lighthouse in Elbow Cay's **Hope Town Harbour,** in Hope Town, is the most photographed man-made attraction in the Out Islands. Sandy dunes back some of the broad, quiet beaches on this long, slim island. Saltbox houses with picket fences make this another contender for a Cape Cod fishing village look-alike. Take a load off at one of the harborside bars and restaurants.

To reach Man-O-War Cay from Hope Town, you must return to Marsh Harbour, where you can catch a ride aboard **Albury's Ferry Service** (☎ 242-367-3147). Ferries leave daily at 10:30 a.m., 4 p.m., and 5:30 p.m.; the cost is $10 per passenger. Once you arrive at Man-O-War Cay, you can wander through its trim streets lined with brightly painted cottages — you'll notice something different right away: Unlike most of The Bahamas (where the majority of residents are of African ancestry), nearly everyone here is a direct descendant of one European American couple who settled the island in the 1820s.

In The Bahamas, you can expect to find at least one small bar for every small church, but not on Man-O-War Cay. You'll see cozy houses of worship, but you won't find any bars or liquor stores at all. Folks on this uncrowded island take their religion very seriously. Don't risk offending anyone by publicly sipping any beer or other alcohol you may have brought along or by walking around in your bathing suit or other skimpy attire.

Residents and visitors celebrate Man-O-War Cay's boat-building history at the waterfront **Sail Shop** (☎ 242-365-6014), which offers colorful bags handmade from the canvas once used for all those sails. The shop is open Monday through Friday from 8 a.m. to 5 p.m. and until 4 p.m. on Saturdays.

To strike out on your own or for a guided charter, contact **Rich's Boat Rentals** (☎ 242-365-8582) or **J.I.C. Boat Rentals** (☎ 242-365-8465). A trip from Treasure Cay to Man-O-War Cay (45 minutes on a good day) takes about an hour on the water. A trip from Treasure Cay to Elbow Cay takes about ten minutes more.

For a different kind of scenic adventure, you can also rent a car in Treasure Cay ($75 a day), drive 35 minutes to Marsh Harbour, and then take the 20-minute ferry ride (through Albury's Ferry Service) to Elbow Cay or Man-O-War Cay. To either island, the fare is $8 each way or $15 same-day round-trip for adults; and $8 one-way or $6 same-day round-trip for children ages 6 to 12. Your time is limited by the ferry schedule, however, so you'll probably make it to only one of the two islands. (For information about Elbow Cay's hotels, restaurants, and sightseeing opportunities, see Chapter 19.)

Fast Facts: Treasure Cay

American Express and ATMs

No Amex services or ATMs are available on Treasure Cay. You can access your cash at an ATM in Marsh Harbour.

Emergencies/Police

Call ☎ 242-365-8048.

Hospital

If health problems arise, contact the Corbett Medical Center (☎ 242-365-8288), behind the Treasure Cay administration building and near the marina.

Information

For visitor-related information, contact the Abaco Tourist Office (☎ 242-367-3067).

Internet Access

Resorts generally offer Internet access, so check with your hotel about Internet access. No cybercafes are available on Treasure Cay.

Pharmacy

A new pharmacy, The Hair Depot, has opened in the National Insurance Building in the hamlet of Coopers Town, directly north of Treasure Cay.

Post Office

In the Treasure Cay shopping center near the marina, the post office (☎ 242-365-8230) is open Monday through Friday from 9 a.m. to 5 p.m.

Safety

Although Treasure Cay is a safe resort, don't forget to take the same precautions that you should whether you're at home or on vacation: Keep valuables in a safe place and don't go into deserted, unfamiliar areas alone at night.

Taxis

Taxis meet incoming flights at the airport. During your stay, staff at your hotel can call one for you whenever the need arises.

Part VI
The Out Islands

The 5th Wave   By Rich Tennant

TRAGICALLY DOUG HAD JUST COMPLETED THE VOCABULARY PORTION OF HIS SAT EXAM BEFORE SETTING SAIL THAT DAY.

©RICHTENNANT

AMELIORATE!!
AMELIORATE!!

Anyone here know what "ameliorate" means?

In this part . . .

We journey to four of The Bahamas' most appealing Out Islands. This section reviews one of the most intriguing of all Bahamian islands — actually a series of islands — called Eleuthera. A slender wisp of an island, visitors go to Eleuthera mainly for its offshore Harbour Island. Harbour Island is known for its attractive 18th-century harborside houses and its small hotels overlooking a pink sand beach. Although the island of Exuma is sailing heaven, avid scuba divers also flock to San Salvador.

In this part, you find all the information that you need for a great trip to the Out Islands. We include tips on how to get there, what to see and do when you're there, and where you can find the best accommodations and food and the liveliest nightlife.

Chapter 22

Harbour Island

●●●

In This Chapter

▶ Getting around Harbour Island

▶ Reviewing Harbour Island's best accommodations and restaurants

▶ Exploring the best beaches, watersports, and historic attractions

●●●

*1*f you're looking for a small, sophisticated hotel on a never-crowded sandy shore, head to **Harbour Island.** This little cay off northern Eleuthera is home to The Bahamas' coziest collection of distinctive oceanfront accommodations. This sandy stretch is *pink.* Mother Nature created this stunning pastel hue over the eons by pulverizing coral and shells. Scoop up a handful of the speckled sand, and you'll see what we mean.

Arriving in Harbour Island

Harbour Island, 2.4km (1½ miles) off the coast of Eleuthera (see Chapter 23), is one of those special places that requires a bit of work and patience to reach. If you come by air, you need to fly into the small, unassuming **North Eleuthera Airport** (from Miami, Ft. Lauderdale, or Nassau). Then you take a five-minute taxi ride to the dock (about $4 per person) and a ten-minute ferry ride to Harbour Island's **Government Dock** ($5 per person). Next, unless you're staying at The Landing, which is just across the road, you take a short taxi ride to your hotel ($4 per person).

Another way you can get to Harbour Island is to board a speedy 177-passenger catamaran in Nassau. Just contact **Bahamas Fast Ferry** (☎ 242-323-2166). You begin this two-hour trip at the **Potters Cay Dock,** which is under the bridge leading from Paradise Island to downtown Nassau. The fare for one of these daily excursions is $110 round-trip or $65 one-way for adults and $70 round-trip or $45 one-way for children ages 2 to 11. This ferry also pulls up to Harbour Island's Government Dock, where taxis wait to take you to your hotel.

Harbour Island

HOTELS ■
Coral Sands **2**
Dunmore Beach Club **3**
The Landing **7**
Pink Sands **1**
Runaway Hill Club **4**
Tingum Village **5**

RESTAURANTS ◆
Angela's Starfish **9**
Beach Bar **2**
Coral Sands **2**
Harbour Lounge **8**
The Landing **7**
Ma Ruby's **5**
Pink Sands **1**
Rock House Restaurant **6**
Runaway Hill Club **4**

FISHERMAN'S DOCK

Nesbit St.
Grant St. **9**
Duke St.
Pitt St. Munnings St. Chapel St.
King St.
Princess Crown St.
Murray St. Barrack St. Court Rd.
GOVERNMENT DOCK Church St. **8** Hill St.
Harbour **7** **6** Colebrook St. Love Ln.
York St. Dunmore St. Clarence St.
5
South St. **5**
Up Yonder Dr.
Surf Dr.
Alice St.

PINK SAND BEACH

1 **2** **2** **3** **4** **4**

HARBOUR ISLAND
area of detail
Dunmore Town

●Miami
FLORIDA
HARBOUR ISLAND □
Nassau ★ ELEUTHERA ISLAND
ANDROS ISLAND EXUMA ISLANDS
0   50 mi
0   50 km

0   1/8 mile
0   100 meters

Choosing Your Location

If Harbour Island (called "Briland" by locals) only had the beautiful beach and the great hotels, it still would be a top-notch vacation choice. But this island also offers the well-preserved 17th-century **Dunmore Town,** the first capital of The Bahamas. Dunmore Town is within walking distance (or biking and golf-cart reach) of all accommodations. The western shore offers panoramic sunsets, and **Pink Sand Beach** along the eastern coast is the only place to be at sunrise.

What little after-dark action the island does have "jumps up" on weekends at or close to the hotels.

Getting Around Harbour Island

Harbour Island is very small — just 5km (3 miles) long and less than a kilometer (½-mile) wide — so you can get where you need to go easily. Here's a closer look at transportation choices.

- ✔ **Taking a taxi:** The island is so small that you really need a cab only when arriving and leaving with luggage. Taxis wait for incoming ferries at Government Dock, and the staff at your hotel can call a cab for you whenever you need one.

- ✔ **Hoofing it:** On this compact island, Dunmore Town (which is ideal for strolling), restaurants, nightspots, and most other places are within walking distance of the hotels. The best place to go for a leisurely walk is the 5km (3-mile) Pink Sand Beach along the eastern shore.

- ✔ **Wheeling around:** You don't see many cars on Harbour Island's nearly deserted roads. If you do feel the need to move faster than your feet can carry you, call **Michael's Cycles** (☎ **242-333-2384**), on Colebrook Street. You can choose among bicycles ($10 a day), two-seater scooters ($35 a day), and four-person golf carts ($47 to $65 a day).

Staying in Style

Most hotels in Harbour Island are expensive. Some daily rates appear high — until you notice that the rates also include breakfast and dinner.

If you stay in a moderately priced or inexpensive hotel, you can still treat yourself to the fancy resorts and restaurants by dining at them now and then, and you always have access to that dreamy pink beach. See the map on in this chapter for more information on the island's accommodations.

No matter your location, you receive as much — or as little — personal attention as you want. Your accommodation may even have an honor bar, where you just sign for whatever drinks you fix yourself.

Most hotels and restaurants close during parts of September, October, and November. Also, because most of the resorts are on a bluff high above the sand, stairs lead from them down to the coast.

Coral Sands
$$$ On the beach

You can sleep especially well at this sprawling 39-room beach resort where the owner, who also owns a Connecticut-based bedding company, replaced all the mattresses with the company's super-durable, super-comfortable brand. Coral Sands, which dates back to the 1960s, exchanged its former retro look for a totally fresh face. Done in tones of pink and turquoise, guest rooms are decorated with wicker furniture and attractive artwork. Some units contain balconies or patios. The rooms have various sizes and views, but all are in buildings surrounded by greenery. In the newest of these blocks of buildings, four oceanfront one-bedroom apartments with wraparound decks can be turned into two- or three-bedroom units by adding adjoining rooms.

A favorite spot is the spacious **Beach Bar,** on a deck hanging high over the pink shore. Lunch and light supper are served here. You can have elegant dinners at **Coral Sands Restaurant,** located on a broad veranda in the main building.

See map p. 286. Chapel Street. ☎ *800-468-2799 or 242-333-2350. Fax: 242-333-2368.* www.coralsands.com. *Rack rates: $215–$450 double, $450 one-bedroom apartment, $450–$695 two-bedroom suite. AE, MC, V.*

Dunmore Beach Club
$$$$$ On the beach

On a bluff above the pink sand beach, this 15-room inn is the quintessential elegant hideaway, with 3 hectares (8 acres) of lush, well-manicured grounds. The rooms, simply decorated in tranquil colors, are perfectly comfortable. "Rooms" are scattered cottages with private patios that have views of the water. The bathrooms in ten of the rooms contain hot tubs that are large enough for romantic trysts, and the shower stalls are spacious as well. A tennis court is on-site, and rates include three top-notch meals a day. A stairway connects the hotel to the beach.

 If you'd rather have a root canal than wear a jacket or a cocktail dress to dinner, don't check in here. Dunmore Beach Club isn't the only Harbour Island hotel where guests dress up at night, but it is a bit on the stuffy side. This hotel was once the hangout of the Duke and Duchess of Windsor and their friends, and a subdued, slightly stiff atmosphere of the private club it once was still lingers.

See map p. 286. Colebrook Street, eastern coast. ☎ *800-891-3100 or 242-333-2200. Fax: 242-333-2429.* www.dunmorebeach.com. *Rack rates: $499–$649 double, $749 suite. Rates include breakfast, lunch, and dinner. MC, V. Closed Sept–Oct.*

The Landing
 $$$– $$$$ Dunmore Town

This intimate inn is understated, tasteful, and lovely, giving you a touch of class like Dunmore Beach Club but for less money. Set in buildings that have stood here since the early 1800s, this small inn is located in the heart of historic Dunmore Town. Its owner is India Hicks, the daughter of the famed London decorator, David Hicks, and a bridesmaid to Lady Diana during her wedding to Prince Charles. The seven guest rooms are decorated plantation-style, with mahogany-stained four-poster beds and hardwood floors. Some rooms have broad verandas and ceiling fans, and most of them look out to the harbor across the road. **The Landing's restaurant** is reason enough to stay here (see a review of this restaurant in the "Dining

Out" section later in this chapter). To reach the beach, you have to go all the way across Harbour Island — but, this feat is hardly a difficult one. If you're traveling with children, ask for a room with an extra single bed.

See map p. 286. Bay Street, across from Government Dock. ☎ 242-333-2707. Fax: 242-333-2650. www.harbourislandlanding.com. Rack rates: $205–$295 double. Rates include breakfast. MC, V.

Pink Sands
$$$$$ On the beach

This 25-room inn, set on 8 landscaped hectares (20 acres) adjacent to the beach, is the epitome of Out Island chic. It's a classier joint than even the Dunmore Beach Club, its chief rival. You won't find a better hideaway or honeymoon retreat in all The Bahamas. The Pink Sands is also less snobbish and a lot hipper than the Dunmore. Jamaican-born Chris Blackwell, who brought Bob Marley to world attention, took over Pink Sands in 1992 and transformed it from a hurricane-ravaged inn into the pocket of posh that it is today.

The airy, spacious bedrooms have either an ocean or a garden view. Smaller units contain Art Deco touches straight out of Miami's South Beach; larger, more expensive units feature Indonesian (especially Balinese) furnishings and art, as well as huge decks. All rooms have kitchenettes or kitchens, central air-conditioning, pressurized water systems, walk-in closets, satellite TV, CD players and a CD selection, wet bars, private patios with teak furnishings, and beautifully tiled bathrooms. The rooms also have dataports, and the staff can supply you with fax machines and cellphones, if you need them.

When not on the beach, guests head for the swimming pool, the tennis courts (one of the three lit for night play), the exercise room, or the library. You can have breakfast and dinner surrounded by leafy greenery on the main dining terrace. (The daily rates include a full breakfast and the four-course candlelit evening meal.) The beachside **Blue Bar** serves lunch and hosts the Saturday night Bahamian barbecues. For a few extra bucks, you can even order room service, an alien concept at most Out Island hotels.

See map p. 286. Chapel Street. ☎ 800-OUTPOST (800-688-7678) or 242-333-2030. Fax: 242-333-2060. www.islandoutpost.com. Rack rates: $655–$765 one-bedroom cottage, $1,150–$1,575 two-bedroom cottage. Rates include breakfast and dinner. AE, MC, V.

Runaway Hill Club
$$$$ On the beach

Guests who first meet at Runaway Hill often book their next vacations together here the following year. Because this inn has only ten rooms (most with patios or balconies), everyone quickly gets to know each other. Set on a rise high above the swimming pool and beach (accessible by staircase), the main building was once a private home. With its individually and beautifully decorated rooms, it looks as if it still is. Our favorite place to sleep is the huge downstairs room with ceramic floor tiles in an intricate pink pattern and a spacious bathroom with twin sinks. The more modern rooms, in a separate hilltop villa, are more similar in size and decor. No matter where you stay, you find artfully arranged furnishings and well-maintained private bathrooms. Guests dress up for the elegant candlelit dinners here, joined by those lucky non-guests who've managed to reserve tables as well. The friendly staff is always on hand to help make arrangements for watersports and other activities.

See map p. 286. Colebrook Street, Central Harbour Island. ☎ 800-728-9803 or 242-333-2150. Fax: 242-333-2420. www.runawayhill.com. *Rack rates: $250–$285 double. MAP $60 extra per person. MC, V. No children under 18 accepted. Closed Sept–mid-Nov.*

Tingum Village
$ Southern Harbour Island

You won't find anything fancy about Tingum Village, and with just 19 rooms in cottages with large terraces, "village" is certainly a misnomer. However, the village's proximity to the island's beach (a four-minute walk away), its excellent Bahamian restaurant, **Ma Ruby's** (see our review in the "Dining Out" section), and the friendliness of the staff all make up for the lack of bells and whistles common at pricier Harbour Island hotels. A local family runs this quiet, low-key establishment. The hotel feels more like the "real" Bahamas than most of the island's more polished but foreign-owned and managed accommodations. The neat, clean rooms look out to a grassy expanse edged by palms, hibiscus, and other vegetation. If you want a hot tub in your room, book one of the two suites. Adjoining the pleasant bar, Ma Ruby's sits on a breezy patio at the edge of the garden.

See map p. 286. Colebrook Street. ☎ 242-333-2161. Fax: 242-333-2161. Rack rates: $95–$125 double, $115 triple, $150–$150 suite, $250 cottage. AE, MC, V.

Dining Out

For such a small island, a surprising selection of first-rate dining rooms, most of them at hotels, await you.

Dinner reservations are crucial, and you may need to make yours in the morning. Vacationers tend to dress up for dinner, especially at the more expensive resorts during the winter season. On the other hand, local spots featuring home-style Bahamian cooking are casual affairs. The majority of restaurants close between meals, and some restaurants also close completely for various chunks of time between September and November.

Angela's Starfish
$–$$ Just outside Dunmore Town BAHAMIAN

For more than a quarter century, this family-run restaurant has been churning out Bahamian dishes that keep folks streaming through the doors. Sit inside, where the casual décor has nautical touches, or on the palm-shaded lawn overlooking the water and mainland Eleuthera. At night, tiny bulbs hidden inside conch shells illuminate the tables. The honey-brown cracked conch is the perfect combination of crispy on the outside and tender on the inside. You can order fish, chicken, and pork chops, all served with mounds of peas and rice and all of which are also well prepared. Key lime and coconut pie are the featured desserts.

You're welcomed here as long as you heed the sign that requests that patrons refrain from swearing and wearing bare-backed clothing.

See map p. 286. At the top of the hill at Dunmore and Grant streets. ☎ *242-333-2253. Breakfast: $5–$8; lunch: $5–$10; dinner main courses: $13–$25. No credit cards. Open: Daily 11 a.m.–8 p.m.*

Beach Bar
$$–$$$ **Northern Harbour Island   BAHAMIAN/INTERNATIONAL**

At the Coral Sands resort, this casual restaurant and bar has a long lunch hour and is one of the most popular places along this broad strip of pink sands. You can sit at tables on a sunny deck hanging high above the rosy sand — the spot is perfect for a long, tall rum punch. You can order an early lunch or a very late lunch. Begin with conch fritters, the conch salad, the conch chowder, or the cracked conch. Main courses focus on sandwiches; one is made with rock lobster, and another with roast beef. If you like something more substantial, order the grilled New York strip steak or the catch of the day cooked to your specifications.

See map p. 286. Chapel Street, at the Coral Sands hotel. ☎ *242-333-2350. Sandwiches: $12–$18; main courses: $16–$19. AE, MC, V. Daily 11:30 a.m.–4 p.m.*

Coral Sands Restaurant
$$$ **Northern Harbour Island   BAHAMIAN/INTERNATIONAL**

If you prefer more elegant dining, stick around for dinner at this hotel's more formal restaurant. This establishment is Harbour Island's only oceanfront bar and restaurant. If the weather's right, everybody tries to get a table on the breeze-swept terrace overlooking the pink sands and the ocean.

Signature dishes include white conch chowder and lobster served with asiago cheese and a sauvignon blanc white sauce. Taste these dishes and you'll know at once why this dining room is one of the island's finest. Most diners wisely opt for one of the delectable fish dishes, including herb-crusted grouper or filet of snapper with fresh citrus chunks and a pinot sauce. Meat dishes, all imported, range from a tender prime Angus beef sirloin steak to New Zealand lamb chops. For dessert, you can finish off with a yummy chocolate torte.

See map p. 286. Chapel Street, at the Coral Sands hotel. ☎ *242-333-2350. Reservations required. Main courses: $25–$33. AE, MC, V. Open: Daily 7–8:30 p.m.*

Harbour Lounge
$$$– $$$$ Dunmore Town   BAHAMIAN

Arrive early to stake out a spot on the terrace so you can watch the sun slide into the harbor while you sip a Bahama Mama. Because you're right on Bay Street, the main thoroughfare, this restaurant is also the place to see and be seen. Along the water across the street, vendors sell straw goods, fruit, and vegetables. After dinner, a very local crowd gathers at the bar. Specialties include the blackened grouper, garlic shrimp with pasta, lobster, cracked conch, and Key lime pie. The food is some of the most satisfying and authentic on the island.

See map p. 286. Bay Street, in front of Government Dock. ☎ *242-333-2031. Reservations recommended for dinner. Lunch: salads, sandwiches, and platters: $9–$17; dinner main courses: $14–$35. MC, V. Open: Tues–Sun lunch 11 a.m.–3 p.m., dinner 5–9 p.m.*

The Landing
$$$$$ Dunmore Town   INTERNATIONAL

The cozy atmosphere of this intimate restaurant makes it clear that the owners enjoy their hands-on involvement. Dating back to 1800, this handsome building is part of The Landing hotel, which has a handful of guest rooms. Both dinner and Sunday brunch are special events here. You can dine in the bright yellow and white dining room or in the garden. Linens and fine china dress the tables, where you sit in saddle-back chairs. The restaurant always features a first-rate chef whose cooking pays tribute to the aristocratic credentials of the place. For your evening meal, you can choose among rock Cornish hen, cappellini with lobster, and Angus beef. The golden-brown, pan-fried grouper with mashed potatoes, eggplant, and green salsa is another bestseller. Dessert offerings may include ice cream, sorbet, and rich but surprisingly light chocolate cake, followed by various gourmet coffees.

See map p. 286. Bay Street, across from Government Dock. ☎ *242-333-2740. Reservations recommended for dinner. Lunch main courses: $12–$22; dinner main courses: $22–$40. MC, V. Open: Thurs–Tues 6:30–10 p.m., Sun brunch 8 a.m.–2 p.m.*

Ma Ruby's
$–$$ Southern Harbour Island   BAHAMIAN

Matriarch Ma Ruby is known for her cheeseburgers, which Jimmy Buffett — "Mr. Cheeseburger in Paradise" himself — ranked as among the ten best in the world. But we'd come back on another day and sample her conch burger, which we feel is worthy of an award as well — that and her hearty, flavorful Bahamian meals, such as conch fritters, stewed grouper, and baked chicken. Main dishes are accompanied by Ma Ruby's peas and rice. For dessert, try the Key lime pie or cheesecake. You dine on a courtyard patio by a grassy garden enclosed by palm trees.

If you want to use a credit card to purchase your meal, the restaurant requires a minimum charge of $65.

See map p. 286. Colebrook Street, at Tingum Village. ☎ 242-333-2161. Reservations not required. Breakfast: $6–$12; lunch: $5–$12; dinner main courses: $18–$26; set price four-course meal $26–$35. MC, V. Open: Daily 8:30–2 p.m. and 6–9 p.m.

Pink Sands

$$$$$ Northern Harbour Island   INTERNATIONAL

The four-course dinner menu is prix fixe at this snazzy beach resort that attracts celebrities. You can dine on a garden patio where the candlelit teak tables are tucked away into private leafy corners. Chefs sometimes jazz up the mainly European gourmet food with Caribbean and Asian influences. You can begin with leek and potato soup with smoked mahimahi or a savory tiger shrimp bisque with cognac. Your main course may be filet of grouper with saffron-scented risotto, grilled beef tenderloin with roasted portobello mushrooms and braised potatoes, or salmon baked in an herb crust and served with tomato-scallion *beurre blanc* (white butter). The mango cream pie is a luscious dessert. A lengthy wine list features excellent choices from France, South Africa, Australia, Chile, and the United States.

See map p. 286. Chapel Street, eastern coast. ☎ 242-333-2030. Reservations required. Four-course dinner: $70. AE, MC, V. Open to non-guests for dinner only, daily 7–9 p.m.

Rock House Restaurant

$$$ Dunmore Town   INTERNATIONAL

This restaurant feels like a hip bodega in Miami. It has lots of varnished mahogany, pale yellow walls, spinning ceiling fans and, in addition to the table groupings for groups of two and four diners, a very large "chef's table" with 16 chairs (originally reputed to have been among the furnishings in Washington, D.C.'s White House before a long-ago refurbishment). Lunches are charming but rather simple affairs, with dishes such as burgers, rock lobster salad sandwiches, and conch chowders. Dinners are more elaborate and more of a showcase for the chef. The best menu items include "Ying-yang" soup, crafted from roasted red and yellow peppers with smoked mozzarella and chili oil; chicken with Asian noodles and a tahini-flavored aioli; crab cakes served with a confit of sweet peppers and béarnaise sauce; grilled lobster tail with clarified butter; and tiger-shrimp spaghetti with local goat cheese, peppers, and parsley. Especially flavorful is a crispy pan-fried chicken breast with a citrus-flavored herb sauce.

See map p. 286. In the Rock House Hotel, at Bay and Hill streets. ☎ 242-333-2053. Reservations recommended. Lunch main courses: $15–$24; dinner main courses: $31–$42; Fri night buffet: $35 per person. AE, DC, MC, V. Open: Daily noon–4 p.m. and 6:30–10 p.m.

Runaway Hill Club

$$$$$ On the beach   CONTINENTAL

To see the daily prix-fixe menu, stop by in the morning to read what's on the old brass music stand by the entrance to the inn. Showing up early helps you for two reasons: First, dinner reservations go quickly at Runaway Hill. Second, this wonderfully decorated former home overlooking the ocean is gorgeous by daylight. See it and you just may want to book a room here for your next vacation. At night, the small, elegant dining room glows with candlelight. The chef turns out cuisine with skill and a certain flair, although it doesn't ever rise to spectacular highs. Your four-course meal may include lobster bisque followed by seafood pasta with scampi, pork tenderloin, rack of veal, or veal piccata. For dessert, you may try the chocolate pie with walnuts or an imaginative strawberry creation.

The restaurant has just one seating (8 p.m.), following cocktails (7:30 p.m.), so tables are at a premium. Men wear shirts with collars, and women really dress up.

See map p. 286. Colebrook Street, central Harbour Island. ☎ *242-333-2150. Reservations required. Complete four-course dinner: $60. AE, MC, V. Open: Mon–Sat. Closed from Sept–mid-Nov. No children.*

Enjoying the Sand and Surf

Fishing (especially bonefishing), scuba diving, and snorkeling are the main aquatic diversions. Relaxing on the beach, wandering around historic Dunmore Town, and socializing with residents round out the roster of activities.

Combing the beach

Pink Sand Beach is truly amazing. Nearly five exquisite kilometers (3 miles) of mostly unpopulated pink sand run along the eastern coast of the island. Take a stroll or plan a picnic here, and don't forget to watch the sunrise — it's spectacular. Sunbathing along this calm strand is best in the morning.

Playing in the surf

You may not be able to see forever in these waters, but on a clear day, visibility is often as good as 61km (200 ft.). This area boasts a diversity of dive sites.

In **Current Cut,** between Eleuthera and Current Island, experienced scuba divers can drift dive at exhilarating speeds with the current that rushes through an underwater chasm. The current carries divers between the rock walls for about a kilometer (a half-mile), along with a blizzard of reef fish, stingrays, and even some mako sharks. Another exceptional dive site is the wreck of a 60m (197-ft.) **steel freighter** that sank in 1917.

For both scuba and snorkeling trips, the place to go is **Valentine's Dive Center** (☎ 242-333-2080; www.valentinesdive.com), on the harbor side of the island in the heart of Dunmore Town. A scuba resort course costs $85. A one-tank dive for certified divers runs $45 and a two-tank trip is $65. Half-day snorkeling sails cost $45 per person.

For an unusual adventure, certified divers can try **reef running,** a ride on an underwater scooter ($120); decked out in your scuba gear, you cover much more marine territory than you do with regular diving.

Climbing aboard

You can rent a motorboat through **Michael's Cycles** (☎ 242-333-2384 or 242-464-0994) on Colebrook Street near Seagrapes nightclub. Plan to spend about $65 for a half-day or $75 for a full day on a 4m (13-ft.) boat and $100 for a half-day or $150 for a full day on a 5m (17-ft.) boat. Kayaks here go for $40 a day.

You can make arrangements for fishing guides and charters through your hotel or by contacting **Valentine's Dive Center** (☎ 242-333-2080), on the harbor side of the island in Dunmore Town. Deep-sea fishing trips start at $550 for a half-day or $750 for a full day.

Exploring on Dry Land

Dunmore Town, located on the harbor side of Harbour Island, was named for the 18th-century royal governor of The Bahamas who helped develop it and who had a summer home here. You can walk around these narrow, virtually car-free lanes in less than 20 minutes, or you can stroll slowly to savor the sight of the old gingerbread cottages that line the waterfront. Overhung with orange, purple, and pink bougainvillea, white picket fences enclose these wooden houses painted pastel blue, green, and lilac. Wind chimes tinkle in front of shuttered windows, and coconut palms and wispy casuarina pines shade grassy yards.

Americans and Canadians own some of these houses, which have whimsical names, such as "Up Yonder" and "Beside the Point," instead of house numbers. You can rent a few of these houses when you vacation here. One of the oldest, **Loyalist Cottage,** was built in 1797. It survives from the days when the original settlers, loyal to the British Crown, left the American colonies after the Revolutionary War. The porches along the harbor make for prime sunset watching. Lucky for you, some porches aren't connected to private homes. The terrace at Harbour Lounge Bar and Restaurant is an idyllic perch. Just across the road from Loyalist Cottage, you can browse through straw goods, T-shirts, fruits, and vegetables at the vendors' stalls.

On Sundays, residents dressed to kill stand in sociable clusters outside churches before and after services. Two of The Bahamas' first churches are in Dunmore Town and are still going strong: **St. John's,** The Bahamas' oldest Anglican church, established in 1768, and **Wesley Methodist Church,** built in 1846.

Spend some time wandering the streets — some hilly, some flat — away from the heart of town. You can see roosters doing their jerky marches through front yards and horses grazing in small fields. You'll find unassuming but perfectly good Bahamian restaurants, bars, and nightclubs in this locals' area.

A Shopper's Guide to Harbour Island

Dunmore Town is no Nassau, but you can find several stores carrying items that are worth a look, such as local artists' works, Androsia resort wear (made from the colorful batik fabric created on the Bahamian island of Andros), and handicrafts like music boxes in the shape of Harbour Island cottages and one-of-a-kind toothbrushes.

The standout boutique is **Miss Mae Tea Room and Fine Things** (☎ 242-333-2002), on Dunmore Street. Among the ever-changing, always-artful, mostly imported merchandise, you may find Haitian-style paintings, silver jewelry from Bali, local painted boxes, antique chests, gourmet wine vinegar from France, and Italian olive oil

Blue Rooster (☎ 242-333-2707), in the center of town, offers what might be the most upscale and stylish collection of men's and women's clothing and (casual) evening wear on the island. Come here for something sporty to wear to a posh hotel's dining room, especially if the button-down look appeals to you. **The Shop at The Landing** (☎ 242-333-2707), at The Landing Resort, usually wins as the most stylish clothing store on the island. It focuses on fashionable sportswear and clothes that you can wear to a casual island cocktail party, a posh brunch, or a buffet dinner aboard a yacht.

You might also check out **Princess Street Gallery** (☎ 242-333-2788), where Charles Carey restored an ancestral home and uses it to display works by local artists.

A few vendors sell fruit, vegetables, T-shirts, and straw goods (baskets, bags, hats, place mats) along **Bay Street,** at the edge of the harbor. You can hone your bargaining skills at this open-air mini-marketplace.

Living It Up After Dark

During the week, life after dark means hanging out at hotel and restaurant bars. Some resorts offer live music with dinner two evenings a week. The other nightspots see most of their action on weekends. The youngest, liveliest local crowd gravitates toward **Seagrapes** (no phone), a large club at Colebrook and Gibson streets. On Friday or Saturday, you're likely to catch a live band here, but the dance floor is packed even when a DJ reigns.

The poolroom at the **Vic-Hum Club** (☎ 242-333-2161), on Barrack Street, is another popular haunt. Calypso, American pop, and R&B pumps from the speakers, and classic record album sleeves decorate the walls and ceilings. Ask the owner to show you "the world's largest coconut," which measures some 84cm (33 in.) around.

Pool, satellite TV sports, and periodic live music entertains patrons at hilltop **Gusty's** (☎ 242-333-2165), on Coconut Grove Avenue in the north. Get here early enough and you'll have the perfect perch for sunset watching.

Fast Facts: Harbour Island

American Express and ATMs

No Amex services are available on Harbour Island. An ATM is available at First Caribbean Bank (☎ 242-332-3328), on Queen's Highway at Governor's Harbour.

Emergencies

Call the police at ☎ 242-333-2111 or contact the Harbour Island Medical Clinic at ☎ 242-333-2227.

Information

In the unlikely event that your request stumps the staff at your hotel, try the Harbour Island Tourist Office (☎ 242-333-2621), across from the ferry dock on Bay Street.

Internet Access

Resorts usually offer Internet access. Arthur's Bakery, located in the center of town, has also installed Internet service. You can use its computer or bring your own laptop. Hours are Monday through Saturday from 8 a.m. to 2 p.m., costing $10 for 15 minutes.

Police

Call ☎ 242-333-2111. The police station is on Gaol Alley between Dunmore and Colebrook streets.

Pharmacy

You can get prescriptions filled at Briland's Pharmacy (☎ 242-333-3427), located at Johnson's Plaza, Dunmore Street. Hours are Monday through Saturday from 9 a.m. to 5 p.m.

Post Office

The post office (☎ 242-333-2215) is on Gaol Alley, and it's open Monday through Friday from 9 a.m. to 5:30 p.m.

Chapter 23

Eleuthera

In This Chapter

▶ Getting around Eleuthera

▶ Reviewing Eleuthera's best accommodations and restaurants

▶ Enjoying the island's beaches, watersports, and land attractions

*V*isitors flock to Harbour Island, a small island off the coast of Eleuthera, to be coddled in comfort, but adventurous travelers head for "mainland" Eleuthera. Although Harbour Island is flourishing, the great heyday of tourism for mainland Eleuthera has dwindled since The Bahamas became independent. Many embittered locals blame the late Prime Minister Lynden Pindling for discouraging foreign investment.

At one time, some of the best-known names in the world visited Eleuthera. If celebs come today, they visit Harbour Island, not the mainland. However, Eleuthera's natural attractions, which made it alluring in the first place, are still here to welcome you.

Arriving at the Airports

Eleuthera has two main airports. **North Eleuthera Airport** (☎ 242-335-1242) serves the northern part of the island along with the two major offshore cays, Harbour Island and Spanish Wells. **Governor's Harbour Airport** (☎ 242-332-2321) serves the center of the island. A third airport at Rock Sound no longer receives as many flights as it used to and is used mostly by local residents.

 When you make your reservations, be sure that your flight will arrive at the appropriate airport; one visitor flew into Rock Sound Airport only to face a $100 taxi ride and a water-taxi trip before reaching his final destination of Harbour Island in the north.

Bahamasair (☎ 800-222-4262; www.bahamasair.com) offers daily flights between Nassau and the three airports in Eleuthera. In addition, several commuter airlines fly from the Florida mainland with either nonstop or one-stop service. Many private flights use the North Eleuthera Airport, with its 1,371m (4,500-ft.) paved runway. This airport is an official Bahamian port of entry, and a Customs and Immigration official is on hand.

Eleuthera

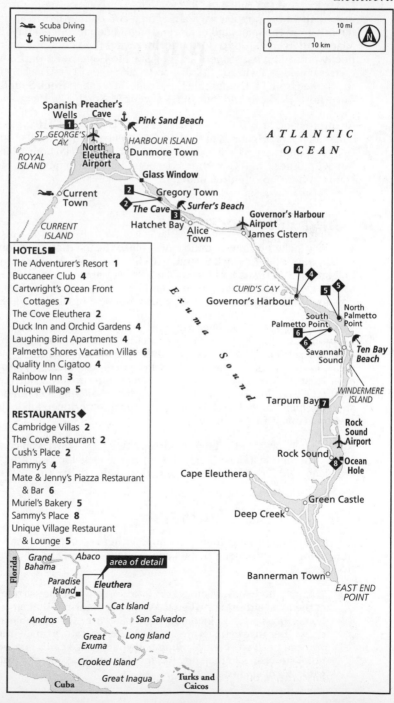

Scuba Diving
Shipwreck

0   10 mi
0   10 km

Spanish Preacher's
Wells Cave **1** Pink Sand Beach

ST. GEORGE'S CAY.

HARBOUR ISLAND
North Dunmore Town
Eleuthera
Airport

ROYAL ISLAND

ATLANTIC OCEAN

Glass Window

Current **2** Gregory Town
Town **2** The Cave Surfer's Beach
3
CURRENT Hatchet Bay Alice Governor's Harbour
ISLAND Town Airport
James Cistern

HOTELS
The Adventurer's Resort **1**
Buccaneer Club **4**
Cartwright's Ocean Front
   Cottages **7**
The Cove Eleuthera **2**
Duck Inn and Orchid Gardens **4**
Laughing Bird Apartments **4**
Palmetto Shores Vacation Villas **6**
Quality Inn Cigatoo **4**
Rainbow Inn **3**
Unique Village **5**

RESTAURANTS
Cambridge Villas **2**
The Cove Restaurant **2**
Cush's Place **2**
Pammy's **4**
Mate & Jenny's Piazza Restaurant
   & Bar **6**
Muriel's Bakery **5**
Sammy's Place **8**
Unique Village Restaurant
   & Lounge **5**

CUPID'S CAY
Governor's Harbour **4** **4**
5 **5**
North
South Palmetto
Palmetto Point Point
6
Savannah Ten Bay
Sound Beach

WINDERMERE ISLAND
Tarpum Bay **7**

Rock
Sound
Airport
Rock Sound
8 Ocean
Hole

Cape Eleuthera

Green Castle
Deep Creek

Florida
Grand Abaco
Bahama *area of detail*
Paradise
Island *Eleuthera*
Cat Island
Andros San Salvador
Great Long Island
Exuma
Crooked Island
Cuba Great Inagua Turks and
Caicos

Bannerman Town

EAST END POINT

USAir Express (☎ 800-428-4322; www.usairways.com) operates what may be the most popular way of reaching two of Eleuthera's airports directly from the mainland of Florida. Flights depart once a day from Miami and fly nonstop to North Eleuthera and then continue on, after briefly unloading passengers and baggage, to Governor's Harbour. Small carriers include **Twin Air** (☎ 954-359-8266; www.flytwinair.com), which flies from Ft. Lauderdale three times a week to Rock Sound and Governor's Harbour and four times a week to North Eleuthera.

 An inter-island link, **Bahamas Fast Ferries** (☎ 242-323-2166; www.ferry bahamas.com) originates in Potter's Cay, beneath the Paradise Island Bridge. From there, it leaves at regular intervals for Harbour Island, North Eleuthera, and Governor's Harbour. Round-trip fares are $110 for adults and $70 for children under 12.

Choosing Your Location

The very lack of accommodations will make the location decision for you. In days of yore, **Rock Sound,** with its fabled Windermere Club or Cotton Bay Club, was far chicer than today's Harbour Island. Chartered planes carrying CEOs landed several times a day, but those days are now memories. Except for private villas, Rock Sound is devoid of rentals.

As you leave Rock Sound heading north of its airport, you come to **Tarpum Bay,** where you find only a handful of simple inns. North of here, the settlement of **Palmetto Point** has a cluster of other modest villas. In the middle of the island further north, **Governor's Harbour —** or at least its economy — never recovered from the day a hurricane washed away Club Med. However, a number of offbeat accommodations, such as Duck Inn and Orchid Gardens, are far superior to any place south of Governor's Harbour.

As you move north into **Hatchet Bay** and **Gregory Town,** you come upon some other modest digs. Although simple, the little mom-and-pop places are clean, comfortable, well maintained, and affordable. Check them out.

Getting Around Eleuthera

It's virtually impossible to get lost on Eleuthera — only one road meanders along the entire length of its snake-shaped form, and you stray from it very rarely.

  ✔ **Taking a taxi:** Most visitors take a taxi only when they arrive at one of the local airports or when they have to return to that airport to go home. Taxis meet all incoming flights and are also available at ferry docks. Because cabbies are independent operators on Eleuthera, you can't call one central number. If you need to call a taxi, your hotel staff can summon one for you, but you may have to wait a while, so plan ahead.

✔ **Hoofing it:** You can easily traverse all the settlements — really, hamlets, in most cases — on foot. With little traffic on the island, walking is an enjoyable experience here.

✔ **Wheeling around:** You don't find any American car-rental agencies on the island. Usually, your hotel staff can arrange for a car rental (prices are around $80 a day). Often, we've ended up with someone's private car. The best bet for car rentals is the North Eleuthera-based **Fine Threads Taxi, Rental Cars & Tours** (☎ **242-359-7780** or 242-335-1556). Here, owner Frederick Neely (nicknamed "Fine Threads" because of his well-tailored clothes) either rents you a car or takes you on a private island tour. An eight-hour experience for two or three people costs $200; 8 to 12 people, $300. Tours usually begin at 9 a.m. and take in a series of bars, restaurants, and geological or historical attractions in Rock Sound, Lower Bogue, Palmetto Point, and Gregory Town. If you negotiate with your driver, you may also visit Preacher's Cave.

✔ **Sailing on a ferry:** For information about how to reach Harbour Island from Eleuthera, refer to Chapter 22. To reach the other off-shore island, Spanish Wells, take the convenient "on demand" ferry service (☎ **242-554-6268**) to North Eleuthera. A ferry runs between Gene's Bay in North Eleuthera to the main pier at Spanish Wells. The ferries depart whenever passengers show up, and the cost is $8 per person round-trip or $4 one-way.

Staying in Style

Because all the luxury properties on Eleuthera have gone belly-up, nearly every place you stay on the mainland is affordable. If you like to spend big bucks, you can always sail over to Harbour Island. Otherwise, you can expect a reasonably priced vacation.

 Although we personally like Eleuthera in the late summer and fall when most visitors have departed, not all inns and hotels are likely to be open, especially in late September, October, and November. If business is slow, hoteliers simply close their doors.

Don't come expecting a lot of personal attention. Eleuthera caters to self-sufficient types. We often met the hotel owner when checking into a rental and didn't see him or her again until we paid the bill.

The Adventurer's Resort
$ **Spanish Wells**

Because the 1999 hurricane demolished all the competition, this hotel has emerged as the most appealing and most recommendable spot in Spanish Wells. It occupies a two-story, pale lavender-colored building in a well-tended garden about a half-kilometer (½-mile) west of the town center. The resort doesn't have an on-site restaurant or bar, but a staff member can direct you to nearby eateries and to the beach, which lies about a kilometer away. The 18 small bedrooms have simple, durable furniture with tropical upholstery; six of the units are apartments with kitchenettes. All accommodations are equipped with air-conditioning and TV but no phone. The resort provides maid service when you rent a regular double room but not when you rent an apartment.

See map p. 299. Harbourfront. ☎ *242-333-4883. Fax: 242-333-5073. Rack rates: $75 double, $127 one-bedroom apt with kitchenette, $190 two-bedroom apt with kitchenette. MC, V.*

Buccaneer Club
$ **Governor's Harbour**

This three-story, five-room farmhouse, built more than a century ago, offers views of the harbor. Today, it sports yellow-painted plank siding, white trim, and an old-fashioned design. The beach lies within a ten-minute stroll, although the house has a small saltwater pool on-site. Bedrooms are comfortable, unpretentious, well maintained, and outfitted with simple but colorful furniture. Rooms have air-conditioning but no TVs or phones. Your host and hostess are Michelle and Dwight Johnson, an Indian/Bahamian entrepreneurial team who foster a calm, quiet atmosphere. The Johnsons prepare lunch and dinner and serve it daily in an airy annex with island murals. Tasty specialties include Bahamian and American standbys: steaks, burgers, club sandwiches, cracked conch, grilled grouper with lemon butter sauce, and chili.

See map p. 299. Haynes Drive at Buccaneer Drive. ☎ *242-332-2000. Fax: 242-332-2888. Rack rates: $105 double. DISC, MC, V.*

Cartwright's Ocean Front Cottages
$ **Tarpum Bay**

Cartwright's is a cluster of three simple cottages right by the sea, with fishing, snorkeling, and swimming at your door. This spot is one of the few places where you can sit on your patio and watch the sunset. The small cottages are fully furnished, with utensils, stove, refrigerator, pots and pans. The inn also provides maid service. You're within walking distance of local stores and restaurants. Rooms are air-conditioned but contain no phones. Regular hotel services are skimpy, although laundry service is available, as well as baby-sitting, if arranged in advance.

See map p. 299. Bay Street. ☎ *242-334-4215. E-mail:* cartwrights@hotmail. com. *Rack rates: $100 one-bedroom cottage, $130 two-bedroom cottage, $150 three-bedroom cottage. No credit cards.*

The Cove Eleuthera
$$ **Gregory Town**

On a private sandy cove 2.5km (1½ miles) northwest of Gregory Town and 5km (3 miles) southeast of the Glass Window, this 30-unit resort is set on 11 hectares (28 acres) partially planted with pineapples. The property consists of a main clubhouse and seven tropical-style buildings, each containing four units, nestled on the oceanside. The resort, a favorite with families, was devastated during the hurricanes of 1999, and a radical rebuilding program was implemented. By late 2000, rooms were back in shape. Each one has tile floors and a porch, with no TVs or phones to distract you. The restaurant serves three good meals a day, and the lounge and the poolside Pineapple Patio are open daily for drinks and informal meals. Kayaks, bicycles, two tennis courts, and a small freshwater pool compete with hammocks for your time. You also have access to fabulous snorkeling right off the sands here.

See map p. 299. Queen's Highway. ☎ *800-552-5960 in the U.S. and Canada, or 242-335-5142. Fax: 242-335-5338.* www.thecoveeleuthera.com. *Rack rates: $130–$165 double, $155 triple. One child under 12 stays free in parents' room. MAP (breakfast and dinner) $45 per person extra. AE, MC, V.*

Duck Inn and Orchid Gardens
$$$ **Governor's Harbour**

The accommodations you rent here are larger, plusher, more historic, and more charming than what you'd expect in a conventional hotel. The complex consists of three clapboard-sided houses, each built between 80 and 175 years ago, and each almost adjacent to another, midway up a hillside overlooking the sea. All cottages come with kitchenettes, air-conditioning, and TV, but no phone. Nassau-born John (J.J.) Duckworth and his Michigan-born wife, Katie, along with their son John Lucas, are your hosts. They spend much of their time nurturing a sprawling collection of beautiful orchids that they cultivate for export to Europe and the U.S. The collection of orchids, some 4,000 strong, is one of the largest in North America.

See map p. 299. Queen's Highway. ☎ *242-332-2608.* www.theduckinn.com. *Rack rates: $110 studio for two, $220 four-bedroom cottage for up to eight. AE, DISC, MC, V.*

Laughing Bird Apartments
$ **Governor's Harbour**

These four simple apartments lie near the edge of Governor's Harbour on a beach in the center of Eleuthera, and they're a good bet if you want to settle in for a week or so. Efficiencies come with a living/dining/sleeping area and a separate kitchen. Apartments face the beach on an acre of landscaped property. The units are bright, clean, and airy, and they have air-conditioning and TV but no phone. The staff offers bike rentals, tables and chairs for outdoor eating, and a garden barbecue. The staff can also make arrangements for water-skiing, surfing, fishing, sailing, tennis, golf, and snorkeling.

See map p. 299. Haynes Avenue and Birdie Street. ☎ *800-688-4752 in the U.S., or 242-332-2012. Fax: 242-332-2358. Rack rates: $95–$105 double, $115–$120 triple, $125–$130 quad. DISC, MC, V.*

Palmetto Shores Vacation Villas
$$ Palmetto Point

This accommodation is a good choice if you want your own apartment and value independence and privacy over hotel services. Asa Bethel rents 12 villas that are suitable for two to four guests. Units are a plain Bahamian-style, with living rooms, kitchens, and wraparound balconies that open directly onto your own private beach. Furnishings are simple but reasonably comfortable. Rooms have air-conditioning and TV/VCRs, and the villas lie within walking distance of local shops and tennis courts. The staff can help arrange car rentals, snorkeling, deep-sea fishing and can also provide free Sunflower sailboats.

See map p. 299. Palmetto Point. ☎ *888-688-4752 in the U.S., or 242-332-1305. Fax: 242-332-1305. Rack rates: $100–$120 one-, two-, and three-bedroom villas. Extra person $30 winter. MC, V.*

Quality Inn Cigatoo
$$ Governor's Harbour

This 22-room inn is on a hill and offers panoramic views of the ocean. Owners Franco and Katherine Ostini, two world travelers, try to bring some of the polish of Europe to the laid-back aura of Eleuthera. Nothing much happens here; you create your own amusement. You can lounge in a deck chair by the freshwater pool or take in a view of the tropical gardens. A good sandy beach, ideal for both beachcombing and swimming, is only a five-minute walk away.

Although comfortable and well maintained, the décor of the bedrooms wouldn't seem out of place in Miami in the 1960s. Built around the pool, the bedrooms open onto ocean or garden views. Each has a private balcony with chairs. If you're just passing through, consider a stopover here for lunch, because the Bahamian-style food is good.

See map p. 299. Haynes Avenue. ☎ *242-332-3060. Fax 242-332-3061.* www.choice hotels.com. *Rack rates: $89–$129 double. MC, V.*

Rainbow Inn
$$ Hatchet Bay

Three kilometers (2 miles) north of Alice Town and near a sandy beach, the Rainbow Inn is a venerable survivor in an area where many competitors have failed. Quirky and appealing to guests who return for quiet getaways again and again, it's an isolated collection of seven cedar-sided octagonal bungalows. The accommodations are simple but comfortable, spacious, and tidy; each has a kitchenette, lots of exposed wood, a ceiling fan, a porch, and a TV but no phone. A sandy beach is a few steps away, and the inn offers an on-site saltwater pool along with a tennis court. You can rent cars, although the inn provides you with bikes and snorkeling gear.

One of the most appealing things about this place is **Dolcevita Restaurant and Lounge** — a destination for residents far up and down the length of

Eleuthera. It has live Bahamian music twice a week and one of the most extensive menus on Eleuthera. The owners take pride that the menu hasn't changed much in 20 years — a fact that suits its loyal fans just fine. Table number two, crafted from a triangular teakwood prow of a motor yacht that was wrecked off the coast of Eleuthera in the 1970s, is a perpetual favorite of guests.

See map p. 299. Hatchet Bay. ☎ *800-688-0047 in the U.S., or 242-335-0294. Fax: 242-335-0294.* www.rainbowinn.com. *Rack rates: $120–$150 studio, $200–$220 two- or three-bedroom villas. MAP (breakfast and dinner) $40 per person extra. MC, V. Closed Sept 7–Nov 15.*

Unique Village
$$ Palmetto Point

Located on a steep rise above the Atlantic coast of Eleuthera, this 14-room hotel is the creative statement of a Palmetto Point businessman who also owns the local hardware store (Unique Hardware). The hotel, built in 1992, offers everything from conventional single or double rooms to a one-bedroom apartment with a kitchenette to two-bedroom villas with full kitchens. All rooms come with air-conditioning. Wooden steps bring you to the beach, where a reef breaks up the Atlantic surf and creates calm waters on this sandy cove. There's a bar and restaurant, also called Unique Village (see our review in the "Dining Out" section later in this chapter), but few other luxuries. Although no sailing, scuba, or tennis is on-site, the staff can direct you to other facilities within a reasonable drive. (If you stay here, you'll probably want to rent a car; for more information on renting a car, see "Getting Around Eleuthera" earlier in this chapter.)

See map p. 299. North Palmetto Point. ☎ *800-688-4752 in the U.S., or 242-332-1830. Fax: 242-332-1838. Rack rates: $120–$140 double, $160 one-bedroom apt for two, $190 two-bedroom apt for up to four. Extra person $25. MAP (breakfast and dinner) $35 per person per day. MC, V.*

Dining Out

Food on Eleuthera can be good and substantial, but don't expect fancy international restaurants. Your best bet for dining is at one of the few resorts. Branch out during the day to sample some "Bahama Mama" type places for island specialties. If you order as many Goombay Smashes as some of the locals do, you'll end up loving whatever is served.

Cambridge Villas
$ Gregory Town   BAHAMIAN

This restaurant occupies a large cement-sided room on the ground floor of a battered hotel (the accommodations aren't as appealing as the restaurant). Harcourt and Sylvia Cambridge, the owners, serve conch burgers, conch chowder, and sandwiches, usually prepared by Sylvia herself. This restaurant is just a simple spot where you may be entertained by the continually running soap operas broadcast from a TV over the bar.

See map p. 299. Main Street. ☎ 242-335-5080. Reservations not accepted. Sandwiches and platters: $5–$10. MC, V. Open: Mon–Sat 7:30 a.m.–9 p.m.

The Cove Restaurant
$ Gregory Town   BAHAMIAN/CONTINENTAL

Located at The Cove Eleuthera hotel, this spacious dining room is your best bet in the area. The Cove Restaurant is nothing fancy, but it offers good homemade local fare. The restaurant is decorated in a light, tropical style. Lunch begins with the inevitable conch chowder; we recommend you follow it with a *conch burger,* a generous patty of ground conch blended with green pepper, onion, and spices. Conch also appears several times in the evening, including in the best cracked conch in town, which is tenderized, dipped in a special batter, and fried to a golden perfection. The kitchen serves the best fried chicken in the area, too.

See map p. 299. At The Cove Eleuthera, Queen's Highway. ☎ 242-335-5142. Breakfast: $6–$18; lunch: $8–$18; main courses: $14–$30. MC, V. Open: Daily 8–10:30 a.m., 11:30 a.m.–2:30 p.m., and 5:30–9 p.m.

Cush's Place
$ Gregory Town   BAHAMIAN

Macushla Scavella ("Cush," for short) is the owner of this big yellow stucco-sided building set less than a kilometer (a half-mile) south of Gregory Town. Inside the somewhat sterile-looking interior, you find a jukebox, a pool table, and a bartender named Walter. Generous portions of Bahamian food are (slowly) served throughout the day and evening. Pork chops and chicken à la Cush (fried chicken) are staples, along with sandwiches, lobster tail, and steamed conch with black-eyed peas and corn on the cob. Come here to hang out with the locals, perhaps over drinks and a platter of food.

See map p. 299. Queen's Highway. ☎ 242-335-5301. Sandwiches: $3–$4; lunch and dinner main courses: $12–$18. No credit cards. Open: Daily 10 a.m.–midnight.

Mate & Jenny's Piazza Restaurant & Bar
$$ Palmetto Point   BAHAMIAN/AMERICAN

This popular restaurant, known for its conch pizza, has a jukebox and a pool table. It's the most frequented local joint, completely modest and unassuming. In addition to pizza, the Bethel family prepares pan-fried grouper, cracked conch, or light meals, including snacks and sandwiches. Lots of folks come here just to drink. Try their Goombay Smash, Rumrunner, or piña colada, or just a Bahamian Kalik beer.

See map p. 299. South Palmetto Point, right off Queen's Highway. ☎ 242-332-1504. Pizza: $7–$22; main courses: $12–$25. No credit cards. Open: Wed–Sat and Mon 11 a.m.–3 p.m. and 5:30–9 p.m.

Muriel's Bakery
$ Palmetto Point   BAHAMIAN

Locals hail Muriel Cooper, a grandmother in her 70s, as the best baker in Eleuthera. Located across from the post office, her little bakery is simple yet warm and welcoming and filled with pictures of her grandchildren. You can stop in to stock up on freshly baked cakes, pies, tarts, rolls, and loaves of bread, which can be ideal for a picnic. Should some fishermen bring her some fresh conch, she'll make a tasty chowder to go or else the island's best conch fritters. You'll fall for her rich, moist pineapple and coconut cakes as well.

See map p. 299. North Palmetto Point. ☎ *242-332-1583. Menu items: $1–$10. No credit cards. Open: Mon–Sat 10 a.m.–5 p.m.*

Pammy's
$ Governor's Harbour   BAHAMIAN

Tile-floored and Formica-clad, this restaurant is just a little cubbyhole with a few tables. At breakfast, you can order ham or corned beef and eggs, along with such sides as grits and bacon. Lunchtime features sandwiches, although you can also order hot plates of food (most often fried grouper). The dinner menu includes platters of cracked conch, pork chops, and either broiled or fried grouper. Don't expect anything fancy. It's a true local joint, serving up generous portions of flavor-filled food.

See map p. 299. Queen's Highway at Gospel Chapel Road. ☎ *242-332-2843. Reservations accepted for dinner only. Breakfast: $2–$7; lunch: $3–$10; dinner main courses: $14–$20. No credit cards. Open: Mon–Sat 8 a.m. –5 p.m.*

Sammy's Place
$ Rock Sound   BAHAMIAN

Hot gossip and cheap, juicy burgers make Sammy's the most popular hangout in Rock Sound — come here for a slice of local life. Sammy's is on the northeastern approach to the settlement in a neighborhood that even the owner refers to as "the back side of town." Sammy Culmer (who's assisted by Margarita, his daughter) will serve you drinks (including Bahama Mamas and rum punches), conch fritters, Creole-style grouper, breaded scallops, pork chops, and lobster. If you drop in before 11 a.m., you may be tempted by a selection of egg dishes or omelets.

 This spot is primarily a restaurant and bar, but Sammy does rent four rooms with air-conditioning and satellite TV, plus two efficiency cottages with two bedrooms and a kitchen. These accommodations can be yours for $66 per night, double occupancy. An on-site cottage rents for $93 per night.

See map p. 299. Albury's Lane. ☎ *242-334-2121. Reservations recommended only for special meal requests. Breakfast: $7–$10; lunch: $5–$12; dinner main courses: $10–$25. No credit cards. Open: Daily 7:30 a.m.–10 p.m.*

Unique Village Restaurant & Lounge
$ Palmetto Point BAHAMIAN/AMERICAN

This is the best place for food in the area, offering the widest selection. You can drop in for a Bahamian breakfast of boiled or stewed fish served with johnnycakes or steamed corned beef and grits. (You can also get "regular" breakfasts, such as hearty omelets.) Lunch offerings include zesty conch chowder and an array of salads. You can order burgers or the steamed catch of the day. At night, the choices grow, and you find the best New York sirloin available in mid-Eleuthera. Cracked conch fried in a light beer batter is one of the better versions of this dish on the island.

See map p. 299. In Unique Village hotel, North Palmetto Point. ☎ *242-332-1830. Main courses: $14–$32. MC, V. Open: Daily 7:30–11 a.m., 11:30 a.m.–5 p.m., and 6–8:30 p.m.*

Enjoying the Sand and Surf

Eleuthera possesses some of the finest beaches in The Bahamas, although none is as fine as the 5km (3 miles) of pink sands at Harbour Island (see Chapter 22).

Now relatively deserted, **Cape Eleuthera** was once home to a chic resort and yacht club that drew some of the movers and shakers from America's East Coast. They're all gone now, but the three splendid white sandy beaches remain the same, and locals claim the deep-sea fishing is as fine as it ever was. Directly north of the town of Tarpum Bay lies **Gaulding's Cay,** a lovely beach of golden sand with exceptional snorkeling.

None of Eleuthera's beaches has facilities or lifeguards. Whatever you need on the beach, you should bring with you, including sunscreen and water. Don't expect any touristy kiosks selling drinks, snacks, or souvenirs, because everything is pristine and undeveloped.

Even without its posh hotel, **Windermere Island** is worth a day trip. **Savannah Sound,** with its sandy sheltered beaches and outstanding snorkeling, is particularly appealing (bring your own gear). You also find excellent beaches for shelling and picnicking, and bonefishing is good — with some catches weighing in at more than 4.5kg (10 lbs.).

West Beach, a good place for sunning, swimming, and children, is about a ten-minute walk from the shutdown Windermere Club. The beach is on Savannah Sound, and this body of calm, protected water separates Windermere from the main island of Eleuthera.

Visitors can enjoy a number of activities, from bonefishing to windsurfing. The dockmaster at West Beach is well qualified to guide and advise you on bonefishing, or perhaps you prefer going deep-sea fishing for white marlin, dolphinfish, grouper, wahoo, Allison tuna, and amberjack. Because no permanent outfitter is on the island, you have to ask around locally about who can take you out.

At **Palmetto Point,** site of some villa rentals, you find **Ten Bay Beach,** one of the best beaches in The Bahamas, with its sparkling turquoise water and wide expanse of soft, white sand. The beach is a ten-minute drive south of Palmetto Point and just north of Savannah Sound. You won't find facilities here, only idyllic isolation.

Near the center of **Governor's Harbour** you find two sandy beaches known locally as the **Buccaneer Public Beaches;** they're adjacent to the Buccaneer Club, on the sheltered western edge of the island, facing Exuma Sound. Snorkeling is good here; it's best at the point where the pale turquoise waters near the coast deepen to a dark blue. Underwater rocks shelter lots of marine flora and fauna. The waves at these beaches are relatively calm.

On Eleuthera's Atlantic (eastern) side, less than a kilometer (a half-mile) from Governor's Harbour, is a much longer stretch of mostly pale pink sand, similar to what you find on Harbour Island. Known locally as the **Club Med Public Beach,** it's good for bodysurfing and, on days when storms are surging in the Atlantic, even conventional surfing.

 Diving isn't a big sport on mainland Eleuthera where outfitters come and go quickly, few getting enough business to hold out until another winter. But diving is excellent off Harbour Island, with some of the best scuba-diving experts in The Bahamas (see Chapter 22).

Exploring on Dry Land

We like to drive the full 161km (100-mile) length of Eleuthera, stopping wherever something enchants us. The island doesn't have any historical attractions, only those that nature created. We begin our tour in the south and head north.

Located in South Eleuthera, **Rock Sound** is a small, shady village. It is the island's main town and was once its most exclusive enclave. The closing of two old-time landmark resorts, the Cotton Bay Club and the Windermere Club, has — at least for now — halted the flow of famous visitors, who once included everybody from the late Princess Diana to a parade of CEOs. No reopenings are yet in sight, but that means you can have many of South Eleuthera's best beaches practically to yourself.

Rock Sound opens onto **Exuma Sound** and is located to the south of **Tarpum Bay.** The town is at least two centuries old, and it has many old-fashioned homes with picket fences out front. Once notorious for wreckers who lured ships ashore with false beacons, it used to be known as "Wreck Sound."

The **Ocean Hole,** which is about 2km (1¼ miles) east of the heart of Rock Sound, is said to be bottomless. This saltwater lake, which eventually meets the sea, is one of the most attractive spots on Eleuthera. You can walk right down to the edge of the water, and you can see many tropical fish here; they seem to like being photographed — but only if you feed them first.

After leaving Rock Sound, head south, bypassing the abandoned Cotton Bay Club, and continue through the villages of **Green Castle** and **Deep Creek.** At this point, you take a sharp turn northwest along the only road leading to **Cape Eleuthera.** Locals call this Cape Eleuthera Road, although you won't find any markings other than a sign pointing the way. If you continue following this road northwest, you'll reach the end of the island chain, jutting out into Exuma Sound.

When you get back on the main road again, you can head north of Rock Sound for 14km (9 miles) until you come to **Tarpum Bay,** a charming old waterfront village. This tiny settlement, with its many pastel-washed, gingerbread-trimmed houses, is a favorite of artists, who have established a small colony here with galleries and studios.

Continue heading north, and you find **Windermere Island,** which lies between the settlements of Rock Sound and Governor's Harbour. To reach the island, you must cross a small bridge. Once the most exclusive vacation retreat in The Bahamas, many rich Americans still have second homes here, and security guards patrol the island.

 You may have to do some sweet-talking to get past the security patrols. They generally let you drive along the island if they think you're a sightseer and not a burglar.

On the east side of Queen's Highway, south of Governor's Harbour, **North Palmetto Point** is a little village where visitors rarely venture (although you can get a meal here). This laid-back town will suit you if you want peace and quiet off the beaten track.

At some 300 years old, **Governor's Harbour** is the island's oldest settlement, reportedly the landing place of the Eleutherian Adventurers, the island's original settlers. The largest town on Eleuthera after Rock Sound, it's situated midway along the island. The town today has a population of about 1,500, with some bloodlines going back to the Adventurers and to the Loyalists who followed some 135 years later. Many old homes line streets amid the bougainvillea and casuarina trees.

Leaving Queen's Highway, you can take a small bridge, thought to be about 150 years old, to **Cupid's Cay.** As you explore the offshore island, you come upon one of the most interesting buildings in the area, an old Anglican church with its tombstone-studded graveyard.

Forty kilometers (25 miles) north of Governor's Harbour is the village **Hatchet Bay.** Hatchet Bay was once known for a sprawling British-owned plantation that had 500 dairy cattle and thousands of chickens. Today, the plantation is gone, and the village is now one of the sleepiest on Eleuthera, as you can see if you veer off Queen's Highway onto one of the town's ghostly main streets, Lazy Shore Road or Ocean Drive.

Gregory Town, north of Hatchet Bay, stands in the center of Eleuthera against a backdrop of hills, which break the usual flat monotony of the landscape. This village of clapboard cottages was once famed for growing pineapples. Although the industry isn't as strong as it used to be, the locals make a good pineapple rum out of the fruit, and you can visit the Gregory Town Plantation and Distillery where they produce it. You can sample it, and we almost guarantee that you'll want to take a bottle home with you!

Dedicated surfers come here from as far away as California and Australia to test their skills at **Surfer's Beach,** 3km (2 miles) south of Gregory Town on the Atlantic side. The waves are at their highest in winter and spring; even if you're not brave enough to venture out, the surfers are fun to watch.

South of Gregory Town on the way to Hatchet Bay are several caverns worth visiting, the largest of which is called simply **The Cave.** It has a big fig tree out front, which the people of Gregory Town claim that area pirates planted to conceal the cave because they had hidden treasure in it. Local guides (you have to ask around in Gregory Town or Hatchet Bay) can take you into the interior of the cave, where the resident bats are harmless (even though they must resent the intrusion of tourists with flashlights). At one point, the drop is so steep — about 3.6m (12 ft.) — that you have to use a ladder to climb down. Eventually, you reach a cavern studded with stalactites and stalagmites. At this point, a maze of passageways leads through the rocky underground recesses. The cave comes to an abrupt end at the edge of a cliff, where the thundering sea is some 27m (90 ft.) below.

After leaving Gregory Town and driving north, you come to the famed **Glass Window,** Eleuthera's chief sight and narrowest point. A natural rock arch once bridged the land, but it's gone now, replaced by an artificially constructed bridge. As you drive across it, you can see the contrast between the deep blue ocean and the emerald green shoal waters of Exuma Sound. The rocks rise to a height of 21m (70 ft.). Often, as ships in the Atlantic toss about, the crew looks across the narrow point to see a ship resting quietly on the other side (hence, the name "Glass Window"). American artist Winslow Homer was so captivated by this spot that he once captured it on canvas.

The inhabitants of **Current,** a settlement in North Eleuthera, are believed to have descended from a tribe of Native Americans. A narrow strait separates the village from **Current Island,** where most of the locals make their living from the sea or from plaiting straw goods. This small community often welcomes visitors. It has no crowds and no artificial attractions. Everything focuses on the sea, a source of pleasure for visitors, but a way to sustain life for the local people.

From Current, you can explore some interesting sights in North Eleuthera, including **Preacher's Cave,** where the Eleutherian Adventurers found shelter in the mid-17th century when they were shipwrecked with no provisions. (Note that your taxi driver may balk at being asked to drive there; the road is hard on his expensive tires.) If you do reach it, you'll find a cave that seems like an amphitheater. The very devout Eleutherian Adventurers held religious services inside the cave, which has holes in the roof to allow light to intrude. The cave isn't far from the North Eleuthera Airport, in a northeasterly direction.

Living It Up After Dark

Eleuthera is rather sleepy, but it does have a hot spot or two. The place to be in Gregory Town, especially on a Saturday night, is **Elvina** (☎ 242-335-5032), on Main Street. Owners Ed and Elvina Watkins make you feel right at home and practically greet you at the door with a cold beer. Their place has a funky charm, with local artwork, license plates, and surfboards as decorations. Surfers and locals alike flock here to chow down on burgers, Bahamian dishes, and Cajun grub, served daily from 10 a.m. to "whenever we close." Elvina's husband, "Chicken Ed," is from Louisiana, and does he ever know how to make a great jambalaya!

Also at Governor's Harbour, **Ronnie's Smoke Shop & Sports Bar** (☎ 242-332-2307), on Cupid's Cay, is the most happening nightspot in central Eleuthera. It's adjacent to the cargo depot of Cupid's Cay, in a connected cluster of simple buildings painted in combinations of black with vivid Junkanoo colors. Most folks come here just to drink Kalik beer and talk at either of the two bars. But if you want to dance, it has an all-black room just for disco music on Friday and Saturday nights. You also find the only walk-in cigar humidor on Eleuthera. If you get hungry, order up a plate of barbecue, pizza, chicken wings, or popcorn. The place is open daily from 10 a.m. 'til at least 2 a.m., and sometimes 5 a.m., depending on business.

Going Beyond Eleuthera

Of course, the most enticing day trip is to **Harbour Island** (see Chapter 22). But **Spanish Wells** is intriguing, too, as a journey back to a distant past. Called a "quiet corner of The Bahamas," Spanish Wells is a colorful cluster of houses on **St. George's Cay,** less than a kilometer (a half-mile) off the coast of northwest Eleuthera. It's characterized by its sparkling bays and white beaches, sleepy lagoons, excellent diving, and fine fishing colony.

You can walk through the village and look at the houses — some more than 200 years old — which have New England saltbox styling but bright tropical coloring. You can see handmade quilts in many colors, following patterns handed down from generations of English ancestors. Homeowners display these quilts that are for sale on their front porches or out their windows.

Regardless of the time of day you arrive, a ferryboat is either waiting for passengers or about to arrive with a load of them (see "Getting Around Eleuthera" earlier in this chapter for more details).

If you're on Spanish Wells at lunch, head for **Jack's Outback** (☎ 242-333-4219) along the harbor front. Unpretentious and well scrubbed, this little place stands along the waterfront in the heart of town. Known for its home-cooking, it offers the usual array of sandwiches and cheeseburgers, as well as Bahamian foods like cracked conch, conch burgers, and conch chowder. It also offers steaks, barbecued ribs, and cheesy shrimp poppers. The interior is air-conditioned, with views of the sea. Sandwiches cost from $3.50 to $10, with main courses priced from $11 to $25. It's open daily from 9 a.m. to 10 p.m. Credit cards aren't accepted.

Fast Facts: Eleuthera

American Express and ATMs

No Amex services are available on Eleuthera, but an ATM is available at the Bank of Canada (☎ 242-333-2230), on Dunmore Street near the library.

Emergency

Call ☎ 242-332-2111.

Hospitals

The Governor Harbour's Medical Clinic (☎ 242-332-2001), located on Queen's Highway, is open Monday through Friday from 9 a.m. to 5:30 p.m. The clinic is also the site of a dentist's office. The dentist is here from 9:30 a.m. until 3 p.m., Monday through Wednesday and Friday only. Call for an appointment before going. A doctor and four resident nurses form the staff of the Rock Sound Medical Clinic (☎ 242-334-2226). Office hours are daily from 9 a.m. to 1 p.m.; after that, the doctor is always available to handle emergency cases.

Information

The Eleuthera Tourist Office (☎ 242-332-2142) is on Queens Highway. It's generally open Monday through Friday from 9 a.m. to 5 p.m.

Internet Access

Check with your hotel for Internet access. An Internet cafe has opened on the second floor of the Haynes Library (☎ 242-332-2877)

at Governor's Harbour. The charge is $10 per hour, and the library is open Monday through Saturday from 9 a.m. to 5 p.m.

Police

If you need the police, call the Governor's Harbour Police Station (☎ **242-332-2111**), located on Queens Highway.

Pharmacy

The Governor Harbour's Medical Clinic (☎ 242-332 2001) fills prescriptions. The clinic is located on Queen's Highway, and is open Monday through Friday from 9 a.m. to 5:30 p.m.

Post Office

At Governor's Harbour, you can find a post office on Haynes Avenue (☎ 242-332-2060). Hours are Monday to Friday from 9 a.m. to 4:30 p.m.

Safety

Eleuthera is one of the safest Bahamian islands. Of course, take all the same precautions you would here that you would when traveling anywhere. Keep valuables in a safe place and don't wander into deserted, unfamiliar areas at night.

Taxis

Cabs meet incoming flights at all three airports. During your stay, your hotel staff can call a taxi for you.

Chapter 24

Exuma

● ●

In This Chapter

▶ Finding the best accommodations and restaurants

▶ Enjoying spectacular sailing and kayaking

▶ Exploring George Town, the charming harborside capital

● ●

*E*xuma — or the Exumas — is a string of some 365 cays, one for each day of the year. Most cays are either barely populated or completely uninhabited. The little archipelago is prime sailing, kayaking, fishing, scuba diving, and snorkeling territory.

Arriving at the Airport

Fourteen kilometers (9 miles) from George Town, **Exuma International Airport** is the official port of entry for this archipelago. Flights come in from Nassau and Florida (Miami, Ft. Lauderdale, St. Petersburg, and Sarasota). At the small, well-kept airport, you have to clear Customs unless you're coming from Nassau. Taxis wait just outside, and the cab fare to George Town hotels is about $25 for two passengers.

If you're going on to **Stocking Island,** an islet in **Elizabeth Harbour,** you can make prior arrangements with your hotel for boat transfers.

Choosing Your Location

George Town, on **Great Exuma,** the main island, is the easiest to reach. At the edge of Elizabeth Harbour, this postcard-pretty village isn't known for its beaches. However, just across the harbor from town, **Stocking Island** boasts some of the country's best sandy shores. A ferry links "mainland" hotels to this beach-rimmed island. If you want to stay on Stocking Island, your choice of hotels is limited to one: Hotel Higgins Landing. Although a few George Town hotels have their own beaches, the swimming is far better on Stocking Island. For guests of Higgins Landing, ferry service is free between this sandy harbor islet and George Town.

Great Exuma/Little Exuma

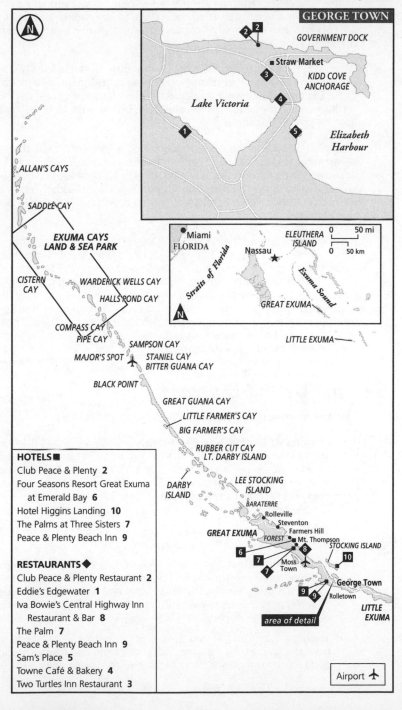

GEORGE TOWN

GOVERNMENT DOCK

■ Straw Market

KIDD COVE
ANCHORAGE

Lake Victoria

*Elizabeth
Harbour*

ALLAN'S CAYS

SADDLE CAY

EXUMA CAYS
LAND & SEA PARK

CISTERN
CAY

WARDERICK WELLS CAY

HALLS POND CAY

COMPASS CAY

PIPE CAY

SAMPSON CAY

MAJOR'S SPOT   STANIEL CAY
                 BITTER GUANA CAY

BLACK POINT

GREAT GUANA CAY

LITTLE FARMER'S CAY

BIG FARMER'S CAY

RUBBER CUT CAY
LT. DARBY ISLAND

DARBY
ISLAND

LEE STOCKING
ISLAND

BARATERRE

Rolleville

Steventon

Farmers Hill

FOREST   Mt. Thompson

STOCKING ISLAND

Moss
Town

George Town

Rolletown

LITTLE
EXUMA

area of detail

●Miami
FLORIDA

Straits of Florida

Nassau ★

ELEUTHERA
ISLAND

0   50 mi

0   50 km

Exuma Sound

GREAT EXUMA

LITTLE EXUMA

GREAT EXUMA

HOTELS ■

Club Peace & Plenty **2**

Four Seasons Resort Great Exuma
   at Emerald Bay **6**

Hotel Higgins Landing **10**

The Palms at Three Sisters **7**

Peace & Plenty Beach Inn **9**

RESTAURANTS ◆

Club Peace & Plenty Restaurant **2**

Eddie's Edgewater **1**

Iva Bowie's Central Highway Inn
   Restaurant & Bar **8**

The Palm **7**

Peace & Plenty Beach Inn **9**

Sam's Place **5**

Towne Café & Bakery **4**

Two Turtles Inn Restaurant **3**

Airport ✈

Sailing is excellent from any home base. Rent a boat, and you can anchor off some of the nearby uninhabited islets, where snorkeling and fishing are top rate. No matter which hotel you select, you can arrange scuba diving and fishing.

When you're ready to explore dry land, George Town is the starting point for renting a car or taking a taxi tour. A bridge links Great Exuma to **Little Exuma,** which you can skip without suffering cultural deprivation. It's like wandering back into another day, because its heyday has been long gone with the wind.

Accommodations in Exuma are as distinct as they are small. If you like being in the middle of island action, book a room at Club Peace & Plenty in town. Guests who prefer a secluded, elegant eco-resort can choose solar-powered Hotel Higgins Landing on Stocking Island. (To find out more about both these hotels, see the section "Staying in Style" later in this chapter.)

No one ever heard of the rat race in sleepy Exuma. Hotel rooms may not have phones, and the few TVs may get only a couple of centrally con-trolled channels (meaning that you watch whatever the bartender turns to). The liveliest entertainment "jumps up" on weekends, usually at Club Peace & Plenty, where the Saturday and sometimes Wednesday night dance parties are legendary. Hotels are close enough to each other that you can dine among them and mingle in a variety of settings. Some good local restaurants besides the ones in the hotels are also conveniently located in and around George Town.

Getting Around Exuma

Exuma is very accessible, and you don't have to rent a car.

- **Hoofing it:** George Town is designed for strolling, but don't expect sights that scream tourist attraction. This spot is a handsome little waterfront village where browsing at the tree-shaded straw market, sampling fresh conch salad at the dock, and mingling with resi-dents and fellow vacationers over drinks and home-style meals are the big draws. The most idyllic walk is around **Lake Victoria.**

   Shuttle service is provided to town from **Peace & Plenty Beach Inn,** or you may want to walk the scenic mile.

   If you don't succumb to taking wheels, you can leisurely enjoy the glimpses of the turquoise and neon blue water through the wispy casuarina pines and bushy coconut palms lining **Queen's Highway.** "Highway" is a serious overstatement, so walking here is fine because traffic is sparse.

- **Taking a taxi:** You have no problems finding a taxi to take you to and from the airport, far-flung restaurants, or on-land tours around Great and Little Exuma. Your hotel can assist you. Fares are regulated, but drivers don't use meters, so agree on a price before setting out. Taxi driver **Kermit Rolle** (☎ 242-345-0002), who also farms and runs local restaurants, seems to know everything anyone could ever want to know about Exuma.

✔ **Boarding a boat:** For ferries between George Town and the beaches on Stocking Island, call **Club Peace & Plenty** at ☎ 242-336-2551. With departures twice a day, the ferries are complimentary for Club Peace & Plenty guests. If you're not staying at the hotel, the cost is $8 round-trip and free for children under age 10. For renting boats, see "Climbing Aboard" later in the chapter.

✔ **Pedaling by bike:** A bicycle is a pleasant way to get around Exuma. To rent one, contact **Starfish Activity Center** (☎ 242-336-3033) in George Town. Mountain and cruiser bikes run $10 for two hours, $15 for a half-day, $20 for a full day, and $100 per week. Those rates include a helmet and a map. Starfish Activity Center also hosts guided bike tours.

✔ **Driving around:** Vacationers based in and around George Town have no real need to rent a car. If you want to see the rest of Great Exuma and Little Exuma, you can hire a taxi. But if you prefer striking out on your own, try **Thompson's Car Rental** in George Town (☎ 242-336-2442 or 242-345-4189), where autos begin at about $65 per day, or **Don's Car Rental** (☎ 242-345-0112), conveniently located right at the airport; daily rates start at $75.

The George Town area has two gas stations: one near Exuma International Airport and the other in Farmers Hill. They're generally open Monday through Saturday from 8 a.m. to 5 p.m., Sundays from 8 a.m. until noon, and on holidays from 8 to 10 a.m.

Staying in Style

Most hotels lie in and around George Town. Of the handful of hotels, most have fewer than 16 rooms. For escapists, one of Exuma's best accommodations is an offshore "one-to-one": one island, one resort.

Club Peace & Plenty
$$$ In the heart of George Town

This pink and white harborside hotel is the virtual social center of the Exumas. Club Peace & Plenty was once a private home built on the site of a slave market during Loyalist days when British supporters fled to The Bahamas after the Revolutionary War. A former kitchen has been transformed into the indoor tavern, decorated with old anchors, rudders, lanterns, and other maritime artifacts. During the National Family Island Regatta each April, visiting and local yachties flock to this hotel's cozy lounge.

The handsome two-story building faces the main road on one side and Elizabeth Harbour on the other. With balconies, satellite TV, and queen, double, or twin beds, the 32 bright guest rooms overlook the harbor, fresh-water pool, or greenery. Although perfectly well maintained and comfortable, the rooms have a somewhat dated feel. Dine indoors or alfresco at Club Peace & Plenty's popular restaurant, where local seafood is the specialty. Twice a week, the hotel features a poolside cocktail party for guests. Snorkel gear is available, and a shuttle runs several times a day between the hotel and its closest sibling, **Peace & Plenty Beach Inn** (see the review later in the chapter). Guests can also take the complimentary ferry just across the water to Stocking Island beaches.

Peace & Plenty is Exuma's "chain" hotel. Peace & Plenty Beach Inn is about a half-kilometer (1 mile) up the road. Six kilometers (10 miles) southeast of George Town is **Peace & Plenty Bonefish Lodge,** an inn for anglers. The lodge serves dinner several nights a week, and guests of Club Peace & Plenty recieve free transportation to it.

See map p. 315. Queen's Highway. ☎ *800-525-2210 or 242-336-2093. Fax: 242-336-2550.* www.peaceandplenty.com. *Rack rates: $150–$165 double. AE, MC, V.*

Four Seasons Resort Great Exuma at Emerald Bay
$$$$$ North of George Town

The sleepy Exumas might awaken with the opening of this 183-room resort. The Out Islands have seen nothing like this in their history, and the resort is expected to change the entire character of the archipelago. All accommodations here open onto private terraces and balconies with scenic views of Emerald Bay. Your choice of rooms ranges from generously sized gardenview units to oceanview rooms opening directly onto the bay. For the big spender, the resort also offers a series of executive suites and one- and two-bedroom beachfront properties.

So much is going on at this resort that you may never get around to exploring the surrounding islands. This resort's facilities include two outdoor pools and four tennis courts, along with a well-defined watersports program, well-organized children's programs, and a business center. The most spectacular feature is a championship 18-hole golf course designed by Greg Norman. The full-service spa and health club is the finest in The Bahamas, and you can swim at either the hotel's crescent-shaped white sand beach or in one of the pools. And the cuisine is among the best in the Out Islands, with both indoor and outdoor dining options and a selection of Italian, Caribbean, Bahamian, and international dishes.

See map p. 315. Emerald Bay. ☎ *800-819-5053 or 242-358-4185. Fax 242-336-6081.* www.fourseasons.com. *Rack rates: $495–$775 double, from $800 suite. Rates include continental breakfast. Children 17 and under free in parent's room. AE, DC, DISC, MC, V.*

Hotel Higgins Landing
$$$$$ Stocking Island

This intimate resort is on a tiny, virtually uninhabited, beach-rimmed island. Not only is it the only hotel on luscious Stocking Island, just a

Houseboats

The most offbeat way to stay in the Exumas is on a brightly decorated floating house-boat. Each boat is like a hotel suite that you can use to explore Elizabeth Harbour and the coast of the Exumas. In between moving your houseboat from anchorage to anchorage, you can go fishing, snorkeling, scuba diving, or just beachcombing. Each houseboat sleeps six to eight people and is fully equipped with air-conditioning, hot and cold running water, a marine radio, an inflatable dinghy, a fully equipped galley, all linens, purified water, and a propane barbecue grill. Boats range from an 11m (35-ft.) one-bedroom to a 13m (43-ft.) two-bedroom. You don't need a special license or even much experience to operate one of these boats. For reservations, contact **Bahamas Houseboats**, P.O. Box EX29031, Government Dock, George Town, Exuma, The Bahamas (☎ **242-336-BOAT**; fax 242-336-2629; www.bahamahouseboats.com). Weekly rentals range from $1,750 to $2,700, with a required security deposit of $500.

half-kilometer (1 mile) across Elizabeth Harbour from George Town, but it's also accessible only by ferry. No roads or cars are on the island, so feet and boats are the modes of transportation.

This upscale resort is solar powered. Hilly twists and turns along rocky paths lead to the five cottages, which sport large decks. Strategically placed to ensure both privacy and proximity to the beach, each unit is beautifully furnished with antiques, four-poster queen-size beds, and Oriental rugs. You're asked to conserve water, but running out of water isn't a problem. Ceiling fans cool the air, which circulates through glass-free screen windows. Cottages are equipped with enough voltage for fans and reading lights, but you have to go elsewhere at the resort to use standard 110-volt electricity. Instead of television, you can visit the hotel's little library. Bob Higgins, who runs the hotel with his wife, Carol, is in charge of breakfast, which the staff serves on a deck overlooking **Silver Palms Beach.** One day, Bob may whip up coconut pancakes; the next, eggs Benedict. Carol takes over for lunch (lobster rolls or salad Niçoise, perhaps) and the candlelit, multicourse dinner may be black mushroom soup followed by grilled beef or seafood and espresso chocolate custard. Room rates may seem high, but they include a gourmet breakfast, lunch, dinner, and hors d'oeuvres daily, the boat trip to and from the island upon arrival and departure, and a variety of watersports equipment. You can make arrangements for scuba diving, snorkeling, and fishing trips.

Smoking is not allowed inside the buildings, but it is permitted on your deck or at the beach bar. Children under 18 are not allowed unless you rent the entire resort.

See map p. 315. Across Elizabeth Harbour from George Town. ☎ *242-357-0008. Fax 866-289-0919.* www.higginslanding.com. *Rack rates: $495 and up. Rates include three daily meals. MC, V.*

The Palms at Three Sisters
$ Northwest of George Town

In 1994, this 14-room low-key resort opened on an isolated spot 11km (7 miles) from its nearest neighbor on a stretch of lovely white sand. Rooms are within a two-story, motel-like building and have English colonial details and simple, summery furniture. This hotel is a great place for privacy and seclusion. Bedrooms are comfortable but basic. You have meals and drinks in a low-slung annex, with views stretching out over the Atlantic (for a full review, see The Palm in "Dining Out," below). You can hear live music every Saturday on a flowery patio. The resort, incidentally, is named after a trio of rocks (the Three Sisters) with a composition that differs radically from the coral formations throughout the rest of the Exumas. They jut about 4.5m (15 ft.) above sea level, just offshore from the beach.

See map p. 315. Queen's Highway, Bahama Sound Beach. ☎ *888-688-4752 or 242-358-4040. Fax: 242-358-4043.* seaoats@batelnet.bs. *Rack rates: $128 double. MC, V.*

Peace & Plenty Beach Inn
$$$ Northwest of George Town

More subdued than its older sibling **Club Peace & Plenty** (see the review earlier in this chapter), this 16-room hotel sits on a small beach. Built in the early 1990s, it draws many snorkelers and bonefishermen. Everyone from newlyweds to families feel comfortable here. In the spacious, attractively decorated guest rooms, French doors open onto large patios or balconies overlooking the swimming pool and ocean. Steps from the saltwater pool lead down to the sand, with expansive views of Stocking Island across the water; guests can take the complimentary ferry to the beautiful beaches. Chefs give the Bahamian favorites a gourmet twist in the striking bar and dining room. Regular shuttles link Peace & Plenty Beach Inn with Club Peace & Plenty, the center of the George Town social scene.

See map p. 315. Queen's Highway, 1.6km (1 mile) northwest of George Town. ☎ *800-525-2210 or 242-336-2250. Fax: 242-336-2253.* www.peaceandplenty.com. *Rack rates: $170–$190 double. Ask about bonefishing package rates. AE, MC, V.*

Dining Out

Most of Exuma's restaurants are in George Town, but you can take a rental car, taxi, or hotel shuttle to some offbeat places in outlying areas. Visit hotel dining rooms for the most sophisticated and priciest dining. When these upscale accommodations serve local dishes, they often have Continental and American influences.

For the most authentic — and the least expensive — Bahamian cooking, try a local restaurant. The food stall near George Town's Government Dock makes a great fresh conch salad prepared to order, but its hours are limited: It's open only on Monday, Wednesday, and Friday.

Most hotels fix reasonably priced picnic lunches for beach excursions and other ramblings. Dining rooms in and outside hotels close between meals, and the smaller spots don't accept credit cards. **Peace & Plenty Beach Inn** (see the review in "Staying in Style" earlier in this chapter) provides shuttle service into town.

Club Peace & Plenty Restaurant
$$$ **In the heart of George Town   BAHAMIAN/CONTINENTAL/ AMERICAN**

Go here for the finest island dining, with plentiful and good home-cooked meals that leave most guests satisfied. Boiled fish and grits is a popular breakfast choice at this hotel dining room with harbor views. But, you can also order eggs, French toast, and other American favorites. For lunch, try the conch burgers. Appetizers include a savory conch chowder, pumpkin soup, or hearts of palm salad. Grouper — pan-fried or steamed with peppers and onions — makes frequent evening appearances, along with Bahamian lobster and T-bone steak. You can also order pasta with shrimp or a spicy tomato sauce.

See map p. 315. Queen's Highway. ☎ *242-336-2551. Reservations required for dinner. Breakfast: $8.50; lunch: from $10; dinner main courses: $18–$30. AE, MC, V. Open: Daily 7:30 a.m.–midnight.*

Eddie's Edgewater
$ **George Town   BAHAMIAN**

On Monday nights, this is the place to be for the weekly "rake 'n scrape," when a band transforms rakes, saws, washboards, and other household items into instruments and turns the restaurant into a party — a wonderful, traditional Bahamian moment. At the edge of Lake Victoria, this casual hangout gets raves for its turtle steak and steamed chicken. If you have your heart set on either of those dishes, call ahead to make sure that they're on the menu that day. Other well-prepared dishes for lunch and dinner include okra soup, conch chowder, and pan-fried grouper. Breakfast is standard but reliable, with pancakes, French toast, and omelets, along with grits, ham, and bacon.

See map p. 315. Charlotte Street, by Lake Victoria. ☎ *242-336-2050. Main courses: $10–$15. MC, V. Open: Mon–Sat 7 a.m.–9 p.m.*

Iva Bowe's Central Highway Inn Restaurant & Bar
$ **Northwest of George Town   BAHAMIAN**

Islanders tell you that this restaurant is *the* place for that local favorite, cracked conch, and they're right. The chicken, fish, and lobster dishes are all excellent, too, and so are the crawfish salad and the shrimp scampi. The dining room isn't fancy, but the home-style food makes a trip — or two — here well worth your time. When you're tooling around Great Exuma, this eatery is a great choice for takeout.

See map p. 315. Central Highway, about a half-kilometer (¼ mile) from the International Airport. ☎ *242-345-7014. Main courses: $10–$20. Open: Mon–Sat noon–11 p.m.*

The Palm
$–$$ Northwest of George Town   INTERNATIONAL

Set beside a sandy, isolated beach, 14km (9 miles) northwest of George Town, this airy, oceanfront restaurant is associated with one of the island's best resorts, the **Three Sisters Hotel** (see the review earlier in this chapter in the "Staying in Style" section). Breakfasts are hearty steak-and-egg fare, although you can also get Bahamian coconut pancakes. Lunches include lobster salads, conch chowder, grouper fingers, burgers, and sandwiches. Dinners are more formal (casual resort wear is best, with collared shirts for men). Although the food is familiar, the chefs prepare it well. Flame-broiled grouper is your best and freshest choice.

See map p. 315. At the Three Sisters Hotel, Queen's Highway, Bahama Sound Beach. ☎ *242-358-4040. Reservations recommended for dinner. Breakfast: $5–$10; lunch platters and sandwiches: $5.95–$12; dinner main courses $16–$28. MC, V. Open: Daily 6:30 a.m.–10 p.m.*

Peace & Plenty Beach Inn
$$–$$$ Near George Town   BAHAMIAN/INTERNATIONAL

The well-chosen Bahamian menu changes nightly at this hotel restaurant. A stained pine cathedral ceiling makes a dramatic statement in the restaurant's attractive dining room. The chicken breast Alfredo is a good choice and so is the tender blackened mahimahi. The chef also prepares New York-cut Angus steak well.

See map p. 315. Queen's Highway, 1.6km (1 mile) northwest of George Town. ☎ *242-336-2250. Reservations required. Main courses: $15–$35. AE, MC, V. Open: Daily 7 a.m.–9 p.m.*

Sam's Place
$ George Town   BAHAMIAN/AMERICAN

Overlooking the marina in George Town, the broad veranda of this second-story restaurant provides a scenic setting for a morning, afternoon, or evening meal. The boating crowd comes here in droves to enjoy its ever-changing menu. Lunch may be conch chowder and a sandwich or maybe a succulent pasta dish. For dinner, your choices include local lobster tail, pan-fried wahoo (our favorite), tender roast lamb, or steamed chicken.

See map p. 315. Main Street, at the marina. ☎ *242-336-2579. Main courses: $15–$25. MC, V. Open: Daily 7:30 a.m.–9 p.m.*

Towne Café & Bakery
$ George Town   BAHAMIAN/BAKED GOODS

For a good alternative to breakfast at your hotel, stop at this bakery-plus. Bahamians come for the filling pancakes and the boil fish, cooked with onions and peppers and grits. The restaurant serves chicken souse with delicately sweet johnnycake (a mildly sweet bread). Coffeecake, fresh doughnuts, and bran muffins are the best choices for pastries here. Antique household items decorate the simple dining room. If the lunch menu includes grouper fingers, go for it.

See map p. 315. Marshall Complex, by the Shell gas station. ☎ 242-336-2194. Main courses: $5–$10. No credit cards. Open: Mon–Sat 7:30 a.m.–5 p.m.

Two Turtles Inn Restaurant
$ George Town   BAHAMIAN/AMERICAN

A popular meeting place, this hotel dining spot within view of the marina has the feel of a sidewalk cafe. Laid-back, but often busy, it is the only outdoor restaurant in town. Dishes prepared with fresh local seafood are excellent. For many years, the zesty Friday night barbecues have been drawing scores of residents and those visitors who make the discovery — now you know all about it, too.

See map p. 315. Across from the village green and the straw market. ☎ 242-336-2545. Main courses: $12–$25. AE, MC, V. Open: Breakfast daily 8–9 a.m.; lunch daily 11 a.m.–3 p.m.; dinner Tues–Sun from 6 p.m.

Enjoying the Sand and Surf

Most of the excitement on Exuma is all wet. However, you can spend a day driving to and through some of the drowsy settlements scattered along Great Exuma and the adjoining Little Exuma. If you don't, you end up missing some sights, such as historic gravesites, pink salt ponds, brightly painted tiny houses, a little museum-boutique, small farms, vestiges of plantation ruins, and plenty of island greenery.

Walking around George Town gives you plenty of opportunities to meet and greet residents and other vacationers. Instead of spending a whole day touring the island on dry land, you may have more fun seeing the sights by water — in a sailboat, speedboat, or kayak. This way, you can explore some of the smaller offshore uninhabited cays.

 With a finger in many different pots, the George Town-based **Starfish Activity Center** (☎ 242-336-3033) makes booking everything from kayaking and snorkeling to bicycle tours as simple as one phone call.

Combing the beaches

George Town's best beaches aren't in George Town but are across Elizabeth Harbour on a pencil-thin slip of land known as Stocking Island. Not even 8km (5 miles) long and barely a kilometer (a half-mile) wide, Stocking Island protects the harbor from the open ocean. Club Peace & Plenty provides ferry service to this beach-rimmed island (free for guests of Club Peace & Plenty, $8 for non-guests, and free for children under age 10).

A regatta to remember

George Town may be known as a quiet, restful place, but in April the **National Family Island Regatta** changes all that. If you visit at this time of year, book your hotel room many, many months in advance. Although the regatta brings many a far-flung Bahamian back home for this week-long event, the maritime competition seems almost incidental to the festivities occurring on *terra firma*.

As the handcrafted sloops, owned and sailed by Bahamians, compete in Elizabeth Harbour, vendors along the waterfront sell grilled chicken, fried fish, and conch in all its varieties. Reggae fills the air. Men huddle around card tables, slapping dominos down with dramatic arcs of their arms. A Junkanoo parade — complete with loud drums and whistles, cowbells, and horns — pulses down the street. Spectators sit on the walls near the Government Building as cars with blaring horns festooned with rainbow-hued streamers pass in a slow line.

When the police band takes center stage in **Regatta Park,** people surge onto nearby steps for the best views. Band members look distinguished in their white tunics, wide red belts, red-banded hats, and black trousers with red side stripes. But nothing is formal about the way their lively music stirs up the crowd. Feet tap, fingers snap, and hips swing, whether they belong to tiny tots or elderly grandmothers.

 You can traverse Stocking Island only by foot or boat. For the calmest swimming, your best bet is the soft, white sands on the harbor side of the island. If you prefer rougher surf, take the path across the island to the Atlantic coast; shelling is also ideal on the Atlantic side of the island. If you didn't pack a picnic lunch, just visit the snack bar. Scuba divers and snorkelers are lured to Stocking Island by the *blue holes* (ocean pools of fresh water floating on heavier saltwater), coral gardens, and undersea caves. **Mystery Cave,** for example, meanders for some 121m (400 ft.) beneath this virtually uninhabited island.

Playing in the surf

Exuma's best asset is, of course, its surrounding sea. Here's a guide to the best watersports so you can get started on your ocean adventures.

Kayaking

You can best appreciate some of Exuma's most dramatic scenery from the peaceful perch of a sea kayak. In fact, many areas — including mangrove lakes, rivers, manta ray gathering spots, and bonefish flats — are too shallow for other boats to enter. Don't worry if you haven't hit the gym lately. Anyone in at least average physical condition — from children to seniors — can kayak with a smile. The **Starfish Activity Center,** based out of George Town, (☎ **242-336-3033**), rents sit-on-top kayaks for singles and doubles. Singles cost about $10 an hour, $20 per half-day, $30 a day, or $120 a week. Doubles cost $15 an hour, $30 per half-day, $40 a day, or $150 a week.

For more adventure, book one of Starfish's guided kayak trips, which the company offers daily. You don't have to spend the whole time paddling your kayak. During half- and full-day excursions, you get lunch and beverages, and the price covers all gear, including snorkeling equipment. You may find yourself watching a blizzard of fish swarm a shipwreck, searching for sand dollars on a deserted beach, snorkeling into a sea cave, or finding out about bush medicine while you hike along a nature trail. Guided trips begin at $35 an hour for adults and $25 an hour for children.

Another good outfitter is **Ecosummer Expeditions** (☎ 800-465-8884). Ecosummer is especially skilled in exploring **Exuma Cays Land and Sea Park** (☎ 242-357-8344), a government-protected natural preserve with excellent wildlife viewing opportunities.

Scuba diving

Surrounding the Exumas, fields of massive coral heads, eerie blue holes, and exciting walls covered with marine life are exposed to scuba divers. Many excellent reefs are just 20 or 25 minutes away from the George Town area, so long boat rides don't cut into your underwater time.

For scuba divers, the great attraction here is the **Exuma Cays Land and Sea Park,** which is 35km (22 miles) long and 13km (8 miles) wide. It draws scuba divers to its 453 square kilometers (175 sq. miles) of sea gardens with magnificent coral reefs, flora, and fauna. The park, inaugurated in 1958, lies some 35km (22 miles) northeast of **Staniel Cay.** Call your hotel to ask whether it offers a hotel/dive package or try **Exuma Scuba Adventures** (☎ 242-336-2893; www.exumascuba.com) at Peace & Plenty Beach Inn for information about scuba-diving excursions. A one-tank morning boat dive goes for $55, and a two-tank dive costs $75. You can also take an afternoon one-tank boat dive for $55 or a one-tank night dive for $60. A reef boat trip for snorkeling costs $25.

Snorkeling

The best bet for snorkeling is the magnificent waters off the coast of **Stocking Island,** across Elizabeth Harbour from George Town, a distance of 1.5km (1 mile). Stocking Island is a long, thin barrier island known for its crystal clear waters, white sands, and blue holes. The island is also ringed with a series of undersea caves and stunning coral gardens in rainbow colors. You can take a boat trip from George Town to Stocking Island; boats depart twice a day. Call **Exuma Scuba Adventures** (☎ 242-336-2893; www.exumascuba.com) if you want to snorkel around some of Exuma's most well-preserved reefs. These three-hour-plus excursions cost $25 per adult and $10 for children under 12.

Climbing aboard

If you like the water but want to keep your feet dry, George Town makes a good home base for skimming the waves.

Through the **Starfish Activity Center** (☎ 242-336-3033), based in George Town, you can rent *Hobie Waves,* high-performance sailboats that are easy to use. These stable, lightweight-yet-durable, 4.5m (15-ft.) catamarans are ideal for families, because they're simple to maneuver. With a minimum of two people, you can take a two-hour lesson for $30 per person. Renting one of these babies runs you $35 for two hours, $50 for a half-day, $75 for a full day, or — if it really looks good to you — $300 for a week.

If motor boats are more your speed, **Minns Water Sports** (☎ 242-336-3483 or 242-336-2604), based out of George Town, rents these 5-, 5.4-, and 6.7m (17-, 18-, and 22-ft.) boats for $88, $120, and $170 per day, with daily rates dropping the longer you rent. **Exuma Dive Center** in George Town (☎ 800-874-7213 or 242-336-2390),where boat rentals start at $80 per day, also offers more economical rates when you keep a boat for a week or longer. With your boat, you can set out to sail the most stunning waters in The Bahamas, rivaled only by those in the Abacos. The best territory for recreational boating is the government-protected **Exuma Cays Land and Sea Park,** which stretches south from Wax Cay to Conch Cay, with their magnificent sea gardens and coral reefs.

Many visitors come to the Exumas just to go bonefishing, deep-sea, or bottom fishing, pursuing the likes of wahoo, dolphinfish, tuna, bonito, and kingfish, among other species. You can make arrangements for outings through **Club Peace & Plenty** (☎ 242-345-5555), the central office for the Peace & Plenty properties, located on Queen's Highway. The Exumas offer kilometers of wadeable *flats* (shallow bodies of water), where trained guides can accompany you. The resort also offers fly-fishing instruction and equipment.

Exploring on Dry Land

George Town is one of the prettiest settlements in the Out Islands. Spend some time wandering around this small village that borders both a harbor and a serene lake.

Touring George Town and Little Exuma

The **Government Building,** an impressive flamingo-colored edifice with white columns, stands at the harbor's edge. This location provides one-stop shopping for the post office, the police station, the courts, the jail, and the Ministry of Education.

Under the shady canopy of enormous trees out front of **N&D's Fruits and Vegetables,** women sit at their posts selling T-shirts, shell jewelry, various straw goods, and snacks. You can also stop for an inexpensive breakfast or some ice cream or other sweet treats.

Up the road a bit, **St. Andrew's Anglican Church** sits on a bluff. For a good view, go up the hill and around back to the gravesites. This resting place overlooks sparkling **Lake Victoria.** You may see small boats making their way toward the narrow opening that leads to the harbor. On your trek up the road, you pass small square houses with chickens running in front yards, a few mom-and-pop restaurants, and magnificent petite churches.

During your walk, you'll come to a table piled high with conch shells. Here you can watch this fish vendor hammer a shell, deftly cut out the dark mollusk and then skin it, exposing the white flesh that tastes so delectable in so many Bahamian specialties, such as cracked conch or conch chowder. Then spend some time sitting quietly on the pier at the water's edge.

 Set aside part of a morning or afternoon for a taxi tour or a rental car drive down to **Little Exuma,** connected to Great Exuma by a bridge.

Little Exuma is a far away retreat, the southernmost of the Exuma Cays. It has a subtropical climate, despite being in the tropics, and lovely white sand beaches. The waters are so crystal clear in some places that you can spot the colorful tropical fish more than 18m (60 ft.) down. Less than 1.6km (1 mile) offshore is **Pigeon Cay,** an uninhabited island. You can go snorkeling here and visit the remains of a 200-year-old wreck, right offshore in about 2m (6 ft.) of water. Visitors often come to Pigeon Cay for the day and later have a boat pick them up to take them back to Little Exuma. On one of the highest hills of Little Exuma, you can explore the remains of an old pirate fort. Several cannons are located nearby, but no one knows who built the fort or when. (Pirates didn't leave too many records lying around.)

Coming from Great Exuma, the first community you reach on Little Exuma is called **Ferry,** so named because the two islands used to be linked by a ferry service before the bridge was built. If anyone's around, see whether you can visit the private chapel of an Irish family, the Fitzgeralds, erected generations ago. Along the way, you can take in **Pretty Molly Bay,** site of the now-shuttered Sand Dollar Beach Club. Pretty Molly was a slave who committed suicide by walking into the water one night. Many locals have reported seeing her reincarnated as a mermaid sitting on a rock combing her hair.

Many visitors come to Little Exuma to visit the **Hermitage,** a plantation constructed by Loyalist settlers — the last surviving example of the many that once stood in the Exumas. The Kendall family, who came to Little Exuma in 1784, originally built it. They established their plantation at **Williamstown,** and, with their slaves, set about growing cotton. But they encountered so many difficulties in shipping the cotton to Nassau that in 1806 they advertised that the plantation was for sale. The ad promised "970 acres more or less" along with "160 hands" (referring to the slaves). Chances are a local guide will offer to show you around for a fee. Also ask to see several old tombs in the area. At Williamstown (look for the marker on the seaside), you can visit the remains of the **Great Salt Pond,** a shallow estuary separated from the ocean by a narrow barrier beach.

Keeping active

Four Seasons Resort Emerald Bay Golf Club (☎ 242-358-4185) is one of the great oceanfront golf courses in the Caribbean. This Greg Norman designed course features six oceanfront holes. The par-72 course stretches a challenging 6,284m (6,873 yds.), yet accommodates golfers of various skill levels. The course uses environmentally friendly seashore paspalum grass and finishes on a rocky peninsula with a panoramic view of the bay. The club also boasts a pro shop. Greens fees are a steep $175 for 18 holes ($210 for non-guests), and the club requires reservations. The resort also has six Har-Tru courts and a state-of-the-art fitness center.

Living It Up After Dark

The best place to head for some after-dark diversion is **Club Peace & Plenty** (☎ **800-525-2210** or 242-336-2093), located in George Town. Although summer nights are slow here, something is usually happening here in winter, ranging from weekly poolside bashes to live bands that keep both locals and visitors jumping up on the dance floor. Also consider dropping by **The Palms at Three Sisters** (☎ **242-358-4040**), which presents live music every Saturday night on its flowering patio. The little resort draws a lively crowd of both locals and visitors.

Fast Facts: Exuma

American Express and ATMs

No Amex services are available in Exuma. You'll find an ATM at Scotia Bank (☎ 242-336-2652), located on Charlotte Street in George Town. The bank is open Monday through Thursday from 9 a.m. to 3 p.m. and Friday from 9:30 a.m. to 4:30 p.m.

Emergencies/Police

Call ☎ **242-336-2666**.

Hospital

For medical care, contact the government-run clinic (☎ 242-336-2088), located on Queen's Highway, about 15 minutes west of Club Peace & Plenty in George Town.

Information

The Exuma Tourist Office (☎ 242-336-2430) is across the street from St. Andrew's Anglican Church, not far from Club Peace & Plenty in George Town.

Internet Access

Check with your hotel for access. You can also go to the ABC Exuma Internet Café at

the Exuma International Airport (☎ 242-345-6038).

Pharmacy

To fill a prescription, go to the clinic on Queen's Highway (see "Hospital" earlier in this listing).

Post Office

The post office is located in the Government Building in George Town. It's open Monday through Friday from 9 a.m. to 4:30 p.m.

Safety

The Exumas is one of the safest archipelagos in The Bahamas. Of course, the usual precautions are advised. Keep your valuables in a safe place and don't go into deserted, unfamiliar areas alone at night.

Taxis

You can find taxis easily, and your hotel's staff can assist you, but we recommend trying Kermit Rolle (☎ 242-345-6038 or 242-345-0002)

Chapter 25

San Salvador

● ●

In This Chapter

▶ Getting around the island

▶ Reviewing San Salvador's hotels and restaurants

▶ Enjoying the best beaches, watersports, and historic land attractions

● ●

Drowsy San Salvador is so undeveloped that it has just two hotels and a handful of restaurants, most located at the larger hotel. Fabulous scuba diving brings most visitors to these tranquil shores. Beautiful empty beaches and easygoing, friendly residents also keep vacationers coming back. If bar hopping, nightclubbing, and eating at a different restaurant every night of the week is what you have in mind, then San Salvador isn't the island for you.

Arriving in San Salvador

San Salvador's small airport is a cinch to access. If you're staying at Club Med, you'll arrive on a direct charter flight from Miami or New York. Club Med's all-inclusive rates cover airfare. You can arrange charter flights through the Riding Rock Inn Resort and Marina as well. Both hotels provide their guests with group transportation to and from the airport. If you're flying into New Providence, you can catch a flight to San Salvador on **BahamasAir** (☎ 800-222-4262).

Choosing Your Location

Deciding where to stay on San Salvador is like choosing between pizza and filet mignon — the two beach hotels, **Club Med–Columbus Isle** and the **Riding Rock Inn Resort and Marina,** are both good, just different. The Riding Rock resembles a pleasant motel, while the larger Club Med resort is decked out in art and artifacts from around the globe.

 The two beach hotels have one thing in common: They both offer excellent scuba-diving programs that allow you to take advantage of the island's main attraction — its underwater wonders. Some 40 well-preserved dive sites are no more than 45 minutes away from both hotels by boat. **Cockburn Town** (pronounced "CO-burn"), the sleepy

San Salvador

capital of the island, is a comfortable stroll or a quick bike or taxi ride away. However, calling the capital a town is like calling a caterpillar a snake. Cockburn Town features a restaurant, bar, and a bank that's open once a week, but the chance to mingle with friendly residents is the real reason for heading to town.

Getting Around San Salvador

Renting a car isn't necessary in San Salvador. If you want to tour the island, ask your hotel staff to help you with arrangements.

✔ **Taking a taxi:** Your hotel staff can arrange taxi service for you. If you have the staff at **Club Med** (☎ **242-331-2000**) arrange an island tour for you, the cost is around $25 per person for a half-day ramble.

✔ **Driving around:** On San Salvador, you don't need to rent a car unless you want to explore far-flung places on your own. You can rent a car through **Riding Rock Inn Resort and Marina** (☎ 242-331-2631) for about $85 a day.

✔ **Pedaling bicycles:** Club Med guests have use of bikes for cycling around the property and for guided tours around the island. If you're not staying at Club Med, you can rent two-wheelers at Riding Rock Inn Resort and Marina for about $10 a day.

Staying in Style

Club Med–Columbus Isle
$$$$$ **North of Cockburn Town**

Until something better opens, this resort is the poshest in all the southern Bahamas, and it's far better than your typical Club Med vacation village. Set on the edge of one of the most pristine beaches in the archipelago, with 3km (2 miles) of white sand, it employs some 30 percent of the island's work force. This 280-room behemoth even operates on its own time clock: Clocks are set one hour earlier than Eastern Standard Time to give late-rising gates another hour of daylight.

Built around a large free-form pool, the resort offers public rooms that are among the most lavish in the islands. Bedrooms contain a private balcony or patio, custom-made furniture from Thailand or the Philippines, sliding glass doors, and feathered wall hangings crafted in the Brazilian rain forest by members of the Xingu tribe. Rooms are large (among the most spacious in the entire hotel chain). Most rooms have twin beds, but you may be able to snag one of the units with a double or a king-size bed if you're lucky. The resort offers nightly entertainment presented in a covered, open-air theater and a dance floor behind one of the bars.

See map p. 330. 3km (2 miles) north of Cockburn Town. ☎ *800-CLUB-MED or 242-331-2000. Fax: 242-331-2458.* www.clubmed.com. *Rack rates: $1,329 per person to $1,945 for seven nights in a double room (price depends on what time of year you go and where you fly from). Rates include all meals, most beverages, most activities, gratuities, round-trip airfare, and ground transportation to and from San Salvador's airport. AE, DISC, MC, V.*

Riding Rock Inn Resort and Marina
$$ **North of Cockburn Town**

In stark contrast to the lavish Club Med, with its perky staff, Riding Rock Inn offers a more tranquil atmosphere. The 42 rooms are motel-like, but they're pleasantly decorated and outfitted with all the modern conveniences you need for a comfortable stay. The newer, two-story building houses are the best digs, and each room features two double beds, a TV, a refrigerator, and a balcony or patio with an oceanview. The hotel's older, smaller rooms overlook the pool. Most guests are avid divers who stay wet. (Riding Rock offers excellent scuba packages.) During the day while divers are away, this place seems downright empty. Nighttime is a different story, however. In fact, you could call Riding Rock Inn Resort and Marina San Salvador's social center. During the Wednesday night dance party, the joint is really jumpin', and Friday nights aren't so quiet, either.

See map p. 330. Just north of Cockburn Town. ☎ *800-272-1492 in the U.S., 954-359-8353 in Florida, or 242-331-2631 in The Bahamas. Fax: 242-331-2020.* www.riding rock.com. *Rack rates: $114–$141 double. Ask about the all-inclusive packages. MC, V.*

Dining Out

If you're staying at Club Med, room rates include all your meals. The resort offers reliable food, with all ingredients imported. The cuisine never reaches the sublime, but there is an effort to offer variety. Unlimited food, including snacks, is included, plus drinks during regular meal hours. However, you shouldn't leave the island without sneaking off campus for some local flavor.

Riding Rock Inn Resort and Marina
$$ Near Cockburn Town   BAHAMIAN/AMERICAN

Sit on the deck overlooking the water or eat inside; either way, you can dine on hearty portions of comfort food. Pancakes make a good choice for breakfast, and sandwiches are on the menu for lunch. The price-fixed dinners include soup, salad, main course, dessert, wine, and soft, chewy, just-baked Bahamian bread. Launch your meal with the well-seasoned conch chowder or okra soup and follow it up with steak, prime rib, veal, chicken, or fresh fish. Likewise, the Wednesday-night barbecues, featuring reggae music, are popular social events.

See map p. 330. Just north of Cockburn Town (within walking distance of Club Med). ☎ *242-331-2631.* www.ridingrock.com. *Reservations recommended. Breakfast: $12; lunch: $15; dinner: $28. MC, V. Open: Daily 7:30–9 a.m., 12:30–2 p.m., and 6:30–9 p.m.*

Three Ships Restaurant
$ Cockburn Town   BAHAMIAN

Since the early 1990s, Faith Jones, the owner, keeps visitors coming back for her cracked conch, steamed or fried grouper, and crab and rice, served with mounds of coleslaw, potato salad, or peas and rice. Spend some time here, and you're sure to strike up a conversation or two with Ms. Jones and the townspeople who stop in for food, drink, or just "to chew the fat" in more ways than one. Jones used to cater meals from her home next door before she opened this dining spot.

See map p. 330. In the heart of Cockburn Town. ☎ *242-331-2787. Main courses: $7–$15. No credit cards. Open: Daily noon–6 p.m.*

Enjoying the Sand and Surf

If you're looking for empty beaches or fantastic diving and snorkeling opportunities, you've come to the right place.

Combing the beaches

If you prefer finding a stretch of sand where the only footprints on it are your own, rent a car or a bike at Riding Rock Inn Resort and Marina or call a taxi (see "Getting Around San Salvador" earlier in this chapter). Empty beaches are everywhere. Just remember to take plenty of water, and, of course, sunblock. You won't find much shade. Along the way, you can look for the island's various monuments to Christopher Columbus.

 On the northeast coast, **East Beach** stretches for some 10km (6 miles). Crushed coral and shells turned the shore a rosy pink. The deep turquoise patches in the clear waters are coral heads, but the beach isn't good for snorkeling because people have spotted sharks here. Tall sea wheat or sea grass sprouts up from the sand. Off mile-marker number 24 on the main road, you can pick your way to the *Chicago Herald* Columbus Monument (see the "Exploring on Dry Land" section later in this chapter.)

Playing in the surf

Scuba divers flock to this remote island, which is a major dive destination with some **40 dive sites** that lie no more than 45 minutes by boat from either of the two resorts. San Salvador has such stunning sea walls around it that *wall diving* — diving where the sloping shoreline suddenly drops off steeply and plummets to the ocean depths — is a major preoccupation here.

Riding Rock Inn Resort and Marina (☎ 242-331-2631), just north of Cockburn Town, specializes in scuba packages and offers a good underwater photography program, as well as night dives on Tuesday evenings. For one of the best outfitters, call **Guanahani Dive Ltd.** (☎ 242-331-2631), based at Riding Rock Inn.

 Club Med–Columbus Isle, also just north of Cockburn Town, should really be called an *almost*-all-inclusive resort, because scuba diving isn't included in its rates. Resort courses run $100, and certification courses are $400. A one-tank dive costs $40 and a two-tank dive costs $60.

Following in the footsteps of Columbus, snorkelers can find a rich paradise on this relatively undiscovered island, with its unpolluted and unpopulated kilometers of beaches that are ideal for swimming, shelling, and, of course, snorkeling. If you stay here a week, you've only begun to explore the possibilities. Places such as **Bamboo Point, Fernandez Bay,** and **Long Bay** all lie within a few miles of the main settlement of Cockburn Town on the more tranquil western side of the island. At the southern tip of San

Salvador is one of our favorite places for snorkeling, **Sandy Point,** and its satellite of **Grotto Bay.** The elkhorn coral reefs off San Salvador are worth the trip to Sandy Point and Grotto Bay.

Exploring on Dry Land

For such a small island, San Salvador offers a great deal of history as well as some sights that merit a look.

Rent a bike, hire a taxi, or start walking, and see how many of the **Christopher Columbus monuments** you can hit. All these monuments are supposed to mark the place where Columbus and his crew anchored the *Nina, Pinta,* and *Santa Maria* early that morning in 1492:

✔ **Tappan Monument:** Just south of Cockburn Town, this small, four-sided stone pillar stands on the beach at **Fernandez Bay** (mile-marker number 5 on the main road). The Tappan gas company embedded this monument here on February 25, 1951 in honor of Columbus.

✔ **A tall cross:** At mile-marker number 6, about 5km (3 miles) south of Cockburn Town, stands the tall cross at the edge of the water, which is also a tribute to Columbus. This cross has been here since 1956, along with a third monument that lies hidden on the ocean floor.

✔ **The *Chicago Herald* Monument:** This monument is located at mile-marker number 24 on the east coast. To reach it, turn off the main road and drive a half-kilometer (1 mile) to **East Beach.** Unless you meet a resident who can give you a ride in a four-wheel-drive car, you have to get out and walk. Turn right and hike 3km (2 miles) parallel to the beach until the sandy road ends. You'll see a cave to the left, at the water's edge. Follow the path to the right. Cupped by vegetation, a stone structure lies on the slice of land between the ocean and the bay. Although many historians dispute the claim, the marble plaque boasts, "On this spot Christopher Columbus first set foot upon the soil of the New World, erected by the *Chicago Herald,* June 1891." (Two reporters from the newspaper marked the site to commemorate the 400th anniversary of Columbus's landfall.) The only problem with the monument's claim is that the treacherous reefs here make this a dangerous — and highly unlikely — landing spot.

Another **monument,** located next to the Columbus cross south of Cockburn Town, commemorates the **1968 Olympic Games** in Mexico. A spiral walkway leads to the top of this structure, where the bowl of the dark metal sculpture held the Olympic flame that was brought from Greece. The flame burned here until it was taken to the games in Mexico City.

In the northeastern portion of the island, the **Dixon Hill Lighthouse,** built in 1856, sends out an intense beam two times every 25 seconds. This signal is visible for 31km (19 miles). The oil-using lighthouse rises

49m (160 ft.) into the sky, and the lighthouse keeper still operates it by hand. For permission to climb to the top, just knock on the door of the lighthouse keeper, who's almost always in the neighboring house.

After huffing and puffing your way up, you'll be surprised when you see how tiny the source of light actually is. From the top of the lighthouse, you can take in a panoramic view of San Salvador's inland lakes, a distant Crab Cay, and the surrounding islets. Ask the lighthouse keeper to show you the **inspector's log,** with signatures that date back to Queen Victoria's reign. Be sure to leave at least a $1 donation when you sign the guestbook on your way out. The lighthouse lies about a 30-minute taxi ride from Riding Rock Inn Resort and Marina or Club Med.

Staying Active

Club Med–Columbus Isle offers ten **tennis courts** (three lit for night play), and Riding Rock Inn Resort and Marina has one (often empty) court. Fishermen test their skills against blue marlin, yellowfin tuna, and wahoo on fishing trips, which you can arrange through **Riding Rock Inn Resort and Marina** (☎ 242-331-2631), north of Cockburn Town. The trips run $400 for a half-day and $600 for a full day. Bone fishermen enjoy **Pigeon Creek,** and some record catches have been chalked up here. Rent a boat from a local or get your hotel to help set you up.

Living It Up After Dark

Club Med (☎ 242-331-2000), just north of Cockburn Town, keeps its guests entertained every night with musical revues and shows starring vacationers themselves. At **Riding Rock Inn Resort and Marina** (☎ 242-331-2631), also north of Cockburn Town, the Wednesday-night barbecue features reggae music, and many locals come to party. The hotel's **Driftwood Bar** is also hot on Friday nights (call ☎ 242-331-2631 in The Bahamas). If you're still game for some fun after the lodgings' festivities, head to the **Harlem Square Bar** (☎ 242-331-2777), across the road from Three Ships Restaurant in Cockburn Town. This friendly place is open daily from 9 a.m. to midnight.

Fast Facts: San Salvador

American Express and ATMs

No Amex services or ATMs are available on San Salvador.

Emergencies/Police

Call ☎ 242-331-2919.

Hospital

The San Salvador Community Clinic (☎ 242-331-2105), a five-minute drive north of Club Med, is open Monday through Thursday from 8:30 a.m. to 4:30 p.m. and Friday from 8:30 a.m. to 4 p.m.

Internet Access

San Salvador Cyber Center in Cockburn Town just opened at press time.

Pharmacy

The San Salvador Community Clinic (see "Hospital" earlier in this listing) fills prescriptions.

Safety

San Salvador is a safe island. However, you still need to take the same precautions that you should take anywhere you go: Keep valuables in a safe place and don't go into deserted, unfamiliar areas alone at night.

Taxis

Your hotel staff can arrange taxi service for you. Island tours arranged through Club Med cost around $25 per person for a half-day ramble

Part VII

The Part of Tens

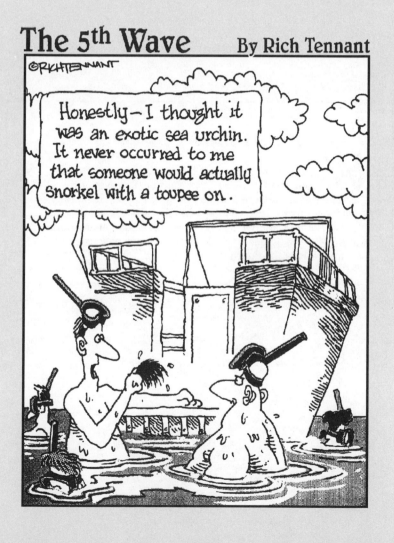

The 5th Wave   By Rich Tennant

©RICHTENNANT

Honestly — I thought it was an exotic sea urchin. It never occurred to me that someone would actually snorkel with a toupee on.

In this part . . .

*W*e give you the ten most common misconceptions about The Bahamas. For example, if you ever thought that The Bahamas were a single, mountainous, casino-packed, Caribbean island, keep reading. We also share our top-ten picks for quintessential island activities, from walking underwater in The Bahamas — without the benefit of scuba gear — to snorkeling with stingrays.

Chapter 26

Top Ten Myths about The Bahamas

• •

In This Chapter

▶ Getting the geography straight

▶ Figuring out the weather

▶ Discovering that no two islands — or islanders — are alike

• •

*I*n this chapter, we explain some of the most common misconceptions about these sunny islands. So the next time someone starts talking about wanting to go mountain climbing in The Bahamas, you can set him straight.

Columbus Definitely Landed at San Salvador

Historians aren't certain whether Columbus's three Spanish ships actually landed on San Salvador (which used to be called Watling's Island until the Bahamian legislature changed it in 1926). The Italian seafarer left no marker to indicate his landfall. Some geographers claim that the landfall occurred on one of the cays of Turks and Caicos; another site in the running is Cat Island. Artifacts of European origin, dating anywhere from 1490 to 1560, were found on San Salvador in 1983. In a meticulously researched article, *National Geographic* published evidence in 1986 that the landfall occurred at Samana Cay, some 104km (65 miles) to the southeast of San Salvador.

The question will probably never be resolved. All we know is that at 2 a.m. on the moonlit night of October 12, 1492, Columbus and his men landed somewhere in the southern Bahamas and woke up some sleepy Lucayans who called them "men from Heaven." In time, when the Spanish killed or sold the Native Americans into slavery, the seafarers may have been more aptly called "men from Hell."

The Bahamas Are One Island

The Bahamas aren't one island — in fact, this archipelago is made up of more than 700 islands, from large landmasses to sandbars. People inhabit only about 30 of the islands, and just a handful of islands actually have hotels.

The Bahamas Are in the Caribbean

Sure, it begins with a *B,* just like Barbados and Bonaire, but The Bahamas (like Bermuda) are in the Atlantic Ocean, not the Caribbean Sea. The Bahamas are close enough that the weather most often feels like the West Indies. Scattered across some 258,998 sq. km (100,000 square miles) of ocean, the islands of the once-British Bahamas have their own special flavor. However, they share a West Indian heritage with their Caribbean neighbors. Therefore, you do find some similarities in architecture, food, music, dance, and the accents of the people.

Beach Weather Is a Given

The weather is *not* always warm enough for the beach. The Bahamas do cool off to often spring-like temperatures around late December to March. Those months are much better for playing golf and tennis than for swimming and sunbathing. The weather can change quickly during this time of year, moving in a flash from beach days to cool days, and then back again.

The Islands Are Mountainous

In the low-lying islands, mountains are more like molehills. The highest point in all The Bahamas — on sleepy Cat Island — is just 63km (206 ft.). Unlike the often-majestic volcanic islands of the Caribbean, these Atlantic isles were created by coral reefs, which make for phenomenal scuba diving and snorkeling, starting in unusually shallow waters.

Palm Trees Are All Over the Place

Except around resorts and residential developments, where people planted palms, most of the trees you see are long-needled casuarina pines. Palms line some beaches, but wispy-looking evergreens (that lean in the direction of the prevailing wind) border the majority of beaches.

For Casinos and Hot Nightlife, Pick Any Island

If you want to gamble into the wee hours or dance 'til the sun comes up, you need to choose the island(s) you visit carefully. In The Bahamas, head to Nassau, Cable Beach, or Paradise Island (all on or attached to the island of New Providence), or to Freeport or Lucaya (on Grand Bahama Island). The rest of the islands don't have casinos, and what little nightlife they do have is liveliest on weekends.

All Bahamians Are of African Descent

On some islands, you find lots of locals with blue eyes and white skin. For example, almost everyone is of European ancestry on Spanish Wells, off the island of Eleuthera, as well as on Man-O-War Cay and Guana Cay, both in the Abacos. Most of these residents are direct descendants of some of The Bahamas' earliest settlers: the Eleutherian Adventurers. Arriving in Spanish Wells in the mid-1600s, these settlers came from Britain in search of religious freedom. In the late 1700s, after the Revolutionary War ended in America, Loyalists (Euro-Americans who sided with the British Crown) also fled to both Eleuthera and the Abacos.

Islanders Resent Tourists

Bahamians are some of the most personable folks around — that is, as long as visitors treat them with respect. For example, if you need to ask someone for directions, say "Hello" first, and don't assume that every local you see works at the resort, store, or restaurant that you're visiting. Strike up a conversation with a resident, and you're sure to come away with a tip about a popular nightspot or a little-known beach. You may even end up with a new friend.

Reggae Music Is the Local Sound

Although you certainly hear reggae music in The Bahamas, it was born in Jamaica, not in these islands. You also hear plenty of calypso (originally from Trinidad), plus lots of American pop, R&B, and rock. But along with all those imports, The Bahamas have their own sound. Traditionally played with cowbells, goatskin drums, whistles, and trumpets, fast-paced **Junkanoo** music is at the heart of the colorful carnival-like festival held on Boxing Day (Dec 26) and New Year's Day.

You may also hear the sounds of **Goombay** (a pared-down version of Junkanoo that's generally played without the elaborate festival costumes). Particularly in the Out Islands, some nightspots still have old-fashioned **rake and scrapes,** where bands turn things like washboards, saws, and barrels into instruments.

Chapter 27

Top Ten Bahamas Moments

- -

In This Chapter

▶ Walking on the ocean floor without scuba gear
▶ Seeing the sights from a horse-drawn carriage
▶ Diving with dolphins and snorkeling with stingrays

- -

*A*re you in the mood for a romantic stroll through manicured English-style gardens? Or is a ride in a horse-drawn carriage along the history-packed streets of Nassau more up your alley? Ever wondered whether pink sand is as soft as the snow-white variety?

Along with scuba diving and snorkeling — which are phenomenal all over The Bahamas — here are other unforgettable adventures you can consider putting at the top of your "to do" list.

Walking on the (Wet and) Wild Side

You can walk on the ocean floor without wearing scuba gear. You don't have to take lengthy classes, either — you just do it. While you're getting up close and personal with fish and coral, your face and hair stay dry. This fun activity is called **helmet diving**. To partake in this adventure, join one of Hartley's Undersea Walks in Nassau. To do so, you wear a lead and glass helmet as you descend a ladder into the ocean. A tank on the boat pumps air through a long tube into your aquatic helmet. For more information, see Chapter 13.

Taking a Carriage Ride through Nassau

Because Nassau, located on New Providence Island, is so full of the country's history, a good way to see this harborside city is from an old-fashioned horse-drawn carriage. You can take a leisurely ride along busy Bay Street (the main thoroughfare) past Parliament Square, with its 18th- and 19th-century Georgian-style government buildings (painted pink and white) and a statue of a young Queen Victoria, among other sights. Turn to Chapter 10 for details.

Wandering through Versailles Gardens

On Paradise Island, you can enjoy a setting that you'd expect to find only in the countryside of France. Studded with bright flowers, shady trees, a lily pond with turtles, and bronze and marble statues, **Versailles Gardens** (see Chapter 13 for details) is the site of a 12th-century monastery. Dramatically perched on a rise, it was built by the Augustinian monks in France. In 1962, Huntington Hartford, the island's original developer, had it moved to the island and reassembled, stone by stone.

Making a Date with Dolphins

Dolphin skin feels like warm, buttery leather. Pet one and you'll see what we mean. (Some marine studies, however, suggest that dolphins don't like human contact. They're such friendly animals, though, you don't get that impression.) You can commune with dolphins on Grand Bahama or an island off New Providence. Some sessions allow you to wade in the water with these mammals while trainers tell you everything you ever wanted to know about them. In other programs, you can scuba dive with Flipper's cousins in the open ocean. For more details, see Chapter 13 (on New Providence) and Chapter 17 (on Grand Bahama).

Feeding the Stingrays

If you find dolphins too tame, try feeding the stingrays that swim gracefully through the shallow waters around a tiny island off Green Turtle Cay in the Abacos (see Chapter 20). If you don't know how to snorkel, your guide can teach you on the spot, or you can take to the water dressed in scuba gear. Either way, you're also treated to a beach picnic after your captain grills the fish or lobster that he just caught.

Digging Your Toes into a Pink Sand Beach

Harbour Island's Pink Sand Beach may be only 2km (3 miles) long, but the soft, broad, pink sand beach along its eastern shore seems to go on forever. The unusual color comes from shells and coral that the waves have pulverized over the years. This beach is pretty enough to make you roll out of bed in time to catch the sunrise. (Turn to Chapter 22 for more details.)

Watching the Sun Set on Dunmore Town

For some of the best sunsets in The Bahamas, head to Harbour Island's western coast. The spectacle is special here because of the glow that the sun casts on the 18th-century wooden cottages along the harborfront. Sip a Bahama Mama or a Goombay Smash at a waterside restaurant while you watch the show. (For more information, see Chapter 22.)

Visiting a Candy Cane-Striped Lighthouse

Sail through **Hope Town Harbor,** which is filled with small pleasure boats, or munch some conch fritters at the water's edge and you can see the whimsical red-and-white striped lighthouse. For a sweeping view of narrow Elbow Cay, edged by fabulous beaches, climb to the top of the beacon, which has stood here since 1838. (See Chapter 19 for more information.)

Living It Up at Miss Emily's

In New Plymouth on Green Turtle Cay in the Abacos stands **Miss Emily's Blue Bee Bar,** the most famous watering hole in the Out Islands (see Chapter 20 for more information). The rum-laced drink, the Goombay Smash, may as well have been invented here. It's called Abacos' answer to atomic fission. Miss Emily is gone now, but she left her secret recipe in the hands of her daughter.

Boating in the Abacos

No matter where you've boated before, nothing compares to sailing the Abacos in one of the vessels that you can rent at Marsh Harbour. (See Chapter 18 for details on how to do so.) Marsh Harbour is aptly known as "The Boating Capital of The Bahamas." In charge of your own vessel, you can visit uninhabited cays and seek out deserted beaches where you can go shelling, exploring, and picnicking in peace — and no one's around to witness if you want to go beachcombing in the buff.

Quick Concierge

Fast Facts

American Express

Representing American Express in The Bahamas is Destinations (☎ 242-322-2931), located on Shirley Street (between Charlotte and Parliament streets) in Nassau. Hours are 9 a.m. to 5 p.m. Monday through Friday. The travel department is also open Saturday from 9 a.m. to 1 p.m. If you present a personal check and an Amex card, you can buy traveler's checks here.

Area Code

On all islands, the area code for The Bahamas is **242**.

ATMs

To find an ATM near you, call or check the Web sites for Cirrus (☎ 800-424-7787; www.mastercard.com) and Plus (☎ 800-843-7587; www.visa.com). See Chapter 5 for more information about using ATMs in The Bahamas.

Credit Cards

If your credit card gets lost or stolen, call the following emergency telephone numbers: American Express, ☎ 336-393-1111 collect; MasterCard, ☎ 800-307-7309 or 636-722-7111 collect; and Visa, ☎ 800-847-2911 or 410-581-9994 collect.

Currency Exchange

You don't have to swap your U.S. dollars for Bahamian currency because American green is accepted everywhere. The exchange rate is $1 to $1, so you won't have any confusion.

Electricity

Electricity is normally 120 volts, 60 cycles, AC. American appliances are fully compatible; British or European appliances need both converters and adapters.

Embassies and Consulates

The U.S. embassy (☎ 242-322-1181 or 242-328-2206) is on Queen Street, P.O. Box N-8197, Nassau, and the Canadian consulate (☎ 242-393-2123) is on Shirley Street, Shopping Plaza, Nassau. The British High Commission (☎ 242-325-7471) is at Ansbacher House (3rd floor), East Street, Nassau.

Emergencies

Throughout most of The Bahamas, the number to call for a medical, dental, or hospital emergency is ☎ 911. In the Out Islands, the number is ☎ 919. To report a fire, call ☎ 411.

Etiquette and Customs

When you encounter someone, even a stranger in the Out Islands, exchanging greetings is customary. A "good morning" or "good afternoon" suffices. But that custom doesn't prevail in bustling Freeport and Nassau. Also, rushing up to someone and demanding that he supply you with directions to a place is impolite anywhere; Bahamians gently lead into conversations with a greeting and friendly comments before getting down to business.

Business in offices is conducted rather formally with exchange of business cards, elaborate handshakes, and the like. If you're doing business in The Bahamas, wear business clothes as you would to any office in America. Don't show up in resort wear or shorts for any formal meetings or functions.

When leaving the beach, men should put on a shirt and pants, even a pair of jeans, before heading into a town. Women should wear a cover-up over their bathing suit, or else slip into a tropical dress or pants.

If you're planning to attend religious services, wear the best clothes you brought along. Bahamians believe in dressing up for their "Sunday-go-to meeting."

Regardless of how colorful an islander may look, photographing anyone without permission is extremely rude.

Internet Access

Access is limited on the islands. Cybercafe, located in The Mall at Marathon (☎ 242-394-6254) in Nassau, is open daily from 10 a.m. to 8 p.m., charging 15¢ per minute; four computers are available. In the Out Islands, you can usually access the Web from your hotel. For more tips about staying in touch, see Chapter 9.

Liquor and Drug Laws

Liquor is sold in liquor stores and various convenience stores; it's readily available at all hours, although it's not sold on Sundays. The legal drinking age is 18.

Importing, possessing, or dealing in unlawful drugs, including marijuana, is a serious offense in The Bahamas that carries heavy penalties. Customs officers may conduct body searches for drugs or other contraband goods at their discretion.

Mail and Postage Rates

Most of the kiosks selling postcards also sell the Bahamian stamps you need to mail them, so you probably won't need to visit the post office. Sending a postcard or an airmail letter (up to ½-oz. in weight) from The Bahamas to anywhere outside its borders (including the U.S., Canada, and the U.K.) costs 65¢, with another charged for each additional half-ounce of weigdt.

Mail to and from the Out Islands is sometimes slow. Airmail may go by air to Nassau and by boat to its final destination. If a resort has a U.S. or Nassau address, using it is preferable.

Pets

You have to get a valid import permit to bring any animal into The Bahamas. You must apply for such a permit in writing, accompanied by a $10 processing fee and a $5 fax fee, to the Director of Agriculture, Department of Agriculture, P.O. Box N-3028, Nassau, The Bahamas, at least four weeks in advance. The phone number is ☎ 242-325-7413.

Police

Dial ☎ 911. In the Out Islands, the number is ☎ 919.

Safety

When going to Nassau (New Providence), Cable Beach, Paradise Island, or Freeport/Lucaya, exercise the same caution you would if you were visiting Miami.

Women, especially, should take caution when walking alone on the streets of Nassau after dark, particularly if those streets appear deserted. Pickpockets work the crowded casino floors of both Paradise Beach and Cable Beach. See that your wallet, money, and valuables are well secured.

If you're driving a rental car, always make sure that you lock the car door and never leave possessions in view. Don't leave valuables, such as cameras and purses, unattended on the beach while you go for a swim. If you're traveling with valuables, especially jewelry, don't leave them unguarded in hotel rooms. Many of the larger hotels provide safes. Keep your hotel room doors locked at all times.

You're less likely to be mugged or robbed in the Out Islands, where life is generally more peaceful. Some resort hotels, even today, don't have locks on the doors there.

Smoking

The Bahamas don't have any general restrictions against smoking in public places, so the smoking policy depends on the individual restaurant or bar. Most of them designate smoking versus nonsmoking areas and keep their premises well ventilated.

Taxes

Departure tax is $15 ($18 from Grand Bahama Island) for visitors ages 7 and up. You're also charged an 8 percent tax on hotel bills; otherwise, The Bahamas don't have sales tax.

Telephone

Communications have improved recently, although some of the Out Islands are still difficult to reach. Direct long-distance dialing between North America and Nassau, Grand Bahama, the Abacos, Andros, the Berry Islands, Bimini, Eleuthera, Harbour Island, Spanish Wells, the Exumas, and Stella Maris on Long Island is available.

To call The Bahamas from the U.S. or Canada, dial 1-242 plus the seven-digit local number. From the U.K., dial 001-242 plus the local seven-digit number.

To make a direct international call from The Bahamas to the U.S. or Canada, dial 1 plus the area code and local number. To call other countries, dial 011 plus the country code (the U.K. is 44, for example), the area code (usually without its initial zero), and the local number.

For local calls within The Bahamas, simply dial the seven-digit number. To call from one island to another within The Bahamas, dial 1-242 and then the seven-digit local number.

Old coin-operated phones are still prevalent in The Bahamas, and these phones still swallow coins. Each local call costs 25¢; you can use either Bahamian or U.S. quarters. But those old phones are gradually being replaced by phones that use calling cards that come in denominations of $5, $10, $20, and $50. You can buy calling cards from any office of BATELCO (Bahamas Telephone Co.).

BATELCO's main branch (☎ 242-302-7000) is on Kennedy Drive, Nassau, although a popular local branch lies in the commercial heart of Nassau, on East Street off Bay Street.

To get directory assistance within The Bahamas, dial ☎ 916. To reach an international or a domestic operator within The Bahamas, dial 0. No distinction is made in The Bahamas between the two types of operators.

To reach the major international services of AT&T, dial ☎ 800-CALLATT from any phone, or head for any phone with AT&T or USA DIRECT marked on the side of the booth. Picking up the handset connects you with an AT&T operator. You often find these phones beside cruise-ship docks to help passengers disembarking on shore

leave for the day. You can reach MCI at
☎ 800-888-8000.

Time Zone

All islands in The Bahamas are on Eastern
Standard Time. The islands also observe
daylight savings time in the summer.

Water

Technically, tap water is drinkable
throughout The Bahamas. But we almost
always opt for bottled. Resorts tend to filter
and chlorinate tap water more aggressively than other establishments; anywhere else, you can get bottled water at
stores and supermarkets, and it tastes
better than water from a tap.

On many of the Out Islands, rainfall is the
main source of water. Definitely drink bottled water when you're there.

Weather

Call ☎ 915 to hear the forecast. Before
your trip or if you have Internet access
while in the islands, check out www.
weather.com.

Weddings

See Chapter 8 for complete details about
getting married in The Bahamas.

Toll-Free Numbers and Web Sites

Airlines

Air Canada
☎ 888-247-2262 in the U.S.
☎ 800-268-7240 in Canada
www.aircanada.com

Air Sunshine
☎ 800-327-8900
www.airsunshine.com

American/American Eagle
☎ 800-433-7300
www.aa.com

Bahamasair
☎ 800-222-4262
www.bahamasair.com

British Airways
☎ 800-247-9297
☎ 0345-222-111 or 0870-77-9850
in U.K.
www.britishairways.com

Chalk's International Airlines
☎ 800-424-2557 in U.S.
☎ 242-363-1687 in Bahamas
www.chalksoceanairways.com

Continental Airlines
☎ 800-321-0856
www.continental.com

Delta Air Lines
☎ 800-221-1212
www.delta.com

Gulfstream/Continental Connection
☎ 800-231-0856
www.continental.com

Lynx Air International
☎ 888-596-9247
www.lynxair.com

Twin Air
☎ 954-359-8266
www.flytwinair.co

U.S. Airways/U.S. Airways Express
☎ 800-428-4322
www.usairways.com

Major hotel chains

Best Western International
☎ 800-528-1234
www.bestwestern.com

Breezes
☎ 877-467-8737
www.breezes.com

Club Med
☎ 888-932-2582
www.clubmed.com

Comfort Inns
☎ 800-228-5150
www.hotelchoice.com

Crowne Plaza
☎ 800-227-6963
www.crowneplaza.com

Four Seasons
☎ 800-819-5053
www.fourseasons.com

Hilton Hotels
☎ 800-HILTONS
www.hilton.com

Holiday Inn
☎ 800-HOLIDAY
www.basshotels.com

Marriott Hotels
☎ 800-228-9290
www.marriott.com

Radisson Hotels International
☎ 800-333-3333
www.radisson.com

Ritz-Carlton
☎ 800-241-3333
www.ritzcarlton.com

Sheraton Hotels & Resorts
☎ 800-325-3535
www.sheraton.com

Westin Hotels & Resorts
☎ 800-937-8461
www.westin.com

Wyndham Hotels and Resorts
☎ 800-822-4200
www.wyndham.com

Major car-rental agencies

Avis
☎ 800-331-1212 in continental U.S.
www.avis.com

Budget
☎ 800-527-0700
www.budget.com

Dollar
☎ 800-800-4000
www.dollar.com

Hertz
☎ 800-654-3131
www.hertz.com

Where to Get More Information

Tourist offices

The best source to try before you leave home is **The Bahamas Ministry of Tourism Office.** You can browse the Web site at www.bahamas.com or call ☎ **800-BAHAMAS** to request information. You can also go to or call the walk-in branch offices at the following locations:

✔ **Chicago:** 8600 W. Bryn Mawr Ave., Suite 820, Chicago, IL 60631; ☎ **773-693-1500**

✔ **Los Angeles:** 3450 Wilshire Blvd., Suite 1204, Los Angeles, CA 90010; ☎ **800-439-6993**

✔ **Miami:** 1200 S. Pine Island Rd., Suite 750, Plantation, FL 33324; ☎ **800-224-3681** or 954-236-9292

✔ **New York:** 150 E. 52nd St., New York, NY 10022; ☎ **800-823-3136** or 212-758-2777

✔ **Toronto, Canada:** 121 Bloor St. E., Suite 1101, Toronto, ON M4W 3M5; ☎ 416-968-2999

✔ **London, U.K.:** 10 Chesterfield St., London W1J 5JL; ☎ 020-7355-0800

Newspapers and magazines

Three newspapers circulate in Nassau and Freeport: *The Nassau Guardian* (www.thenassauguardian.com), *The Tribune,* and the *Freeport News* (http://freeport.nassauguardian.net). In the Out Islands, newspaper circulation is limited and likely to be slow.

Web sites

The following is a list of our top picks for destination Web sites for The Bahamas. In addition to these sites, we recommend Frommers.com (www.frommers.com), which is full of travel tips, online booking options, and more comprehensive advice from *Frommer's Bahamas* (Wiley).

✔ The Bahamas Ministry of Tourism (www.bahamas.com)

✔ The Bahamas Out Islands Promotion Board (www.bahama-out-islands.com)

✔ Bahamas Tourist Guide (www.interknowledge.com/bahamas)

✔ Bahamasnet (www.bahamasnet.com)

Index

364 Bahamas For Dummies, 2nd Edition

BUSINESS, CAREERS & PERSONAL FINANCE

0-7645-5307-0   0-7645-5331-3 *†

Also available:
- Accounting For Dummies †
  0-7645-5314-3
- Business Plans Kit For Dummies †
  0-7645-5365-8
- Cover Letters For Dummies
  0-7645-5224-4
- Frugal Living For Dummies
  0-7645-5403-4
- Leadership For Dummies
  0-7645-5176-0
- Managing For Dummies
  0-7645-1771-6

- Marketing For Dummies
  0-7645-5600-2
- Personal Finance For Dummies *
  0-7645-2590-5
- Project Management
  For Dummies
  0-7645-5283-X
- Resumes For Dummies †
  0-7645-5471-9
- Selling For Dummies
  0-7645-5363-1
- Small Business Kit For Dummies *†
  0-7645-5093-4

HOME & BUSINESS COMPUTER BASICS

0-7645-4074-2   0-7645-3758-X

Also available:
- ACT! 6 For Dummies
  0-7645-2645-6
- iLife '04 All-in-One Desk Reference
  For Dummies
  0-7645-7347-0
- iPAQ For Dummies
  0-7645-6769-1
- Mac OS X Panther Timesaving
  Techniques For Dummies
  0-7645-5812-9
- Macs For Dummies
  0-7645-5656-8
- Microsoft Money 2004 For Dummies
  0-7645-4195-1

- Office 2003 All-in-One Desk
  Reference For Dummies
  0-7645-3883-7
- Outlook 2003 For Dummies
  0-7645-3759-8
- PCs For Dummies
  0-7645-4074-2
- TiVo For Dummies
  0-7645-6923-6
- Upgrading and Fixing PCs
  For Dummies
  0-7645-1665-5
- Windows XP Timesaving
  Techniques For Dummies
  0-7645-3748-2

FOOD, HOME, GARDEN, HOBBIES, MUSIC & PETS

0-7645-5295-3   0-7645-5232-5

Also available:
- Bass Guitar For Dummies
  0-7645-2487-9
- Diabetes Cookbook For Dummies
  0-7645-5230-9
- Gardening For Dummies *
  0-7645-5130-2
- Guitar For Dummies
  0-7645-5106-X
- Holiday Decorating For Dummies
  0-7645-2570-0
- Home Improvement All-in-One
  For Dummies
  0-7645-5680-0

- Knitting For Dummies
  0-7645-5395-X
- Piano For Dummies
  0-7645-5105-1
- Puppies For Dummies
  0-7645-5255-4
- Scrapbooking For Dummies
  0-7645-7208-3
- Senior Dogs For Dummies
  0-7645-5818-8
- Singing For Dummies
  0-7645-2475-5
- 30-Minute Meals For Dummies
  0-7645-2589-1

INTERNET & DIGITAL MEDIA

0-7645-1664-7   0-7645-6924-4

Also available:
- 2005 Online Shopping Directory
  For Dummies
  0-7645-7495-7
- CD & DVD Recording For Dummies
  0-7645-5956-7
- eBay For Dummies
  0-7645-5654-1
- Fighting Spam For Dummies
  0-7645-5965-6
- Genealogy Online For Dummies
  0-7645-5964-8
- Google For Dummies
  0-7645-4420-9

- Home Recording For Musicians
  For Dummies
  0-7645-1634-5
- The Internet For Dummies
  0-7645-4173-0
- iPod & iTunes For Dummies
  0-7645-7772-7
- Preventing Identity Theft
  For Dummies
  0-7645-7336-5
- Pro Tools All-in-One Desk
  Reference For Dummies
  0-7645-5714-9
- Roxio Easy Media Creator
  For Dummies
  0-7645-7131-1

* Separate Canadian edition also available
† Separate U.K. edition also available
Available wherever books are sold. For more information or to order direct: U.S. customers
visit www.dummies.com or call 1-877-762-2974.
U.K. customers visit www.wileyeurope.com or call 0800 243407. Canadian customers visit
www.wiley.ca or call 1-800-567-4797.

SPORTS, FITNESS, PARENTING, RELIGION & SPIRITUALITY

0-7645-5146-9

0-7645-5418-2

Also available:
- Adoption For Dummies
  0-7645-5488-3
- Basketball For Dummies
  0-7645-5248-1
- The Bible For Dummies
  0-7645-5296-1
- Buddhism For Dummies
  0-7645-5359-3
- Catholicism For Dummies
  0-7645-5391-7
- Hockey For Dummies
  0-7645-5228-7

- Judaism For Dummies
  0-7645-5299-6
- Martial Arts For Dummies
  0-7645-5358-5
- Pilates For Dummies
  0-7645-5397-6
- Religion For Dummies
  0-7645-5264-3
- Teaching Kids to Read
  For Dummies
  0-7645-4043-2
- Weight Training For Dummies
  0-7645-5168-X
- Yoga For Dummies
  0-7645-5117-5

TRAVEL

0-7645-5438-7

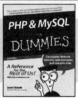

0-7645-5453-0

Also available:
- Alaska For Dummies
  0-7645-1761-9
- Arizona For Dummies
  0-7645-6938-4
- Cancún and the Yucatán
  For Dummies
  0-7645-2437-2
- Cruise Vacations For Dummies
  0-7645-6941-4
- Europe For Dummies
  0-7645-5456-5
- Ireland For Dummies
  0-7645-5455-7

- Las Vegas For Dummies
  0-7645-5448-4
- London For Dummies
  0-7645-4277-X
- New York City For Dummies
  0-7645-6945-7
- Paris For Dummies
  0-7645-5494-8
- RV Vacations For Dummies
  0-7645-5443-3
- Walt Disney World & Orlando
  For Dummies
  0-7645-6943-0

GRAPHICS, DESIGN & WEB DEVELOPMENT

0-7645-4345-8

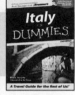

0-7645-5589-8

Also available:
- Adobe Acrobat 6 PDF
  For Dummies
  0-7645-3760-1
- Building a Web Site For Dummies
  0-7645-7144-3
- Dreamweaver MX 2004
  For Dummies
  0-7645-4342-3
- FrontPage 2003 For Dummies
  0-7645-3882-9
- HTML 4 For Dummies
  0-7645-1995-6
- Illustrator cs For Dummies
  0-7645-4084-X

- Macromedia Flash MX 2004
  For Dummies
  0-7645-4358-X
- Photoshop 7 All-in-One Desk
  Reference For Dummies
  0-7645-1667-1
- Photoshop cs Timesaving
  Techniques For Dummies
  0-7645-6782-9
- PHP 5 For Dummies
  0-7645-4166-8
- PowerPoint 2003 For Dummies
  0-7645-3908-6
- QuarkXPress 6 For Dummies
  0-7645-2593-X

NETWORKING, SECURITY, PROGRAMMING & DATABASES

0-7645-6852-3

0-7645-5784-X

Also available:
- A+ Certification For Dummies
  0-7645-4187-0
- Access 2003 All-in-One Desk
  Reference For Dummies
  0-7645-3988-4
- Beginning Programming
  For Dummies
  0-7645-4997-9
- C For Dummies
  0-7645-7068-4
- Firewalls For Dummies
  0-7645-4048-3
- Home Networking For Dummies
  0-7645-42796

- Network Security For Dummies
  0-7645-1679-5
- Networking For Dummies
  0-7645-1677-9
- TCP/IP For Dummies
  0-7645-1760-0
- VBA For Dummies
  0-7645-3989-2
- Wireless All In-One Desk Reference
  For Dummies
  0-7645-7496-5
- Wireless Home Networking
  For Dummies
  0-7645-3910-8